They Went to Portugal

Dame Rose Macaulay was born in 1881 and died in 1958. She was associated with the Bloomsbury Group in the 1930s and was well known as a society wit and woman of letters. Even as a small child she was an enthusiastic writer; later her talent found expression in many essays, three collections of verse and a number of travel books and novels. She was a frequent contributor to BBC programmes and her talks and articles often appeared in the *Listener*. Her novels include *The Valley Captives* (1911), *Potterism* (1920), *Told by an Idiot* (1923), *Orphan Island* (1924), *They were Defeated* (1932) and *The Towers of Trebizond* (1956). *They Went to Portugal* was first published in 1946. Written with impeccable style, it is a vivid and intoxicating account of British travellers in Portugal from the times of the Crusades.

Rose Macaulay had an insatiable appetite for adventure; after her death a tribute to her in the *Listener* said: 'She was paper-thin, transparent, almost as if a light shone through her; yet it was always she who was first up the hill, or the last out of the sea, the untiring explorer, and examiner of ideas and places and people.'

ROSE MACAULAY

THEY WENT TO PORTUGAL

PENGUIN BOOKS

Penguin Books Ltd, Harmondsworth, Middlesex, England
Viking Penguin Inc., 40 West 23rd Street, New York, New York 10010, U.S.A.
Penguin Books Australia Ltd, Ringwood, Victoria, Australia
Penguin Books Canada Ltd, 2801 John Street, Markham, Ontario, Canada L3R 1B4
Penguin Books (N.Z.) Ltd, 182–190 Wairau Road, Auckland 10, New Zealand

First published by Jonathan Cape 1946
Published in Penguin Books 1985

Made and printed in Great Britain by
Richard Clay (The Chaucer Press) Ltd, Bungay, Suffolk
Typeset in Baskerville

CONTENTS

5

CONTENTS

Portugalers with us have trouth in hand:
Whose Marchandy commeth much into England.
They bene our frendes wyth there commoditez,
And wee English passen into there Countrees.
Lybelle of English Policye (1436)

How often, contrasting my present situation with the horrid disturbed state of almost every part of the Continent, did I bless the hour when my steps were directed to Portugal!
WILLIAM BECKFORD (1794)

Em Inglaterra não ha nenhum tolo que não o faça um livro de *tourist* nenhum architolo que não o faça sobre Portugal.
ALEXANDRE HERCULANO (1854)

(In England there is no foolish person who does not write a tourist book, no one extremely foolish who does not write it about Portugal.)

ACKNOWLEDGMENTS

I HAVE received so much help and kindness while writing this book that it is difficult to know where to begin or end thanks. First, while in Lisbon I owed a great deal to the Lisbon branch of the Historical Association, and in particular to its president, Mrs. Jayne, who, with her unrivalled knowledge of Lisbon Anglo-Portuguese life, put material in my way, allowed me to read in her library, and gave me much information which she had collected, including an admirable unpublished article on English merchants in Lisbon, a highly interesting narrative (to be published soon), of a Jacobean prisoner of the Inquisition, and several delightful articles in the Association's Reports.

To Dr. West and the British Institute in Lisbon I am indebted for permission to read at the Institute, and for the loan of books and periodicals; and to my friend Mr. C. D. Ley in particular for much help, both in Lisbon and since; I owe him many pointers and suggestions, and a great deal of interesting and entertaining information. One cannot reach the end of the hospitality and helpfulness of the English (and Portuguese) in Portugal to stray visitors and inquirers; from the Portuguese Propaganda Ministry, to those who so hospitably entertained me in Lisbon, Cintra, and Oporto; here I would thank in particular my friends Susan and Luiz Marques. The British Association in Oporto allowed me to read in the library of their Factory House, and very many other Lisbon and Oporto residents gave me news of their respective cities. Mr. Fulford Williams gave me interesting information about chaplains and St. George's Church and cemetery, and let me read his own account of these. Mr. A. R. Walford presented me with his history of the English Factory, an invaluable source of information.

In this country I have to thank Dr. Prestage, the greatest English authority on Portuguese history, for lending me books unobtainable elsewhere, and for supplying me with information. Dr. Armando Cortesão also gave me much help, including the use of his library and the elucidation of some linguistic difficulties. Sir Claud Russell was most kind in giving me information about Lord and Lady William Russell, and lending me their portraits for reproduction, Lord Ilchester and Sir John Murray in allowing

ACKNOWLEDGMENTS

me to read and quote from Lord Ilchester's still unpublished *Letters from Lady Holland to her Son*. In the matter of port wine, M. André Simon and Mr. Gerard Sandeman generously lent me books, brochures and pamphlets not otherwise to be come by, and Mr. Max Graham of Oporto and Major Gerard Graham answered inquiries with admirable fulness, kindness and patience. Mr. Arthur Bourke, of Harper's *Wine and Spirit Gazette*, was most helpful in putting me on the track of Baron de Forrester's picture of Oporto wine-shippers, Mr. L. E. De Rouet, of Messrs. Offley Forrester, Oporto, not only lent me this picture for reproduction, but presented me with a print of old Oporto bar for my frontispiece. I am grateful, too, to Miss Marion Jennings and to Colonel C. P. Hawkes for information about Oporto life. And to the late Lady Abbess of Syon Abbey, and the Sister who so skilfully and kindly copied for me the manuscript letter of Sister Catherine Witham, and furnished me, as did also Canon Fletcher, with much information about the Bridgettine nuns (whose romantic story lack of space in the end excluded from this volume). Also excluded, for the same reason, is a chapter on the Lisbon English during the Peninsular war, for which Mr. Arthur Bryant supplied me with many useful references. Mr. S. Jacomb-Hood kindly lent me the earthquake letter of his ancestor Thomas Jacomb; Bishop David Mathew called my attention to the adventures of Sir Thomas Stukely, about whom he has so admirably written himself; Mr. Guy Chapman was a helpful and essential guide through the tangled web woven by the Beckford papers. I am grateful to the Hamilton Trustees for permission to look at and quote from these papers, and to the Curator and staff of the Edinburgh Register House for making this task so easy and pleasant, and to Sir Herbert Grierson and Mr. Charles Bell for their friendly help. I have to thank Lord Bearsted for permission to reproduce his Romney portrait of Beckford, and Mr. Roger Senhouse for lending me his print of this. Miss Jaqueline Hope-Wallace kindly lent me her print of the British Museum engraving of Prince Rupert, and the Hudson Bay Co. a photograph of the portrait in their possession.

As always, the officials of the British Museum and the Public Record Office and the staff of the London Library maintained their traditions of helpfulness in difficult times; I should in particular like to thank Mr. F. G. Rendall and Mr. A. I. Ellis of the

ACKNOWLEDGMENTS

British Museum for their frequent help in difficulties, and the officials of the Record Office Search Room who kindly reclaimed evacuated State Papers for me, and even gave me access to some of these in their country lairs. Miss L. Drucker's skilful copying of some of the letters of our earlier and less legible Lisbon consuls has saved me much time and probably many errors.

Finally, Mr. Daniel George has, by his patient reading, criticisms and suggestions, rid this book of some, at least, of its flaws.

PREFACE

IF ever I had the notion of putting into this book all the British people who have been to Portugal down the ages about whom I could discover anything, I soon abandoned it. They are too many; they have gone too much. So, out of the eight centuries with which I have dealt, I selected some travellers and tourists, some writers, some soldiers, some ambassadors and consuls, some priests, some nuns, some adventurers, some merchants, some kings, queens and princes, some missionaries, a few exiles, a murderer. And even these selections have had, in the end, to be halved, so that my book, as it here appears, is really only selected specimens of all that I have so voluminously written about these Peninsula visitors.

For it is a long story. Beginning with the pirate-crusaders whom the first kings of Portugal called in as they were on their way to the Holy Land, to help them rid Portugal of its Saracens, the tale of those who went to Portugal rambles down the centuries like a Cook's tour, conducting to that lovely, improbable, often distracted, usually, to the British, rather incomprehensible land, medieval royalty and knights; Elizabethan and Jacobean Catholic exiles, fugitives and plotters; pirates, soldiers and sailors; seventeenth-century poets and ambassadors (I regret having had to discard from this volume the admirable Sir Richard Fanshawe, who was both); Anglican, Roman and non-conformist clergymen; the pioneers of the great port wine trade colonizing the ports of the north, swelling in the eighteenth century into a magnificent aristocracy of commerce, the most robustly British colony ever to settle abroad; the rising tide of tourists through the same century (alas, I have here only found room for three of them), inquisitive, gushing, practical, disdainful, or merely consumptive (for no one heeded the wise medical counsel of Sir Thomas Browne uttered in the century before, 'those who are tabidly inclined would do well not to live in Portugal', and to the Lisbon English burial ground under the green Estrella trees the phthisical English travelled to stay); the aesthetic dilettante tourist making his fantastic discontented paradise at Cintra; the rush of romantic travellers all gushing over this paradise that they found so like Eden, so like Malvern, so much too good for the Portuguese.

The selections in this volume may seem capricious, as selections always must. I have found no space for Wellington and his army; but these have been described well and often by better campaigning pens than mine. I myself miss more all the diplomats and consuls. Reading the many fascinating volumes of manuscript correspondence from our Lisbon envoys over three centuries, I regretted that I could not include most of these bland, skilful, informed, industrious beings, who had to walk their tight-ropes over such perilous political and personal quicksands, who so seldom lost their urbane good manners or their tempers (Sir Frederick Lamb is an exception to this rule; but then he had to cope with Miguel in Lisbon and a Tory government in London), so almost never their discretion. But I have only found room here for two ambassadors and one consul; it is a pity about the consuls, for some of these had less urbanity, manners and discretion, and wrote racier letters, and all of them bring one in touch with the British community for which they laboured, that tough, free-spoken, grumbling, quarrelsome company of merchants, Sir Benjamin Keene's 'jolly free Factory' which deserves a book all to itself.

I have not included the living; that always raises questions too delicate. I regret it, for there is among them tempting material; but it must wait. Nor have I put in the more recent of those British who have laboured to do good to the Portuguese, founding schools, instructing them in birth control (as did a nineteenth-century Viscountess Cook of Monserrate), in the protestant religion, in how to start a Lusitanian church on Anglican model — only, since the model came out of Ireland, the Lusitanian church became, despite its Anglican liturgy in Portuguese, 'low, low, low', as one of its clergy expressed it to me, holding his hand a few inches from his church floor. How greatly this church would have vexed the tractarian souls of Dr. Neale and Mr. Oldknow, no one who loves tractarians can care to reflect.

Finally, having been myself only a tourist in that enchanting country, and for how brief a time, I am filled with abashment at my temerity in attempting such a theme, which had been better tackled by a long-term resident. The Oporto wine-shippers, for instance: what a magnificent story for nearly three centuries is theirs, how picturesque their calling, how excitingly beautiful its setting, how rich their history in characters and incidents. Not a theme that can possibly be adequately dealt with by an outsider;

Oporto and the wine-shippers wait their historian. Let me suggest this noble theme to some Oporto resident who knows it from the inside of that remarkable city, whose magnificent pile on its steep hills above its sweeping golden river so stirs the imagination, from the inside of those mountain quintas that stand among the terraced vineyards up in the wine country. There is here a great romantic history: but it must be written by an Oporto pen, and Oporto pens have so far been regrettably idle in the matter. There is here also a novel not romantic (if anything about Oporto can be not romantic) — a comedy of manners and of Oporto British social life. There are, no doubt, those now in Portugal who could write it.

All I can say of my selected gallery is that it has given me pleasure to live with them and their rejected companions for three years; they have given me the entertainment of a very varied and miscellaneous society, and I hope that some others may like them a little too. If not, I do myself, and that, though by no means everything, is something.

EARLY VISITORS

GOING to Portugal was, no doubt, a common enough habit among British Islanders many centuries before they left any records of it, and many centuries before either Britain or Portugal was a nation. The Phoenicians had their trade routes between Iberia and Britain; as Ezekiel remarked in the sixth century B.C., apostrophizing the fallen Tyre, 'Tarshish [i.e. Tartessius in south-west Spain] was thy merchant by reason of all kinds of riches; with silver, iron, tin and lead they traded in thy fairs'; and from Tarshish the Tyrian ships crept up the Peninsula coasts to get tin and wine from the north-west, braved the gales of the Bay of Biscay, seeking the tin mines of the questionable Cassiterides, and put in to Cornish ports, to barter merchandise with those 'shy traffickers, the dark Iberians' of Britain, who could supply pearls and jet, copper and tin and gold and furs, in exchange for amber, silver, embroidriees, coral, spices, purple and precious stones. Lured by such rich merchandise from overseas, it would be natural for the shy traffickers to voyage in their turn to the trading ports of the western continent, where small dark men like themselves spoke a variant of the tongue they both knew. Later, when both Britain and the continent were reinforced by the vigour of the adventurous Celts, who never failed to get about, such visits would be more frequent; later still, the trafficking Britons of the Roman Empire were probably quite well acquainted with the ports of Felicitas Julia, and would put in to the mouths of the Douro, the Lima, the Mondego and the Tagus, to trade metals, furs and wolf dogs for cargoes of oranges, oil and wine. Some Britons, less fortunate than these sailors and merchants, were themselves shipped, cargoes of captured slaves, by their Roman masters for sale in the markets of these gay, staring and chattering ports, where, however, they are said to have not fetched much. One may imagine that they did not compare favourably with Circassians and other eastern barbarians; indeed, they probably looked sulky, disobliging and arrogant, and as if they considered themselves insulted by being auctioned to Portuguese.

That British-Iberian traffic had always been common enough seems assumed by a twelfth-century reference to the Tower of

Hercules on the Coruńna peninsula as having been built by Julius Caesar (perhaps during his governorship of north-west Spain) 'as a centre through which the revenues of Britain and Ireland and Spain might pass to and fro. For it is so situated that it offers the first landing-place for travellers coming directly over from Britain'. In one way and another there must have been in Roman Britain a fair knowledge of that fruitful peninsula south-west of Gaul, where the olive, the vine and the orange tree so agreeably flourished, where great-horned oxen drew cargoes down to the quays in creaking carts, and long-capped Phoenicians went fishing for tunnies, and dragged in heavy nets of sardines from the rich sea.

Later, the pirate hordes of barbarians on the move did not cease to ravage and raid the coasts and mainlands of Europe from their new island home; but until the ninth century records are few, and such adventures are swallowed up in the engulfing darkness of their age. After the exciting and remarkable discovery of the corpse of St. James the Apostle in Galicia, about the year 800, religion reinforced cupidity, and devout pilgrims and pirates from Britain made the Santiago trip in great numbers; many of them thus heard for the first time the accents of Galicia, which were also those of Portugal. Some proceeded from the Groyne down the Lusitanian coast, to trade with or plunder the people in the ports of Viana, Lima and Portus Cale. Venturing further, they put into the great mouth of the Tagus and trafficked with the wealthy infidels who held Lisbon and the south, and in whose hands commerce, art, science and literature had formed a civiliza-tion far richer, more learned and more refined than any European Christian culture was for centuries to be. With it the Saxon and Norman visitors could make few intellectual contacts; to them the Moors were infidels, resplendent in luxury and given over to vice; but traders and pirates made their own crude contacts, and the merchant ports of Lusitania were pillaged continually by Norse and English seafarers, zealous against the infidel and avid for his possessions. Such raids and excursions were probably the first experiments made by the English in the crusading technique in which they were later to become experts. History does not relate whether English adventurers assisted the Christian Visigoth princes in their winning of the Minho and Douro districts and the capturing of Oporto from the Moors in the tenth and eleventh centuries, nor whether Portugal, by that time partly redeemed from Moslem, received any of the Saxon exiles who fled their country after Hastings.

It is not until the Crusades that we have detailed accounts of those English irruptions into Portugal which have continued, under one mode and another, ever since.

CRUSADERS

IT was permissible, even laudable, the pope said, and might easily be profitable, the crusaders hoped, to break an expedition to the Holy Land in Spain or Portugal, where Moors were almost as obnoxious to God as in Palestine, and a good deal more obnoxious to the Christian princes of those lands. So, when crusading fleets put in to Oporto for rest and refreshment after the buffeting of the Biscay seas (called by the Moors the Sea of the English) on the way to Palestine, some emissary was not unlikely to meet them there and persuade them to such Iberian diversion. Whether any large number of the personnel (mostly Frankish) of the first crusade was thus diverted is uncertain; what is apparent is that when a band of English pirate-crusaders stopped off in Galicia in 1112 to give their services (running true to form in the matter of English intervention in Iberian civil war) in a rebellion against the Bishop of Santiago de Compostella, their kind was already well known, and they were recognized as English a great way off. All along the Iberian coast, and even inland till expelled by the bishop and by his patron St. James, they pillaged and plundered, murdered and violated churches, keeping up their shocking reputation as a people 'not seasoned with the honey of piety', a reputation not new, and well sustained throughout the crusading period.

The affair of 1140 took much the same pattern as that of seven years later; except that the English contingent was very small compared with that of the Franks; but English there were, and they remembered the expedition unfavourably when their help was asked against Lisbon again. As in 1147, the crusading fleet put in at Oporto, and was persuaded to sail to the Tagus and help Affonso I to capture Lisbon from the Moors. The siege was unsuccessful; the crusaders were happy in being able to ravage and lay waste the districts round the Tagus, but departed finally without having achieved their object, and with a disillusioned distaste for besieging Lisbon, for the Portuguese, and for their king, who had, in their view, and in some of the many ways customary between allies, let them badly down. This rankled; and particularly in the resentful breasts of those two enterprising and egotistic pirates, the Veal brothers, whose isolationist attitude with regard to the Moorish problem in Portugal in 1147 nearly crashed the whole Lisbon affair.

There must have been more crusading attempts on Lisbon than find mention in the chroniclers. 'How many times within our memory', the beleaguered Moorish alcayde bitterly cried from the Lisbon castle walls during the siege of 1147 to the Archbishop of Braga who parleyed with him for the king, 'have you come hither with pilgrims and barbarians to drive us hence!' And the pilgrims and barbarians were to come to Portugal against them again, though they broke them in Lisbon by that bitter four months' siege in the summer of 1147.

It was the second crusade. A fleet of Flemish and Rhineland crusaders, under the Counts Arnulf of Areschot and Christian of Gistel, called at Dartmouth to collect the Anglo-Norman contingent for the Holy Land. These were four groups — the men of Suffolk and Norfolk, under Hervey of Glanville, the men of Kent under Simon of Dover, the men of London under Andrew, the west countrymen (very difficult, especially those from Bristol, and much influenced by professional pirates), and a few Scots and Bretons. They were, as has been pointed out, an essentially lower-class crowd, hardy sailors and adventurers, both Saxon and Norman by race. Before setting forth on their holy enterprise (says the priestly English reporter of the expedition, traditionally, but probably wrongly, known as Osbern) the company drew up regulations and ordinances for their conduct abroad; laws of retribution, such as eyes for eyes, teeth for teeth, and so on; rules for weekly confession and communion, for the division of spoils, for the behaviour of the women they were taking, who were on no account to walk out in public. (Precisely what services were to be rendered to the army by these women the writer does not mention. Richard I, forty-five years later, ordered that no women were to accompany the crusading army out of Acre 'except the washerwomen, who would not be an occasion of sin'; possibly these also were washerwomen.) Anyhow, such as they were, the miscellaneous fleet set sail for Palestine on a day in May, a hundred and ninety ships in all, and a pretty tough crowd, including the squadron of west countrymen under the brothers Veal.

They met, of course, with rough weather in the Bay, and were also annoyed by sirens, who made a horrible noise of wailing, laughter and jeering, like the clamour of insolent men in a camp. Alarmed by these and beaten by storms, the crusaders became penitent, and 'atoning with a flow of tears' for their misdeeds, they were rewarded by so many divine visions and miracles that 'it would be tedious to enumerate them in detail'. They called at Whitsuntide at Santiago, to make the usual pilgrimage to St. James of Compostella, and then sailed down to the Douro, where, on June 16th, they put in to Oporto for refreshment.

They had been anxiously awaited. The sight of that storm-battered fleet entering Foz to anchor off the quays of Oporto and Gaia while an international crowd of tough armed men disembarked, with an air of being ready for anything, from piracy to Moor-killing, cheered the expectant eyes of the Bishop of Oporto, charged by his king to receive and welcome the fleet. His job was to divert them from going after Moors in the Holy Land to going after Moors in Portugal: their assistance was essential to the king's plan of taking Lisbon. As an earnest of the pleasures of Lusitania, the bishop had them served with 'good cheap wine and other delights', which enabled them to listen, when herded into the cathedral cemetery, to a long and persuasive address from him, delivered in Latin and translated by interpreters into the several tongues of the different contingents. He addressed them as repentant pirates who had now turned to God (no doubt he was familiar with their plundering expeditions on the Spanish coasts). Praising their sacrifice in undertaking this crusade, he urged them to switch their anti-infidel fervour from Palestine to Portugal, told them of the king's dire need and generous offers, and begged them to embark forthwith for the Tagus to meet and treat with the king. 'Do not be seduced', he begged them, 'by the desire to press on with your journey, for the praiseworthy thing is not to have been to Jerusalem, but to have lived a good life while on the way.' Thinking there was something in this, the crusaders decided that Portugal, King Affonso and his proposals were worth their cautious attention; they presently set sail for the Tagus, carrying with them the bishop and his colleague the Archbishop of Braga.

Osbern (or who ever he was) was an appreciative, even an enthusiastic, traveller, though too well read, for he adorned his descriptions of the country with chunks from Solinus and other geographical scribes. He was a little fanciful too, and sometimes threw up a palace or castle where there were none. But he gave a good account of the country between Oporto and Lisbon, and when the fleet entered the Tagus his admiration overflowed, and he struck the authentic note of British tourism, which so many sailing up the same river were to follow. This noble river, said he, was most abundantly fishy, and there was gold on its banks. To English eyes, used to nothing better than apple, pear, plum or cherry orchards, the vines, pomegranates and figs were most agreeable. The country round was admirable; corn, honey and hunting abounded; mares conceived, with great fecundity, by the west wind; all was opulent, all cultivated, all fertile. There was salt, oil, wine, game in profusion. At Cintra, which seemed to him to be only eight miles off, there was a spring of water in the Moorish castle which cured consumption and coughs. In the rich and populous city of Lisbon, there were gold and silver and hot baths, as was usual with Moors. As was equally usual with Moors, there was also every lust and abomination; the city was, in his opinion, a breeding-ground of these. It was also steep; it had 'steep defiles instead of ordinary streets'. It had magnificent walls, and, rising high above the labyrinth of narrow, crowded and climbing streets, a castle that looked impregnable. Certainly a city worth sacking, if it could be taken. The crusaders looked at it with wary and covetous eyes from the hill west of the town where they were encamped to await the arrival of the king, whom the two bishops had gone north of the city to fetch. King Affonso arrived and made his proposals, flattering and bribing them. He was heard with attentive caution. Most of the English contingent voted for staying. Not, however, those who had been to Lisbon before and had seen through besieging it; these took the king's promises for treachery. Some were swayed by the Veal pirates, practical men to whom crusades were not only partly, as with most crusaders, but exclusively, plundering expeditions, a legitimate and industrious means of laying up capital against old age. They and their followers were for going pirating along the Spanish and African coasts, and making Jerusalem while weather and winds were good. About eight of the English ships were for doing this. Noisy disputings broke out; Hervey of Glanville addressed the pirate group, entreating them for their honour's sake to stay with their comrades; even the Scots, said he, who were universally agreed to be barbarians, had not failed in the duty of friendship. Finally the pirates agreed; still strictly businesslike, they would remain as long as they were fed and paid, and not a day longer.

A firm agreement with the king was drawn up and sworn to, though there were crusaders of experience who believed that it made little difference what Affonso swore. However, the agreement looked good; if Lisbon were taken, the crusaders were to keep all enemy property, and to possess the city until it had been searched and spoiled, after which it was to be handed over to the king. Afterwards the city and lands would be shared out among them, according to rank. Also the ships and goods of the besiegers would be freed for ever from goods and tolls (possibly the first Anglo-Portuguese trade agreement, possibly not). These terms having been accepted, the bishops and some of the crusading leaders went to parley with the Moors. The alcayde and others stood on the city walls to hear them. The Archbishop of Braga addressed the enemy, telling them they had no right there and should go back to the land of the Moors without causing bloodshed. The alcayde replied with a bitter tirade. 'How many times within your memory have you come hither with pilgrims and barbarians to drive us hence? Do your possessions give you no pleasure, or have you got into trouble at home, that you are so often on the move? Surely your frequent coming and going proves your mental instability, for he who cannot control the flight of the body cannot control the mind. This city did, I believe, once belong to your people, but now it is ours. It may be yours in some future time, but this will be decided by the will of God. While God willed, we have held it; when he wills otherwise, we shall no longer hold it. Go away, for you shall not enter the city but by the sword. Why should I delay you longer? Do what you can. We will do what God's will determines.'

The Bishop of Oporto replied tartly, 'What end awaits you, you will learn by experience', and they parted with no mutual salutations to make them ready for battle, which began at once. The Moors shut themselves up in the Mouraria and threw stones at the Christians from the roofs. Fierce skirmishes went on day after day. Mutual insults were bandied; the Moors alternated the time-honoured gibe about the probable conduct of the crusaders' wives at home and the number of bastards being born by them, with odious remarks about the Trinity. The Christian repartees are not recorded, but no doubt they thought up equally good insults to the wives in Moorish harems and to the Prophet. After a fortnight they began to construct engines of assault, such as movable towers. Meanwhile some of the English crusaders went fishing on the Almada coast, and were captured there by Moors; in revenge, their comrades made a brilliant commando raid on Almada, returning with two hundred captives and eighty Moorish heads: this exploit greatly sent up Anglo-Norman stock in the army, and henceforth fishing expeditions to Almada were unimpeded.

The Lisbon garrison meanwhile were starving, and the worse for pestilence (they had nowhere to bury their dead) and sent fruitless appeals for help to their comrades in Evora. From time to time starving infidels would creep out of the city and give themselves up to the enemy, who would baptize them and were then apt to cut off their hands and pelt them to death with stones. The desperate garrison must have known it was only a question of time before the end came. The Germans and Flemings sapped terrible breaches in the eastern walls; when the Anglo-Normans came over to see how they were getting on, they were repulsed with anger and bidden to go back to their own engines; for international jealousies raged, and the allies got on together in the manner usual with allies on the battlefield. The crusaders thought the Portuguese inclined to retire at crucial moments, and that the king sent away forces and equipment to Santarem. Portuguese historians regard this as unlikely.

According to the English narrator, it was the Anglo-Norman movable tower, an engine eighty feet in height and equipped with a drawbridge that finally broke the spirit of the besieged. The account of the assault on the walls with this strange but powerful erection is Cromwellian in its mixture of violence with prayer. The long exhortation addressed to the manipulators of the machine by the priest who accompanied them might have been spoken by Oliver himself. 'Brothers, the work grows hot, the enemy presses . . . Trust in the Lord, and he shall give you the desires of your hearts. Be reconciled again with God, and put on Christ once more . . . Remember the marvellous work of the Lord which he has wrought in you, how he has brought you unharmed over

the vast waters and the violent storms, and how he has brought
you here, where through the inspiration of the Spirit we have
invaded this suburb . . . The enemy will not stand against us,
because those whom the error of ignorance of the faith degrades
will be struck with difficulty of action . . . Strike your guilty
breasts while you await the aid of the Lord. For it will come, it
will come . . . I am persuaded that'neither famine nor the sword
nor tribulation nor distress shall separate us from Christ. Now,
being certain of victory, fall upon the enemy . . . Glory be to our
Lord Jesus Christ . . . Amen.'

At this the engineers fell on their faces with groans and tears.
And so, in a loud voice calling on God for aid, they moved the
engine forward. After three days of desperate fighting, with
heavy losses on both sides, during which the tower was nearly
lost, it was placed within four feet of the wall, and the scaling-
bridge thrown out. That was the end: the heroic but beaten and
starving infidels laid down their arms and asked for a truce until
morning. This was granted, and Moorish hostages were handed
over to the king.

Jealousies and rioting broke out in the army, each nation fearing
to be done out of its due spoils. The Portuguese heard a rumour
that all the gold and silver in the city would go to the crusaders;
the crusaders clamoured to have the hostages. Mutiny raged
among 'fatuous English seamen', incited by a Bristol clergyman
of doubtful morals, who asked why so many brave men should obey
a few unworthy leaders. The fatuous seamen saw no reason why;
they rushed out of camp, shouting vengeance against Glanville.
The Moorish hostages, dignified men who disapproved such unseemly conduct, said firmly that they would negotiate terms with
the king and his army, but would have no dealings with those
base, disloyal and ferocious men, the crusaders. A council was
held with the king; it was agreed that if the alcayde and his son-
in-law might keep their property and the other citizens be fed, the
city should be surrendered. The English and Normans at once
agreed, saying very properly that upright conduct should be preferred to spoil; the Germans and Flemish, however, 'in whom there
is always innate cupidity', were determined that the city should be
completely despoiled. It was finally agreed that only the alcayde
should be allowed food and his property (except his Arabian mare,
on which the Count of Areschot had set his heart). Tumults and

clashes continued, and the king, now thoroughly sick of foreign crusaders, remarked that he did not care to associate with such people any more.

It was agreed that a hundred and sixty Germans and Flemings and a hundred and forty Anglo-Normans were to enter the city first, and occupy the upper castle, where the Moors were to bring their money and possessions, after which the city would be searched for what they might have neglected to bring; later the despoiled citizens would be let out through the three gates.

The gates were opened, and, needless to say, the Germans and Flemings cheated, for with the agreed hundred and sixty there rushed in over two hundred more, and proceeded to behave in the most shocking fashion. Of course, says Osbern, no Anglo-Normans beyond the agreed quota presumed to enter; these followed the bishops and watched them plant the banner of the cross on the castle tower, while clergy and people, not without tears, intoned the *Te Deum* during the ceremony of aspersion which purified the city defiled by unbelievers. These holy doings made small impression on the men of Flanders and Cologne, who, seeing so many temptations to greed all round them, quite succumbed, rushing hither and thither, pillaging, breaking down doors and robbing houses, insulting citizens and maidens. They took for themselves what should have been common property, they cut the throat of the aged Mozarabic bishop, they seized the alcayde and pillaged his house. Count Areschot struggled for the coveted mare so roughly that the poor animal had a miscarriage. All Germans and Flemings, in fact, behaved in the most brutal and licentious manner imaginable.

'But the Normans and English, to whom good faith and scruples of conscience were matters of the greatest import' (this apparently went for the Veal brothers too) 'remained quietly at the posts to which they had been assigned, preferring to keep their hands from all rapine rather than violate their promises; an occurrence which greatly shamed Areschot, Christian and their followers, since their unmixed greed now stood openly revealed.'

It should in justice be observed that the Teutonic accounts read rather differently, and that, as a Portuguese historian acidly points out, there is little in the antecedents of the Anglo-Norman crusaders to make it easy to believe that they stood quietly as spectators of these wild scenes, converted suddenly into models of moderation and virtue. As an Anglo-Norman, it would ill become me to take a side in this international squabble. Better to hasten on to Saturday morning, when the despoiled citizens, Moors and Christian Mozarabs in about equal numbers, began to file out through the three city gates; so many were they (as those acquainted with Mouraria and Alfama can readily believe) that the procession lasted till Wednesday. After they had gone out, great quantities of wheat, barley and oil were found stored in their cellars.

It does not appear that there was any organized feeding or sheltering of the dispossessed, whether unbelievers or Christians. Among them pestilence, starvation and conversion raged. 'Among ruins and vineyards and villages, countless thousands of corpses lay exposed to birds and beasts, and living men resembling bloodless beings went about the earth and kissed the cross as suppliants, and declared that Mary, the Mother of God, was good.' Whether they gained anything by this gesture is not clear. But even the Christians were moved almost to pity, though they 'thought the prophecy of Isaiah happily fulfilled'. Osbern's narrative ends with a religious discourse — 'We are inclined to feel pity for our enemies in their evil fortunes, and to feel sorry that the lashes of divine justice are not yet at an end.'

So ended the seventeen weeks' siege. Lisbon was won for the King of Portugal, and it was the only lasting gain of all that the crusaders attempted in Portugal on their various incursions. They had been promised half the city in reward; but they did not feel inclined for Lisbon, and renounced their claims on it; a large number requested instead grants of land, and settled in colonies up the Tagus valley and elsewhere. The fifteenth-century historian Galvão, a man of pleasing fancies, mentions various places thus settled; he puts the English particularly in Villa Franca, which he says they called Cornogoa, after Cornwall. The name was said to have been changed to Villa Franca because of the freedoms and franchises it enjoyed, and because, said the English chaplain in Lisbon, the learned Dr. Colbatch, writing in 1700, well-bred and delicate-minded Portuguese did not care to say 'corn'. Like the alleged English derivation of the name Almada, ('all made it') the story is not inherently probable. All the tales of crusaders' settlements are difficult to prove, and seem to have a mythological element. Still, Affonso I and his successors, do seem to have

wanted for military reasons an infiltration of northern blood in
Portugal. Affonso did not care for the crusaders' manners and
habits, nor did his subjects; but no one could deny that they were
tough fighting men and useful against Moors and Spaniards, and
he was probably glad that they should settle about the country.
'Factaque est illic cristicolarum colonia usque in presentem diem',
says Helmold. There are families in Portugal now which trace
their descent from those crusading colonists. How many stayed is
not known. The majority, after wintering in Lisbon (many of
them in the monastery of S. Vicente de Fora), appear to have
departed for Palestine in February.

Among those who stayed in Portugal was the new Bishop of
Lisbon, Gilbert of Hastings, an English priest, who was selected
for the office by his countrymen, approved by the king, council
and bishops, and consecrated immediately after the city's fall by
the Archbishop of Braga. That he was chosen for the first bishop
of the restored Christian see shows high qualities in himself and
the intention of the king to keep in with England. Of his past
little is known; it has been suggested that he must have been of
good birth, since, in a snobbish age, his countrymen treated him
with respect and chose him from among all the crusading priests
for the episcopacy. Whatever his birth, he was esteemed as a high-
minded and learned prelate. 'There was chosen,' says a Portuguese historian, 'a virtuous man who was called Gilbert, of very
good life and habits, and learned in degrees.' He proved also an
able administrator. He is said to have induced many of the
crusading chaplains to stay and work under him; the king gave
him thirty-two houses for his canons, with lands, vineyards and
olive groves, which must have been a pleasant change for these
northern clergymen. The king further recognized the Anglo-
Norman crusaders' help by dedicating to them the church, St.
Mary of the Martyrs, built during the siege on the burial-ground
of their slain. Over the altar was placed a Madonna who had
travelled with the English fleet, and the church became a crusaders' centre.

Gilbert, an energetic bishop, set to work to organize his enormous diocese that stretched north and south from Leiria to
Alcacer do Sol and east to Evora. He helped in building the
cathedral, established the Sarum use (which was continued in
Lisbon until 1536), and endeavoured (in the end successfully) to

subjugate the Templars, those proud and difficult men, who had their own jurisdiction round Santarem, claiming independence of the Portuguese primacy and direct dealings with Rome. It took Gilbert ten years of argument to get these arrogant transmontanes down. He also had a pacifying and Christianizing effect on Moors. In 1151 he undertook a mission to England to enlist crusaders for an attack on the Saracen stronghold of Alcacer do Sol; he induced an English fleet to sail to Portugal and assist, but the Saracens were stubborn and the attack failed. The English military continued, however, to be in and out of the peninsula, both in Portugal and Spain; they would stop off *en route* for Jerusalem, casually destroy a castle or two, and proceed on their way refreshed.

But the next time there is specific mention of English incursion was at the siege of Silves in 1189, where they and the other crusaders behaved with the utmost ferocity. King Affonso was dead; his son Sancho inherited the task of clearing Portugal of infidels and the habit of roping in war-like foreign crusaders to assist him in doing it. The crusaders, for their part, had acquired the habit of regarding the peninsula ports as richly rewarding stages on their journeyings to the Holy Sepulchre; many of them got no further, but returned home with their pockets full of the spoils and wages of the Christian war in Iberia. Their habit was to call at ports along the northern Spanish coast, stopping for religious reasons in the river Tambre in Galicia to make their way to St. James of Compostella, then sailing south down the Portugal coast, looking in on Oporto and Lisbon to refresh themselves and see if anyone had a job for them. The sight of these large and odious armed men (for large and odious they seemed both to the Moors and the Portuguese) sailing in fleets up the rivers and disembarking with barbarian northern cries, only too ready for anything, became familiar to the Galicians and the Portuguese. So familiar and so disconcerting that the crusaders who landed to perform their Lenten duties at Santiago in 1189 were driven off by an exasperated populace which too well knew their habits, and had to retreat with their duties unfulfilled. Many of this particular band were Danes, even larger and more odious than the Germans, Dutch and English who formed the rest of the armada. Somewhat annoyed with the obstructive Gallegos, they sailed down to the Tagus. There, according to precedent, they met King Sancho, set on conquering Algarve. The crusaders took a favourable view of this enterprise, and, joined by a Portuguese fleet, sailed south, rounded Cape St. Vincent, and entered the pleasant bay of Portimão. Landing, they found themselves in a rich, fertile, semi-tropical land, lovely with almond and orange-blossom, strangely, to northern eyes, grown with dark, glossy carobs and sticky-leaved figs. But an empty land, for the evil news 'the Christians are in the bay' had sent the Arab peasantry fleeing for shelter into the walled stronghold of Alvor; all in vain, for the Christians followed them there and made short work of them and their castle, scaling the walls, sacking, destroying and looting, and massacring nearly six thousand persons. One raid by northern barbarians is very like another; the Saracens of Algarve experienced now what the Britons had suffered from the invading Saxon hordes long ago, what the Saxons had endured from Norse vikings, what Roman Europe had from Goths, Visigoths and Huns. Satiated for the moment with infidel blood and loot, the crusaders tarried no more, but continued their voyage to the Holy Land.

Another fleet of them, this time with more English, mostly Londoners, on board, arrived in July of the same year. Their goal was the Algarve capital, the rich, beautiful and strong city of Silves, whose loot King Sancho promised to the foreigners. A Portuguese army joined them; they encamped up the river Drade outside Silves. Again the fertile countryside was emptied of its people; this time they had sought shelter inside the strong walls of their capital, and Silves was a much tougher proposition than Alvor had been.

Algarve lay in oppressive African heat; the figs were ripe and bursting on the sticky trees, the largest and sweetest figs in Europe. As they ate them, the men from the north looked up at the proud and rich Saracen city, dazzlingly white, surrounded by gardens and orchards in luxuriant leaf, flower and fruit, built about with arcaded and mosqued dwellings and churches, crowned with a castle that seemed impregnable. There was a high city, a lower city, a suburb, and each was guarded by moats and by stubborn, watch-towered walls. Silves looked, in fact, as hard to take as it proved. The Portuguese regarded it dubiously; but the foreign crusaders, indomitable and avaricious men, were undaunted.

They besieged it through August. On September 1st the garrison, perishing from thirst, surrendered, asking to be allowed to leave the city with such of their goods as they could carry. The king was for consenting; the crusaders however insisted on their last pound of flesh, and would allow the infidels nothing but their lives.

So the starving and bereft procession filed out through the gates. Seeing the Moors thus at their mercy proved too much for the crusaders, who fell on them with blows and insults and stripped them even of their clothing, which angered the king and the Portuguese army greatly. The Portuguese occupied the city that night, which they and their allies spent largely in torturing the remaining inhabitants to make them reveal the whereabouts of their treasures. Next day the crusaders sacked the city. The king, by now thoroughly disgusted with his assistants, turned them out, and resentfully they returned to their ships with their spoils; failing to extract more loot from the perfidious king, as they indignantly called him, they refused to remain and assist in an attack on Faro, but sailed away, some to Palestine, some to spend the rewards of their labour in their own lands. The affair had ended, like so many allied campaigns, with the greatest mutual ill feeling; the Portuguese accused the northerners of rapacity and turbulence, and were accused in their turn of having been defaulting in battle and stingy in reward.

But next year, like migratory sea birds, a fleet of these turbulent beings, *en route* to join Richard Coeur de Lion in the Mediterranean, swam into Portuguese seas once more. The fleet had been scattered by storms, and each vessel sought shelter where it could. One shipful, driven into the Bay of Silves, acceded to the bishop's request that they should help to defend Silves against an infidel attack; the rest of the fleet arrived in the Tagus, and proceeded to behave very strangely. By now accustomed to attacking and sacking Portuguese towns, and doubtless having indulged too freely in Portuguese wines, the crusaders landed in Lisbon and began to treat it as if they were come to capture it. Some of them may have had old scores to pay off; some may have mistaken the situation, and, seeing Moors and Jews about, and remembering their fathers' tales of forty years ago, may have supposed it their task to wrest the city once more from the infidel; or all may have been moved, quite simply, by the ruling crusading passion for destruction, blood and loot. Anyhow they fell on Lisbon, as a Portuguese historian puts it, like a pack of wild beasts got loose, running through the city and attacking the citizens with violence, more particularly the Saracens and Jews, but not sparing the Portuguese, their persons, their property, or their female relations. For several days the violence, sacking and burning went on in the city, the suburbs, and the country round. The king, hearing of these distressing scenes, hurried down from Santarem to stop them; a tactful man, he did not return violence in kind, but requested the commanders of the marauders to make them desist and observe the rules made for crusaders by King Richard, who knew their temptations and habits. The commanders failed to confine the unruly mob to their ships; violent Anglo-Portuguese fighting broke out; the king sent his troops to arrest and endungeon all the seven hundred English in the town. They were locked up until pledges had been given for their good conduct and the restitution of plunder; this arranged, the English fleet, to Portuguese relief, sailed off to the Mediterranean.

They were back in the Tagus in 1217. Some Portuguese historians eliminate the English from this adventure, disguising the Earls of Wight and of Holland, their leaders, under the names of Count de Wythe and the Count of Holland from Flanders; but this seems to be merely the pardonable confusion customary among the Portuguese when it comes to distinguishing the nationalities of northern crusaders. The expedition consisted of the mixture as before — Rhinelanders, Flemings, Frisians and English, all set for the Holy Land, and it took the usual course — storms at sea, arrival, after six weeks of tossing and straying, in the Tagus, appeals for help from the local clergy, who nobly entertained the arrivals and told them that it was too late in the summer for Palestine, that God had sent them to Lisbon to besiege Alcacer do Sol, and that its spoils when captured would be great. A hundred ships decided to stay, including the two English earls and their fleet.

A two months' fierce siege followed. A Saracen army joined furious battle with the Christians. These, when drawn up for battle in the early morning against their tremendously outnumbering foes, saw among the brilliant stars a great cross, and perceived that they would win. Indeed, God seemed with them, for when the sun rose they also observed in the sky an army of Templars engaged in aerial combat with Mussalmen. So every augury was with them, and three days of fierce mutual slaughter ended with the rout of the infidels. The garrison of Alcacer, however, held out till mid-October, when at last surrender was forced.

It is a relief not to have to record subsequent excesses on the part of our ancestors and their colleagues, who seem on this occaion to have behaved with no more impropriety than the situation warranted. The Portuguese prelates, anxious to keep them for further operations against the Saracens, wrote to ask the Pope if they might stay in Lisbon for another year, earning thereby the same indulgences as if they had proceeded to Palestine. The Pope said this would not do; he was beginning to think Palestine neglected for Portugal. So the crusaders had to proceed to the Holy Land in the spring; they wintered, however, in Lisbon, and apparently enjoyed themselves greatly. The English taste for wintering in Portugal was now well launched.

This was, so far as we know, the last irruption of English crusaders (as such) into Portugal. It was a habit perhaps better broken. Fine fighters as the Anglo-Norman adventurers were, they were too covetous, too tipsy, and too rough. *Bebido inglez*, English drunkard, became and remained a term of abuse among a people whose intemperance has never taken the form of excessive drinking. Contemporary Portuguese comment singled out the Germans as more coarse and brutal than the Anglo-Normans; still, one must ask oneself, as a Portuguese historian says, if the comradeship in arms did not leave odious memories in Portuguese souls. The answer, obviously, is yes. Not the less, perhaps all the more, because of their courageous fighting efficiency, the effectiveness of their help, and their sometimes insulting scorn for their smaller and less war-like allies.

Besides memories, there remained in Portugal a few English settlements up the Tagus, some Portuguese versions of some English names, and some English blood — large frames and blue eyes scattered about among a small dark people up and down the country where the adventurers of the Cross had roved and pleasured.

It would be interesting to have more light on the confused darkness which obscures the numbers and careers of the English crusading settlers. Most, presumably, lived by cultivating their lands; some may have taken to trading, and formed the core of the Anglo-Portuguese commercial relations that were, a little later, so rapidly and strongly to develop and thrive. If the behaviour of the crusaders in general fails to suggest suitability or taste for a steady business career, it must be remembered that piracy and trade have traditionally been twin activities of the English seafaring adventurer, and those who have landed sword in hand have often stayed to buy and sell.

BIBLIOGRAPHY

De Expugnatione Lyxbonensi, edited and translated by C. W. DAVID (1936).
Narratio de itinere navali peregrinorum Hierosolymam tendentium et Silviam capient-ium. A.D. 1189. Edited by C. W. DAVID (*Proceedings of the American Philosophical Society,* vol. 81, 1939).
De Itinere Navali . . . a Peregrinis Hierosolymam Petentibus MCLXXXIX.
Historia de Portugal, ALEXANDRE HERCULANO (Lisbon, 1846-53).
Lisboa Antiga, JULIO CASTILHO (Coimbra, 1884).
A Aliança Inglesa, ARMANDO MARQUES GUEDES (Lisbon, 1938).
Chronica de Affonso Henriques, DUARTE GAVÃO (Lisbon).
Imagines Historiarum, RALPH OF DICETO.
Chronica Gothorum.
Historia Compostelana.
English Crusaders in Portugal, H. A. R. GIBBS (Chapters in Anglo-Portuguese relations. Edited E. Prestage, 1935).
History of Portugal compiled from Portuguese histories, EDWARD MCMURDO (1888).

ROYALTY

1. ENGLISH QUEEN OF PORTUGAL
Philippa of Lancaster
(1386-1415)

JOHN OF GAUNT, Duke of Lancaster, Edward III's fourth son, having his full share of the continental illusions of his family, believed himself to be the King of Castile. This faith (which superseded and put in the shade his earlier view that he was the Count of Provence) was encouraged and crystallized by his taking for his second wife in 1371 the ex-Infanta Constance, the elder of the two surviving daughters of the dispossessed and by then murdered King Pedro the Cruel of Castile. (To keep the Spanish crown safely in the family, Lancaster's brother of Cambridge married the younger ex-Infanta.) John of Gaunt took for his style 'King of Castile and Leon', was called 'My lord of Spain', 'Monseigneur-d'Espagne', and, by the Black Prince, 'my very dear and well-beloved brother of Spain'. It was, for the English, quite settled: it only remained to convince the Castilians, and in particular the *de facto* reigning King of Castile, and to take possession. This could not, naturally, be done in a hurry; it was advisable first to secure the assistance and connivance of the King of Portugal. Diplomatic envoys plied to and fro between Portugal and England, lavishly entertained; commercial favours were showered on the merchants of each country by the sovereign of the other; in 1373 the Treaty of Windsor was signed, by which both allies agreed to help one another against all enemies. An odd alliance, a little wary on both sides, and rather treacherous and half-hearted on Ferdinand of Portugal's, for he continually wavered away from his ally towards Spain his enemy; but John of Gaunt, his eyes unswervingly on his Spanish dream, pursued Portuguese friendship with a single mind. He waited his chance, seeing always his Castilian crown shining, an intoxicating mirage across the seas.

It was not till 1386 that he took his army over to fetch it. He took, of course, his family too; no military expedition was complete without the female relatives of its leaders. Lancaster had his wife

Constance, all eagerness to avenge her murdered father; he had his two *filles à marier*, the devout and virtuous twenty-six years old Philippa (so like his beloved first wife her mother) and her young half-sister Katherine. Besides his legitimate offspring, he took also his bastards Blanche and Joanna to the wars. To complete the domestic party, there was Katherine Swynford, in her double function of mistress to the duke and to his daughters. The ladies kept on the voyage the most ceremonious pomp and luxury; it was more like a pleasure cruise than a military expedition. The party were seen off at Plymouth by the king and queen; Richard, rather relieved to be getting rid of his uncle, whom, according to Shakespeare, he habitually and unnecessarily called 'aged Gaunt', presented him and his wife each with a golden crown, to impress their subjects the Castilians.

The expedition arrived at Santiago, which it occupied with ease and distinction; Lancaster prayed at the shrine of St. James of Compostella, expressed his views on the papal feud by changing the Clementine archbishop for an Urbanite, notified the kings of Castile and Portugal of his arrival, and settled down to wait events. Seldom had the quiet ancient town of the apostle known such gaiety or been so extremely full. The duke and duchess set up a magnificent court, as befitted Castilian royalty, and Philippa and Katherine, to be out of harm's way, were placed in an abbey; the *filles à marier* had to be carefully guarded.

So gaily enough, three months passed. King John of Portugal sent noble presents of fine ambling mules to the duke and duchess and their daughters; Lancaster sent him in return two peregrine falcons and six greyhounds, for without these sporting birds and beasts English gentlemen seldom embarked on foreign campaigns. Then the duke and the king, with companies of knights and troops, met each other in state on the river Minho, exchanged courtesies and rich banquets, and negotiated a treaty for the invasion of Castile, by which King John supplied an army and received the hand of Philippa. After nine days of festive and tipsy emulation and good will, Lancaster returned to Santiago, where his duchess, eager to know everything, awaited him. She asked him, says the omniscient Froissart, how he had liked the King of Portugal. Very well, replied the duke; his people say they have had no king this hundred years whom they liked so much; he is only thirty-six, and strong and brave. Yes sir, said the lady, but what says he to any marriage? The duke said he had offered him one of the girls, and he had, with many thanks, chosen Philippa. The duchess, perhaps a little huffed at the passing over of her own child, said, He has good reason, for Katherine is yet too young for him.

So the Lancasters settled down in Galicia through the mild damp green winter to await the day when it should please the king to make the next move and ratify the marriage. For the next two months, while the English army skirmished in a desultory way about Spain, King John, occupied in preparing his own army for the invasion, from time to time sent polite salutations to Philippa and her parents, but made no move to see her. Philippa, a patient young woman, may have thought that her nuptials were once again to fall through. Different reasons have been given for the king's dilatoriness, as that he was told that the young woman was plain, and he had other and more attractive attachments. Or, since her father was dissolute, might she not, under that calm and cold English exterior, be dissolute too, and no fit queen? She had, after all, grown up with the worst examples before her . . . Or he had to wait for a papal dispensation from the vows of celibacy of his Order of Aviz. Or he was still hesitating, in the traditional Portuguese manner, between the English alliance and the Castilian, weighing the advantages of each. And so on. Most probably he saw no occasion for haste, and it never actually occurred to his Iberian mind that a month or two of delay would cause speculation. When he was ready, and the dispensation to hand, he sent a message to Santiago to say so.

There seems some confusion and vagueness among the historians as to the sequence of events after that. Froissart's story is that the Archbishop of Braga came to Santiago accompanied by a special envoy from the king, who was to marry Philippa by proxy; the marriage was performed and the couple laid in the same bed, according to what the Portuguese believed to be the English custom. After that the duke sent his daughter to Oporto, with a retinue of English and Portuguese ladies, bishops, high military and naval officers, and companies of lancers and archers. They had a great ceremonial reception, and Philippa was lodged in the episcopal palace, where she spent many days before the king came to her. He, still in no hurry, at last arrived in Oporto and met his bride for the first time. He took her by the hand, kissed her and all her ladies, conducted her to her room, took his leave, and went south again. His gentlemen behaved in similar fashions with the other ladies. The wedding date in due time arrived, and so did the king, just in time for the ceremony. This was only the religious ceremony; the actual wedding was twelve days later, and was a magnificent festal occasion. Oporto was decorated up to the nines; in the streets, bright with banners and strewn with sweet herbs, people danced; in the gardens by S. Domingos jousts and tournaments were held. The whole city gave itself up to feast for the wedding of their popular king with the young English princess Filippa de Alemcastre, a member of the most powerful royal family in Europe and daughter to the future King of Castile.

There may have been felt some not unreasonable disappointment that the great duke her father did not attend the nuptials; but he was occupied in subduing Galicia and in planning the Castilian invasion, and could not get away.

Out of the courts of the bishop's palace rode King John on a fine white horse, all in cloth of gold, and the new queen on another; they wore crowns of jewelled gold; the archbishop led the queen's horse by the rein. Before them went the pipes, the trumpets and the other music, drowning the singing of the matrons (for only matrons might sing at weddings; the maids looked enviously on). Oporto was full to overflowing; companies of English troops came in from the country round to see the procession and join in the revelries; confusion was immense. The wedding was followed by a magnificent banquet, after which the archbishop, bishops and priests processed with all the pomp of religion to the royal apartments to bless the nuptial bed. A company of English and Portuguese noblemen, carrying torches, went too, and all entered the bedroom. The matrons meanwhile, presumably still singing, had laid the bride in bed. The groom entered, attended by a crowd of knights and servants, uttering the dissolute expressions and jests suitable to the occasion, an old Portuguese custom which survived till 1834, when the modest young Maria da Gloria ended it. The archbishop and priests, entering on this scene, prayed over the *novios* and blessed them according to the English custom. After which, again according to the English custom, they were given wine in the nuptial goblet, which was passed round to all present. Then, after placing the king in bed, the assembly withdrew.

There followed a fortnight of national revelry throughout

Portugal. Tourneys, jousts and feasts consumed the days, dancing and singing the nights. 'The good people of Porto,' said a Lisbon historian, 'broke the hard monotony of their lives in that hour of rejoicing. The very sun penetrated into the dismal streets, and lent the faces of the citizens a luminous vivacity.' In Lisbon they emulously prepared great doings against the arrival of the court; up and down the country townsfolk and peasants made merry, lit bonfires and danced. It was an auspicious beginning to a happy partnership and a popular reign.

For Philippa, one can believe it a happy change. The good, religious and studious child of a mother who died when Philippa was eight years old, she had passed into the care of a governess who was also her father's mistress, and later of a passionate Spanish step-mother who involved the family in preposterous and humiliatingly fruitless continental excursions in search of a throne. At home, she saw her ambitious and intractable father hated by the people, befriending the heretic Wycliffe and to that extent sharing the shame of his pernicious doctrines, intrigued against by court fac-tions and patronized by his young nephew the king, who mainly wanted to be rid of him. The nation was plague-struck, the peasantry wretchedly hungry and destitute, the church and orders corrupt, the nobility factious. She herself had been hawked round as a possible match to various foreign princes and to her cousin Richard, seven years her junior, but had found no takers. Finally, here was this wild crown-hunting adventure into the peninsula, and she and her sisters dragged along in the heat with the army, dumped into abbeys or bishops' palaces to keep them safe while their father offered them as make-weights in his negotiations with kings.

But at last this was over. Philippa was a queen; her marriage was a triumphal procession, her husband handsome, victorious, beloved of his own people, a friend and ally of hers, an assistant to her father in his adventure into Spain. She, while they pursued this chimera, maintained her court at Oporto or Coimbra, sur-rounded by the English ladies and gentlemen she had brought from home and by affable, if incomprehensible, Portuguese. She received a visit from her stepmother and her sister Katherine; she accompanied them and her husband to Bragança to see the joust-ing between her brother-in-law Holland and a French knight; they had a delightful time there, and after it was over she returned to Coimbra to wait with her court until her husband should have finished helping to conquer Castile for her father. News of that disastrous and plague-stricken summer campaign, and of the deaths, one after another, of the flower of the English army, crossed the frontier to the English queen; at last failure was admitted; the King of Portugal and the sick, weary and embittered Duke of Lancaster returned from the inimical, burnt Spanish soil, defeated by illness and by Spanish indifference to their cause. On his way to Coimbra, King John fell dangerously ill; Philippa and Portugal besieged heaven with anguished prayers; he recovered, and together the king and queen went to Coimbra, where a Castilian tried to poison the queen's father and stepmother, failed and was burnt alive. After that the Lancasters left Portugal for Bayonne; Philippa was left with her king, her adopted country, and her English retinue.

The court had, and kept, strong English elements. The queen's personal officials were English; her chancellor was an English priest, Adam Davenport, a former prebendary of St. Paul's; her major-domo was called William Arnold. Her ladies were English; many of them married into Portuguese noble families, infusing English blood into the pedigrees of the fidalgos. Many English came out after the court; the prospect of living under an English queen gave a fresh impulse to merchants in pursuit of trade and gentlemen hoping for royal patronage. There was a constant Anglo-Portuguese coming and going to and from that brilliant court under its genial king and its gentle, high-minded, studious queen. Its language became French; the strange, Anglo-Norman kind of French that the English court spoke at home. Philippa of course learnt Portuguese; but French became the mode. A fashion of French clothes and manners set in among the higher ranks of Portuguese, and never quite died out. The court moved permanently to Lisbon, instead of, as before, alternating with Coimbra. Lisbon became larger and more magnificent; wealthy merchants from all countries brought their ships up the Tagus and filled the streets with their booths; gaieties and entertainments enlivened city life, while at the palace a brilliant Anglo-Portuguese circle surrounded the royal family. During the summer the court was much at Cintra, where the king had restored and enlarged the Moorish palace.

Children frequently occurred; they were given names alternately

English and Portuguese. There were five princes, all gifted and all to be illustrious; Edward (or Duarte), named after his great-grandfather Edward III, who wrote philosophical treatises, studied law, and succeeded to the throne; Pedro, a great traveller and man of letters; Henry, the greatest of them all, named for his English uncle, born in the Rua dos Inglezes in Oporto, to become the Navigator, the founder of Portuguese exploration; John, Grand Master of the Order of Santiago and Constable of Portugal; Ferdinand, the religious and monastic, the Master of Aviz, the martyr of Fez. There was also a girl, Elizabeth (or Isabel), who married Philip the Good of Burgundy. They were a magnificent set of Infantes, and had a mutual affection and a devotion to their mother quite unusual in royal families. Philippa, a studious and bookish woman, whose parents had been Chaucer's friends and patrons, had them well educated; several of them had an English look, tall, spare and ruddy (though Isabel looked Portuguese, being short, plump and brunette); Henry in his portraits might be an English squire. They had, says a Portuguese historian, English tenacity and constancy, and great chastity; their English blood was an 'influxo glacial', and caused Henry to live a life quite un-Portuguese, shutting himself up in his observatory at Sagre and devoting his time to the science of navigation, undistracted, it was said, by any female interests. They did not get this from their genial father, who had not permitted the vows which had to be annulled by the pope before he could marry to hamper him unduly, and owned two sizeable children, a son and a daughter, whose mother, at his marriage, he made superior of the Santos convent in Lisbon. Philippa, quite used to bastards in her home life in England, took in these children the interest of a good stepmother, and helped to arrange a match between Beatrice and the English Earl of Arundel; her letter about it to her brother Henry IV is kindly and businesslike. The boy, Affonso, was made Duke of Bragança; he was bitterly jealous of his legitimate half-brothers: but two hundred and fifty years later it was his line that followed the ousted Spaniards on to the throne of Portugal, and stayed on it for another two hundred and fifty.

That the English queen was, in fact, a particularly nice and good woman seems to have been the general view. She was tall, fair, white-skinned, regular-featured, with small English blue eyes, which she modestly turned down as she walked. Her mien was indeed almost too modest, her piety impressive. She did not, it seems, at first charm her husband as a woman, but she dominated him with time, and, adopting her standards of chastity in court life, he, with southern fervour, carried them to extremes, and burnt at least one adulterer alive. And 'in the vigour of life', writes a Portuguese historian, 'in the thirties, forties and fifties, the king got no bastards. What a singular change in our court customs!' The court, in fact, became most peculiar: no amorous encounters short of matrimony were tolerated. Every now and then, some gentleman and lady would receive a note from a secretary commanding that they got married forthwith; over a hundred ladies thus had their positions regularized. The court became like a school, where the headmistress, pacing gently about with hands holding her veil across her breast, her eyes, which nevertheless observed so much too much, raised conventually to heaven or cast conventually down to earth, enforced standards too rare for human understanding. It was said that she never forgave lapses. The king, caught kissing pretty ladies-in-waiting (those formidable temptations of kings) had to explain, shame-faced, that it meant no harm. Gravely she left the room. Here one must again quote a Portuguese commentator. 'Was she jealous? No, only those are jealous who know passion. It was that sentiment extraordinarily Saxon, for which there exists only an English word — cant, that unconscious mixture of pride and convention which is below religion and duty, but above hypocrisy.' King John became by her influence gradually transformed; he may in the end even have ceased to kiss ladies-in-waiting; there are, in fact, no rumours that his affections seriously strayed from his wife, though one need not actually suppose him so eccentric a Portuguese as to emulate his English wife and sons. He took to translating devout books; the piety that was to characterize the Portuguese royal line, though not yet become, as it later did, delirious, had firm roots in him. In that grave court learning, science and philosophy also flourished; the Infantes were indeed well bred and reared.

History does not relate that any of them were so English as to be continually drunk; possibly in this respect their Portuguese blood, breeding and environment prevailed over their northern strain. Henry, at least, may have recognized the danger, for after his youth he left off wine altogether; he could not risk intoxication in his navigational studies. The court, however English, sounds sober; the queen was certainly so; though her sister Katherine of Castile practised this British vice so patriotically that she became bibulously stout. But Katherine never had Philippa's principles or piety.

Philippa died of plague in 1415; she was fifty-five. The fleet was preparing for the Ceuta expedition against the Moors, on which the king and three Infantes were going, together with half the nobility of Portugal and many rich English adventurers. Philippa, who saw it as a glorious and chivalric crusade, was concerned not to delay its start by her illness and death. She sent away the king lest he should catch the plague, but sent for the three princes and gave them the swords she had had made for them against their knighting. To Duarte, the heir, she spoke of ruling his people with justice and pity.

'I give you this sword with my blessing,' she said, 'and that of your grandparents from whom I descend. Though it be strange for knights to take swords from the hands of women, I ask you not to object, for, because of my lineage and the will which I have for the increase of your honour, I think no harm can come to you by it; nay, rather I believe that my blessing and that of my ancestors will be of great help to you.' Duarte kissed her hand and said he would carry out her orders with good will. The second sword she gave to Pedro, giving ladies and damsels into his charge, for, said she, she had observed him from childhood engaged in honouring and serving them. Pedro replied that it pleased him much to continue in this occupation, and he would do so without any doubt. Then she gave the third sword to Henry, her favourite, saying, with a certain aristocratic partisanship (for she was a Plantagenet), 'This one I kept for you, for I think it is strong like yourself. To you I commend the lords, knights, fidalgos and squires; it often happens that kings, owing to false informations and unfair petitions from the people, take measures against them that they should not.'

The wind rose with great noise; the queen asked from what quarter it blew. From the north, they told her. 'I think,' said she, 'that that will be favourable for your voyage.' She added that she had looked forward to seeing them start, but that this could not now be. Duarte told her she would recover and see it, but she knew better; she would only see it from aloft, and they must start on the Feast of St. James, a week hence. The next day she made a very good death, surrounded by her sons; her expiry was preceded by an eclipse of the sun, which seemed to the people a seemly tribute and symbol.

For they had loved this good and religious English queen, so devoted to her family, her church, her books, and her principles, so generous, chaste and kind, so quietly courageous that for herself she seemed to fear nothing. It was remembered how, thirteen years ago, when expecting the birth of Fernando, she had been so ill that the doctors had predicted that she would die unless she took something to cause abortion; showing the resolute spirit of her line, she said she would sooner die than that; and, amid the fervent prayers of the nation, Fernando was safely born, inheriting a most religious spirit and the self-sacrificing devotion of the martyr.

Mourned by a nation and by a bereaved family, Philippa, smelling sweetly, but by no means unexpectedly, of violets, was buried at Odivellos where she had died. A year later, her body was transferred to Batalha, that English-looking Gothic abbey built by John to commemorate the battle of Aljubarrota, and partly designed by an English architect. John and Philippa had watched it building; their bodies, after the king's death, lay there together; on their tomb their stone figures lie together too, hand in hand; the English queen holds in her free hand a book; both are beautiful.

Thus was English Plantagenet blood infused into the royal line of Portugal, and at the same time much other English blood into other Portuguese lines. Two seafaring races blended, and Portugal burgeoned into maritime glory, under the guidance of the most English of Philippa's sons. Slow, careful, studious, a little unapproachable to those who did not know him well, Prince Henry the Navigator shunned delights and lived laborious days in his observatory on the cape of Sagre, dreaming mathematical, exploratory, cartographical, and navigational dreams, sending out expeditions of discovery to the coasts of Africa to find the sea route to India. This the mariners did not find; but they returned with fresh knowledge of ocean geography and of Africa, with gold, ivory and spices, with ship-loads of negroes; and all these fruits of travel were approved by Prince Henry, who used his share of the negroes to cultivate the Algarve, and to give him information about their native lands; in return, though they lost their homes, their families and their liberty, their souls were saved for God. Henry, like the rest of his family, was very devout.

BIBLIOGRAPHY

Cronica del Rey D. João I, FERNÃO LOPES (1644 edition).
Cronicas del Rey Dom João I, NUNES DE LIAM (1780 edition).
Cronicas de los Reyes de Castilla, PEDRO LOPEZ DE AYALA.
Chronicles of Fernão Lopes, etc. (edited EDGAR PRESTAGE, 1938).
Chroniques, FROISSART.
As Rainhas de Portugal, FONSECA BENEVIDES (1878).
D. João I e la Alliança Ingleza, VILLA FRANCA (1881).
Os filhos de João I, OLIVEIRA MARTIN (1891).
Historia de Portugal, ALEXANDRE HERCULANO (1848).
Quadro Elementar das relacões politicas e diplomaticas de Portugal, VISCONDE DE SANTAREM (1842-60).
John of Gaunt, S. ARMITAGE-SMITH (1904).
The Expedition of John of Gaunt to the Peninsula, C. H. WILLIAMS (*Chapters in Anglo-Portuguese Relations.* Edited E. PRESTAGE, 1935).
History of England under Henry IV, J. H. WYLIE (1884-98).
Henry the Navigator, ELAINE SANCEAU (1945).

2. THE ROYAL CAUSE AT SEA

Prince Rupert

[1649-50]

'THE royal cause was now at sea.' After the 'bloody and inhuman murder of my late uncle,' Prince Rupert, then with his 'revolted fleet' of seven ships or so off Kinsale, was made by his cousin, the new king, Lord High Admiral of England, and took to a running war of piracy and capture about the Bay of Biscay, the Atlantic off Portugal, the Mediterranean coast of Spain, and the islands of the new world. He was a soldier, not a sailor; so was Blake, the parliament's Admiral of the Fleet; the 'generals now at sea' all had their marine trade to learn. Rupert, with his little ill-rigged fleet and motley crew of English cavaliers and Irish adventurers, must depend on captured prizes for maintenance; he must, he knew, have safe harbours to sell them in, and to lie in. He sent from Kinsale in March 1649 to his Majesty King John IV of Portugal a knight, Sir Arnold Delisle, with proposals that he should use the Portuguese ports for his operations. He asked for liberty for his fleet to cast anchor in all the ports, rivers and roads of the kingdom and its dominions overseas,

44

to stay there as long as they liked, to sell their captured prizes there free from duties and free from inquiries as to how they had been acquired. Further, should any ships of the parliamentary enemies of the King of England happen into any port while the king's fleet lay there, they were to be detained for three days after the fleet had put to sea.

King John, friendly to the royal cause, and his class solidarity badly shocked by what the rebels had just done to his brother of England, replied with cordial caution that any ships of the English nation might come and trade in any Portugal ports; they should be received with benignity and allowed to sell their goods, however they might have acquired them, since it was no business of his Majesty to inquire into this. Should Prince Rupert come in person, he would be entertained and assisted with all due respect, and his fleet, though it could not be allowed to trade with the king's dominions overseas, might victual and supply its needs in any port, whether in Europe, Africa or the Indies. So much King John, 'out of the desire to give content in all things to his Majesty of Great Britain', conceded. One reads in the polite, wary and somewhat nervous document some anxiety. It was only nine years after Portugal's liberation from Spain; the king, however royalist in feeling, however well-wishing to the dashing young princes who were carrying on the fight for the royal cause, recognized that it was, anyhow for the present, a mislaid cause, that the new Commonwealth was that disagreeable thing, a *fait accompli*, and must, in the interests of political and economic welfare, be accepted and not flouted: the English trade was the largest in Portugal, their merchants greater in number and wealth than any other foreigners, the English alliance essential to meet the Spanish menace that growled always across the frontier. It simply would not do to quarrel with that unpleasant and powerful regime, the Commonwealth; nor would it do to excite the rage and jealousy of the French and Hollanders by giving to Prince Rupert's pirating fleet privileges above what these possessed. Further, King John knew this reckless dare-devil prince and his brother Maurice by hearsay and reputation; he must have been aware, or if he was not his ministers told him, that Rupert was a stormy petrel in any port, and unlikely to go about his business peaceably. There was among the Council a strong party against admitting the English royal fleet to any point of vantage; for one thing, most of that powerful and vocal body, the English Factory in Lisbon, would resent it. King, ministers and people were united in wanting peace, in their desire not to be dragged into any disturbances by foreign factions at odds with one another: non-intervention was their admirable slogan. The only would-be militant was Prince Theodosio, the young heir to the throne, a youth of great spirit, a champion of the princes and of the royal cause, whose ardour had with difficulty to be restrained.

The king's permission, such as it was, was enough for Rupert, who swung out from Kinsale across the Bay of Biscay and down the Portugal coast in the *Constant Reformation*, with his seven ships behind him and the Union Jack at his mast, capturing merchantmen as he sailed; one was the English *Roebuck*, freighted by Portugal and bound for Lisbon from Brazil.

Anchoring in Cascais Bay in late November, Rupert received on his flagship a polite and noble embassy from the king, who invited him to proceed up the river to Lisbon. Bearing into the Tagus, the fleet was saluted by the forts on either side, all the coast along. They sailed up the north channel, and came to anchor in the bay of Oeiras, where they remained for some time victualling the fleet and treating with merchants for the sale of their prizes. The king sent another embassy, to invite the princes ashore and 'assure them of all the assistance his kingdom could afford them' (the narrative is by one of Rupert's officers, Captain Pyne). Their Highnesses landed at Belem, 'where they were received by many of the nobles and treated in very great state for some days, until preparation was made for their reception at court, which being ready, the king sent his nobles with a great train to attend them to his palace, where he received them with great kindness'. One of the kindnesses he did them was to grant their request that the leading members of the parliamentary faction among the English Factory should be forthwith imprisoned. With these gentlemen safely out of the way, there was the less chance of British protests against this royalist intrusion into their commerce. The British consul was a royalist; he made no complaints of the arbitrary incarceration of his compatriots, who had for long been annoying him by refusing to pay him his consulage.

While Rupert and Maurice feasted at the court, made themselves popular about Lisbon, and hunted daily with the royal family, and their subordinates sold their captured merchandise, victualled, and fitted out their prizes as men of war, the Portuguese Secretary of State, a careful, cautious and worried man with an increasingly anxious council behind him, was requesting the restitution of the *Roebuck*, the English ship chartered by King John to carry Portuguese settlers overseas. His Majesty, wrote the Secretary, could not suffer the retention of this ship. Nor, he added, becoming irritated and tough, though always polite, could his Majesty allow the ships of the English Commonwealth to be taken and sold in Portugal — 'considering the present state of this kingdom and its commerce, it would be in no way convenient to make a war or shew any hostility. His Majesty should rather equally entertain and receive all of the English nation, since with them he had renewed the contracts of peace and friendship that have always been between the two nations. Your Serenity's navy should come in for repair to the ports of this kingdom, but not go out in hostile manner against the ships of the same nation, returning to port to sell the goods thus taken, then with new refreshing sail out and do more damage, in notorious hostility to the English nation and contrary to the friendship which the Portuguese nation always had with it; moreover, it is wholly to take from this kingdom the commerce with England, wherein not only the king's custom-house but a great part of his subjects are interested', and might cause many English residents to leave Portugal. 'Then let your Serenity be pleased to weigh these reasons, and with them to consider that the joy and pleasure their Majesties conceived and demonstrated at the arrival and sight of your Serenities, together with the applause and content wherewith all the court entertains and desires to serve you, deserve that your Serenities should reply with benefits, and not to our hindrance and prejudice, a thing not suitable to the greatness of your Serenities.'

Rupert saw nothing in this argument; he had no notion of either desisting from piracy or of restoring the *Roebuck*, which he said belonged to London rebel merchants; his reply was unsatisfactory. The Secretary wrote again a month later, more curtly. The owners of the ships and goods captured by the Prince and sold in Lisbon had demanded justice, and his Majesty 'commands me to tell you that to avoid embargoes and sequestrations of your goods, as also the arresting of the buyers, your Serenity should re-embark every one into your ships and with all brevity hasten your departure'. From the urgent tone, one may infer that the Portuguese ministry had learned that the Commonwealth fleet, under General Blake, was about to arrive on their coasts. The Secretary went on to deplore that Rupert, with no authority in the port of Lisbon, should compel passing ships with his artillery to strike their flags to his admiral. 'And now the country with great resentment begins to present to his Majesty that he can never consent to do any offence against the Commonwealth, by reason of the damage that might thereby result to their commerce with the City of London ... His Majesty expects that, as he did what he could to procure quietness and union between the parliament and king of Great Britain, so you would procure the same between him and his subjects, taking away all occasions of disgust to a nation that with so great joy and content received and entertained your Serenity.'

Learning of these letters, and of the growing tension between their government and the visiting princes, the Portuguese merchants who were buying the pirated goods took alarm, 'flew from their bargain', and would neither buy what they had agreed for nor pay for what they had already bought; the market became sticky, the customers wary, the sellers angry. Even the ships' victuallers stopped giving credit, fearing to wake one morning and find the birds flown. Rupert, furious at the insult and injury offered him and his ships, began an angry letter to the Secretary in his own hand, then decided that what was called for was a public protest in Latin, to be posted about everywhere, so that the whole world should understand how Portugal had broken faith with the King of England. News of this poster reached and alarmed the court; the Secretary of State came in person on to Rupert's ship to stop it, explaining away the interpretation put on his Majesty's letters and assuring the prince that of course the royal agreement would be honoured. The Latin poster, having done its work, was withdrawn. But still the Portuguese merchants would not pay for the goods they had bargained for.

The moment was unfortunate, for Blake and the Commonwealth fleet — twelve ships of war, newly painted and in fine fighting trim, with cannons firing a salute — were arriving, to Portuguese consternation, in Cascais Bay. With them was Mr. Charles Vane, the new Commonwealth's agent to the crown and people of Portugal. He was politely received by the king in audience, but His Majesty could not consent to his demands that the princes and their fleet, that gang of vagabonding pirates, should be either delivered to Blake or else immediately sent out to sea that they might fight it out. King John was not to be shaken from his friendship or his loyalty to English royalty. Nor would he allow Blake's fleet to enter the river; the guns from the forts on either side barred the entrance, and the fleet had to retreat and anchor beyond Belem.

So the English civil war was joined in Lisbon river, and the Portuguese king and people awaited developments in alarm. This bringing of the internal squabbles of their formidable ally to their coasts was the last thing they had desired: it was most unfair. They watched a duel of intrigue and invective waged between the rival commanders. Rupert, relying on his personal popularity with the Portuguese populace, 'showed himself frequently among them, hunting daily'; this, with his liberality and genial manners to all sorts of people, they having been accustomed to Spanish gravity (and, one may imagine, with his striking and arrogant beauty, the curled upper lip, cleft chin, fine dark eyes, gallant, swaggering carriage) delighted the people, and convinced them more than ever of the soundness of the views that were being promulgated from every pulpit on how shameful a thing it was for a Christian king to treat with rebels; the people grew so incensed about it that the king could not drive out without hearing remarks passed. Having got at the clergy and got in with the people (who even, on occasion and from a safe distance, stoned the members of the Council), Rupert felt himself on a good wicket, and the faction at court against him were held in check.

Charles Vane meanwhile, with less glamour and an unchristian rebel cause, was having less success. He could neither get his fleet into the Tagus nor his enemy's sent out of it; and though he had considerable backing at court, the king was politely unaccommodating; he would not offend the new Commonwealth, but neither would he truckle to it; these people had murdered their king, and all his class feeling, reinforced by that of his wife and sons, was in arms, warring with his anxiety for his country's welfare. He could not be expected to see the rival English fleets as the Council in London saw them when it instructed its generals to go to the Lisbon river 'in pursuit of the revolted fleet who now ride there . . . the treacherous fugitives, renegados and sea robbers' who had made off with ships of the British navy 'on a design to disturb trade and to prejudice peace, to infest merchants and others in their passing to and fro from the ports of the Commonwealth'. To John IV, that lately restored king of a long-frustrated royal line, it was Blake who commanded the revolted fleet, Rupert who was loyally contending for the right, and he did not much care to see Mr. Vane, with whom conversation was awkward.

Neither did Mr. Vane have much success with the Factory, when he called together those members of it who were still out of prison (naturally the more royalist-minded) and proposed that they should petition the king to order both fleets out to sea, that they might not hinder the trade of the city. 'His drift being smelt out by the merchants, that he hoped to engage the two fleets to a fight, the greatest part of the best and ablest among them refused to sign it', not desiring 'the effusion of so much English blood'. Vane's other suggestion was that they should stop paying consulage to Mr. Chandler the consul, and await the new consul to be appointed by parliament. This too the Factory rejected (it must have been about the only occasion in their history when a suggestion that they should not pay consulage was coldly received) and the consul, not unnaturally, 'complained to the king of the insolence of the man, who, being in no way qualified and having no order from the king, durst persuade men to deny him these duties'.

Nor could Vane get any satisfaction as to the release of the merchants in prison, who seemed likely to stay there.

Meanwhile, in the magnificent war of abuse being waged between Vane and Rupert one cannot award the palm. Rupert issued a declaration to the kingdom of Portugal concerning the coming of the English fleet of rebels into the river of Lisbon. It opened with a righteous swagger.

'The insolent and horrid proceedings of the rebel party in England commonly known by the name of Parliamentary, whereas indeed they are nothing else but tumultuous, factious, seditious soldiers, and other disorderly and refractory persons conspiring together, should awaken all Christian princes seriously to attend the designs of these conspirators, lest the fire now kindled in England should come to their own doors . . . As they are sworn enemies to all settled government both in church and common wealth, what may they attempt in neighbouring countries when time and occasion serve?' The declaration went on to reveal a plot calculated to curdle the blood of all Spain-fearing Portuguese. The enemy fleet, Rupert explained, was in league with Castile to attack and overthrow Portugal; had it not carried to Spain an agent to the Spanish court? True that it had also carried an agent to Portugal, but this agent was only meant for a spy, to report to his colleague in Madrid the means for overthrowing this realm. 'For these persons to come into this port with so many ships of such strength, under pretence of assailing us, and to advance as they did without leave, was as audacious as if they held the laws of all nations in as great contempt as their own.' It was to be feared that if the forts and castles had not hindered their coming in, they would have attacked the city and the harbour and made an entrance for the Spaniard, who now lay on the frontier with his army. In spite of its repulse, the fleet lay just beyond the port, blocking its mouth, so that ships could not go in or out; it was a high affront to a nation that its principal port was thus abused by a company of declared rebels. 'We hope,' Rupert grandly concluded, 'that the Portuguese nation will not endure such insolence by rebels who are to be esteemed pirates and sea robbers, but will seriously join with the King of Great Britain's fleet . . . for the prevention of the design of their and our implacable enemies, and to give demonstration to the whole world how little the insolency of these people is to be endured.'

After some days an answer to this was hatched out on Blake's flagship, and 'there was a paper scattered up and down the city so scurrilously invective against the Prince his person, so audaciously boasting of the insolencies they have committed in England', that Mr. Vane disclaimed having composed it. In the matter of style, it is better than Rupert's effort.

' . . . neither do we take it for any disparagement to us our parliament and nation that we are vile in the esteem of this Vagabond German, a Prince of Fortune, whose highness is nothing else but haughtiness, his Principality mere piracy, the plurality of his person an affectation so singular that no real prince can choose but smile at it, who, after he was cudgelled out of England for his trade of plundering, did in a short time set up at sea, and was even now ready to set forth of this harbour and to take pastime with Leviathan in the great waters, had not the audacious fleet of rebels come in the very nick of time to put an embargo upon his highness. And truly it's no marvel if he hath ever since been so exceedingly transported with choler, and foams so beastly at the mouth, calling us rebels, thieves, professed enemies to all government, thereby endeavouring to render us (as much as in him lies) odious to all nations and princes.'

There followed a refutation of the Spanish plot charge, an assertion of the Commonwealth's desire for 'a firm and perpetual league of amity' with Portugal, and a suggestion that there would be greater advantage in trusting in those sent out by the Commonwealth of England for the protection of trade than in 'those who make it their business to spoil and rob whomsoever they meet . . . us who are only English, the most ancient allies and affectionate friends of this nation', rather than 'that fleet whose strength doth most consist of Irish, who have ever been and are most passionately and almost superstitiously devoted to the Spanish nation and party'. The rest of the document dealt fully with the extreme vileness of the Irish.

There is little sign that either of these declarations was particularly appreciated by the King of Portugal or his subjects. All they wanted was to be well rid of both combatants. Blake's fleet lay outside the bar, lying in wait for and capturing ships. A kind of guerilla warfare was carried on between the two fleets. Blake set an ambush to trap the princes as they rode back from hunting; surprised and routed, the ambuscade were captured or killed. In repartee, Rupert devised a bomb in a barrel and had one of his sailors dressed up as a Portuguese and sent to place it in a stern boat on board the admiral's ship; unfortunately the messenger, naturally flustered, forgot himself and exclaimed in English (very probably with an Irish accent) so was taken.

The situation had become intolerable, with one English fleet outside the bar waiting for the Brazil ships, the other inside it taking and selling prizes, and the daily expectation of a clash. The Secretary of State tried to get rid of Rupert, the king of Blake. The only person they did get rid of was Vane. The Commonwealth government had perceived that their agent's embassy was not being a dazzling success. In June (1650) the Council wrote to Mr. Vane recalling him from his agency with the King of Portugal, 'perceiving by his letters and papers, and by those of the generals, that it will be of no advantage to the Commonwealth for him to remain'. So Vane left Lisbon, having accomplished none of the purposes of his mission, and leaving his servants in prison behind him.

Meanwhile the generals at sea were still busy taking ships, and Rupert selling his in Lisbon port. The exasperated Secretary admonished him again that his behaviour was outrageous. 'Your Serenity knows very well that this and other things done by you in this port have been a mighty hindrance to trade, with the oppression and irreparable damage of this people, directly opposite to what was agreed with M. du Lisle . . . All of which nevertheless his Majesty for this time has winked at and tolerated from his great love to his Majesty of Great Britain.'

The king meanwhile was urging Rupert to attack Blake's fleet, and ordering his own navy to assist him in this enterprise. The Commonwealth, angered at the royal attitude, sent out a second fleet under Colonel Popham, to protest against the exclusion from the bay of Oeiras of Blake's fleet. 'For that the said king, having first permitted those treacherous fugitive pirates to come in thither with those ships, part of the English navy which they ran away with, it were against all right and justice to deny the Commonwealth that liberty to come in with their ships of war.' Therefore Popham is to desire the said king to open his ports and admit the fleet into the Bay; and if he won't, then seize his ships.

As usual, the king was of one mind, the Council of another. Prince Theodosio, 'a young man', says Clarendon, 'of great hope and promise', declared that 'he would have all the ships in the port made ready, and would himself go on board and fight for Prince Rupert, and so fight the English and drive them from hence'. But he was not allowed to do this; the Council were not going to jeopardize the English connection by taking sides; instead, they besought the king to send Rupert's fleet out of the river.

The waylaying by Blake of the Brazil fleet setting out from the Tagus brought the king's anger to a head; he put his own fleet at Rupert's service and urged an attack. The attack was a failure; the Portuguese sailors had no mind for it, and the odds were too great; Rupert returned to the safe side of Belem, and there, for the next few weeks, his fleet lay, dodging Blake's, which continued its work on the Brazil ships.

Rupert's mother, Queen Elizabeth of Bohemia, wrote to the

Duchess of Richmond a typically maternal account of her son's doings:

'Rupert has been out to have fought with the rebels' fleet, but they would not stay him, and sailed from him. He followed them three days; but not being able to overtake them he returned to Lisbon, which they did within two days after, to the same place they were before, and Rupert was to go out again, with more ships, to fight with them if they will stay him. The King of Portugal gives him all kind of assistance, and is extreme kind to him and Maurice.'

To this effect, no doubt, were Rupert's letters home. But the port of Lisbon was getting, what with Blake's fleet and what with Portuguese resentment, too hot to hold him much longer; at the first safe opportunity he resolved to sail. He wrote to his cousin Charles that he thought his prizes would fetch £40,000. 'All the ships lie now between Belem and Lisbon, out of command, from whence either I will sell or carry the prizes, in spite of all this kingdom.'

At Michaelmas, the fleet being ready and the enemy out of the road, Rupert sailed out, intending for the Straits and Spain. 'So that now', wrote Captain Pyne, 'misfortunes being no novelty to us, we plough the seas for our subsistence, and, being destitute of a port, we take the confines of the Mediterranean for our harbour: poverty and despair being companions, and revenge our guide.'

What he meant was that they were to go pirating off the Spanish coasts. It brought them little good; they were dogged by the enemy fleet, and by Commonwealth threats to Spain should she advantage them. They were now flattered, now fired on, by a time-serving Spanish government, according to the ups and downs of Commonwealth prestige: finally the ups gained the day; the draggled royalist fleet was forbidden access to Spanish ports, and sought the Barbados, whose wide tropic seas and rich coasts were more rewarding. But the royal cause was sunk beyond Rupert's salvaging; four years of piracy enriched him, and killed Maurice, his dear companion, but could not restore his cousin Charles.

The Portuguese king and government, relieved of the marauding and distasteful rival fleets of their ancient ally, looked wisely at facts, and came to terms with the successful rebel rulers of Britain. In the end, after long negotiations and much hard work on the part of the Council in London, the king even freed the imprisoned British merchants. Soon afterwards the treaty was made that was to define English rights and privileges in Portugal for the next century and a half; and the first of our permanent envoys to the court of Portugal took up his duties in Lisbon. The regicide rebels of Britain found favour even with Europe's more impassioned monarchists a good deal more quickly than did the regicide rebels of Russia some years later. When a nation has naval strength, commercial energy and resources, is a valuable ally and a formidable foe, its ideological flaws sink into the background; so, as Prince Rupert found, do its revolted fleets and their gallant pirating admirals.

BIBLIOGRAPHY

Relation of passages at Lisboa. Camden Miscellany, vol. 10. Edited S. R. GARDINER (1902). (Add. MSS. 35,251).
Captain Pyne's Relation. Memoirs and Correspondence of Prince Rupert and the Cavaliers, B. E. G. WARBURTON (1849).
Memorials of the Great Civil War in England, 1646-52, HENRY CARY (1842).
History of the Rebellion, EDWARD HYDE, EARL OF CLARENDON (pub. 1702-4).
Cal. Dom. State Papers, 1649, 1650, 1651.
Clarendon State Papers, 1650.
State Papers, Portugal, 89/4 (Record Office).
2nd Report of the Lisbon Branch of the Historical Association. Article by M.S. JAYNE (1938).
Rupert, Prince Palatine, EVA SCOTT (1899).

3. THE PATRIOTIC HORSE

Edward Prince of Wales   King Edward VII
　　　[1876]　　　　　　　　　　　　　[1903]

AT the time it was called by the English newspapers the first official visit of an English prince to Portugal. One would think that the visit of John of Gaunt and his daughter Philippa might have merited the adjective, even if it was denied to the Duke of Sussex, with his asthma and his Freemasonry. But it is true that the reception of the heir to the English throne, with illuminations, processions, court ball and banquets, was a state event, on a grand scale. It had been mooted at the time of the prince's departure for his tour of India in the autumn of 1875. He was to call at Lisbon, if not also at Oporto, on his way home in the spring. By February, preparations for the Visit were busily proceeding. English carpenters came out from London to build pavilions, English illumination experts to illuminate city and river, English pyrotechnicians (the same who had lit the Thames for the Shah of Persia) to make fireworks, an English musician to teach Portuguese bands to play 'God save the Queen' and 'God bless the Prince of Wales'. Even an English glass of water was arranged for, lest the prince should hesitate to partake of Portuguese water (in the improbable event of his desiring water at all). It was said by a spiteful Portuguese journalist that efforts had been made (whether successful or not he did not mention) to produce an English fog. The court saloons where the ball was to be held were decorated and furnished à l'anglaise; at the hippodrome English jockeys raced English steeds.

How many of the Portuguese people besides Senhor Ramalhão Ortigão, who set it down in great malice in an 'Epistola a John Bull', took exception to this Anglo-Saxon note in the preparation of their capital for British royalty, there seems no way now of ascertaining. It was seventy years ago; the Portuguese press was flatteringly correct; such critics as there may have been are long dead; there is no one left in Lisbon to remember this royal visit, except a few who were too young to care who made the fireworks or built the pavilions.

The prince had visited first Madrid, where he had spent a few days doing the royal round of sight-seeing and feasting, but had declined to attend a bull-fight; the *Soir* correspondent said because of the English affection for roastbeefs; more probably it was the English affection for horses, combined with advices from his entourage that such attendance would not have a good press in Great Britain, which was at that time definitely humanitarian. Probably a Portuguese bull-fight might have been more possible, but this was not offered. Anyhow, the prince left Madrid for Lisbon on April 30th in a special Spanish train, was met at the frontier by a special Portuguese train, and arrived at Lisbon station at three in the afternoon, to be met by King Luis and his ministers and suite. There were cordial greetings, and the well-taught band struck up 'God save the Queen'. The royalties then drove to the palace of Belem, where the prince was to stay, calling on the way on Queen Maria Pia. The city was full of people, many of them up from the provinces to see the fun, the Tagus was full of the battleships of various nations, of which the British and Portuguese fired salutes as the procession drove by. The windows of the offices of British merchants were crowded with British merchants, who gave loyal and hearty cheers as their prince passed.

There was only one hitch, which very likely entertained the gazing street crowds more than if all had gone smoothly. The procession was halted abruptly in the square outside the station by the obstinate decision of one of the horses of the royal carriage not to proceed. He stopped dead. We have of the distressing, contretemps the delighted account of Senhor Ortigão, who found it the one incident in the prince's visit that he could applaud. He respected and admired the resolution of this fine horse, who, in the face of all persuasion, threats, blows, prods from bayonet points and parasols, remained inflexibly stationary. The coachmen, the police, the military, officials, ordinary citizens and their families, all had a try to move him. They recited to him, says Senhor Ortigão, the law, the police regulations, extracts from the patriotic speeches of Senhor Thomaz Ribeiro; they praised the monarchical regime, telling him that under it he might become a consul like the horse of Caligula; they reminded him that he was a public servant, that he must on no account incur the odium of a traitor. It was no good; he resisted everything, neighing, biting, rearing, tearing his harness. The only thing was to unharness him and proceed a horse short.

The newspapers next day, to minimize the scandal, said the horse had gone mad. But, said Senhor Ortigão, that was not true. He had himself observed the horse being led quietly home, wearing an expression reflective and composed. The horse was in full possession of his faculties. He did not draw the prince's carriage because he did not wish to. 'And that', said Senhor Ortigão, 'seems to me important, John' (he was addressing John Bull), 'that among those who triumphantly received His Royal Highness, there was one who protested.'

Everything else seems to have gone without a hitch. The prince took part in a great court ball, where eight salons were decorated with royal arms, and the buffet was extremely recherché; he attended military and naval reviews, dined the king on the battleship *Serapis* and was dined by him at the Ajuda Palace, went to the races to see the English jockeys ride English horses, admired the English fireworks on the Tagus, where the fleets were all lit up, and thousands of spectators displayed intense gratification, visited the Jockey Club at Belem and smoked a cheroot there, conversed with fidalgos, duchesses, other exalted ladies, and the queen, received deputations from British merchants of Lisbon and Oporto, visited Cintra, with the king, where they rode up to the Moorish castle on donkeys and lunched with Dom Fernando d'Edla in his chalet. In Cintra His Royal Highness bought a donkey (perhaps that which had so nobly carried him up the hill to the castle of the Moors), and ordered it to be sent to the *Serapis* to accompany him home; no doubt he wanted it for the little princes and princesses at Sandringham. Another day he walked from the Belem palace to visit the Dominican Irish Convent and school of Bom Successo; the nuns were charmed with him and he with them; he invited them to visit the *Serapis*, but the rules of their Order forbade. The Superior, Father Smyth, showed him over the house and grounds, the children asked him for a holiday, and nuns sang 'Kathleen Mavourneen' very pleasingly to a harp. He became from that time the friend and protector of Bom Successo, requesting the Portuguese government, whenever they had an anti-religious-order fit, to spare both this convent and the Irish Dominican friars of Corpo Santo, which they obligingly did (as a matter of fact, they always had).

The last day of His Royal Highness's visit was Sunday. He attended the Anglican church at Estrella, which was much crowded with English, partook of a few more banquets, and sailed for England in the *Serapis* on Monday, seen off by the king with cordiality and, doubtless, relief.

There followed the violent and unusual 'Letter to Mr. John Bull' of the vitriolically anglophobe Senhor Ortigão. It was directed less against the prince personally than against the whole British nation. Portugal, he complained, had since the beginning of the century imitated, against its natural genius, English institutions, dress, food. The Portuguese had taken to beer instead of their national drinks; this gave them bile, enlarged their tongues, and gradually brutalized them. Anglomania had adopted such words into the language as *sport, turf, jockey* and *pale ale*. All this, said Senhor Ortigão, is nonsense, for our culture is really French, the foreign tongue we know is French, the books and journals we read are French. When the royal visit was proposed, everything was done to make His Royal Highness believe that he was not in a free country, with its own customs and traditions, but in a fief of Great Britain's. Was there, then, no Portuguese national life which could have been exhibited, no national costumes, villages, fishing-boats? Did the prince visit any of our national monuments or buildings, talk to any of our men of science, industry, or letters? What did he take out of Portugal to England? Two shirts given him by a manufacturer, and a donkey bought at Cintra. He was a good donkey, honest, hard-working, independent; for years he had bravely carried Cintra tourists, and the burdens of those who went in to market. He was no snob, and had no craving for grandeur; he was indifferent whom he carried on his back, only preferring lighter weights. What would he feel, poor *burro*, idle, melancholy and expatriate, at the English court? 'What the devil do these people want me for?' he would wonder. 'For the Epsom races?' The notion that a Portuguese *burro* could be happy carrying English royal children about Sandringham heath did not occur to Senhor Ortigão; the two faults of Englishness and royalty would be enough to make a self-respecting Portugal *burro* kick them off and behave like the patriotic horse who refused to draw the prince's carriage in Lisbon.

As to the prince, the disapproving writer went on, he is stout, strong and bald. Thirty-four years old, he has no events in his biography. For his position, his fine beard, his correct profile, he is a fine figure at banquets, but not in the chapters of history. Was he received with enthusiasm in Lisbon? As well as anyone, His Royal Highness knows what real enthusiasm can be, for not long since he saw Garibaldi march through London amid a crowd gone mad. That was enthusiasm for a hero. The prince's visit may be compared profitably too with another visit — the unapplauded visit to London last year of a Portuguese prince, only brother of our king. As for you, friend John Bull, you live in such a dreadful climate on your bitter and implacable island, that you have to work at high pressure all the time, and have no time to cultivate imagination, amiability, or human sympathies. No wonder you and all your institutions are so detestable; but we don't want you in Portugal.

That is the sum of this oddly-timed essay in hate. It is improbable that it was ever translated into English, but probable that its gist was reported. Royalty has to learn to be tough.

Anyhow, King Edward visited Portugal again, twice. It was to our oldest ally that he paid his first state visit abroad after his coronation. The preparations were enormous. The royal yacht would arrive in the Tagus on April 2nd, 1903. A squadron lay in the harbour, seven thousand troops would line the shore. Windows were hired on the procession routes for immense sums, while for a box at the gala performance at the opera house people paid £75. Balconies were hung with rich embroideries, all hotels brimmed with visitors, plans were made for illuminations, concerts, banquets, pigeon-shooting, Cintra, entertaining six thousand poor.

The weather was superb; Lisbon April sunshine. King Edward in his yacht *Victoria and Albert* was escorted by the squadron up the shining river, King Carlos in the royal barge, with the Bragança dragon as figurehead, was rowed out to the yacht. The monarchs landed together on the steps of Black Horse Square, where the ancient painted state coaches were drawn up in line; the royal party entered them and drove to the palace, and this time no horse was patriotic enough to strike.

The days (four) passed in the usual round. King Edward occupied silk-tapestried rooms in the Necessidades; from these he issued forth to visit Cintra, to receive loyal deputations from his subjects in Lisbon and Oporto, to dine, lunch, preside at pigeon-shooting, attend the concert and the play, open the Royal British Club, see the fireworks, go to the English church at Estrella, watch fireworks, spend a morning with the gratified Irish Dominican nuns at Bom Successo, make speeches about his illustrious cousin the King of Portugal and his people and the integrity of the Portuguese colonies.

The press was friendly; even the Oporto press, usually slightly anglophobe, was kind. The comment of the perhaps over-feasted Lisbon correspondent of the *Times*, that 'the golden hours under these untarnished skies bring him day by day the ripened fruit of Portuguese hearts' may seem a trifle flowery and fruity; nevertheless the Portuguese were kind and did not seem displeased. Crowds which had twelve years ago smashed windows of pro-British newspapers because of the Ultimatum, now cheered. In a cordial atmosphere the King of England opened the new Parque de Eduardo Sétimo, seating himself on a seat which his grandson the Duke of Kent was shown nearly thirty years later. 'Impossible,' said the Duke. 'It is not large enough.'

And so, in the glorious blue weather, after he and his illustrious cousin had toasted one another and their ancient allied countries for the last time, the King of England sailed away in his yacht. If any horse or man registered a protest during this visit, it has not been recorded.

BIBLIOGRAPHY

The Times, (May 1876, April 1903).
As Farpas, Epistola a John Bull, 1876, COSTA RAMALHO ORTIGÃO (1887).
The Convent of Bom Sucesso (1926).

WRITERS

I. HUMANIST

George Buchanan

[1547-1552]

FOR the men of the New Learning, the faggots and flames were always just round the corner, throwing sinister flickers of menace like bad dreams on to the paths which wound so alluringly towards new horizons, paths which a man might start to tread with the eagerness and the aesthetic pleasure of a scholar, and which might land him any fine day in some market square chained to a stake among brushwood for a heretic. Most scholars, like most other men, had no mind for such an end; to do them justice, they were, when they perceived whither their path was taking them, as quick as the next man at doubling on their tracks; they had not good wits for nothing. It is difficult to imagine Erasmus burning. George Buchanan, the Scotch humanist, Latinist, poet and historian, was an Erasmist. No one, until after that long-drawn bout with the Inquisition in Portugal, could have called him a Lutheran; that is, not truly or justly; they did call him a Lutheran, because 'Lutheran' was what 'Fascist' later became, a vague term of reprobation for anyone whose opinions were suspect. But he was not a Lutheran, nor yet (as he later became) a Protestant: he was a modernist Catholic, interested in the new ideas, ready to investigate and assess them, even, as he afterwards owned, to be swayed by them this way and that; and, first and last, he was not a theologian, but a scholar, a dramatist, and a poet, with a natural keen-witted scorn for stupidity, nonsense and bigotry.

He escaped by the skin of his teeth from Scotland in 1539, the year when Castle Hill was a blazing pyre for heretics. Cardinal Beaton and the Bishop of Dunblane set it going; five died in it, four priests and a gentleman of Stirling; others recanted or fled in time. Some had been present at the wedding of a priest, the Vicar of Tallibody; they had eaten meat at this festive occasion, which had occurred in Lent. One was an Augustinian (in the bad

62

sense). One had written a play on the Passion, acted before King James on Good Friday, in which the Pharisees were got up to resemble the clergy of the day. The layman, Mr. Forrester, had read and possessed 'sic bukes as are suspect of heresy' and were forbidden by the Kirk. Buchanan regarded their fate with a shudder; there, but for the favour of the king, whose bastard son he was tutoring, went he; he had done worse than most of them, for he had not only attended that wedding and eaten meat at it, but had written satires (no less than three) on the Franciscans. He was imprisoned; with King James's connivance (so one gathers from a confused story) he slipped his guard and came to England. There he had no money and no influence and no strings to pull. He spent six months there, from Lent to August; he heard sermons from divers points of view, kept company with all kinds of people, his mind wavered to and fro. He found English religious politics confused, 'for men of both religious parties were being burnt on the same day and in the same fires', which seemed to his Scots mind silly.

He left England for the clearer-headed Paris, his spiritual home, where he had lived from eighteen to thirty (he was now thirty-three), first as student in the Scots college, then as professor in the college of Ste. Barbe. Paris had then been the home of eager discussion of the new reforming notions; Buchanan, with his free tongue and sharp satiric wit, always felt more himself in France than anywhere else. But this time he gave Paris one apprehensive look and left it, for his enemy Cardinal Beaton was there on an embassy from Scotland; hastily he turned his back on this peril and went south to Bordeaux, where he was invited by his Portu-guese friend and old Ste. Barbe colleague, André Gouveia, to be professor of Humanity at the new Latin College of Guienne, of which Gouveia was principal. There, in a congenial company of teachers and scholars, he spent three happy years, lecturing, writing tragedies and poems, having his plays acted by eager pupils (among them was Michel de Montaigne), and, if his own 'Defence' written for the benefit of the Inquisitors at Lisbon is to be believed, settling his theological problems and returning to orthodoxy. In 1543 he left Bordeaux for Paris, was a regent in the Collège du Cardinal du Moine for a time, kept company with the most distinguished intellectuals of all nations there assembled, and, as he pointed out, with men of the most unimpeachable orthodoxy. It was at this time that he made, so he said, his peace with the Church, took advantage of a Bull of general pardon for repentant waverers, was absolved. (But neither the Inquisitors nor modern historians can trace this Bull.) After a period of illness and absence from Paris, he reappears in 1547 as one of the brilliant band of scholars who accompanied André de Gouveia, at the invitation of the King of Portugal, to Coimbra, to staff the new College of Arts there. King John requested Gouveia to bring with him some Greek and Latin scholars, 'men who should expound the classics in the educational institutions which the king was then erecting'. The university had just been restored from Lisbon to Coimbra, its original home; the king was anxious to make it a university where Portuguese youth could be educated instead of going, as now, to Paris. King John seems to have been inspired rather by Portuguese patriotism than by love of learning, though he took a detailed interest in the university. The contemporary verdict on his intelligence was poor; he had been regarded, while his father lived, as intellectually almost an imbecile; he may have desired others to know Latin, but he could never learn it himself; he had two ideas only — he loved and wished to exalt the Church and the religious orders, and he passionately hated the Jews and the New Christian converts. 'How hateful to him from his very childhood those who cherish errors against our holy Faith', as a Seville Inquisitor remarked. Under his despotic but intelligent father, King Manuel, the New Christians had been protected by the law; directly John stepped into his shoes, they discovered their mistake; the campaign against Jews and Jewish converts raged. 'Give me a Jew, and I will give you a burned Jew', cried the Tenebrero, the terrible Inquisitor of Cordova, and John did his best to implement this by doing, ten years after his accession, what his father had refused to do — he established the Inquisition in Portugal, on the best Spanish models. This 'intelligence below mediocrity', inspired by fanatic hate, let the tiger loose on his Hebrew subjects, and they quailed before it.

But Buchanan did not see that he had anything to fear in Portugal. Rather the contrary. Approached on the matter of going there, he 'gave a ready assent'. 'For, while perceiving that all Europe was already ablaze with civil or foreign wars, or soon would be consumed by the flames, he observed that that one corner would be free from disturbances.' It sounds familiar. So off to this peaceful spot he went, pleased with his company, who were old friends and distinguished scholars, French and Portuguese.

The college made a brilliant start; then, after the first year, the principal, André de Gouveia, died, 'a bitter blow to his colleagues', wrote Buchanan, 'yet a not untimely departure for himself. For all the hostile rivals to the enterprise made an attack, first under cover, then openly like hired ruffians; and after holding a secret inquest through agents bitterly hostile to the accused, they arrested three men. . . .'

The three were Buchanan, de Teive, and da Costa, who shared rooms together. It was on August 10th, 1550. Buchanan and de Teive were seized in Coimbra, on an order from the Cardinal Prince, da Costa in Lisbon, where he was visiting. They were locked in the bishop's palace while their rooms were searched for suspicious books and writings; they were brought such money and clothes as they requested; the proceedings were strictly honest as regards property. Then the prisoners were taken to Lisbon. Buchanan was delivered to the gaoler of the Inquisition prison on August 15th, and shut away *incommunicado*, awaiting examination. It was three days before his first examination; it apparently seemed longer to him, for he wrote afterwards that they 'after long experience of prison filth were brought to trial, violently attacked day after day with many insults, and again remanded to their secret cells. Not even yet were their accusers named'. There is no doubt that Buchanan touched up the story a good deal when he set it down; he gave his time in prison as a year and a half; actually it was under a year; and its end was not quite so triumphant for him as he described it. Nor do the Inquisitors, from the records of the examinations, sound so brutal or so violent as he says.

The affair had been brewing for some time. The Order for Inquest had been signed by the Cardinal Prince last October. 'It is necessary for the service of our Lord and the welfare of the Holy Office that we should be informed as to the mode of life and habits of both the Portuguese and foreigners who came to this kingdom to the University of Coimbra . . . Take with all secrecy the evidence of Friar Joam Pinheiro, a Portuguese Dominican in Paris, with other evidence that he may indicate.'

This Pinheiro was the chief witness. It has been thought that the original informer may have been not he but Diogo de Gouveia, former principal of the College of Ste. Barbe in Paris, uncle of André de Gouveia, jealous of his nephew's position as head of the new Coimbra college, jealous of the college itself, which was intended to supersede Ste. Barbe as a resort for Portuguese youth; no doubt also a religious and orthodox old gentleman, who suspected the views and morals of his brilliant nephew and his circle of friends. So he planned his attack. But André died before it could be launched; da Costa, succeeding him, became its target, and his friends Teive and Buchanan were included. Buchanan, with his free tongue, chequered past, and devotion to the new learning, was an obvious suspect. The Jesuits also may have been concerned to make trouble; not only were they hostile to the new thought, to humane and scientific studies, and to the least smell of heresy or immorality (and there was a smell of both among the professors of the Royal College), but they stood to gain by the fall of these scholars; a few years later the college passed into their hands. But they did not instigate these proceedings; it is, in fact, uncertain who did. Whoever it was had been able to collect plenty of witnesses. The Licentiate sent to Paris to open the inquiry examined seven of these. Pinheiro said he had always suspected those who had gone from Bordeaux to Coimbra of being Lutherans; they had jested with him on religious subjects, such as meat-eating on fast days, monastic orders, etc.; he remembered in particular a certain conversation at Bordeaux . . . They had often when in Paris conversed with atheists and suspected persons; Pinheiro cited many witnesses as to this. The three had usually been considered Lutherans; they had argued dubiously on matters of faith. Teive had held loose moral views, while as to Buchanan, there was the rumoured scandal of the paschal lamb, which he was said to have eaten in Scotland with five others, who had been burnt for it; Buchanan, escaping, had only been burnt in effigy. Diogo de Gouveia endorsed this; he had heard say that 'Buchanan had fled from Scotland as a heretic and a Jew, who thought he might eat paschal lamb.' Others had heard that Teive and Buchanan thought wrongly of the Faith, that Teive was given to epicureanism and atheism, as shown by his friendship with men who had since had to be burnt. Costa had known a blasphemous Gascon nobleman; he and Teive had been at a banquet at which noblemen had blasphemed. In most of these iniquities Buchanan was by association involved, as well as having a good few to his own account, such as eating meat in Lent, having odd ideas about free will and confession, and always that paschal lamb.

There were certainly plenty of charges to bring, when Buchanan, three days after his arrival in prison, came up for interrogation before the Inquisitors. Neither the accusations nor the names of the accusers were mentioned; the prisoners had to infer them from the questions; the strain of uncertainty as to what they were accused of, the dread of inadvertent self-incrimination, the problem of defending themselves from unknown assailants and charges in the dark, the terror of saying the wrong thing, the sense of a great weight of undisclosed evidence, some true, some false, behind the trapping questions, was unnerving. Some defendants were apt to throw in their hands, break down, and confess more than they were asked, more than they had said or done, and so clear themselves of the heinous crime of concealment. George Buchanan was too canny for that; but he did make some needless confessions, being, and remaining throughout his life, under the impression that the gravamen of the charge against him lay in the satires he had written long ago against the Franciscans, and that the chief informer was his old enemy Cardinal Beaton; as a matter of fact the Inquisitors had not heard of these Scottish misdemeanours until he mentioned them. They were busy with his life in France. The satires (in an innocent and modified form) came out at his first interrogation, and that he had read while in England some heretical books. At the second examination they questioned him about the Bordeaux conversation mentioned by Pinheiro. He said that he remembered little of this, except that he had joked about monastic orders and perhaps been a trifle unorthodox about the Eucharist. Pinheiro had remembered much more; he had remembered such jests about the orders and the Church that he had thought the jesters true Lutherans; they had said that the Church fasting seasons were man-ordained, and that Christ had said there need be no difference in victuals on certain days; they had gone on (assisted by a French physician) in such a way that Pinheiro had lost his temper and told them they had better be careful what they said.

The matter of the paschal lamb came up. Portuguese inquisitors naturally had Jews on the brain, and saw nothing odd in the notion of Jewish rites in the all-Gentile British Isles, so different from Portugal that they could not imagine it. So they asked the surprised Scot, 'Do you recollect ever having practised Jewish ceremonies?' 'No,' he replied. 'Did you ever eat Passover lamb in company with any one?' 'I neither ate it nor said it might be eaten. And there are no Jews in Scotland.' 'Do you recollect any persons being burnt in Scotland for eating paschal lamb?' 'No, (one imagines a note of ironic impatience in the sharp Scotch voice at this idiotic inquiry), 'nor did I ever hear of such a thing till now.' After this, the lamb seems to have been shelved.

It was after this second examination that Buchanan wrote his Defence, which he read aloud at the third interview. It is an interesting and coherent document; its author kept his head, and managed to combine a certain amount of admission of error and repentance with putting his past in a favourable, but not impudently favourable, light. He emerges as a repentant and (he trusts) reconciled and forgiven one-time waverer in the faith, who had for a short time doubted on some points, but had later ascertained the truth and cloven to it. He ran over his past spiritual career: the Franciscan business (in which he had retorted on insolent monks of profligate lives — but of course only some monks were like that); slanders about his being a Lutheran spread by a lady enemy, King James's mistress, who, seeing him reading Ecclesiastes, thought it was the New Testament (which only Lutherans are believed to read); his advice to a sick friend, in peril of his life, to cure himself by eating meat on fast days, which, to encourage him, he ate with him (and a famous Dominican preacher used to say that even Christ ate meat with his apostles in Lent). 'Hence, I suppose, originated the fable of the paschal lamb, of which I heard to-day for the first time. And thus I received the first taint of evil, and my earliest intercourse with Lutherans.' He described his months in London after his escape from Scotland; this was his shadiest period, and he owned that he had been to many controversial meetings. 'The result was that my feeble intellect sometimes wavered and was tossed by the waves of argument now this way, now that.' When he heard Catholic sermons, the faith of the Church seemed to him the right one, when a Lutheran sermon, the views of Luther struck him as correct (a curious and rather unusual effect of sermons). 'Likewise I read many books on both sides.'

Then to France, where the customary freedom of speech

allowed discussion of everything without offence, and where he had been, no doubt, franker than one would be elsewhere. Jesting with Pinheiro at Bordeaux, he had said 'no more than custom allows to be said publicly in France, and what can be said everywhere between friends . . . When a troublesome fellow asked me who first made monks, I casually replied, the barber and the tailor. Nowhere in France are men wont to be offended by this kind of talk.'

At Bordeaux he had written a sketch that was acted, attacking fathers who drive their children to the cloister without considering their suitability for it; it was a sketch 'such as custom permits to be acted in France', and no one had condemned it.

He outlined his views on some controversial points. Of Free Will he sensibly washed his hands — 'I have always considered that the idea of God involved foreknowledge, and the idea of man free will. But I did not consider that I ought anxiously to inquire how these principles mutually agree, nor have I investigated the subject except in the schools'. He went on to his views on vows, religious orders, the marriage of priests, Franciscan garb, miracles, purgatory, indulgences, justification, transubstantiation, the Mass, prayer, rules, confession, images, Judaism ('of Judaism I have never thought'), Anabaptists ('I am still ignorant of the nature of this sect'), Epicureans (he had always hated them), the King of England's headship of the Anglican Church. As to the Anglican Church, the English 'could never explain to me its essence or its nature'.

'These are the matters stored up in my memory on which my mind wavered or sometimes thought wrongly for about two years in Scotland and England, or in connection with which I held company with those who thought wrongly. But all the time I was at Bordeaux I spent in anxiously seeking out the truth . . .' At Bordeaux (so mistaken was Pinheiro about him) he learned the authority of the Church, resolved to be less self-confident in future, and trusted the authority of Scripture, of which he acknowledged the Church the sole interpreter. 'My mind was so subdued by this reflection that for the last two years I was at Bordeaux I think no word at all out of the ordinary fell from my lips, except such as I could easily account for in France, where sportive conversation and theatrical comedies enjoy the utmost freedom.'

This exception probably seemed to the Portuguese Inquisitors to have permitted him quite enough licence, and his boast that no one had sullied him with the slightest suspicion did not cut much ice with interrogators who had in their hands such a mass of evidence from informers who had known him in France.

The apologist knew that repentance was his best defence. He related how, at the end of 1543, he made up his mind to return to Scotland and be reconciled there with the Church which he had offended; how he got as far as Paris, and while he was there the Pope announced a Bull of pardon for all who had strayed into heresy and desired reconciliation; how he had taken advantage of this, confessed his errors and done penance, and, though he had . still desired to return home and give public satisfaction for the scandal he had caused there, he decided to impose on himself the voluntary penance of life-long exile instead. Further, he fell ill and could not leave France; further again, the English were occupying Scotland. So, for these several excellent reasons, and perhaps others, he had abandoned the design of going to his native land, stayed some time at Paris keeping excellent, distinguished and religious company, then looked about him for some post where he would be so far from Scotland that he would not even hear news of Scottish woes. Honourable posts in France had been offered him, but he preferred the less important Coimbra one, as being a long way off; so to Coimbra he came, and there had led the most innocent orthodox life in the world. Far behind him now were those three years of doubt, those perilous years during which he had done and said much that was wrong and irreligious, partly through ignorance, partly through carelessness, the fire of his youthful age, and evil communications. When, in Paris in '44, he had accepted pardon and done penance for those sins, he had thought men would bury the memory of them for ever, as he trusted God had already done. 'I did not think I should now have to answer for these acts . . . But the later nine years I have spent in such a manner and in such company in the light of Christendom that I imagine I have given no opportunity even for fabricated charges . . . If a harmless nine years is not enough indication of a changed life, if a return to the Church and pardon count for nothing, I know not to what harbour of refuge sinners can fly.' The tone here becomes almost Russian in self-accusation; he confesses that he has sinned grievously against God and man, and has been a scandal to the Church of God; 'yet I have confessed my sins often, and especially when indulgences were announced, and since then have taken pains to offend no one, so far as I can remember.' He asks that, in respect of Portuguese sins (if any) he should be judged in Portugal, but that for sins committed in France he should be sent there in chains to be judged, so that he could call his witnesses and cite well-known names. 'Besides', he adds, 'here I perceive many acts are regarded as criminal which in France are free even from the suspicion of crime'. As to what had occurred in Britain, he abhors it, though he does not ask to be sent there for judgment. But he asks his judges to consider the nature of youth, how weak it is, how apt to be roused by insults, set aflame by ambition, deceived by the crafty, incited by the learned, swept on by passions, beset by ambushes of the devil, corrupted by evil communications. The cause of his fall had been that he had thought he ought to listen to arguments on both sides. So, when Lutherans attacked their opponents, and Christians, 'brooking ill the public questioning of what they considered stable and sound beliefs, answered by abuse rather than argument' (here a note of irritation and malice unwisely sounds from the repentant apologist) 'the minds of weaker brethren would waver, because they believed it was from lack of proofs that the orthodox resorted to abuse' — and so, not daring to seek help, they were bogged in the mire. But after he came to France he had grasped the truth when he heard it, and in no matter had he ever been stubborn. . . .

Thus George Buchanan's Defence, which his judges considered for a week before examining him on it. At the fourth examination they questioned him on the marriage of priests and other points. At the fifth, they succeeded in inducing him to remember a little more of his conversation with Pinheiro at Bordeaux — how he had discussed whether friars need fast when travelling. At the sixth, Buchanan failed to remember anything fresh, or to denounce anyone with whom he had talked (he was admonished 'to declare the whole truth, because it was not easily to be believed that he had not held converse with many suspicious persons'; to his credit, he failed to remember any of them). The seventh turned on meat on fast days; he owned that he had eaten meat in Lent at Salamanca, because his stomach was out of order, and he had not liked the wholemeal Spanish bread. His companions, da Costa and Teive, had also eaten meat, 'it being his opinion that they had the same complaints in their stomachs as he had'. At Coimbra last Lent he had again eaten it, because he had been suffering from double tertian fever (for fever or any other illness meat was apparently his sovereign remedy). A French master had eaten it with him, because he too had been ill; and Dom Sancho had also partaken, because he had stone in the bladder. The eighth examination was awkward and disconcerting; it concerned the papal Bull of pardon of 1543 or '44, which, after painstaking and honest inquiries, the Inquisitors had quite failed to trace, nor could anyone tell them anything about it. Buchanan could only declare that he had 'taken' it; it had been granted by Paul III, and granted plenary indulgence for crimes of heresy. Buchanan had fulfilled its requirements (confessing and fasting for three days and taking the Holy Sacrament) and gained it; it was unfortunate that he could produce no witnesses. Asked who had confessed him, he said it was an aged Franciscan, whose name he had not known. He knew of no one who might have a copy of the Bull. But he had told M. de Byrom, a gentleman of Perigord, that he could not sup with him because he was in the middle of his fast. However, as the Bull could not be traced, he took the advice of the Inquisitors and did not take his stand on it. It has not yet been traced. It was thought that he might be confusing it with a general pardon issued by the King of France some time ago, which would avail him nothing. The Inquisitors went on seeking for it; no one could say that they were not conscientious. While the search proceeded, the interrogations were held up until May. It may have been during these three months, which must have been months of some anxiety, that the prisoner began his Latin translation of the Psalms. Possibly the first edge may by now have worn off his fear: it must have grown to seem less likely that he would be put to the torture to drag from him confession or the names of fellow heretics, a contingency which the reputation of some of his judges must have suggested: one of them was the redoubtable Jeronymo d'Azambuja, famed for his torture of New Christians. But the failure of the attempt to smell out Judaism and paschal lamb, and there being no Jews in Scotland, was fortunate. On the other hand, the stake might still be at the end of the road; though surely not for such a repentant heretic, even if no Pardon could be traced.

Considering that it could not, Buchanan got off lightly. His tenth examination, in May, consisted of questions on theological points, justification and so on; his eleventh and last was merely an interview with the notary about the alleged Pardon. Then they had done with him; and in July sentence was pronounced. It declared that

'George Buchanan, a Scot, being a Christian, separated himself from our Holy Catholic Faith and from Holy Mother Church, vacillating and doubting in things of the Faith, during three years, inclining often to Lutheran opinions, holding that the Body of our Lord was not present in the Sacrament of the Altar, but only figuratively; and at other times doubting and vacillating thereon; doubting if the Mass was a sacrifice, and on Purgatory; holding mentally that by confidence only we were justified, that it was not sin not to confess at the times ordered by the Church if scandal was not caused; that confession was human not divine . . . that it was not necessary to obey the Church about meat-eating; that it was better to go direct to God than to the saints; all of which errors are heretic, Lutheran, damned, and reproved by Holy Mother Church . . . In view of the fact that the Defendant, moved by true and sound counsel, came at length to recognize his errors, and with many signs of repentance begged pardon for them of Our Lord and for the mercy of Holy Mother Church, the Deputies of the Holy Inquisition are agreed to receive Defendant to reconciliation, union and mercy of Holy Mother Church, as he has begged to be. His penance is that he make a public and formal abjuration of his errors before the Inquisitors and their officers in court, and that he reside in a monastery, which they assign to him as a prison, for such time as appears good to the Inquisition, where he will employ himself in some virtuous exercises and in things necessary to his salvation.' In conclusion, the defendant was absolved from excommunication.

So Buchanan read to his judges the abjuration they had written for him. He swore on the Gospels 'that of my own free will I renounce all and any heresies, especially those which I have confessed' (there followed the list of these, as set forth in the Sentence), after which he confessed the Holy Catholic Faith as set forth by the Holy Mother Church of Rome, swore to be obedient to it and to remain always in its bond, and to denounce and publish all those opposed to it, and 'God grant I may not fall into the penalty of backsliding'. It was an abjuration *de vehementi*; the penalty of relapse was the stake. Having sworn to it, he was sent to the convent of St. Bento for four months: he found the monks good-humoured but ignorant, and spent his time translating the Psalms into Latin and possibly doing exercises in classical erotic verse. He was released in December and allowed to live in Lisbon but not to leave it. Two months later he was set free entirely; requested by the king to remain in Portugal (or so he later said) he saw no life for him there, and only longed for France, which he reached at last, *via* England, in 1553. He was happy to be there, and safely out of Portugal. His *Adventus in Galliam* is a cry of relief. It had been a close thing, his bout with the Holy Office, a damned close-run thing, and he was taking no more risks. One result of it was to make of him what all his theological researches and his Lutheran dabblings of the past had failed to make him — a Protestant; he ranged himself with the Reformed Church soon after returning to Paris, if not officially (in the dangerous state of religious persecution that prevailed at that time in France) then by sympathies; returning to Scotland in 1560, he openly declared for it. He had indeed fallen into the penalty of backsliding, and remained in it for the rest of his successful and influential life, as eminent scholar, poet, preacher, historian and theologian, adviser and preceptor at the Scottish court, tutor in turn to Queen Mary and to her son James. The Inquisitors in Portugal, and King John himself, must have gazed rather sourly across the seas at the distinguished figure of their ex-prisoner, who had once been in their power, in whose repentant abjuration they had so rashly trusted.

What went on in Buchanan's own mind and soul about the whole business? It is impossible to be certain. That, having once shaken off Catholicism and become one of its fiercest opponents, he was ashamed of the rather ignominious figure he had cut before the Inquisitors, is apparent, from his own version of the affair, as told in his brief autobiography, and, more fully, by his friends and apologists, who must have got it from him. His indignant version in his Life is that 'it was on Buchanan, as a foreigner, that they heaped the greatest insults and injuries . . . After the Inquisition had for a year and a half worn out his and their own patience, lest they should be supposed to have persecuted to no purpose one not altogether unknown to fame, they shut him up for some months in a monastery, in order that he might be more accurately instructed by the monks, who proved neither unkindly nor ill-disposed, though utterly ignorant of religious truth'.

His story is inaccurate in details, and markedly omits any mention or implication of abjuration or sentence. According to him, his persecutors simply got tired of persecuting him and let him go.

A still more triumphant version was put about by his friend Thomas Smeaton, in reply to an attack on him from the Catholic Archibald Hamilton. According to this story, the Inquisitors had not merely got tired of persecuting him, but triumphantly and completely acquitted him of heresy. Smeaton quotes long and grandiose speeches which Buchanan had made, he said, to his judges on the vexed topic of transubstantiation, supporting his declarations by the weighty evidence of Augustine. So 'as he could not be convicted by any argument or witness, he was acquitted by the votes of his judges, and returned to France', the loss to Portuguese culture being so great that King John afterwards tried to recall him with the most loving letters. 'But it was in vain; for, once set free by the great kindness of God out of the most cruel hands of the Inquisitors, he refused to enter a second time into that peril.'

There is little here to suggest that scene of dictated abjuration and repentance and ignominiously worded, though merciful, sentence in the Lisbon Inquisition House eighteen years ago. The great scholar, poet and controversialist of European fame, the Grand Old Man of learned Scottish Protestantism, had done nothing so humiliating as to abjure Protestant errors before a board of Portuguese Inquisitors. Archibald Hamilton, well primed against the bitter enemy of the Church he had joined, but over-painting the picture, retorted that the Lisbon records bore witness that Buchanan had not been delivered by quoting Augustine, but by the verse of the Psalmist, which, prostrate at the Cardinal Prince's feet, he had uttered in a voice broken by sobs — 'Remember not the sins of my youth, nor my transgressions, O Lord.' The records do not, as a matter of fact, bear out either the presence of the Cardinal Prince or the use of this psalm; but the picturesque story is true in spirit if not in detail.

'I have mentioned this abjuration,' Hamilton goes on, 'so that Scotland may understand how authoritative and steadfast is its patriarchal leader in religion whom now the country follows, regarding as the surest oracles of the Holy Spirit every paradox of a wanton poet and abjured heretic.'

Buchanan cannot have relished this bringing up of the unflattering ghost of a past that he had spent many years in twisting into a different and more agreeable shape, these unpalatable memories of that dreadful year in a dungeon cell of the Holy House in the Rocio, when days and weeks of comfortless and solitary fear had been punctuated only by terrific, incriminating, trapping interrogations before seven quiet, nagging, patient, evidence-primed judges and a scribbling notary in the corner; when questions, sometimes silly, sometimes alarmingly to the point, had been shot at him in the bigoted, nasal voices of men who tortured and burnt, who half thought he might be a Jew in disguise, like so many of their Portuguese prisoners, and were certain he was three parts a Lutheran. The memory would still bring the sweat of fear to his brow. And then, after the humiliating, lenient sentence, which showed that his judges had tried to be just, even in the face of that untraced Bull of pardon, those absurd months in St. Bento among the amiable, ignorant monks, when he had translated the Psalms into Latin and written, for relief and recreation, Latin verses so different. . . .

It was all a buried nightmare now: he did not care to think of it.

BIBLIOGRAPHY

The Trial of George Buchanan before the Lisbon Inquisition, J. M. AITKEN (1939).
George Buchanan in the Lisbon Inquisition, G. D. S. HENRIQUES (Lisbon, 1906).
George Buchanan, Humanist and Reformer, P. HUME BROWN (1890).
Memoirs of Life and Writings of George Buchanan, DAVID IRVING (1817).
Coimbra, Boletim Annual (1918).
Da origem e estabelecimento da Inquisicão em Portugal, ALEXANDRE HERCULANO (1854-5).

2. MAC-FLECKNOE'S FATHER

Richard Flecknoe

[1648-50]

THIS rather enigmatic man and mediocre poet, spitefully made by Dryden the father-in-dullness of his *bête noire* Thomas Shadwell, and, less viciously but still rudely, skitted by Marvell, who met him in Rome in 1646, is known to us to-day

only because thus doubly impaled by two poets of the first class.
He was scarcely worth it; he wrote much, but it did not matter;
he said himself, 'There is none that prints more nor publishes less
than I, for I print only for myself and private friends.' Not true,
for there was none that liked better to have an audience, or was
more chagrined when rejected of the great public; still, it is difficult to see just why Dryden picked on him after his death for an
outburst of hate and scorn, coupling him with his loathed rival
Shadwell, saying that he

> In prose and verse was own'd, without dispute,
> Through all the realms of Nonsense absolute.

You would not think that Flecknoe, even in dullness, was as prominent as that. It has been suggested that Dryden hated him for
his attacks on stage obscenity and his pleas for 'a reformed stage'.
For the rest, he had praised Dryden, whose malice was usually
evoked either by those who had slighted him, or by those of whom
he was jealous. And anyhow a Roman Catholic priest seems an
inapt sire for Mac-Flecknoe, the True-Blue-Protestant poet. But
Dryden spat hate as an octopus squirts ink, being so full of it; it is
scarcely worth inquiring his reasons. Obviously Flecknoe must
have been a shocking bore; he was a parasite, a snob, infinitely
vain, and read his verses to everyone he could get hold of, posting
them to the others (if they were persons of any consequence).
Dryden was enough like this himself (most poets were) to hate
him.

Doubts have been raised as to whether Flecknoe was really a
priest. On the grounds that he nowhere alludes to it in his
writings, either letters or any other, and does not seem to have
exercised his functions, some critics have decided that he probably
never took orders, and that to call him a priest was just a mistake
of Marvell's. Yet Marvell not only calls him 'Fleckno, an English
Priest at Rome', but describes his soutane and black habit; Dryden
calls him 'priest by trade', and his name appears in the Pilgrims'
Book of the English College in Rome, on the occasions of his visits
there, as 'D. Ricardus Fleckno Sacerdos Anglus Londoniensis'.
Even if Dr. Joseph Gillow is wrong about his education in an
unspecified Jesuit college, and his having joined the Society and
left it, he remains either a priest or one who posed as a priest. To
be sure, he laid little enough stress on it; there is no hint of it in

the detailed self-portrait that he wrote for a lady correspondent, or anywhere else in his works. But many English Roman Catholic priests contracted a habit of discreet unobtrusiveness; they went about as laymen, and had usually several aliases; and Flecknoe, for other reasons than convenience and safety, definitely preferred himself as writer, musician, and man of the great world. He was devout; his first known work (printed in 1626, when he must have been quite young), was called *Hierothalamium, or the Heavenly Nuptials of our Blessed Saviour with a Pious Soul*; his second, in 1640, shows a mind still running on the same theme. After that he gets away from this discouraging topic, turning to plays, characters, poems, and miscellaneous trifles; though not all pious, they are all virtuous. He was vain; he liked to present himself as a man too retiring and too lazy to push, and more concerned to trifle elegantly than to enter the heat of the battle. He knew the *beau monde*, he was skilled on the lute, he got about Europe and met everyone, he even got to Brazil, for, as he said in excuse for this trans-Atlantic exercise, 'my desire of seeing all the world is so insatiate (whether the more one sees of it the less he is satisfied, or that it satisfies so much, as one has still a desire of seeing more) as just like another Alexander I am seeking another forth'.

He began his prolonged round trip in 1640, smelling trouble in the English air. He went first to Ghent, whence he wrote to his friend Colonel William Ewers, explaining his departure.

'Here are divers Birds that fly away when Storms and Winter comes, one of those Birds am I, for all prognostic Mariners observe of ensuing Storms, and I have observed in England the billows beginning to swell high, and those Porpoises which, were the times fair and serene, should be i'th' Bottom, dancing on the Top. Meantime, let your vast and strong-built Carracks ride out the storm for me; I'm too weak and slight-built a vessel for tempestuous Seas. Besides educated as I am in the Arts of Peace (Music and Poetry) . . . England is no place for me. And this much for my leaving it. Now for my retreat hither, 'twas altogether without design. I, like one who flies an *Incendium*, wholly indifferent whither I went, so I sav'd myself.'

He had a marvellous time at Ghent, among the nobility, who were extremely courteous and obliging — 'there is no Feast nor party without me. In all their sports and exercises I must make one, for their games they teach them me and make me win . . . it were too great a vanity to tell you this if it were not a greater Ingratitude to conceal it.'

But after two years of these gratifying pleasures, he felt he must move on. Ghent became, as affairs grew stormier in England, 'too full of melancholy Englishmen and sad intelligence from home'. 'I,' he wrote to a friend (all his travelling comes to us in the form of letters, whether they were all actually posted or not), 'I, by reducing all to the narrow compass of one Portmanteau, travel lightly up and down, enjoying that Liberty Fortune has bestowed on me, and Nature inclines me to.'

He obviously had a little money, and he saved it greatly by living on friends. So off he went to Brussels, where, as he wrote to Lady Audley, he had a very gay, sociable time, finding the ladies particularly handsome and sprightly, and every one most hospitable. Brussels was delightful; the nobility rivalled that of Ghent in their attentions. 'You will wonder', he writes to Lord Blank, 'living so deliciously as I do ... every day with Mlle de Arschot and the Princess Hoghzollern in the Park, singing and making music at the foot of every tree, every day in Feasts at home or Collations abroad, I can resolve so soon to quit Bruxelles, having scarcely resided here a year.' But he wanted to be further from war. To be near the nobility, to be far from war — these were his aims, and when the nobility went to war, as nobility sometimes will, the second prevailed. Anyhow (and we hear in his words the eternal plaint of Belgium) 'here, where the French and Hollander between them waste and consume this country just like a Taper lighted at both ends ... every place a frontier to some enemy or other', here he would not stay. Italy, he decided, was the safest bet. So for Italy he made, via Paris, which he did not like, for it was all hurry and noise, and Marseilles, which he liked very much, for the women were much handsomer than in most sea towns, and so to Genoa and Rome.

Rome was not a success, except for the ruins. Socially, it fell well below Brussels, Ghent and elsewhere. There are indications that Flecknoe was pinched for money, and that his hopes of getting some out of the Vatican were disappointed.

'I swear I like it not', he wrote. 'Give me good Company, good Nature, and good Mirth, and the Devil of any such thing they have here, all being for their interest ... In a word, when you have seen the Ruins, you have seen all here' (even St. Peter's was nothing) . . . 'For generosity and Magnificence, it seems to have died with the last Pope, for now there's none left here.'

He did not care about the cardinals, who lived like great princes, but their souls were stifled in their narrow breasts. In fact, coming in without influence or contacts to that close though international society of seedy hangers-on, pensioners, exiles, intriguers, and solicitors for favour, which had always haunted the Eternal City, he failed to get on. He explained in a letter from Lisbon that he could not push.

'When good fortune falls, I cannot crowd and slave to catch it; I had rather be silent than solicitous what to say . . . and for Industry, 'tis not in my Nature . . . I came a discontented person from Rome.' For in Rome one cannot speak without caution nor live without extreme industry, 'and all is insidiousness, shoving, shouldering, and soliciting, making business of everything, 'tis no wonder I never agreed with it'. He told the King of Portugal that 'at Rome all studied the Pope's art, which was hoarding up of money and nothing else'.

Such complaints, added to Marvell's account of his cramped lodgings, hunger, and shabby ancient clothes, point to a poor time in Rome. He sometimes dined at the English College; and he saw something of Marvell, who was travelling as tutor to a young gentleman. They exchanged visits.

> Oblig'd by frequent visits of this man . . .
> I sought his lodging,

Marvell's poem begins. His lodging was a narrow, coffin-like room three flights up; directly Marvell entered, Flecknoe began to recite to him in dismal tones his verse, then played his lute. Marvell, to stop him, and perceiving him hungry, took him out to dinner, for which he dressed by wrapping reams of his poems about him under his cassock, to read aloud at table.

It says much for Flecknoe's dread of war that he stayed in Rome between two and three years. He wrote deploring his irksome life; he felt he said, like Adam turned out of Paradise, once among angels, now among beasts. Obviously no one asked him out or entertained him, or supplied him with money. He endured it till 1648, then went to Provence and sailed from Hyères, intending Spain. But on the way the ship fell in with a Holland man-of-war bound for Lisbon; changing his plan, Flecknoe boarded it, and

reached Cascais 'in the mouth of Lisbon Road' five or six weeks
after leaving Hyères. The governor of Cascais decided that he
was a spy, and sent him to Lisbon under a guard, who delivered
him to the Secretary of State, who 'made great difficulty of my
stay in the country, till, spying my lute, the suspicion that I was a
musician soon drove out of his head the suspicion that I was a
spy'. The Secretary then paid him every attention, lodging him
in the house of an English Catholic merchant, Mr. John Muley, a
great confidant of the king's, till he could inform His Majesty of
him. For King John, with whom music was a hobby, liked to
know other musicians. He sent for the English priest to court,
arranged that he should continue lodging with Mr. Muley ('than
which the whole Town afforded not more noble accommodation'),
and tried his musical skill in a test which lasted two or three hours.
Flecknoe acquitted himself creditably, and passed into royal
favour; he was assigned a cavalier to whom he was to address
himself for access to the royal presence whenever he pleased.

> My warbling Lute, the Lute I whilom strung,
> When to King John of Portugal I sung,

as Dryden wrote, having no doubt heard the story often enough.
   Flecknoe enjoyed himself greatly in Lisbon, being looked upon
with particular regard by all (so different from Rome), and 'passing most of my time in Mr. Muley's Kinta, or Garden House, some
three or four miles from Lisbon'. He wrote a poem about it,
which he sent to Lord Charles Dudley.

> When in a Vale near *Tagus* golden side,
> Through all the world renowned far and wide . . .
> A *Kinta* stands so situated 't has
> Resort unto't of every Rural Grace,
> (And Rural Graces are in Summer far
> Jollier than those of Towns in Winter are)
> Whose fairest Garden's planted round with all
> Those Trees we fruitful and delicious call.
> As *Orange*, *Lymon*, *Apricock*, and *Peach*,
> (Whose ruddier side do Nymphs their blushing teach)
> Silk-animating *Mulberries*, spreading wide,
> *Pomegranates*, *Figs*, and hundred more beside. . . .

It is a pity that it was not Marvell who stayed at Mr. Muley's quinta; we should have had a better poem. Still, Flecknoe enjoyed himself. Mr. Muley's views on his royally-imposed visitor are lacking. Flecknoe wrote letters about how pleasant was Lisbon, how objectionable had been Rome, and what he had said to King John about the Pope, which he was not sorry to learn had somehow got round to his Holiness. To his friend the Countess of Berlamont he sent a gay description of his Lisbon life, the spaciousness of Mr. Muley's garden, the fruit — 'figs that make beccoficos of men, and meloons both red and green, beyond their marmalade for meltingness'. As to his company, he called it, archly ironic, 'none but such one would be ashamed to keep compañy withall. The King here, a man of no estate', etc. etc. He was much better when he dropped this playfully sarcastic boastfulness and forgot himself in a lively description of the royal family.

'The King is an honest plain man, changing nothing of the Duke of Braganza by being King of Portugal, faring as homely as any farmer, and going as meanly clad as any citizen . . . his ordinary exercise is hunting and music . . . But for the Queen, she has more of the Majestic in her, and if she be not King, her ambition 'twas that made the King. She has a goodly presence, a stately gait, and uses the Trowel in painting . . . For Prince Theodosio, her eldest son, he is a Prince of great expectation, learned and of great wit and courage, of person tall and slender, about some 18 years of age.'

These comments on Portugal have interest as coming from one of the earliest English visitors who went there merely as tourists; he was an advance guard of a great company of trippers. A born tripper he indeed was; even Portugal, its luscious fruits and gardens, its friendly and musical monarch, could not detain him long. Soon he was writing to Mlle de Beauvais, one of his dearest lady friends, that he was planning a trip to Affrique and Brazil. 'The ardent thirst I had of voyaging, which nothing but the whole *Ocean* could quench', beckoned him thither. Having seen so many Brazil rarities in Portugal, he thought·it worth a voyage there to bring her some of them. The King had kindly presented him with 200 crowns for his voyage. 'I imagined it richly worth my journey, to see the stars of the other Pole, and the Nature of the other Hemisphere. And lastly, my desire of seeing all the world is so insatiate. . . .'

So off he sailed, had a marvellous time in Brazil, and was back in Lisbon for a short time in 1650, before taking off for Flanders. He wrote from Lisbon that he had been trying to explain the English constitution, king and parliament to eminent Portuguese friends, who were doubtless scandalized and puzzled by recent happenings overseas. These had been brought to their very doors earlier in the year, when Prince Rupert and the revolted royalist fleet had been privateering and fighting with Blake and the Commonwealth navy in and out of Lisbon Road. Explanation was certainly called for; whether Flecknoe elucidated the situation much is doubtful. The proper function of Parliament, Flecknoe explained, was to support and uphold the king. But the ruin of the monarchy began long ago, with the Schism, when the king took on himself ecclesiastical authority, and the throne 'has stood wavering and tottering ever since'. A just nemesis for heresy and arrogance, Flecknoe thought it; and no doubt the Portuguese agreed with him.

He was debating the question of his future. 'If there be any settlement in England and subsistence for an honest man who loves to be quiet and let others be so, I may see it again: if not, I have learnt how wide the World is, and to esteem every place for my Country where I may live quiet and without molestation.'

After leaving Portugal he wrote a flattering 'collins' to Mr. John Muley (who was, naturally, not among the English merchants lying in prison for their parliamentary sympathies).

'Worthy Sir. The courtesy I have received in all my Voyages from those of your noble profession, especially from your self, obliges me in gratitude to the publishing every where of the following Character of an English Merchant resident in foreign parts.'

The Character is flattering indeed; it is to be hoped that Mr. Muley turned it into Portuguese and presented copies to the Lisbon Custom House and the Secretary of State for their information. 'To conclude', it ends, 'he is the honour of his Nation abroad, and therefore his Nation should be very dishonourable and unworthy, should it not always honour him.'

Flecknoe then betook himself again to Holland, Brussels and Ghent; presumably, as he calls his collection of letters 'A relation of ten years travel', he was in England again, the civil war being safely over, sometime in 1650. He settled down to versifying, play-writing, and miscellaneous compositions; they included, as was common form, an appreciation of the Lord Protector at his death and another of King Charles II at his Restoration.

We have his own view of what he was like, not only in many letters, but in a Self Portrait, written for a friend. Rather like a portrait of Seneca to look at, he thought; 'he is well enough content with his exterior, but with his interior not so well'... His mind is neither very good nor very bad; he never cares for what he cannot have, nor puts himself out to get it. Above all, he shuns all highways of the vulgar and by-ways in religion. He is shy; familiar with few, and those of the nobler and better sort; 'loves all things cheerful, splendious and noble, and hates sectaries most of all, because they are otherwise'. A cold word freezes him; and a hot makes him boil over at once.

More light is thrown by his epistle to the Reader which prefaces his Travels.

'I write my Travels . . . but to satisfy the curiosity of some noble friends, and make honourable mention of others, to whom I am infinitely oblig'd . . . Nor is it vanity in me, that I make mention of so many and noble ones, all that know me knowing I never willingly converse but with the noblest in every place, finding them still in every respect the best; besides, since Fortune maim'd me and brought me to my Crutches, whom should I rely upon but the best able to support me? which they are the more willing to do because I lean so lightly on them, and always strive to offer them some pleasure for the profit I receive of them.'

But he did not lean lightly on them; he sent them his verses. And when they composed complimentary replies, he printed these at the beginning of his books. The Duke of Newcastle sent him some lines of acknowledgment which probably all the other poets took as irony.

> Flecknoe, thy verses are too high for me . . .
> Thy vaster fancy doth embrace all things,
> And for thy subject ought t'have greatest Kings

Flecknoe, delighted, prefaced his Travels with these lines, with the deprecating comment, that though he did not deserve such a tribute, 'yet must I glory in it, and publish it everywhere . . . How glorious it must be for me to be praised by the most praise-worthy man alive!'

Writers all made fools of one another, and of the nobility; this was not much worse than most.

On the whole, a harmless man, with a certain gift for phrase and imagery in prose (which was better than his verse); as this, about Constantinople — 'every one wearing such various coloured silks, with swelling turbans and flowing garments, as their streets appear just like tulip gardens, whilst ours (with so many's wearing black) appear just like mortuary houses, all mourning for the dead'. With politics he concerned himself little, so long as they let him be, but had the usual view of his party on such matters as liberty. 'I see 'tis a mere cheat this Popular Liberty, the enchantment of the vulgar, the gewgaw they promise children to make them good boys; yet 't has been and ever will be the madness of the Common People to go in quest of it, as Don Quixote did of his Dulcinea ... In reality there is no such thing at all, the true liberty of the people only consisting in being well commanded. ...'

'He seems', said the *Retrospective Review* with the severity of 1822, 'to have been a vain busy coxcomb, who thought it genteel rather to affect a little negligence than too great curiosity.'

Possibly. In fact, certainly. But he wears an air of touching pathos, of being always in forced retreat from a world he believed himself too proud and too negligent to assail, yet never ceased assailing. And he loved his noble friends. On hearing in Ghent of the execution of Strafford, he wrote to Lord Blank, sending him an epitaph that he had composed on the slain earl and adding, 'And now (my Lord) comfort yourself, if you chance to be the next, that you shall not want one to make your Epitaph and Character at least'.

BIBLIOGRAPHY

A Relation of Ten Years of Travels in Europe, Asia, Affrique and America: All by way of Letters occasionally written to divers noble Personages, from place to place, RICHARD FLECKNOE (1654).
Fleckno: An English Priest at Rome, ANDREW MARVELL (pub. 1681).
Mac-Flecknoe, JOHN DRYDEN (1682).
Richard Flecknoe: Eine Literar-historische Untersuchung, ANTON LOHR (Leipzig, 1905).
Biographical Dictionary of English Catholics, JOSEPH GILLOW (1885).
Dictionary of National Biography.
Omniana, ROBERT SOUTHEY and S. T. COLERIDGE (1812).
Retrospective Review (1822).
Letter to *The Times Literary Supplement*, H. M. MARGOLIOUTH (June 5th, 1924).

3. HIC JACET...

Henry Fielding

[August-October 1754]

NEVER can any invalid have taken more pains to recover and live than did poor Fielding. Finding himself, in the winter of 1753, 'in a very weak and deplorable condition, with no fewer or less diseases than a jaundice, a dropsy, and an asthma', and entirely emaciated, he decided that he was no longer a Bath case, gave up hopes of cure from the waters there, and began to look on himself as dying, a martyr to his energetic campaign for clearing the streets of criminal gangs, which had exhausted his strength. He retired to Ealing, and tried everything — milk diet, tar-water, tapping, all the medicines of his physician, Dr. Ward; it was no use, he could not, for all the tappings, keep pace with the dropsy. He was told that the summer would mend him; alas, he was in a country in which there is often no summer; he saw the summer mouldering away, or rather the year passing without intending to bring on any summer at all; in the whole month of May the sun scarce appeared three times. The asthma grew worse, the dropsy grew worse, winter would return and he would not be able to withstand it. The only hope was in a warmer climate; Aix in Provence was thought of, but the overland journey would be too long; it would have to be Lisbon. Lisbon was four degrees south of Aix, it must be milder and warmer, the winter shorter. His brother found a ship, the *Queen of Portugal*, which would sail in a few days; the passage would cost £30. This sum, which presumably covered the transport of Fielding, his second wife, his daughter Harriot, Miss Margaret Collier, William the man and Isabella Ash the maid, seems reasonable. The younger children were to be left at home. Fielding, with his usual spirit, though pretty sure he was dying, took with him, besides his 1578 folio of Plato and other books, the materials he had collected for the refutation of the pernicious doctrines of Lord Bolingbroke on which he was engaged. For this he thought it necessary to go through the Fathers and other eminent controversialists; so his library on the *Queen of Portugal* must have been considerable. When one reflects that he might instead have begun a novel, for which he would have required no library at all, one is driven once more to meditate on the perverse ways in which men of genius so frequently waste their time and their gifts.

The story of the voyage, its delay in beginning, the visit to Ryde, the adventures on the way, the character of Captain Richard Veal, and all the rest of it, are familiar to us as told in the *Journal of a Voyage to Lisbon*; voyages through such known seas are seldom interesting, and for an account of a few weeks of Fielding's two months in Lisbon we would give the whole of it. But, alas, the journal ends abruptly when the party have landed and driven to 'a kind of coffee-house', and for the two months we have only one letter, written to his brother two or three weeks after arrival, and discovered some years ago. It is tantalizing in its racy, fussy gossip, its amusing detail, its hints at uneasy situations not elaborated; there must have been more letters; there may be somewhere other letters, from other Lisboans who met the Fieldings — nice, intelligent Mr. Williamson the chaplain, at whom Miss Collier set her cap; Abraham Castres, the British envoy; Edward Hay the consul; Mr. Stubbs, 'the greatest merchant of this Place, and the greatest corn factor in the world'; the Hakes, the Perochons and other members of the 'jolly free Factory' society which Sir Benjamin Keene, their late ambassador, had so much enjoyed, and who must have met or heard of the famous dying novelist, his wife and daughter, and Miss Collier the 'toast of Lisbon'. There was not, in 1754, so great a rush of English visitors to Lisbon that such a party would have been overlooked, even though factory society was all agog at the time over their commercial grievances at the hands of Pombal; the corn merchants in particular (led, one presumes by Mr. Stubbs, who nevertheless found time to be of service to Fielding) were up in arms against the laws against exporting corn, and every mercantile house of note was busy evading the bullion export prohibition. Letters may yet come to light describing how the Fielding household struck Lisbon. No one familiar with that city can doubt that there was plenty of animated gossip about them, and particularly about Miss Collier's pursuit of the chaplain.

How Lisbon, seen from the sea, struck Fielding, we read in the *Journal*; he thought the country looked burnt and parched and lacked large trees; he felt proud of the British verdure; so far now from British chill, he could think kindly of it. They entered the Tajo, as Fielding persisted in calling it; they were boarded by the quarantine officials, then by the customs, who behaved with great insolence, and for whom the sailors expressed hatred and contempt — the usual British feelings towards the Portuguese customs officials, intensified during these years by new regulations and the feud between the merchants and Pombal. They were now opposite Belem, which Fielding called throughout his acquaintance with it Bellisle; he was not alone among the English in this; but he had no ear for sounds and was a hopeless linguist; it is probable that through his two months in Lisbon no word of Portuguese penetrated correctly. Neither was he a historian; he believed the Queen Catherine buried in Belem to have been Catherine of Aragon.

At last, at midnight, in a calm and moonshiny night, the ship cast anchor off Lisbon; the women, entranced, stayed three hours on deck enjoying the scene, while Fielding lay below and enjoyed their pleasure at second hand. Next morning he saw the view of Lisbon from the deck; medieval Lisbon still, that was to be destroyed next year, rising steeply, tier above tier, white houses, white convents, white churches, climbing in an almost perpendicular mountain against a Lisbon-blue sky. Fielding thought it all lacked ornament, and would compare but poorly with Palmyra and other ancient cities.

Thus musing on a decadent civilization and departed glory, he waited three hours on deck for the return of his man William, whom he had sent ashore to order a good dinner and bring a chaise. When William at last returned at three o'clock, it was to say that no passenger might land without an order from the providore, and that the providore was asleep and might not be roused. It was not until about seven in the evening that Fielding landed, or rather was carried on shore, got into a chaise, and 'was driven through the nastiest city in the world, though at the same time one of the most populous, to a kind of coffee-house, which is very pleasantly situated on the brow of a hill, about a mile from the city, and hath a very fine prospect of the river Tajo from Lisbon to the sea'. It was no doubt in Buenos Ayres, but we know no more of it except that 'here we regaled ourselves with a good supper, for which we were as well charged as if the bill had been made out on the Bath road, between Newbury and London'. We do not even know if the coffee-house was also the inn where they stayed, and which was so much too dear. The *Journal* stops

abruptly, with 'hic finis chartaeque viaeque', and we have no
more news of the Fieldings in Lisbon until the solitary letter to
John Fielding, undated and, according to the irritating habit of
sojourners in Lisbon, not headed with any address. Fielding had
in spite of this received two letters from his brother, but he asks
that even the smallest parcel may be addressed to John Stubbs,
Esq., as the captains of merchant ships who bring the letters pay
no regard to any but merchants. 'The truth is that Captains are
all the greatest scoundrels in the world, but Veale is the greatest
of them all. This I did not find out till the day before he sailed . . .
he is likewise a Madman, which I knew long before I reached
Lisbon. . . .'

He then dismisses Captain Veal, whom he had rather liked on
the voyage before he had found him out, and goes on to say that
his health is much improved, the dropsy gone, and he would now
be quite recovered were it not for every possible accident and misfortune. First Mrs. Fielding, Miss Collier and William had all
fallen ill. William had made himself worse by drinking too much
wine, as the English in Portugal did; in terror of dying abroad, he
had sailed home with Captain Veal, with £3 12s. swindled from
his master. Bell, who is 'only a fool', 'follows Captain Veale to
England, where he hath promised to marry her'; as he certainly
will do no such thing, John is to find her another place. 'My
Family now consists of a black Slave and his Wife, to which I
desire you to add a very good perfect Cook, by the first ship, but
not by Veale.'

Besides these domestic mishaps, there were money difficulties;
'I found myself in the dearest City in the World and in the dearest
House in that City. I could not for my Soul live for less than
2 Moidores a day, and saw myself likely to be left Pennyless 1,000
miles from home, where I had neither Acquaintance nor Credit,
among a Set of People who are tearing one another's Souls out
for money and ready to deposit Millions with Security but not a
Farthing without.' He could not move to a cheaper house, because there were only two others in which he would not be
poisoned, and these were dearer still. It was a bad look out, until
he fell in with Mr. Stubbs, the great corn merchant, who 'hath a
little Kintor or Villa at a place called Jonkera 2 miles from Lisbon
and near Bellisle, which is the Kensington of England, and where
the Court now reside'. What Mr. Stubbs actually had was a

quinta at Junqueira, near Belem. Anyhow, he got Fielding a little house there, unfurnished, without even a kitchen grate, for 9 moidores a year, and here, after furnishing it, the Fieldings moved, and found they could live inside a moidore a week. All would now have been well, but Mrs. Fielding, a spiritless and selfish creature, was ailing and homesick; she pined for her children, believed that Fielding would be quite as well in England, and was 'so dispirited that she cries and sighs all Day to return to England'. It is probable that she did not like the heat and dust of Lisbon in summer, did not care for the black slave and his wife, or for the lack of a kitchen grate; unlike Edith Southey, she was not consoled either by the fruit or by staring at the people in the streets and commenting on their unfortunate appearance and queer clothes; or if she was her husband does not mention it.

Fielding himself would have been happy enough; he was getting better, his fortunes had improved, he had pleasant society round him, and asked his brother to send him out some new clothes for the winter. 'Let me have likewise my Tie and a new Mazer Perriwig from Southampton Street, and a new Hat large in the Brim from my Hatter, the corner of Arundel Street. I have had a visit from a Portuguese Nobleman, and shall be visited by all as soon as my Kintor is in order ... My affairs will soon be in a fine Posture, for I can live here, and even make a Figure for almost nothing. In truth the Produce of the Country is preposterously cheap.' He was preparing to settle down for the winter, and asked his brother to send him out a 'conversible Man to be my companion in an Evening, with as much of the Qualifications of Learning, Sense and Good Humour as you can find, who will drink a moderate Glass in an Evening or will at least sit with me till one when I do'. He asks too for a housekeeper (a Mrs. Hedley) and an amanuensis (Mr. Jones).

The letter is tantalizing, because it seems that parts of it are lost and other parts almost illegible. For much in it we have to rely on a summary by the Fielding family and Mr. Austin Dobson, who first published it in 1911. The parts thus summarized, paraphrased and reconstructed seem particularly interesting, and would have been more satisfactorily dealt with by copying what is not absolutely illegible and leaving gaps for the rest. All reconstruction is suspicious; one does not know how much the reconstructors have to go on. According to Mr. Dobson, accepted and

followed by Mr. Wilbur L. Cross, who adds a few sentences more
to the transcript, Miss Collier was scheming to catch Mr. Williamson the chaplain, and proposing that the homesick Mrs. Fielding
should return to England, leaving her in charge of Harriot. 'The
passages immediately succeeding,' says Mr. Dobson, 'deal with
plans for defeating Miss Collier's machinations. They show much
excusable irritation, and even some incoherency.' There seems
no reason for not quoting them, but this is all we are told. The
domestic disturbances hinted at depressed Fielding immeasurably.
'By these means,' he writes, 'my Spirits which were at the Top of
the House are thrown down into the Cellar.' However, he sends
his friends chests of onions and hogsheads of calcavella, and promises them orange trees, lemons, and wine, 'Port or Lisbon which
you like best'. He was able now, he said, to get in and out of a
chaise by himself and ride all day in it. His chief companion was
Mr. Williamson, whom he called the cleverest fellow he had ever
seen.

With company, sunshine, a house in a pleasant suburb to live
in, and health enough to drive about and see the neighbourhood,
he should have had prospects of happiness. He was in the sumptuous pre-earthquake Lisbon, whose magnificence had been so
enthusiastically described five years earlier by the Welsh traveller
Udal ap Rhys; a Lisbon of churches, convents, gold and jewelled
ornaments, abject poverty, negro slaves, priests, friars, the sumptuous processions which had a few months before the Fieldings
arrived scandalized and fascinated the Reverend Mr. Whitefield,
superstition, squalor, corruption, women eating sweets and playing
guitars at windows, and rich galleys sailing in from Brazil. How
much of this rich and entertaining pageantry Fielding was able
to see, we shall not now know. Did he get as far as Cintra, the
English tourists's Mecca? Or across the Tagus to Almeida? Or
visiting and chatting with the English nuns of Sion? His friend Mr.
Williamson may have shown him the sights, including the new
English cemetery among the cypresses up at Buenos Ayres, his
future home. He has left no such news of his doings as was left by
countless uninteresting and unimportant travellers and writers
who bustled about Portugal and set it all down. These are the
sad lacunae of history. And when unexpected letters from such
as Fielding do turn up after a century and a half, they should, one
feels, be published not piecemeal and in summary, but in full.

The last words we have from him are this letter, and the preface and introduction to the *Voyage to Lisbon*. Fortunately he devoted himself to this rather than to getting on with his commentary on Bolingbroke. That he wrote at least the preface after arrival in Lisbon we know; in it he compares those who are imposed on by the travellers' tales of Pliny and his great fellow liars to the natives of the country 'where I now write, as there is nowhere more pomp of bigotry'; people, if foolish enough, will believe anything they are told, nor, as a rule, do they understand what they believe. It is a gay and racy little essay on travellers, and when he wrote it he must have been feeling ease enough of mind and body to make jokes.

Yet he was dying. When the *Public Advertiser* for October 16th wrote 'Letters by the last mail from Lisbon advise that Henry Fielding, Esq., is surprisingly recovered since his arrival in that climate. His gout has entirely left him, and his appetite returned', he had been dead eight days. He died in the 'little Kintor' at Junqueira on October 8th; he was forty-seven. He was buried by his friend the chaplain in the lovely English cemetery on the hill of Buenos Ayres. Neither his family nor any one in Lisbon put up much of a tombstone for many years; in 1772, when both Nathaniel Wraxall and Richard Twiss visited the cemetery, Wraxall said he saw the grave and tombstone, but the grave was nearly concealed by nettles and weeds, and Twiss 'had the mortification to see many marble monuments with long, pompous flattering inscriptions' erected to the merchants and their families, while 'the great author of *Tom Jones* is here interred without even a stone to indicate that here lies Henry Fielding'. There seems a difference of testimony between the two tourists about the stone; either the one that Wraxall thought he saw had disappeared a little later when Twiss got there, or had become quite hidden by weeds and nettles, or there had been no stone, but perhaps a wooden board. Of the two visitors, Twiss was the closer observer; Wraxall's thoughts were roaming after 'that seductive species of writing, unknown to antiquity, which we denominate novels', and placing famous novelists in order; it is possible that he did not really notice the material of which the sign-post to Fielding's grave was made. In any case, it can have been scarcely worth calling a tombstone. The architect J. C. Murphy, in Lisbon sixteen years later, also complained of the lack of a monument; a few years before this it had shocked even the French consul, who, in 1786, mainly to· annoy the indifferent English, had a marble tombstone made at his own expense and inscribed with a poem in French complaining of the lack of attention paid by the English to their great novelist. The French were in a phase of Fielding enthusiasm (though they preferred Richardson, if a novelist had to be English at all); and the consul was an enthusiast. Murphy condemned the design of his monument as contemptible and its epitaph as unappropriate and unpoetical, and made 'rather from vanity than gratitude, rather with a view to confer honour on himself and his country than to perpetuate the memory of Fielding'. Neither did the English Factory, who owned the cemetery, care for its tone. It urged the seeker after Fielding's remains,

> De la mort et du temps déplore les effets,
> Ou déteste plutôt l'oubli de ses semblables.
> Ils élèvent partout les marbres fastueux,
> Un bloc reconnaissant ici manque à tes voeux. . . .

He, however, would consecrate this marble to Fielding, and it should survive for ever 'pour l'honneur de mon nom et celui de la France'.

But it was not to survive in the English cemetery; it was turned down. Neither, for two or three years, did the English colony take the hint and do anything about a tombstone themselves; they were no great readers — philistines, Southey called them a few years later — though Fielding's novels were probably the kind they liked when they did read. But they presumably took the individualist view that if a man's family did not choose to commemorate his grave, it was no business of any one else's; they put up handsome marble tombstones, as the French consul tartly, and Richard Twiss sadly, observed, to their own families and friends, and let other people's remains alone.

Dom John of Braganza, the queen's uncle, and the founder of the new Lisbon Academy, was the next to plan a monument, for the honour of Portugal. But the Church did not smile on this plan; it had never cared for the English burying-ground, which had been wrested from the Portuguese government after many years of struggle, and did not wish the Duke of Braganza to honour a protestant heretic thus. The duke, a true man of letters and literary enthusiast, liked honouring protestant heretics when they were worthy; he had lately honoured William Julius Mickle by admitting him into his new Academy; but he had to defer to the clerical view.

A few years after the rejection of the French monument, the British did begin to bestir themselves in the matter, and Murphy, then in Lisbon, was asked to prepare a design. He did so; it was engraved, and published in the *European Magazine*, in the hopes of attracting support. But neither Fielding's family, friends, nor admirers came forward with funds, and the plan lapsed. For many years the grave remained unmarked and almost lost, which seems rather odd of the various successive chaplains, many of them intelligent men. One would think that Southey, an enthusiastic Fielding addict, might have induced his uncle Hill to see to it; and that the sophisticated English colony who gathered round Hookham Frere's Legation at the century's beginning might have suggested something; but they were perhaps too much occupied in social gaieties to worry about a dead author. Anyhow, nothing was done; the burying-ground passed through the stormy days of the French occupation and later the British under Beresford (when the Factory had their hands full rejecting the intrusion of the remains of brigadier-generals into their cemetery) and Fielding

> 'neath the green Estrella trees
> Sleeps with the alien Portuguese,

unmonumented and unmarked, until 1830, when a locum tenens chaplain collected money and had the present monument put up, with a long Latin inscription praising the illustrious deceased's virtues and genius and mildly regretting his follies. Ever since, it has been a shrine of pilgrimage to English tourists, kissed by Borrow, sought for in vain by Tennyson, sentimentalized over by by all.

Fielding, with his love of good company and his eighteenth-century taste for sentiment, would have been delighted to watch them all at it. Particularly he might have enjoyed the comment of Wordsworth's daughter, Mrs. Quillinan, who visited the cemetery in 1846 . . . 'the cypress fence within which lie the remains of Fielding and Doddridge (this life and the next), and some other names familiar to our ears. The exact spot where Fielding was buried in this inclosure is not known. His monument, a huge ungainly thing, is on a spot selected by *guess*. The bones it covers may possibly have belonged to an idiot'.

BIBLIOGRAPHY

The Journal of a Voyage to Lisbon, HENRY FIELDING (1755).
The History of Henry Fielding, WILBUR L. CROSS (1918).
A Fielding Find, AUSTIN DOBSON (1912).
Travels in Portugal in 1789 and 1790, JAMES MURPHY (1795).
Historical Memoirs, SIR NATHANIEL WILLIAM WRAXALL (1815).
Travels through Spain and Portugal in 1772 and 1773, RICHARD TWISS (1775).
Journal of a few Months' Residence in Portugal, DORA QUILLINAN (1847).
The Public Advertiser (October 16th, 1754).

4. TRANSLATOR OF CAMOENS

William Julius Mickle

[1778-1780]

THE most industrious way to ensure having a really good time in Portugal has always been to have a shot at translating some Portuguese literature, preferably Camoens, before your visit. This pleases the Portuguese, an amiable and generous people, irrespective of the merits of the translation, which are usually not remarkable. Had Southey been warned by his uncle before his first visit to Lisbon to acquire a little Portuguese and translate a little Camoens, he would have had a better time in the capital and more to say in praise of its natives. Had Byron done so, his head would have been completely turned by the crowns of laurel placed upon it, and several cantos of *Childe Harold* would have read very differently. Camoens certainly gave Sir Richard Fanshawe and Lord Strangford a standing with the Portuguese court and *literati* above that commonly enjoyed by diplomats. Mr. William Julius Mickle, on the strength of his *Lusiad*, was so fêted in Lisbon that he is possibly the only literary British visitor to Portugal who has had literally nothing but good to say of it. And he had, as a rule, a good deal to say of people that was not flattering, for he was a man of strong angers and disapprovals.

His father was a learned Scottish minister who came south, accepted an Anglican incumbency, and wrote many of the notes for Bayle's Dictionary. William, born in 1735, was a failure as an

95

Edinburgh brewer and as a man of affairs and went bankrupt. Coming to London in 1763, he got to know the literary world, and established a good reputation as a poet. He made it his business to cultivate useful connections, flattered Dr. Johnson and was rewarded with kind patronage, got Boswell to recommend him to Garrick, to whom he sent a play which Garrick mortally offended him by rejecting (he was with difficulty dissuaded by Boswell from writing a Dunciad about him), had sharp passages with other literary gentlemen who slighted him, and, in short, pursued the usual quarrelsome and toadying literary life of his period. A firmly orthodox Christian, he viewed deists and atheists with detestation, and could not, without passion, hear mentioned the names of Hume and Voltaire.

It was said by malicious critics that, since his friend Hoole had a good position in the East India Company, he coveted a similar one for himself, and for that reason conceived the notion of translating the *Lusiadas*, which dealt with the Portuguese discovery of India, and into which he could interpolate favourable remarks on the beauty of overseas commerce and on the modern superiority of British methods to Portuguese. Indeed, his plan of surrounding the poem itself with voluminous notes, introduction, dissertation and appendix promised ample opportunity of inserting anything he chose.

So he learned Portuguese (but not quite enough) and settled down in 1771, to the five years' task of translation and preparing the volume for the press: it appeared in 1776, curiously entitled 'The Lusiad', in the singular; Mickle showed no sign of knowing that Lusiadas meant sons of Lusus, or the Portuguese; he treats the word Lusiad as if it were Iliad, referring to the poem's different Books as 'the 8th Lusiad', etc. He thought it would help him if he dedicated it to a nobleman, and selected the Duke of Buccleuch, whom he addressed in the usual flattering terms. Unfortunately the Duke neglected to open his copy, and failed to do his duty as a patron; either he had been got at by Mickle's enemies (Mickle thought the deists), or he feared that the Lusiad might bore him; the poet, bitterly affronted by this negligence, nearly, but not quite, lost faith in the nobility.

The book was imposing: it had an immense introduction and dissertation, extensive notes, a history of the discovery of India, another of Portuguese Asia, a life of Camoens, a learned appendix, and finally the translated poem itself. The frontispiece shows Britannia seated at the temple of fame and receiving the Lusiad from a kneeling and laurel-crowned Mickle. On the title-page is the rather ominous motto from Horace, *Nec verbum verbo curabis reddere, fidus interpres*; and in one of his notes Mickle says that his ambition 'was not to gratify the Dull Few whose greatest pleasure in reading a translation is to see what the author exactly says; it was to give a poem that might live in the English language'. This remark would have come better from him had he not hauled Sir Richard Fanshawe over the coals for the liberties he had taken with his original. In fact, his only predecessor in the field had little mercy from him, in spite of 'the great respect due to the memory of a gentleman who, in the unpropitious age of a Cromwell, endeavoured to cultivate the English Muses'. Fanshawe was obscure, full of proverbs, 'could never have enough of conceits, low allusions, and expressions'; in fact, it was high time he was superseded. Certainly Mickle reads more smoothly; bland and moralizing eighteenth-century pompousness has taken the place of naif, colloquial seventeenth-century charm; and he is, on the whole, more correct, though the Dull Few discovered in Portugal (not in Britain, where reviewers, however dull, had entire confidence in their author's fidelity to the text they could not read) that he had strayed unscrupulously, even composing three hundred lines of his own and calmly writing them in at the end of the ninth book. No one in London knew or cared; Mr. Hoole, the elegant translator of Tasso, James Boswell, Esq., Dr. Johnson, Dr. Goldsmith, Dr. Crowe of Oxford, several gentlemen of the East India Company, several Portuguese gentlemen in London, were all thanked in the Dissertation for their patronage, approval, or help, and they and the general literary public agreed that here was the definitive English translation of the celebrated but unread Portuguese masterpiece.

The Portuguese thought so too. Mickle (or one of his Portuguese friends) sent a copy to Dom John of Braganza, Duke of Lafoens, the queen's uncle, oddly a man of letters in a family, a country and a time little addicted to such interests. Its fame spread; the Portuguese were delighted that a celebrated British poet (for celebrated they understood that he was) should have introduced, in such a magnificent and erudite dress, their epic to his countrymen. If the introduction contained some slightly discouraging comments on their national fall from greatness, it is improbable that many of them could read it; and, after all, Camoens himself had made similar comments.

'But where ignorance characterizes the body of the nobility, the most insipid dissipation, and the very idleness and effeminacy of luxury, are sure to follow ... Thus rose and thus fell the empire of Rome, and the much wider one of Portugal ... Every evil which they have suffered from their acquirements arose, as shall be hereafter demonstrated, from their general ignorance, an ignorance which rendered them unable to investigate or apprehend, even the first principles of civil and commercial philosophy. ... What but the fall of their state could be expected from barbarians like these!'

Possibly even the Duke of Lafoens did not read English very easily. In any case, he and the other barbarian nobility of Lisbon showed every mark of kindness and esteem to the translator when, in the autumn of 1779, he was taken to Lisbon as secretary to his friend Commodore Johnstone on the battleship *Romney*, which was sailing to Portugal with a squadron. Mickle had seen to it that his arrival was advertised, and when the *Romney* reached the Tagus, Dom John and a group of other admirers were waiting on the quay, all cordiality and politeness, in the most charming Portuguese manner. 'By this distinguished personage, he was introduced to the principal nobility, clergy, and *literati* of Portugal, who vied with each other in showing him every mark of respect and attention during a residence of more than six months.' It was very natural that he should take a different view of Portugal and the Portuguese from that expressed by most English visitors of his period. It was not, from a British standpoint, a propitious moment in the country's career; King Joseph was dead, the great Pombal fallen, Queen Maria I, given to devotion and bigotry, was suspending all the late minister's reconstruction plans and building only convents; the Inquisition was returning to power, Pombal's miserable prisoners, set free after many years, were stumbling emaciated from their gaols, another quite different set of prisoners were taking their places, the reign of the Church, which always so shocked Englishmen, had returned. Everything was occurring (as indeed it usually did in Portugal) which to a North Briton of constitutional views and protestant convictions would have seemed obnoxious in ordinary circumstances. It was in this same year and through the year before that the indignant and disapproving officer, Captain Arthur Costigan, wrote his *Sketches of Society and Manners in Portugal*, inveighing against it as a wretched and servile state, sunk in ignorance and barbarism and tyrannized over by indolent and insolent clergy and by imbecile statesmen. The only people whose society Costigan enjoyed in Portugal were his countrymen. Did he meet Mr. Mickle being introduced to the sights of Lisbon by admiring Portuguese? Mickle has not left a full account of his visit; presumably he moved in the social life of the Lisbon English, frequented the gatherings at the houses of the envoy, the consul, and the other hosts of whom Costigan writes, and whose hospitality Hickey too enjoyed two years later; but his brief account refers only to his Portuguese acquaintances. He does not even say where he stayed.

'I have made the best use of my time, in seeing everything in my power, and I have had every assistance from the Portuguese noblesse and *literati*, many of whom understand English and are well acquainted with our literature' (this would have surprised Captain Costigan) 'and who seem well pleased that a translation of their favourite poem has been well received in England.'

More unusual still, we are told that 'of the clergy, though by no means prejudiced in favour of the Romish Church, he always spoke with great respect, and of the courteous and hospitable reception which he experienced at the monasteries, particularly at the royal and noble foundations of Alcobaça and Batalha, he likewise made mention in terms of the warmest approbation'.

Few British visitors have taken about the Portuguese clergy just this tone, which lacks both the shocked contempt of the protestant and the rationalist, and the flippant, friendly cynicism of the amused Beckford. Mickle was ready to be pleased with everything and everyone in Portugal. Many years later he described in a letter to *Literary Panorama* (1809) a 'sacred drama' he had seen at Christmas time in Lisbon; it had obviously delighted him.

'When the curtain drew up, the first scene presented a view of the clouds, where a figure like a Chinese Mandarin sat between St. Michael and Satan. Satan accuses Michael, and Michael scolds like an oyster-woman, and at last kicks Satan on the head and tumbles him down out of sight, telling him to go to hell for his impudence. The Chinese-like figure then walks about the stage, and repeating the words of the Latin Bible, creates the world.' The drama ran through the Old Testament, enlivened with comic scenes in Lisbon, where Noah's carpenter (the King of Portugal's ship-carpenter) lived; and ended with the birth of Christ. An admirable piece, Mickle called it.

More admirable still he found the Royal Academy of Lisbon, which was founded in May, 1780, and of which he had the honour to be admitted a member, under the presidency of his Grace the Duke of Lafoens, that noble patron of letters, who presented to the distinguished Scottish Lusophile his own portrait as a token of his particular regard. No wonder that Mickle went about in a state of pleased vanity and enthusiasm, and decided that a great renaissance had arrived in Portugal, after its long decadence when 'literature was totally neglected and all was luxury and imbecility at home'.

He employed some of his time in writing a poem which he called *Almada Hill, An Epistle from Lisbon*, which describes the city and its environs in glowing terms, contrasting its climate favourably with that of Great Britain, and particularly of Oxford, where he had been working at the Clarendon Press and suffered from fog. No nonsense about Oh, to be in England now that April's there. He detested those

> Lowering wintery plains
> Now pale with snow, now bleak with drizzling rains,
> From leafless woodlands and dishonoured bowers,
> Mantled by gloomy mists, or lash'd by showers
> Of hollow moan, while not a struggling beam
> Steals from the Sun to play on Isis' stream . . .
> In other clime through sun-bask'd scenes I stray. . . .

To Mr. Mickle thus straying, eating oranges as he strayed, stopping every now and then to regard some magnificent marine or mountain view, flattered by the remarkable attentions he daily received from these amiable people, it seemed that

> A dawn of brightest ray
> Has boldly promised the returning day
> Of Lisbon's honours, fairer than her prime . . .
> Now Heaven-taught Science and her liberal band
> Of Arts, and dictates by experience plann'd,
> Beneath the smiles of a benignant Queen
> Boast the fair opening of a reign serene

Of omen high, And Camoens' ghost no more
Wails the neglected Muse on Tago's shore;
No more his tears the barbarous Age upbraid;
His griefs and wrongs all sooth'd, his happy Shade
Beheld th' Ulysses of his age return
To Tago's banks; and earnest to adorn
The Hero's brows, he weaves the Elysian crown.

Ulysses was, of course, the Duke of Lafoens, who had qualified for the Homeric name by travelling about for twenty-two years, visiting courts in Europe, Turkey, Egypt, and even Lapland, and now, less aptly, by founding the Royal Academy of Lisbon and admitting Mickle to honoured membership. 'This,' said Beckford, who encountered him at Cintra seven years later, 'is the identical person well known in every part of Europe by the appellation of Duke of Braganza . . . Were he called Duchess Dowager of anything you please, I think nobody would dispute the propriety of his style, he being so like an old lady of the bed-chamber, so fiddle-faddle and so coquettish. He had put on rouge and patches, and though he has seen seventy winters, contrived to turn on his heel and glide about with juvenile agility. I was much surprised at the ease of his motions, having been told that he was a martyr to the gout. After lisping French with a most refined accent, complaining of the sun, and the roads, and the state of architecture, he departed (thank heaven!) to mark out a spot for the encampment of the cavalry, which are to guard the queen's sacred person during her residence in these mountains.'

So much for Ulysses, seen in the different lights thrown on his person by the flattered and the acid observer. As to the benignant queen whose smiles blessed this new literary and liberal epoch, she was by the British envoy of the time thus described, together with Dom Pedro, that one among her uncles whom, Bragança-fashion, she had married: 'The Queen and the King are very devout. They are of unlimited obedience to the See of Rome and the jurisdiction of the clergy in its most extensive pretensions. The Queen is timid, and consequently easily influenced by the clergy, with whom she has very much conversed . . . She has a great deference for her husband, and the King has a great veneration for her, and speaks of her as a saint. The King is of a very confined understanding, hears three or four masses in the morning in the utmost ecstasy, and attends evening prayers as devoutly.'

The queen, her whole mind (such as it was) set on the exaltation of the Church, suspended all other business in order to build in Estrella the huge baroque church of the Heart of Jesus; she re-established the Nuncio's court, restored convents, pensioned the released Jesuit prisoners of Pombal, and any converts to the faith who offered themselves for baptism in the royal chapel. Her benignant smiles were already the smiles of semi-imbecility, in a few years to change to the shrieks of the insane.

Like other British tourists in Portugal, Mickle aspired to write a history of its ancient and present state, and spent some of his time there collecting materials for this work. But it seems a work seldom destined to be completed by British tourists; they return home laden with material and enthusiasm, but little comes of it, and they expire before its achievement.

Mickle sailed home in the autumn of 1780, as purser in the ship *Brilliant*; on his return he was enriched by a share of the prize money won by his squadron, which relieved him of financial anxiety for life. He settled in Oxfordshire, married, continued to write mediocre but esteemed poetry, and died in 1788, in time to escape the pain of being eclipsed by the new Romantic Poets. Whether or not, like Southey, he lived the rest of his life pining for Portugal, he has not left on record. A consumptive clergyman who met him in Oxford in 1783 wrote, 'Mr. Mickle tells me I cannot do better than winter in Portugal, which he believes would quite restore me.' Whether the clergyman did so, and with what results, we do not know. Mr. Mickle, thus wistfully recommending his dear Lusitania, had perhaps forgotten not only Sir Thomas Browne's counsel to the tabidly inclined, but the number of tabid British, both clerical and lay, who had not been restored, but who had laid their bones beneath the Estrella trees; or perhaps he thought, better lay them there in Lisbon sunshine than in some damp and chill British churchyard mantled by gloomy mists and lashed by showers. Looking back on his own happy sojourn, he may well have felt such a resting-place a desirable end.

As to his Lusiad, it ran through edition after edition; every one read and admired it, it was favourably compared with Pope's Iliad and Camoens' name, as well as Mickle's, was made in Britain. Mickle had the great advantage that few English readers could compare his translation, favourably or otherwise, with the original; those who admired Camoens meant that they admired Mickle. Horace Walpole, whom epic bored, decided that he preferred Camoens to Virgil, Lucan and Dante (Dante he found like a Methodist parson in Bedlam).

It is possible that no British poet has descended so many rungs of the ladder of reputation in the course of a century as did William Mickle between his death and its first centenary. No one could call him a bad poet: but it became increasingly difficult, as the nineteenth century went on, to call him a good one. He had his day, and passed satisfied into the shades to talk it over with Camoens.

BIBLIOGRAPHY

The Lusiad. Translated from Luis de Camoens, W. J. MICKLE (1776).
Poems and Tragedy, with Anecdotes of Mr. Mickle, JOHN IRELAND (1794).
Poetical Works of W. J. Mickle, with Life, J. SIM (1806).
British Poets, vol. 66. *Life of W. J. Mickle* (1822).
European Magazine, ISAAC REED (1789).
Lives of Eminent Scotsmen, CHAMBERS.
Biographical Dictionary, ALEXANDER CHALMERS.
Dictionary of National Biography.
Life of Johnson, JAMES BOSWELL (1781).
Almada Hill. An Epistle from Lisbon, W. J. MICKLE (1781).
La Littérature Portugaise en Angleterre, FÉLIX WALTER (1927).
Sketches of Society and Manners in Portugal, ARTHUR COSTIGAN (1787).
Literary Panorama (1809).
Dictator of Portugal, MARCUS CHEKE (1938).
State Papers Portugal 89/85 (Record Office).
Italy; with Sketches of Spain and Portugal, WILLIAM BECKFORD (1834).

5. SIR FRETFUL PLAGIARY

Richard Cumberland

[1780]

IT was the year after the performance of *The Critic*, which had so delighted Richard Cumberland's enemies, acquaintances and friends (the three categories were almost synonymous) with the antics of Sir Fretful Plagiary. It was generally known that the slightest criticism enraged the poor dramatist; 'he's the sorest man alive', as Sneer remarked of Sir Fretful, 'and shrinks like scorched parchment from the fiery ordeal of true criticism. Yet he is so covetous of popularity that he would rather be abused than not mentioned at all'. Poor Cumberland felt flayed, humiliated, furious. He had somehow to get even with life, to establish himself as a figure more important than any of his tormentors and rivals. 'He is as envious as an old maid verging on the desperation of six and thirty'; and, like her, felt impelled to make some reckless bid for fortune. It would be good to get out of squabbling, mocking, backbiting literary London, to make his mark in some wider sphere, to take a hand in large world affairs, that would bring him reputation as a diplomatist and lead to some preferment above the secretaryship of the Board of Trade, some honourable achievement that would confound his enemies and frustrate the knavish tricks of his fellow dramatists. It must have been in some such mood that he, at the age of nearly fifty, suddenly saw himself as an envoy of his country abroad, entrusted with delicate and important international negotiations. So William Beckford, also a sore and disgruntled man, saw himself nearly twenty years later. But Beckford could get no one else to see him thus; he was snubbed in his project from the outset; whereas Cumberland, oddly, managed to persuade the Foreign Office, and (odder still) the Treasury, that he was fit to be financed and entrusted with a mission abroad.

Looking at the two Romney portraits of the elegant, harassed, fretful-faced dramatist, it is easy to discern the unsatisfied hankerings in those near-set, worried eyes that gaze into some imagined future in which he will play a star part that shall put his rivals in the shade. He might almost be listening to Mrs. Thrale's starling, which was, she had said, to be trained to tease the envious man by crying 'Burney! Burney!' in his ears night and day.

But he would get out of hearing, and forget his mortifications in diplomacy. The idea came to him when he believed himself to have learnt through French and Spanish secret agents some facts which might make practicable the putting out of peace feelers to Spain. 'Of these communications,' he wrote in his memoirs, 'I made that use which my duty dictated and to my judgment seemed admirable.' The exact details of his dealings with his government are obscure; but he contrived to get himself employed on a secret mission to the Spanish minister Florida Blanca, and to get out of the Treasury a thousand pounds on account. He put it to them, it seems, that he had better go abroad with his wife and two daughters, on pretence of travelling through Spain to Italy. They were to go to Lisbon, and with them the Abbé Hussey, chaplain to his Most Catholic Majesty of Spain; Hussey was to travel thence to Spain to sound the government on the usefulness of Cumberland's proceeding further, and report to him at Lisbon; if the report was favourable he was to go, still attended by his family, to Spain, if not, he was to take the next packet for home. It all seems an odd affair, and it is difficult to be certain how much of the plan was authorized, how much was Cumberland's dramatic imagination at work on yet another melodrama, yet another flop.

However this might be, Cumberland, Mrs. Cumberland, Elizabeth and Sophia (who used to attend the opera in such high head-dresses that those sitting behind them hissed), together with Mr. Hussey, sailed for Lisbon at the beginning of May, 1780, and, after the usual storms and actions with the enemy (they captured a French frigate on the way), anchored in the Tagus on May 17th. Cumberland bought a quantity of oranges and established his family at Mrs. Duer's hotel in Buenos Ayres, while the Abbé saw the Spanish ambassador about his passport and prepared for his journey. Cumberland, during his time in Lisbon, may have wished that he had, before starting, thought to translate Camoens, for here was Mr. William Mickle in Lisbon, courted and fêted by royalty and nobility, admitted to membership of the new Academy, and having the time of his life — a painful spectacle for an envious literary man; one can imagine that he said to Mrs. Cumberland, in Sir Fretful's words, 'Now, another person would be vexed at this'. It is not surprising that he says nothing about Mickle. However, he was by no means neglected; he was waited on at Mrs. Duer's by Mr. Walpole, the British ambassador, Sir John Hort, the Consul, Commodore Johnstone (Mickle's friend, who had brought him to Lisbon, which makes it pretty certain that the two authors also met), and several gentlemen of the English Factory, including, no doubt, the Reverend William Allen, the chaplain, with whom he must have been at Trinity in the '40s. The Cumberlands admired the Corpus Christi procession from a friend's house on May 25th; the young ladies, 'as they presented themselves at the open window in their English dresses (and, I may add without vanity, in all their native charms), most evidently arrested the attention' of the processing religious 'in a manner that by no means harmonized with the solemnity of their office'. A son of the Marquis of Pombal annoyed Cumberland by coming into the room and, with a supercilious air, motioning with his hand towards a chair, telling him that he might sit down. Possibly the family head-dresses were again too high; anyhow, Cumberland, as so often, took umbrage. 'There was an insolence in the manner of it irresistibly provoking, and I am not ashamed to say my answer was at least as contemptuous as his address was insolent.'

After nearly three weeks, during which the Cumberlands saw the sights, visited Cintra and Queluz, and all that, came the expected dispatch from the Abbé Hussey at Aranjuez, where he had been sounding the Spanish ministers about Cumberland's mission. Hussey's letter worried him by its lack of precision. His instructions had been to go and see Florida Blanca only if the cession of Gibraltar were by agreement excluded as a topic of discussion; on Gibraltar there could be no negotiation. This was what Hussey had been commissioned to discover. But Hussey did not mention Gibraltar; he only said that the minister was 'very desirous of a happy conclusion', and advised Cumberland to come. Cumberland was puzzled; he was extremely anxious to proceed with his mission, and not to return to England as a failure; on the other hand, would his government back him in it? He consulted Walpole, who cautiously advised against it. But ambition and desire prevailed. He wrote to Lord Hillsborough to say he was going to Spain, and went, three days after he had received the letter, taking with him Mrs. Cumberland and the girls. The ladies disliked the dirt of the inns where they baited. 'At the wretched posada in this place Aldea Gallega we had our first sample of that dirt and loathsomeness which admit of no description, and which every baiting-place throughout Portugal and Spain with little variation presented to us. Men may endure such scenes; to women of delicacy they are, and must be, nauseous in the extreme.' Provisions had to be bought *en route*; their kid dangled from the carriage in the sun and dust; at the inn they had to roast it themselves. Fortunately they also had with them a cold turkey.

The mission to Spain is not here our concern. It was unsuccessful. He spent many months and many thousands of pounds over it, following the court and ministry about from place to place. Florida Blanca and the court were polite and friendly; still, 'they wanted only to talk about Gibraltar, and I was not permitted to hear it named'. A hopeless basis for negotiations. To make things worse, the Gordon No Popery riots broke out in England while the Cumberlands were in Spain, and exacerbated the atmosphere intolerably.

The mission was no use. No doubt realizing this early, the Treasury would pay no money into his London bank; according to Cumberland they had agreed to finance him. His bankers nobly shouldered the burden and advanced him enough to go on with. Life was extremely expensive, what with keeping up a fitting establishment (which included five servants), entertaining and being entertained, which meant clothes for the ladies and himself, and all the travelling about, and no doubt tips and bribes all the time. By March, 1781, when the party at last left Spain for France, time had added to it another Miss Cumberland, 'at the breast of a Spanish nurse, a wild but affectionate creature'. So home they all came, arriving ruined and unsuccessful in the cold and derisive London which Cumberland had hoped to convert to admiring envy and applause. There was no applause and no reward, and no reply to his claims for the refunding of the £4,500 he had spent out of his own purse on the tour. Both the Treasury and Lord North maintained a chilly silence; it seems doubtful whether Cumberland even got slips from clerks saying that they were directed to tell him that his letters were receiving attention. Anyhow, they never received any. The only attention he received was the mockery of derisive literary men like Horace Walpole on his 'successful negotiations in Spain'. 'I hope,' said Horace, 'he will write an ode himself on the treaty he did not make.'

Cumberland did not do this. He merely continued his career as a hugely prolific dramatist and author, rather more embittered than before against his fellow authors. When he wrote his Memoirs, he included 'a long and languishing account' of his mission to Spain.

BIBLIOGRAPHY

Memoirs, RICHARD CUMBERLAND (1806).
Richard Cumberland, STANLEY T. WILLIAMS (1917).
Diaries, MADAME D'ARBLAY (1842-6).
The Critic, RICHARD BRINSLEY SHERIDAN (1779).

WRITERS

6. AESTHETE

William Beckford

[March-December 1787. November 1793-October 1795.
December 1795-March 1796. December 1798-July 1799]

TO read Beckford on Portugal, after a prolonged course of
his fellow tourists, is to lose oneself in an extraordinary,
many-coloured, fantastic drama (or opera) of fun, beauty, gaudy
decor, pomp, luxury, absurdity, vanity, cynicism and wit,
described in supple and easy prose, after making guide-book tours
or disgruntled surveys hand in hand with Mr. Thomas Cook or
with some bitter, underpaid British officer in the Portuguese army,
or some anti-clerical liberal democrat whom the despotism,
superstition, and backward education so often to be met with
abroad caused to see red, or even with some cheerful and sociable
soul who had a jolly time with the British colony in Lisbon or
Oporto. Whether these travellers express enthusiasm, rhapso-
dizing over Cintra's glorious Eden and the parties given by the
British embassy and Factory, or disapproval of Church, State and
natives, or merely set down dry chunks of information as to
population, architecture, produce, commerce and history, the
result, though it may amuse and inform, is seldom literature.
Those in greater sympathy with the religion and constitution of
Portugal did not necessarily write better; they were apt on the
whole to be a little simple. In any case, to write like Beckford is
a rare gift.

He had indeed most of the gifts; not least that sensuous sensitive-
ness to all aspects of beauty often found in those subject, as he was,
to emotional amorous affairs with both sexes at once, and that
delicately articulated expression of it of those whose most constant, cherished, and assiduously cultivated amorous affair is with
themselves. His imaginative receptivity was refined to exquisite-
ness, his gifts trained not to the austere proficiency of the professional, but to the facile dilettantism of the leisured amateur.
Music plunged him into swooning dreams of pleasure or regret;
beauty, whether of art or nature, transported him into ecstasy.
Like his Vathek, he built palaces of pleasure for the gratification
of each sense — the Eternal Banquet, the Temple of Melody, the
Delight of the Eyes, the Palace of Perfumes, the Retreat of Mirth

— and strolled about each in turn. A poet, he fortunately wrote little verse; what he did write was bad. English poets have, before and after Beckford, visited and written of Portugal; when they have celebrated it in verse, it has not been very good verse, not even Byron's; one would give all his abusive cantos about Lusitanians, the lowest of the low, Cintra's glorious Eden, and Vathek, England's wealthiest son, for a few more easy, slangy letters about swimming the Tagus and eating oranges. Beckford was not a poet in verse at all; his poetry lit his imagination and soaked his prose. He wrote of Portugal and life among the Portuguese elegantly, wittily, ironically, beautifully. The fact that when he himself came into the picture he was faking, falsifying, mystifying, concealing and showing off much of the time sometimes confuses and baffles us, but does not cramp his style or our pleasure. It is, from the biographer's angle, of course a pity that his published travels in Portugal were romanced, distorted and fudged up from the facts as set down at the time in his private diary; and one would like to know whether certain odd incidents, such as his interview with the Prince of Brazil in the forest, and his meeting with the poet Bocage at a date when this writer was apparently in exile at Goa, actually occurred, or were, as Beckford's latest and most thorough biographer is convinced, invented; but it does not much matter. And his careful smoothing away of his boycotting by the Lisbon British and their ambassador that so enraged and mortified him only matters in that it shows again his versatile and careful ingenuity as a self-exhibitor.

An unamiable character, said his contemporaries; jealous, *malin*, an actor but no gentleman; 'you see the character is irregular by looking in his countenance; there is a twist in his look'. All that, and more; he was ruthless, unscrupulous, malevolent, vain, a liar, a corrupter of youth; he spent his enormous income almost entirely on himself; he wrote with genius; he must have had immense charm; he was brilliant, fascinating, cultivated, mood-ridden, witty, perverse; he evoked love, wearied of it, slipped from its fetters and began again elsewhere; he did not like the human race, yet had to secure its appreciation; when that failed, life was ashes to him, he was angry, bitter, contemptuous, yet for ever bent on twisting through any side-door into favour. Throughout his writings, said Joseph Farrington, who did not like him, there was a spirit like champagne prevailing, sparkling everywhere; the man had never been to a public school . . . 'the wild youthful William', Louisa, who loved him, called him, 'animated by the fire of Genius and the love of pleasure . . .' he was not quite the thing.

With his oriental sultan complex, his admiration for caliphian luxury, pomp and power, his enjoyment of religious pageantry and music, the Portugal of Queen Maria I in 1787 seemed his spiritual destiny. He had intended Jamaica: the troubles of getting there appeared too great. He had to go somewhere, since his own country hissed and tittered with scandal about him, and his enemies would not let it die. He decided on Madeira and 'the delights of mass' at Funchal — unless, worn out with a fortnight of sailing, he should 'take refuge in some Portuguese convent and give myself up to eating oranges and worshipping my beloved St. Anthony'. The fortnight's sailing proved more than enough; he landed in Lisbon, with Dr. Verdeil, his Swiss doctor, and a retinue of servants, and settled in Belem. Not for him one of the hotels on the slopes of Buenos Ayres among the English merchants; his friend Horne got him a house, the Quinta dos Bichos, from the queen, and into it he presently settled, with his piano, his furniture, and his great train of servants at hand; from twenty to thirty of these, for 'less would not have comported with the figure he desired to make abroad', and he did not see why he should not have a biscuit, properly made, with his glass of sherry, nor couriers to arrange his goings out and comings in, nor valets to see to his clothes, nor lackeys to run his errands, nor a few grooms to mind his horses and chaise, nor a footman to run behind them; in fact, all the attendants, including doctor, tailor, hatter, barber, musicians and chef, of whom a travelling gentleman might find himself in need. It is not known where they were all put up; the Quinta dos Bichos has perished, and its accommodation capacity is unknown.

Anyhow, there he settled, after a few weeks in Lisbon, in the hot end of May, and prepared for the conquest of Lisbon society. Lesser visitors than he, visitors who were not millionaires and had no suites of attendants, had been very civilly waited on at their lodgings by His Excellency Mr. Walpole, Sir John Hort the consul, and other prominent members of the British colony; they had been invited about and hospitably entertained, at dinners, suppers, cards, balls. Beckford waited on the ambassador in correct style; he was not received; and there was no return visit. None of the English called: the word had gone round — the scandalous millionaire in the Quinta dos Bichos was to be boycotted. It must have been disappointing for enterprising Lisbon hostesses not to have the chance of entertaining this fabulous bird of paradise at their parties; women were nearly always taken by him, even when their husbands sneered and looked coldly on the exotic young man with his high, sweet eunuch's voice and dazzling gifts of mimicry, comedy and music. Perhaps even the ambassador's young wife looked after him as he drove by in his chaise with Portuguese or Dutch friends, and sighed for embassy propriety that barred such exciting, shocking attractions from her table. But there it was: the English boycott was inflexible; it was said to be dictated from the English court. If any Lisbon British were sorry to be so inhospitable — and they were a kindly, jovial set, who had not, in a general way, particularly rigid standards — they dared not fly in the face of the social diktat of His Majesty's representative. So, in his richly-furnished quinta by the Necessidades palace, the millionaire, companioned by his physician, taken about by his friend Mr. Horne, and increasingly receiving civilities from the Portuguese nobility, who were attracted by his exuberant pieties and his more than exuberant expenditure, waited in vain for the expected attentions from his countrymen; it did not take long to dawn on him that he was being cut.

Resentment seethed in him; with every weapon he could muster, he opened battle. It is characteristic of him that no hint of the battle or of his defeat appears in his published travel journal, the *Sketches of Spain and Portugal*; so far as this goes, it merely endorses Cyrus Redding's account — 'delivering his credentials, he was soon received into the higher society of the earthquake-shaken capital of Portugal'. As indeed, if higher society means the Portuguese nobility, exclusive of the court, he was. For introduction at court, he angled in vain. It became an obsession with him: he could not be happy without this panache, this triumphant vindication to throw in the faces of his countrymen who had hounded him from England, and in the choleric, malevolent face of His Majesty's envoy in Lisbon. His relations in England, appealed to for credentials, would not help him by a word. He waited in vain for the arrival of the packets with assurances of the intervention which should get him what he wanted; till at last, 'One would think Lady Effingham [his aunt] and my relations were leagued together to make me appear what Walpole has represented me. All I have written cannot bring them to speak one word in my favour — so I must shift entirely by myself in this kingdom'.

Shifting entirely by himself meant enlisting to his aid everyone he met, and in chief his influential and devoted friend, the Marquis of Marialva, who rallied nobly, with unstinting and generous efforts, to the cause of this fascinating, wealthy and injured visitor to his land. The close friendship between Beckford and the Marialvas began soon after Beckford's arrival; the first entries in his journal speak of stopping at the Marialva palace while driving out, and greeting Dom Pedro, the fifteen-year-old, rather dismal son of the Marquis, who had conceived a passion (only tepidly and fitfully returned) for Beckford: 'he coloured to his eyes — I know not why — nor he neither, perhaps'. Among the letters Beckford kept was one written in May and docketed, with another, 'The two first letters written to me by the Marquis of Marialva (D. Diogo)'. Beginning 'Mon très cher ami', it went on in a tone of the most sympathetic flattery, and in French often imperfect, 'Il faut absolument, mon cher, que tout honnête homme et que tous eux qu'ont l'ame bien faite s'interessent dans votre cause ... et je me flatte de voir bientôt se dissiper cette ridicule impression . . .' which, far from injuring you, can only serve to discredit all those who attack you, and expose them to general scorn, 'tandis que votre mérite, ainsi que vos nobles qualités, se répandent généralement'. Beckford was begged to regard with indifference all that a crowd of slanderers had invented to his discredit, 'car tout le monde connait a fond votre irreprochable conduite, et vos talents aussi que votre naissance vous rendent supérieur à tout cela ... et moi je serai le premier a le prôner par tout'.

The marquis was as good as his word; he did preach his friend's virtues everywhere; he induced all his acquaintances to call, and Beckford was free of the circles of the best Portuguese society, as well as of the hospitalities and gaieties of the Marialva palace, where the great family took him to its heart. It was an entertaining society. The Marialvas lived in feudal state, under the patriarchal wing of the old marquis (the father of Beckford's friend), who supported a court of about three hundred retainers;

well on in his seventies, he was still active enough to dance a galliard, to go on excursions attended by his troupes of followers, and to gourmandize on a startling scale, dining, in the Roman manner, between two tubs, and devouring thirty-five courses besides dessert; 'this prince of gluttons', Beckford calls him. In the palace with him lived his descendants and relations; his natural brother the Grand Prior of Aviz; his sons, including the younger marquis, the queen's Master of the Horse, who was so eager to introduce his maligned English friend at court; the latter's children, legitimate and illegitimate; for the lovely bastard Henriqueta, a match with the English millionaire was contemplated; from the fifteen-year-old Pedro Beckford received tongue-tied adoration, which a little bored him, for the boy was melancholy and unattractive; though before he left Portugal he was to write excited entries in his diary — 'he loves me — I have tasted the sweetness of his lips — his dear eyes have confessed the secret of his bosom'. It shows his versatility and sex fairness that he wrote of Henriqueta, soon after their first meeting, 'they think me rather inclined to fall in love — so I am'. Emotion thus catered for, entertainment was offered by the 'swarm of musicians, poets, bull-fighters, grooms, monks, dwarfs, and children of both sexes' who formed the old marquis's heterogeneous menagerie. At dinner there would be at least fifty servants in waiting, and wax torches and over a hundred tapers — style and pomp after Beckford's heart. He greatly admired this beneficent and magnificent patriarchy. The Marialvas were, except for the Duke of Lafoens, the most powerful nobility in Portugal; the late King Joseph had been used to say to the formidable Pombal, 'Do as you like to the rest of the nobility, but beware how you interfere with the Marquis of Marialva'. The Marialva palace had become under Pombal an asylum for the persecuted; the old marquis now led the 'ultra' party of anti-Pombalien reactionary fidalgos and clerics, whose powers had been grudged and clipped by the great Carvalho, and who had since his fall schemed to recover them with interest.

Into this entertaining milieu Beckford entered, and was welcomed *con amore*. There he would be shown round the marquis's apartments full of clocks, watches, antiquated rarities stinking of camphor, by the Grand Prior of Avis; there he met the Viceroy of Algarve, grimacing hospitably in pea-green, pink and silver, extolling in all languages in turn the glories and pieties of the late

John V, deploring the extinction of the Jesuits, and exulting in that of the execrated Pombal. In an adjoining apartment Policarpio, one of the first tenors in the queen's chapel, sang to the harpsichord, while Donna Henriqueta, 'a most interesting girl with eyes full of bewitching languor', examined the strange visitors from a distance. Night approached; lights glimmered from every part of 'the strange huddle of buildings of which this morisco-looking palace is composed; half the family were engaged in reciting the litanies of saints, the other in freaks and frolics, perhaps of no very edifying nature', and all to the monotonous staccato of the guitar and the soothing murmur of modinhas. Then came a glare of flambeaux and a splashing and dashing of water, and back from across the Tagus arrived the old marquis and his son in a scalera, with 'a procession scarcely equalled since the days of Noah'; they had been on a pilgrimage 'to some saint's nest or other on the opposite shore'. Beckford watched the landing entranced; the procession was led by a hump-backed dwarf blowing a trumpet; there followed some shady military officers, a savage-looking monk and two friars, an apothecary in sables, a half-crazed improvisatore spouting verse, and a confused rabble of watermen and servants with bird-cages, lanterns, baskets of fruit, and a bevy of lovely children with wings on their shoulders, for with these little innocents, thus got up as angels, the old marquis loved to surround himself. It was a typical Marialva outing and assembly.

Such was the society into which Beckford was thrown. He ensured his acceptance by the devout Portuguese nobility by orgies of church-going; he achieved a reputation as a *devoto*. 'I hear there is no conversation in Lisbon but of my piety', he wrote; 'really this joke begins to have its inconveniences.' For a joke it was and remained to him. He dedicated himself to the worship of St. Anthony, and attended mass with the most pious devotion and zest, observed by his interested and critical fellow-countrymen, whom one of his purposes it was to annoy. 'Really', he wrote soon, 'these church parties begin to lose in my eyes great part of the charm which novelty gave them. I have had pretty nearly my fill of motets and Kyrie eleisons and incense and sweetmeats and sermons. The heretic Verdeil, who would almost as soon be in hell at once as in such a cloying heaven, would not let me rest till I went with him to the theatre . . . in order to dissipate by a little profane air the fumes of so much holiness.'

Yet all this religious zeal was not entirely malice or policy; the music and operatic magnificence of the Lisbon ceremonial masses played on his senses, reducing him at times to pale and swooning pleasure. A believer he was not; he had the '*scepticisme enjoué*' of the cultured dilettante; a Protestant he had never been, a Catholic he never became; materialism his lively, haunted mystical sense forbade, yet all his foreboding dreams of the supernatural were salted by cynical disbelief. 'Gracious goodness! the Roman Catholic religion is filled with fine stage effects.' He amused himself among prelates and priors, finding some of them excellent company; the simpler monkish clerics he listened to and drew out, occasionally with a revolt of weary disgust at the monotony of their miracles and marvels and the pious simplicities of their minds. As to having changed his religion, of which he was later accused, 'I am just what I have always been in that respect', he wrote to Thomas Wildman, 'an Amateur, a Dilettante, a Connoisseur perhaps, but no Professor . . . Beyond a few genuflexions or expressions in time with the rest of the audience, I defy Mr. W. and all his Set to prove anything. The gravity with which you write of my having changed my Religion from Protestant to Roman Catholic takes away all gravity from me . . . I change indeed! Pray when did you know me adhere to the Sect I am supposed to have relinquished?'

His throwing in his lot with the Portuguese fidalgos, his turning away from the Lisbon British (or rather, theirs from him) has deprived us of what might have been a brilliantly acid account of the English colony. It is not to be supposed that he would have liked most of them: if to Southey they seemed philistines, how much more to Beckford, to whom Southey would himself have seemed so, still more Southey's uncle Hill, the card-playing merchants and their wives, the soulless embassy staff. He might have written, as he had written from Switzerland ten years before, 'Alas, fat Bulls of Basan encompass me around. Tubs upon two legs, crammed with stupidity, amble about me'. And, with feeling, 'Such an animal I am determined not to be'. In 1781 he had poured out to Lady Hamilton his hatred of his countrymen — 'English phlegm and frostiness nips my slight texture to death. I cannot endure the composed indifference of my Countrymen. What possessed me to return among them? The Island is lovely without doubt . . . But such inhabitants! Ye Gods! why cannot I drive them all headlong into the sea . . .' This was at a time when he was fantastically popular, and the only persecutions he suffered were cards of invitation lying at his door 'as deep as snow'. Later, he became more misanthropic. 'If I am shy or savage', he wrote to Lady Craven after his second visit to Portugal, 'you must consider the baitings and worryings to which I allude — how I was treated in Portugal, in Spain, in France, in Switzerland, at home, abroad, in every region . . . I sigh for the pestilential breath of an African serpent to destroy every Englishman who comes in my way.'

Had he been given the chance, he would doubtless have destroyed with breath and pen every Englishman in Lisbon and Cintra, and we should have been the gainers by the artistry of the massacre. But this was not the way he felt about his countrymen's society during the first few days in Lisbon. He would have liked to dine with the British ambassador, not only with the Dutch consul, if only to confound his enemies in England. He was not allowed to do so; instead he went native, and the results of his immersion in that exotic, lavishly un-British world remain, exquisite and rare loot from a fantastic day-dream. There is something piquant in the spectacle of the languid and resentful millionaire arriving in Portugal with Major Dalrymple's *Travels through Spain and Portugal* in his valise (as well he might, he found this work 'dry, tiresome and splenetic'), turning in mortified vanity from his countrymen whom he despised but would fain have impressed, and diving into an orgy of church-going to impress instead the Portuguese court and nobility, not without malicious sideways glances, as he crossed himself and beat his breast, at the 'broad English faces' staring at his antics from the back of the church. His piety 'caught the eyes of the high priest, a good old man, but a determined Bigot', but failed to get him to court.

Marialva and Mr. Horne worked hard for him. The court was at Caldas, taking the baths. Horne stayed there; he wrote to Beckford that the whole court was unanimous in sounding his praises and (with Portuguese politeness and sympathy) cursing Walpole and his colleagues. 'He thinks', Beckford hopefully wrote, 'we shall carry everything before us with a high hand . . . I long to know when and in what manner Her Majesty is to give my audience. Miss Sill and I had a long conversation — she thinks the Factory in great alarm, and the Portuguese open-mouthed with surprise and expectation.' Miss Sill, tactful woman, knew Beckford's taste for an enthralled gallery of spectators; though he wrote, 'I am sick of forming the chief subject of conversation at all the card parties, office boards and counting-houses in Lisbon', he would have been sicker of not forming a subject of conversation at all.

There was another and less satisfactory letter from Horne in a few days. The queen still seemed undecided about the audience; the neglect of Beckford by his English relations caused speculation. 'Mello and the other ministers know not what to make of my being so totally abandoned.' The Prince of Brazil was impatient to see the notorious foreigner. Horne sounded his praises continually, blowing curiosity to a blaze; 'my name is never mentioned without a string of complimentary epithets'. The old Abade, an intimate of the Marialva household, was full of the Marquis's scheme to marry him to Henriqueta, and hinted of her affection. 'If this gossip gets about Lisbon, it will double the number of my enemies.' The Marquis's brother, who was, Portuguese fashion, in love with his niece, was jealous and resentful. The Marquis's plans were obvious. 'Will not the Palace at Belem and a Dukedom tempt you?' Horne wrote.

Beckford was perplexed and worried. 'I know not even now which way to turn myself, and feel fatigued before I begin my course.' He grew more and more depressed; he was homesick for Fonthill. 'Shall I banish myself for ever from those happy scenes of my childhood? Shall I renounce that earth in which my poor Margaret is laid?' Portugal was too hot; no fairies would visit it, for there were no velvet lawns for them to trip about, no bowls of cream to set before them. Lisbon had for long been palling. The climate and noise were intolerable, the company dull. The beauty of sea and sky still gave him pleasure, 'but I am very low and melancholy'. There were, to be sure, Policarpio the tenor and his band of *meninos*, at the Patriarchale, one of whom played remarkably well on the harpsichord; his name was Gregorio Franchi; he was an attractive child, and Beckford felt he must be careful; 'I shall get into a scrape if I don't take care. How tired I am of keeping a *mask* on my countenance. How tight it sticks — it makes me sore ... I have all the fancies and levities of a child, and would give an estate or two to skip about the galleries of the

Patriarchale with the Menino — unobserved. D. Pedro is not child enough for me.' The fear of scandal, and of trouble with the Patriarchale, kept him cautious and prudent with little Franchi. He consoled himself with languid dreams of romance, as he took his evening drive along the shore of Belem, after the day's heat. 'How I should enjoy stretching myself on its sands by moonlight, and owning all my frailties and wild imaginations to some love-sick, languid ~~youth~~ girl[1] [*sic*] reclined by my side and thrown by the dubious light of undecided murmurs into a soft delirium. Alas, will my youth pass away without my feeling myself once more tremblingly alive to these exquisite tho' childish emotions!'

Meanwhile, it was excessively hot, and he missed England and the fresh green country and the lowing of his herds at Fonthill, missed his wife, 'who doated upon her poor William with such excessive fondness' and had now left him 'wandering about the world the object of the vilest calumnies and the most inveterate persecutions', missed London parties and conversation, which, he bitterly reflected, were going on now, even while he was 'sitting meekly and reverently with two holy Fathers from St. Anthony's Convent, talking of martyrdom and miracles . . . This time three years ago I little dreamt of ever having a conference with friars in Portugal — I was then on the high road to fame and dignity — courted by Mr. Pitt . . . worshipped and glorified by my Scotch kindred — and cajoled by that cowardly, effeminate fool, W.C.' (So far and so steeply had his 'lovely William' fallen from any tenderness of memory, though still he could be 'woken by barking dogs from a dream of walking with W.C. in the declivity of green . . . our eyes were bathed in tears of affection and friendship — our hands were joined, and we seemed to have intirely forgotten the miseries we had occasioned each other'.)

Beautiful Lisbon now grated his nerves and sensibilities. 'The more I am acquainted with Lisbon, the more I dislike it . . . A succession of ugly villages', he unfairly called it, 'awkwardly packed together and overpowered by massive convents.' Dom Pedro was more dismal than ever; no amount of burgundy gave him animation; boring visitors came and spent the evening and played sonatas execrably on piano and fiddle; the old marquis danced a minuet to the music, with kicks and flourishes very

---

[1] In the MS 'youth' is cancelled and 'girl' written above it – obviously a later amendment.

unsuitable to his years — 'how can a respectable old marquis, grandfather of so many children, make such a fool of himself?'

The younger marquis returned, with the court, to Lisbon, and Beckford was received at the Marialva palace with great affection. Having still not made up his mind about Henriqueta, he remained aloof from her, and talked to her father about Walpole's behaviour, and Mello's timidity; he had 'gone twisting and turning about to prevent a formal presentation and so keep well with all sides'. The queen was impatient to see Beckford, yet could not bring herself to give the word of command and order Mello to conduct him into her presence with the usual ceremonies. They would gladly have received him as it were by chance at Caldas, but 'the Marquis was above smuggling an introduction, and is determined to carry the point in a decided manner, and in the sight of Walpole and his colleagues and train of satellites'. So they agreed to pay a call on Mello and induce him to 'break through the sacred etiquette of the court and present me himself to the queen in defiance of the English minister'. Marialva asked to be allowed to tell the queen that Beckford had thoughts of establishing himself in Portugal, but Beckford would not commit himself to that. The marquis's inviting description of a life in Lisbon in which all his, the marquis's, friends would show him the kindest attentions did not tempt him. 'I could not welcome the thought. I still remained on the defensive, declaring that unless the queen admitted me into her presence, and immediately gave public proofs of disbelieving the calumnies of Mr. Walpole, I could scarcely continue another month in Portugal.' The marquis was surprised and vexed at his unwillingness to abandon his native land, which he had so much reason to abhor. But Beckford could not decide to. He waited on events. 'Whether I shall be once more safely landed in my native country, or cast away in a foreign one, blind Destiny alone is acquainted ... I have established no fixed rule to act by, am neither one thing nor another, neither vicious nor virtuous, and in the meantime lead the stupidest life imaginable.'

The following Sunday they called on Mello, finding him 'profuse of compliment, but stingy of committing himself with Walpole and the diplomatic set. Not all my noble friend's insinuations could move him from his purpose of strictly adhering to the established etiquette'. He admitted the ridiculous conduct of

Walpole, but urged the impropriety of overturning the accepted system and being presented except by the British minister. They went over the same ground for an hour and a half, the marquis insisting that never before had a minister, through private pique, dared to offer such a public insult, that Beckford's honour was deeply affected, and that 'I must kiss the Queen's hand immediately or quit Portugal, a step which would deprive him of the society of the friend he loved best in the world, and the country of a person whose pious and amiable dispositions served in this degenerate age as a bright example'. This picture of himself set Beckford laughing, but he also burst into angry eloquence on the abominable conduct of Walpole, 'in style that alarmed Mello and obliged him to palliate the Envoy's behaviour. He assured me Walpole had never said a word to him against me, that he was convinced all might be right if I would only tranquillize myself . . . that the dispute had been fomented on both sides by officious meddlers, but he did not despair of seeing me conducted into the presence chamber by the British Minister with every demonstration of respect and kindness. I heard this idea with such contempt and violence that the poor old secretary wished himself a mouse to creep into some crevice of the apartment. The marquis thought I went too far, and employed the usual sort of softening . . . but the wind was up, and not so easily laid'. He left in a passion, leaving the marquis to soothe the alarmed secretary as best he could. He had been home for half an hour when Marialva arrived, to tell him that he had frightened the 'shuffling, timid old man' out of his senses. 'He is returning your visit . . . for my sake, drive him not perfectly mad by your sharp taunts and menacing gestures.' Beckford promised to be gentle, 'now I have had my frolic'. He had made up his mind to leave Portugal when he had been properly presented, and to leave it unless this occurred. All his visitors sympathetically joined in abusing Walpole; they 'foamed and stamped and growled in chorus', which was soothing. As to Marialva, he devoted himself to fomenting his friend's resentment against his country and dissuading him from returning to it. He instanced Mr. North and Lord Edward Fitzgerald, who had been lately in Lisbon and had been full of spiteful reflections on him, though they did not even know him. The marquis besought him to abandon any idea of 'falling once more into this nest of scorpions, and remain with us, who love, pity and respect you. The queen would, in that case, grant you signal favours, and the whole court would unite in treating you with distinction'. The marquis then took a religious turn, explaining that Beckford had been conducted to Portugal by a miracle, and into his own friendship by the will of God. 'In general', said he, 'I avoid strangers, and particularly those of the English nation, whose brutal fierceness and sullen insolence I abhor. But an irresistible impulse draws me to you. Recommend yourself to that bright luminary of Portugal, the blessed St. Anthony, and beseech him to use his powerful intercessions with the Supreme Being to conduct you in the paths of life.' For these persecutions and calumnies were for Beckford's final good, the ways of Providence being inscrutable.

Beckford, rather disgusted by all this superstition, 'received this singular sermon with all due meekness and reverence . . . I am grieved at my heart to find a man I honour and esteem so far gone in the labyrinth of bigotry, so thoroughly persuaded of miraculous interpositions. If the affair of my presentation is to be given out of Mello's hands into those of St. Anthony, I think I may as well pack up and take my leave of Portugal'. However, he agreed to promise in case of success considerable alms to the monks of Boamonte, whose prayers could not fail of disposing the queen to act in his favour. The marquis lifted his eyes to heaven while his friend made this vow, and, after embracing one another with devout tenderness, they parted.

It grew hotter than ever. Beckford 'lay gasping like a perch just hooked out of a rivulet, while the marquis poured into my ears the bitterest maledictions on England. I see he will never rest till he has rooted out the last fibres of attachment to my native country'. Again and again Beckford told him he could not make a violent change unless he had first a distinguished reception from Her Majesty: it seemed a vicious circle. The homesick exile could not bring himself to dash to the ground every hope of re-establishing himself in his own country, among his own lawns and trees. Short of that, 'I am heartily sick of these endless cabals, and would give some thousands to be quietly established with all my books under the canopy of my favourite chestnuts at Evian'. Indeed, so sick was he of 'acting the part of the wandering Jew, and being stared at and wondered at by my ruthless nation as if I bore the mark of God's malediction on my countenance', that he was 'almost ready to abandon the contest, and build my nest in the first regions whose inhabitants will promise to keep the English at a distance. Could the Marquis of Marialva look into the depths of my heart, and see how its blood boils with indignation and rage against England, he would seize the moment of effervescence, lead me to the queen, and make me abjure in her presence my religion and my country. I trust the gust of passion will never drive me into such desperate measures. After all, what would become of me, a follower of the good old Sylvanus . . . in this dusty, sunburnt capital'. What use to him would be a string of pompous titles and the confinement of a drawing-room?

The solicited letter arrived from Pinto, the Portuguese ambassador in London, but Beckford was not pleased with it, it lacked force. 'My being humbly recommended to the protection and *benevolenza* of Mello will flatter the old Bird's diplomatic vanity much more than I could wish, and set him a-crowing.' But the report of this recommendation served, at least, to annoy Walpole, whom Beckford met driving along swelling with malice, with 'new fire in his flaming countenance. If the Grandees distinguish me by hospitality and testimonials the Toad will burst, and the Factory be flooded with venom'.

Meanwhile, more and more grandees called, all execrating the English, and Beckford's party strengthened every day. The marquis said he would even bring his wife and Henriqueta to dine; a most signal mark of esteem in Portugal. In spite of all these civilities and in spite of little Franchi's large-eyed adoration ('these Portuguese youths are composed of more inflammable materials than other mortals. I could keep them spellbound for hours at my side . . . dissolving like snow in the sunshine') Beckford was hideously bored. 'It's a wonder I do not expire with ennui . . . My good friend the marquis bores me with monotonous perseverance, and repeats the same professions of regard for my person and zeal for the salvation of my soul. How I long for the verdure and tranquillity of my beloved haunts in Savoy. Every day in my Lisbon existence is tinted with the same dull colours . . . I rise, gape about me, wipe the dust off my books, receive begging letters from convents, dash into my tub of cold water . . . Verdeil tries to persuade me to make something of my position in Portugal. I might certainly climb upon the shoulders of the Marialvas to lofty dignities, but I have not sufficient strength of nerves or spirits to run risk of tumbles.' He was becoming increasingly tired of the Portuguese. Franchi looked silly and sheepish; while as to Dom Pedro, whom the old Abade suggested as a spouse for his little daughter Margaret, aged two, he decided that it would never do; 'the little spirited thing has too much of her father's and mother's taste for beauty and elegance not to spurn away such a stiff, dismal, pig-tailed sapling. . . .'

But reports of his reputation from England were no better, and 'I cannot yet discover any decisive method of smoothing my way home'.

No hint of all these feuds, mortifications, resentments and defeats, and little hint of ennui, gets beyond the private diaries. The published version of these eight months is a record of sightseeing, social triumphs and felicities, unmarred by humiliation. It has been pointed out with what careful suppressions and emendations this effect was produced, all the writing up by which, later, Beckford turned his experiences not only into a work of art, but into a presentation of himself as a courted personality. He tells of festivals, processions, concerts, parties, excursions, plays and bull-fights (which he detested), the warbling of modinhas, games with lovely girls, fireworks, barking dogs, the gossip of priests, the beauty of Lisbon by moonlight, of Belem beneath the sunset sky, the shell-work and broken china on convent walls and at Mr. de Visme's Bemfica quinta, music in the royal chapel, amusing galas, expeditions to Collares, Mafra and Cintra. It is all a charming and entertaining travelogue, flowing agreeably over the stormy currents of anger, resentment and wretchedness that were the main stream of his emotional life through these months. He enjoyed the fêting, the society, the new scenes and sights, the people; they could not appease his unsoothed heart, or assuage his wounded pride. He fixed his mind firmly on presentation at court as the only remedy against his foes and against his own mortified vanity; without this, life was ashes to him; the ashes stirred into flickers when fanned by some new excitement, flattery, emotion or entertaining scene, but settled coldly again, leaving him sick at heart. 'I am out of order, and hang my head like a broken gilly-flower.'

Cintra revived him. A Portuguese Irishman, Senhor Street-Arriaga Brum da Silveira, had lent him Ramalhão, his quinta, close to the village; he went down with Marialva on July 9th to visit it; the garden was charming, the house spacious, airy and cool. On the 22nd he settled there, surrounding himself with the amenities of living, such as musicians, books, a flock of sheep from Fonthill. The court came down, and the Marialvas were close at hand; Beckford was continually with them. Horne and the Guildermeesters both had quintas near; life was sociable, cheerful, and rather absurd, full of parties, expeditions, sight-seeings, music, funerals and gossip; one would say not a dull moment, though Beckford complained to his diary, 'I am worn to a shadow with doing nothing. Not a book to be seen at the Marialvas. They never read'. Indeed, why should they? They had plenty of more agreeable occupations, into many of which their English friend was swept with them, though they failed to sweep him into the queen's presence, even with the court so near at hand. But Beckford was permitted by Marialva to borrow whenever he pleased a selection of musicians from the queen's chapel, that 'bevy of delicate warblers, as plump as quails and as gurgling and melodious as nightingales', accompanied by violins and wind instruments of the first order, who followed Her Majesty about the country wherever she went. Beckford would place some of these performers in a thicket or orange and bay trees, and pass hours listening to them in his pavilion, plunged by their sweetness into languor and gloom. He had, too, the orchestra collected at his orders by the conductor of the Lisbon opera, and he sang to the accompaniment of young Franchi, who had escaped from the Patriarchal and followed him to Cintra.

Marialva took him on a visit to Mafra, where they spent the night at the great convent, and next morning in the garden had one of those mysterious private conversations — 'a most serious and semi-official discourse about my stay in Portugal, and the means which were projecting in a very high quarter to render it not only pleasant to myself, but of some importance to many others'. No one has succeeded in making anything lucid or convincing out of these curious hints at high political intrigue in which Beckford was to play a part. Some writers, notably M. André Parreaux, have done their best, but there really is not enough to go on; Beckford's hints are too slight a basis on which to build. There is no doubt that the Marialvas urgently desired to secure the English millionaire for their family, and eagerly sought to tempt him with magnificent offers of place and power; beyond this, one cannot go. Beckford's self-glorifying aptitude and his desire to compensate his injured vanity may have magnified this; on the other hand, the Marialva party may well have tried to enlist him and his wealth for their own political purposes. That Beckford wrapped the approaches made to him in a certain amount of mystifying secrecy may merely imply that, though it seemed to him at the time important and flattering, it did not, when put into words, amount to anything very convincing; or that, when he wrote up and published his *Sketches*, in 1834, the liberal tide which had swept over Europe, including Portugal, made it unwise to play up too definitely the aims of the defeated faction and the attempt to involve him in their struggle.

It does not much matter. What matters is the brilliant beauty of the account of Ramalhão and Cintra, the picture of the scene on a furiously hot day in the Ramalhão pavilion, when 'I trifled away the whole morning, surrounded by fidalgos in flowered bed-gowns and musicians in violet-coloured accoutrements, with broad straw hats . . . looking as sunburnt, vacant and listless as the inhabitants of Ormus or Bengal . . . An agreeable variety prevails in my Asiatic saloon; half its curtains admit no light and display the richest folds; the other half are transparent, and cast mild glow on mats and sofas. Large clear mirrors multiply this profusion of drapery . . . One of the party, a very shrewd old Italian priest, told me he remembered an apartment a good deal in this style, that is to say, bedecked with mirrors and curtains, in a sort of fairy palace communicating with the Nunnery of Odivellas, so famous for the pious retirement of that paragon of splendour and holiness, King John the Fifth . . . Oh, said the old priest, very judiciously, had you but heard the celestial harmony of King John's recluses, you would never have sat down contented in your fine tent with the squalling of sopranos and the grumbling of bass-viols. The silver, virgin tones I allude to, proceeding from the holy recess into which no other male mortal except the monarch was ever allowed to penetrate, had an effect I still remember with ecstasy.' And so on. This pleasant morning was interrupted by a summons to the assembled company to attend a particularly merry funeral, of an English heretic lady converted on her death-bed and to be buried in great triumph; it proved a gay and sociable occasion, accompanied by the merry pealing of all the bells of Cintra and a frolicking procession of inhabitants, high and low, with noblemen bearing the bier. The festive ceremony over, some of the distinguished party returned to Ramalhão, ate iced fruit and sweetmeats, and spent the evening talking over the lively scene they had witnessed.

Scene after scene is sketched in luminous colours, ironic, sub-acid and exquisite; person after person enters, lively, charming, absurd; parties occur, at the Guildermeesters', with the host trying in vain to sell his visitors diamonds; at Mrs. Stait's, where most of the English at Cintra were congregated in a damp garden, eating a cold funereal supper in a low tent in imitation of a grotto; the queen arrives at Cintra, attended by dwarfs, negresses, and black, white and piebald horses; Beckford is privileged to watch the royal family party through a lattice window. He is taken by the Grand Prior to call on the archbishop confessor at the palace, and finds him a pleasant, portly, cordial man, walking in his white robes like a turkey in full pride, and informing Beckford that 'that mad-cap Lord Tyrawley was an archbishop at home', from which he had deduced that English archbishops were consecrated in ale-houses.

Beckford was such a pretty blend of poet and wit that one scarcely knows whether he is best in his ironic descriptions of persons and scenes, or when idling away the day in the delicious Elysium of the Collares valley, with citron bushes dropping their fruit into the rocky streams. The gaiety of his social encounters, the beauty of his country ramblings, the sweetness of continual music, make his published journal a record of pleasure. In revenge for the omission from it of his frustrated ambitions, his dark rages, his passions that must be held in leash by prudence, there are some singular scenes in the published book which may be sought for in vain in the private drafts; among these is the remarkable interview in the plains of Cascais with Dom José, the young Prince of Brazil and heir to the throne, which is given great prominence and significance in the published account, but is nowhere mentioned in the manuscript diary; the day (October 19th) ascribed to it in the former contains no such entry in the draft, but is filled with the account of a ride, and subsequent pages are removed. This, with the inherent oddness of the incident, has led Beckford's latest biographer to dismiss it as pure invention, one of Beckford's self-flattering romances. Nothing is impossible with Beckford; but there is no proof that the interview, in some form and on some date, did not take place. A French critic, dealing with it at length, sees it as a move in the Marialva plot to get rid of the heir and his *politique Pombalienne*, that bugbear of the ancient nobility; Beckford, he believes, was sent to him as *agent provocateur*, to make him talk anti-clerical politics and revolutionary reforms, so that these could be passed on to the archbishop confessor and excite in him such anger and mistrust as might lead to the prince's downfall.

It is far-fetched but possible; it would mean that in that case the interview would have been sought not by the prince but by Beckford himself, which Beckford's royalty snob-complex makes anyhow likely enough; as M. Parreaux comments, his insistence that the interview was arranged by the prince and took him by surprise is in itself suspicious. If it was the other way round, he would naturally remove the evidence from his diary. On the other hand, the prince might well be curious to meet the notorious Englishman of whom he had heard so much lately, and who, coming from the land of democratic liberalism and anti-catholicism, yet himself disliking his native country, might be expected to listen to his views (at once radical, advanced, and anti-British) with sympathy.

The interview, as Beckford relates it, reads oddly. He was, he says, summoned mysteriously to the prince's hunting caravan, and treated to a long and enthusiastic monologue, which he did nothing to evoke or encourage, on the advanced political, social and anti-clerical policy that ought to be pursued in order to rescue Portugal from her backward state, and from the embraces of Great Britain. Beckford, who highly disapproved of all that kind of thing (he was always a man of the Right, though later years made him more so) listened in silent amaze and growing horror. The prince discoursed for over an hour; Beckford listened, bowed and smiled. 'The sun set, the dews fell, the prince retired, and I remounted my horse with an indigestion of sounding phrases and the most confirmed belief that *the church was in danger*.'

Tired out and much agitated, he returned to Ramalhão, threw himself on his sofa and had tea; after which he hurried to the palace and related to the archbishop confessor 'all that had passed at this odd, unexpected interview. The consequences in time developed themselves'.

The consequences apparently were that this unfortunate prince, getting smallpox a year later, was clumsily treated and allowed to die: but whether this was contrived by the excellent archbishop, who had become thoroughly alarmed by the prince's revolutionary and unwholesome views, by the Marialva côterie, or by the queen, who, says Beckford, became deranged at this time owing to 'the conflict between maternal tenderness and what she thought political duty', does not seem certain. Beckford would appear, from this remark, to have backed the queen as first murderer. Wraxall observed that she refused to have her son vaccinated; but this seems more likely to have been from superstition than from filiocide. That his death, whoever caused it, was a relief to the Ultra faction, is clear; they felt that the main threat to their re-establishment in their pre-Pombalien importance was removed. That Beckford was a tool in the intrigue against him is possible but unproved.

Another scene in the *Sketches* whose authenticity has been doubted is the meeting at dinner with the young poet Bocage on November 8th. Indeed, it is odd, since Bocage seems, from all the evidence, to have been in Goa from 1786 to 1789. Theophilo Braga, it is true, makes out an ingenious case for his possibly having returned to Lisbon for a short while in 1787; but he seems to be basing this merely on the premise that the 'delicadissimo Lord Beckford', who drew of the young poet so speaking a portrait, must have been speaking the truth. This, it seems from the evidence (which includes the omission of any mention of Bocage in the original diary) he was not doing. He may have met the poet on a later visit to Portugal; the description is lively and plausible, but then so was Beckford's imagination. In short, as in the case of Prince of Brazil, one must leave it to God.

Meanwhile, Beckford's ambitions after a royal audience were still indefatigably championed by his affectionate friend the marquis, who constantly pressed his claims on the undecided though friendly queen (so good a religious woman dreaded both to offend England and to patronize scandalous vice); but on September 28th Marialva told him that a spoke had been put in the wheel by the malevolent Mr. Walpole, who had 'had the audacity to make representations in the name of the Court of England against my being introduced to Her Portuguese Majesty, and the archbishop was thrown into the utmost consternation at

so violent and unexpected a message. The queen knows not how
to act, continued my friend . . . her good inclinations are frustrated by this attack . . . My resolution is taken', Beckford added.
'I shall pack up and· depart; nothing will now detain me.'
Marialva entreated him, but in vain. He saw no future for himself
in Portugal now; the class solidarity of royalty would keep him
from court, whatever Marialva said.

At the end of October he left Cintra for Lisbon. The mule
cortège was put in train once more, the furniture, books, piano,
food and wines loaded up, the retinue of servants, attendants,
friends and musicians took the road. Did the Fonthill sheep
remain to decorate the pastures of Mr. Street-Arriaga's domain?
There is no more news of them. Beckford said farewell to
Ramalhão.

That charming residence was to pass through odd vicissitudes.
It became a royal palace; that fierce virago, Queen Carlota
Joaquina, was exiled there from Lisbon in 1822 for refusing
allegiance to the new liberal constitution; there she plotted
despotic usurpation for her son Miguel against her husband the
mild king, with or without the sympathetic assistance of Dom
Pedro, Marquis of Marialva, who had been Beckford's boy friend
thirty years before and later became the queen's ('there is Don
Miguel, that busy little despot', said Beckford to Cyrus Redding,
according to this enterprising and foolish journalist; 'do you
know whose son he is? The reputed son of D. Pedro, Marquis of
Marialva, whose father was my friend when I was in Portugal.
D. Pedro, it is remarkable, was web-footed.') Queen Carlota
had the walls of one of the rooms painted with Brazilian trees and
birds, to remind her of the Rio forests where she had galloped
for fifteen tedious years. There must have been despotic yearnings
in the air of Ramalhão; in 1833 Don Carlos of Spain stayed there,
and from it issued his fiery anti-niece declaration that launched
the Carlist wars. By the middle of the century the palace stood
empty and falling into ruin; later it was minded by peasant
caretakers who never heard of Beckford, probably never of
Carlota, Miguel, or Carlos of Spain. To-day it is a school for
little girls, kept by kindly and intelligent nuns; in each small clean
cubicle is a small clean bed, on each small clean pillow sits a teddy-
bear. Beckford, who liked children, might have been pleased.

He was leaving Portugal: weary of its provincialism, its pious, unintellectual society, perhaps of the tortuous political intrigues into which they were trying to drag him, reluctant to play a part in them, unwilling to marry Henriqueta and go Portuguese, frustrated in his court ambitions and persuaded by the Portugal-hating Dr. Verdeil, he was for trying his luck in Spain. He spent his last weeks in Lisbon with the Marialvas, hearing music, attending church and the ballet (where the queen and nobility sat surrounded by bedizened African implings, who, 'sweet sooty innocents, kept gibbering and pointing in a manner so completely African and ludicrous') sitting down to prodigious last banquets, having fond and tragical farewell scenes with Marialva and the old archbishop, who both sadly reproached him for deserting them in the crisis they foresaw. Shaken to the depths by the beauty and sadness of Jomelli's requiem mass, he drove to the Marialva palace and had a last melancholy talk with the marquis and the Grand Prior. 'It seemed to cut through my soul, and I execrated Verdeil and all those who had been instrumental in persuading me to abandon such a friend.'

If there was more here than mere regret at parting with friends, we do not know what. Failing fresh evidence, such as might (or might not) be supplied by the publication of letters from Beckford to Marialva now in private hands in Portugal, we must leave Beckford's mysterious hintings unclarified. All we know is that he felt remorseful, melancholy and oppressed when on November 28th he and his retinue embarked at Pampulha stairs to cross the Tagus in the Marialva scalera with its eight and twenty rowers, and landed on the Aldea Gallega shore, his journey to Spain begun.

His journey was comfortable enough. Other travellers have complained bitterly of wretched nights spent at the miserable Aldea Gallega posada; not so England's wealthiest son, who put up very commodiously at the postmaster's, though there was the usual racket all night. But he had no cause to grumble at his accommodations during the fortnight's journey to the frontier. At Vendas Novas he was lodged in the unused palace built by John V for a night's accommodation for the cortège of his son's Spanish bride in 1729 (a piece of extravagance after Beckford's own heart; it was a pity those two lordly spendthrifts could not meet); at Arroyolas the governor sent him a mandate for milk for breakfast (one may be sure that he would not have gone short of any scarce foods even to-day), and here he laid in a stock of bright carpets for his journey, lest he should find himself in an uncarpeted room; in the Estremos posada he spread them all round his bed, they made a flaming, exotic appearance and protected his feet from the damp brick floors. His own bed, of course, travelled with him, and was put up every night. Even crossing the frontier stream into Spain was made easy, the custom-house was all mildness and moderation, the baggage was not ransacked, and 'at sight of my passport, such a one, I believe, as is not frequently granted, all difficulties gave way'. In these days when passports are so much alike, this must cause some wistful emotions . . . 'allow the bearer to pass freely without let or hindrance, and afford him or her every assistance and protection of which he or she may stand in need'. Beckford must have had something warmer and more imposing than that on his. So, what with one thing and another, and in spite of jolting roads, some rain, and the misfortune of reading Major Dalrymple's dry travel book in the coach, the journey did not go too ill. It landed him at last in Spain, and he passes out of the Portuguese scene for six years.

He entered it again at the end of 1793. He was now thirty-three; life, while embittering him increasingly, owing to the cold attitude of the British about past scandals, had also enriched itself, become more luxurious and extravagant; at Fonthill he had lived *en fidalgo*, with an immense establishment, three male cooks and a confectioner, nine men and his Italian dwarf to wait at table when there was a dinner for three, Gregorio Franchi, who had become his pianist, assistant, courier travelling-companion and confidante, whom the neighbourhood called contemptuously 'the Portugal orange', a physician, a heraldic adviser, and other specialists. For a camping holiday on Lake Evian, he had pavilions 'planned, executed and adorned by the first artists of Paris, who are all here in my suite, with the addition of the best clarionets, oboes, drums, major and minor, of the ci-devant Gardes du Roy des Français'. A little later, when the Terror was raging over France, he retreated to Italy with a reduced band of seven musicians 'for these are no times for much suite in travelling'.

To Portugal in November 1793 he took his physician, Dr. Errhardt (who came from the French court and had attended the king's execution, and was therefore a suspicious character in the eyes of French émigrés in Lisbon) the indispensable Franchi, the still more indispensable chefs, confectioners, valets and footmen, and, of course, the band. Which others of the household of eighty-seven (of whom he wrote when in Lisbon) he brought with him, which collected in Portugal, he does not mention. A slight air of craziness had accrued to his establishment and his methods of travelling; he grew more Caliphian; was he drawn back to Portugal because there he found, in a Europe disconcertingly becoming jacobinized and drab, the rich ripe sultan style?

Not that even Portugal was quite what it was. The queen was quite mad, and her second son in charge; unlike his brother José, who, as Beckford hinted, had been allowed to die of smallpox for his Pombalien and Voltairean opinions, D. João was a mild reactionary bigot, good-natured and weak, whose views gave no cause for alarm. But, wrote Beckford to Sir William Hamilton, 'this country is by no means quiet — the priests are chop-fallen, the oracular images of our Lady and St. Anthony are as mute as the fishes to whom he preached, and the ministers scared by the terror of France out of the scanty remains of their senses. Poor Mary Portugal fancies herself damned to all eternity, and there-fore, on the strength of its being all over with her, eats turkey and oyster sauce Fridays and Saturdays, and indulges in conversations of rather an unchaste tendency. Were there ever such times, such vertigos, such bedevilments? Society is almost totally dissolved in every part of Europe ... However, there is no saying what is going forwards at home at this hour, for we are perfectly newsless at this dirty fag-end of Europe. ...'

To enliven the dirty fag-end, he plunged again into music and devotions. 'I am a pattern of sanctity, and have set St. Anthony a-going again so effectually that the patriarch, the Inquisitor, and the heads of religious houses stuff me with sweetmeats and smother me with caresses ... This very evening the monks of St. Vincent ... give me a grand entertainment in the open air. We shall feast like Absalom on the house-top, to the sound of the lute, the harp and the sackbut; but we shall not have the pleasure, like that graceful young gentleman, of being surrounded with concubines — snug's the word in Lisbon — in that particular.'

So he once again picked up the threads of his Portuguese life, settled in the Belem quinta he had taken, S. José de Ribamar, resumed his intimacy with the Marialvas and his prelate friends (the old archbishop confessor, whom he had loved, had died soon after the Prince of Brazil) and passed the winter and spring pleasantly enough in society, feasting, music and church-going. He was still campaigning to defeat the British ambassador and be presented at court; he was to achieve this eight-years-old aim eventually, but not until May, 1795. Meanwhile he enjoyed the return to Roman ceremonial, its 'fine stage effects, glittering crosses . . . processions, perfumes, clothes and music, from the deep tones of the organ to the delightful squeakings of the Pope's eunuchs'. He had no intention of changing his religion, unless as a bargaining counter for place and power; he mocked at Romanism, grew impatient with its pieties and superstitions, but enjoyed its splendours and pomps; the chilly calm of eighteenth-century Anglicanism was never his spiritual home.

It has been guessed that he was not received in Portugal with quite the old warm welcome, and that he regretted the offers he had once refused. These offers, so far as they concerned the hand of Henriqueta, were common gossip in Lisbon. 'M. Becfort, riche anglais, qui vient de s'établir en Portugal, et qui devait épouser la bâtarde de Marialva', wrote a Lisbon Frenchman of him in 1796; the bastard was now espoused elsewhere, and the rich Englishman had never become a Portuguese grandee. Did he regret it? We have fewer clues to his inner life during this second visit to Portugal, for this time he kept no private diaries that we can compare with his published account; or if he did, they have perished. There are some letters; and there are the *Recollections of an Excursion to the Monasteries of Alcobaça and Batalha*, published forty years later from notes which we have not seen. There are no means of checking most of the facts and conversations recorded in the *Recollections*; how much was genuine, how much embellished, how much invented, it is impossible to know. There are incidents which seem unlikely: his audience with the Prince and Princess of Brazil, for instance, in June 1794, with the implication of previous interviews, though he was not presented at court until the following May; but his excitement about royalty always produced some queer tales. Again, as in the *Sketches*, he throws out mysterious hints of some high destiny or mission on which he had turned his back, and which he recalled with regret in his reverie by the side of the stream near Batalha, when, throwing himself on the ground, he 'thought (alas! how vainly now!) of offers I had slighted with so much levity, of opportunities which, had they been grasped with a decided hand, might have led to happy results, and stemmed a torrent of evils. Since that period, the germ of destructiveness, which might then have been trodden down, has risen into a tree fraught with poisons, darkening the wholesome light, and receiving nourishment, through all its innumerably varied fibres, from the lowest depths of hell.'

At what date did he set down this? Had the poison-tree grown to its hellish state before or since he thus meditated in vain regret? Is he referring to the French occupation, to the liberal Constitution of 1820, to the Miguelist reign of terror and the civil war that followed it and the victory of liberal and anti-clerical forces that extinguished the ancient nobility? He may have been commenting on all this as a violently Tory old man; the streak of craziness that always ran turbulently in him did not calm with age. That streak has to be taken into account in his description of his Batalha reverie; it is futile to inquire too closely what can have been those great, those fateful offers which, had he accepted them, might have saved Portugal. It is obvious that, whatever position he had been put into, it would have made no difference to Portugal, and that this stemming of a torrent of evils is the fantasy of a megolomania that grew in him steadily as he aged.

Already in his mid thirties it was well developed. Already he saw himself as the head of a caliphian establishment, a miniature court, in the style of the Portuguese fidalgos; though he derided the Marialva medley of dwarfs, musicians, monks, negroes and the rest, who skipped about their master where he went, he adopted the fashion at Fonthill, and even abroad; he wrote to Sir William Hamilton that his establishment at Montserrate consisted of eighty-seven, 'and exceeds in splendour and talents that of any prince in Europe'. This is the language of slight madness; and it is partly this madness, partly his deliberate self-glorification, that throws a veil of confusion over much that he wrote; it is like a glinting dream, whose parts need not logically fit together. For fact-seekers it is tantalizing; for those who are content to accept his narration as a lovely and amusing chain of incidents, humours and descriptions, partly memories, partly dreams, waking thoughts and inventions, the *Excursion* is almost without a rival. Written in rich, supple, easy prose, Beckford's prose, so unlike the prim, stilted, ponderous, didactic style of most of his fellow travellers, it is decorated with delightful scenes, lovely landscapes, comic persons; its conversations are ridiculous and gay; it is by someone who saw sharply, beautifully, with the artist's eye. It has few of Beckford's complacencies and fatuities; to read it is to stroll, with a perceptive guide, through beautiful scenes and odd, amusing society. It never flags, from the morning when the old Grand Prior of Aviz and the Prior of St. Vincent's, 'than whom a more delightful companion never existed since the days of those polished and gifted canons and cardinals who formed such a galaxy of talent and facetiousness round Leo the Tenth', called at Beckford's house in Lisbon on a fine June morning to take him to visit the two famous monasteries, until, twelve days later, with the shriekings of the crazy queen in his ears, he drove home from the palace of Queluz.

It would be tedious to summarize the familiar excursion. Agreeable pictures decorate almost every page, and everyone acts in character throughout. Beckford himself is alternately satirist, wit, poet, moralist, sympathetic observer, and occasionally vulgarian, as when he describes with complacency the astonishment of the monks at the plethoric hampers of rich food brought by their guests and the carrying into their precincts of grand beds and silver basins and ewers for a night's lodging; he is untouched by any regret at hurting the feelings of his amiable hosts, or by any shame at this so excessive ostentation. He is more likeable when wandering alone through enchanted woods, yielding to melancholy nostalgia, running races and dancing with the Princess of Brazil's girls-in-waiting, or looking down his nose at the unfinished chapels at Batalha, which he found very fussy, Manueline, and unlike Greece.

The excursion lasted twelve days, ending with a pretty scene of running and dancing before the Princess of Brazil 'in the deepest recesses of the odoriferous thickets', and an audience with the Prince Regent, at which 'the Prince honoured me again with those affable expressions of regard which his excellent heart never failed to dictate'. The passage which follows, about 'this beneficent sovereign' (he became king in 1816) and the baneful intrigues of his wife, was obviously written after King John's death in 1826, though it begins 'Let me observe, whilst the recollections of the interviews I have had with him remain fresh in my memory

. . .' a good example of the mixture of periods in the composition of the narrative.

The *Recollections* must, in the main, have been written at the time, or soon afterwards; perhaps during the leisured autumn at Montserrate that followed the excursion. Beckford's own account of it, prefaced to the publication in 1835, was that coming the other day, in examining some papers, on some 'very slight notes of this Excursion' and 'flattering myself that perhaps they might not be totally unworthy of expansion, I invoked the powers of memory — and behold, up rose the whole series of recollections I am now submitting. . . .'

A characteristically Beckfordian falsification. The slight notes must have been a full narration, written at a time when its memory was still clear and sharp. No doubt it was added to, altered, faked up here and there; there are a few apparent additions, elderly reflections, comments on later history, words and phrases that belong rather to the 1830s than the 1790s; but in essentials it must have been contemporary. The wealth of closely-observed (or beautifully invented) detail, the sharp loveliness of the descriptions, the life-like conversations, the richness of the fun, the irony and the poetry and the decoration, can neither be a memory forty years old suddenly invoked, nor the composition of a man in his mid-seventies; it has all the fresh power, poetry and enjoyment of youth. It had possibly, like the manuscript of *Dreams, Waking Thoughts and Incidents*, gone about among his friends for years, though there seems no record of leakages and plagiarisms such as had annoyed him in that case, or, indeed, of any comments at all, so perhaps he kept it to himself.

That summer, after the Alcobaça excursion, he gratified an old desire: he rented Montserrate, Mr. De Visme's Cintra quinta, which he had coveted on his first visit to Portugal for its magnificent grounds, situation and views. 'It was,' he told Cyrus Redding, 'a beautiful Claude-like place, surrounded by a most enchanting country. It belonged to a Mr. De Visme, a merchant, of whom at the time I could not obtain it. Afterwards, however, he pulled down the house, and built another in barbarous Gothic. On my return I rented the place of him; for, although he had knocked down the old edifice, he could not level the hills nor root up the woods. I build it! 'twas built by a carpenter from Falmouth.'

Tradition at the time and since has fastened the building on Beckford; indeed, it seems strange that the sensible and level-headed Mr. De Visme should have knocked down his quinta and replaced it by another in barbarous Gothic, which was not the style of the solid merchant who built the square and solid British Factory hospital; on the other hand, it was a style of which Beckford was capable, his taste being erratic and uncertain and easily distorted by immense cost, as his collection of curios shows. And he would, as we know, put up towers in a hurry that collapsed and fell down. Montserrate, which twelve years or so after he had left it seems to have been a ruin, must have had flaws in its structure. But the suspicion that Beckford rebuilt the house, and later, finding it despised by good taste, disowned it, is modified by Lady Craven's letter to him from Cintra in 1791, in which she remarked that 'De Visme is building at a Place called Montserrate. Beautiful situation, but a Vile Planned house', to which Beckford added the comment 'perfectly true'. Yet he is not entirely let out, for he was writing from Montserrate in August, 1795 to Sir William Hamilton of 'my proceedings here in building, gardening, etc,' and in September of having 'built houses'. So how much of the barbarous Gothic must be blamed on him, how much on Mr. De Visme, we do not know. Both at least are absolved from the barbarous orientalism of the Montserrate of to-day, constructed in a Moorish delirium by the Visconde Cook of 1856.

Beckford threw himself with ardour into the improvement and planting of the already beautiful garden and grounds. Landscape gardening always showed him at his most likeable; his enthusiasm was unaffected, his energy boundless. He wrote to his friend Senhora Bezerra in July, 1795, inviting her to stay. 'Montserrat with all its bloom and fragrance is at your absolute command whenever you choose to honour it with your presence ... I have been too much engaged with the Royalty of Nature, with climbing roses and corktrees, with tracing rills and runnels to their source, and examining every recess of these lovely environs, to think of inferior Royalties. Not once have I left this enchanted Circle. Here I remain spellbound, and no talisman in the prince's power could draw me away ... I have been extremely lucky in the choice of my *location*[1] (a fine new word fresh from the mint of

---

[1] It is interesting to note that the first use of this word in this sense quoted in the Oxford Dictionary is dated 1827.

Mr. Cumberland) which is as dry, as healthy, and as gloriously cheerful, as the most classical spots in Arcadia'. All he wants is Senhora Bezerra's company and some good wine, if her husband can get him some, expense no object.

By this time he had been at last presented at court; that long battle was won, and the irate British ambassador wrote a curt note to Sousa Coutinho the foreign minister, inquiring why. Later he explained that his note had been private and unofficial. No doubt this was so: the duel between him and Beckford had become a matter of personal spite and pride with both; Beckford's belated victory must have been a bitter pill. As to Beckford, his hatred for 'those things called envoys and ambassadors' remained venomous through his life, even when he was intriguing to be made one.

What inducements finally prevailed with regent and ministers to make them thus flout the British ambassador and receive the black sheep, we do not know. Perhaps the good-natured and undecided Prince Regent hoped the English would not notice; or perhaps money talked; it was an argument which the Portuguese royal family and their ministers usually heard readily; perhaps Beckford persuaded them that, as he wrote a few months later to Sir William Hamilton, à propos the reception he demanded from the King of Naples, he was '*worth* humouring'.

His terrific royalty complex was unsatiated by his Lisbon victory; he had long been wanting to visit the Hamiltons at Naples, but for some time did not dare to face the French-infested ocean — 'If the season was less boisterous, and the French cruizers not quite so busy at the very mouth of the Tagus, I should sail forth with the first fair wind and pay you a visit,' he wrote on arrival in Portugal. The French cruisers remained busy; he became absorbed in Montserrate; and it was not until September, 1795 that he wrote that he had 'engaged a Danish ship bound to Leghorn', and might be expected in Naples early in November. 'I have worn Portugal threadbare, have built houses and given fêtes, and spent money by cartfulls, and outcanted the most furious adorers of St. Anthony. I own a gentle transition from the Portuguese would not come amiss for the sake of variety.'

He contemplated a temporary transition only. A letter to Sir William written a month before shows him well dug in at Montserrate and even in Lisbon, where he was building a new house.

'My new house in Lisbon is almost finished, and a glorious habitation it bids fair to be. St. Anthony conducted my furniture safe — and inspires me with a supernatural affection for this moonish silly country ... There still lurks in my bosom an inviable desire of visiting Naples. ...'

The moonish silly country was boring him a little by the end of September, and he was eager to be off on the Neapolitan trip. He assured Sir William that he had no intention of meddling in Neapolitan politics. 'I could not help laughing at the notion of such a determined *ipso facto* aristocrate as yr. loving cozen being set down on the Jacobin list. Of all the calumnies which have been floating about the world to my prejudice this is the plumpest ... No, my dear Sir William, you may assure His Majesty of Naples that a more loyal subject, a more hearty well-wisher to established forms of government exists not in all Europe ... and the very distinguished and unprecedented manner in which I have been received at the Court of Lisbon shows plainly the opinion entertained by the Prince of Brazil of my conduct and sentiments. My suite will consist of the following persons. ...' He enumerates them: physician, maître d'hôtel, baker, cook, footmen, valet de chambre, all were staunch royalists. 'I cannot travel with fewer servants than the above ... They are picked out of eighty-seven, for my establishment consists of that very large number. ...' He proceeded to mention in what manner he would wish to be treated by the Neapolitan court (the ferocious Bourbon Ferdinand IV). 'I think it would be fair to let the King know that I am *worth* humouring, and that no person in Europe can spend more money in his country, *if I am properly cherished and attended to* ... I bring very little baggage, and only wish for a pleasant airy apartment in the Albergo Reale, or any other Albergo ... The less I spend in show the more I shall have for collecting and real comfort, so *trêve de parade* till times change for the better, or His Majesty should animate me to a display of magnificence by *peculiar* graciousness and distinction.'

Alas, he never got to Naples, and we shall never know to what displays of magnificence King Ferdinand and his strong-minded consort might have animated him, or how the hated 'English swarm' would have behaved. It is a pity. Frightened from the seas by a Barbary corsair, he took refuge at Alicante: 'I was pretty well laden with the good things of this world, so I have had a narrow escape.' As it was, he doubted whether he could face further navigation, and, after waiting for a time in Valencia, he renounced the idea. Unfortunately he had already sent to Naples some of his 'very little baggage' — 'a cargo of cases containing wines, linen in a large trunk, liveries, a very fine forte-piano, and I hardly know what else besides; if they arrive have the kindness to let them remain — unopened and untumbled if possible — under your protection'.

At the end of the year Beckford returned to Portugal; he stayed only three months, and there is no record of what he did there, except his own statement that he had been 'entrusted with a very important mission by His Highness the Regent'. He was back in England by the end of March, full of importance and high diplomacy and the mission from 'my royal friend in Portugal'. This mission, whatever it was, excited no interest in His Majesty's ministers. 'I think myself shamefully trifled with,' he wrote to his mother. 'I have received no answer to that important communication with which I was entrusted, no invitation to consult upon them, no mark of attention or gratitude. Things at Lisbon are advancing to such a Crisis that ... the consequence will be confirming the triumph of the Spanish Faction to the utter destruction of our commerce with Portugal ... unless a very different line of conduct is adopted towards me, and the services I have it in my power to render are treated with less contempt and reserve, I shall be obliged to communicate such observations to my royal Friend in Portugal as' ... etc.

All this diplomatic fuss probably amounted to little enough, and no doubt the British government thought they could get all the information they required about Portugal from their Mr. Walpole. 'You are not aware, perhaps', said Beckford to Cyrus Redding, 'that I offered my services to the government, at a critical period, as an envoy to the court of Lisbon. My acquaintance with the Prince Regent, and my intimacy with the Marialva family, adapted me for such a post. It came to nothing; but I think I could have done the country some service.'

Snubbed in the matter of Portugal, Beckford, in his ambition to be one of those things called envoys, turned his attention to France, with no better luck; he was snubbed again. Perceiving that international troubles must take their course unchecked by his efforts, Beckford went off to Portugal again in a huff; he was there from the end of 1798 to July of next year; presumably he saw his royal friend and his other intimates, and disposed of any houses he still owned there; the only record there seems to be of his doings is a police record committing to prison one Antonio, who had let him down in the matter of some horses and delayed a journey he intended to make.

He never, so far as we know, went to Portugal again.

But, in a sense, he never left it. Fonthill, and the Fonthill life, that so amazed, mystified, fascinated and scandalized the neighbours through so many years, with its grandiose luxury, its dwarfs, its troupes of exotic musicians, its rich banquets, its ceremonious pomp, its curios, beauties and extravagancies collected from all parts of the world, its patriarchal armies of retainers, its gourmandizing off rich plate to the accompaniment of elaborate orchestral performances, derived from an imagination which had found in the Portugal of Maria I, of the rich eighteenth-century fidalgos and prelates, of the feudal Marialva and his friends, its home. The fabulous, crazy loveliness of that lotus-eating, comicopera, devout, ridiculous, moonish world had evoked in him a response at first delightedly (however cynically) amused and charmed, later ennuyé, bored, but still willing to be pleased, and always sensuously enchanted by its bizarre beauty and unconscious wit.

He kept his travel diaries by him, wrote them up, showed and read them to friends (who plagiarized from them), though there is no record of the kind of publicity which *Dreams, Waking Thoughts and Incidents* had achieved even before the printing and suppression of the 1783 edition called attention to it. But even more aptly than of the *Dreams* it could have been said of the two Portugal travel books that 'they were written with genius . . . throughout the whole there was a spirit like champagne prevailing — sparkling everywhere'. He wanted them published; in 1818 he suggested to Rogers that Moore might edit them; Moore was reluctant; Beckford gave up the idea and let them alone until 1833.. The *Sketches* appeared in 1834, the *Recollections* the year after.

The *Sketches* were prefaced by a wistful note — 'Portugal attracting much attention in her present convulsed and declining state, it might not perhaps be uninteresting to the public to cast back a glance by way of contrast to the happier times when she enjoyed, under the mild and beneficent reign of Donna Maria the First, a great share of courtly and commercial prosperity.' The date was March, 1834; the war of the two brothers was nearing its bitter end, and Portugal enjoyed no prosperity at all. Beckford would have found in it nothing to please him; had he returned, he would have been a stranger and exile there, hostile to everything he saw and heard; his Portugal was indeed dead, slain by Napoelon's destroying armies, never to return.

To live with and prepare and expurgate and embellish his memories of it for publication perhaps gave him, besides gratifying ambition, a melancholy solace. That he should claim them as a new composition, written up from 'very slight notes', was natural, and part of the drama in which, at seventy-five, he still lived. Re-living those earlier acts of the long drama, the gorgeous, exotic scenes of beauty, levity, passion, romance and travel on the grand scale, which he had enacted in Portugal, he seemed to himself once more the gifted, fêted, enigmatic, youthful tourist, who had met, in the drama as written by himself, with no rebuffs, but had been courted by Portugal with homage, feasting and music all the way.

BIBLIOGRAPHY

Italy; with Sketches of Spain and Portugal, WILLIAM BECKFORD (1834).
Recollections of an Excursion to the Monasteries of Alcobaça and Batalha, WILLIAM BECKFORD (1835).
Hamilton Papers (Register House, Edinburgh).
Beckford, GUY CHAPMAN (1937).
Life of William Beckford, J. W. OLIVER (1932).
Life and Letters of William Beckford, LEWIS MELVILLE (1910).
Memoirs of William Beckford of Fonthill, CYRUS REDDING (1859).
Le Portugal dans l'oeuvre de William Beckford, ANDRÉ PARREAUX (1935).
Diary, JOSEPH FARINGTON (January, 1797).
Letters, HORACE WALPOLE (To Mann. 1783).
Tableau de Lisbonne, J. B. F. CARRÈRE (1798).
Bocage. Sua vida e epoca litteraria, THEOPHILO BRAGA (1876).
Viagems de Beckford a Portugal, L. A. REBELLO DA SILVA (*O Panorama*) (1855).
Lagrimas e Thesouros, L. A. REBELLO DA SILVA (1863).
D. Maria I, CAETANO BERÃO (1928).
La Littérature Portugaise en Angleterre à l'Époque Romantique, FÉLIX WALTER (1927)
F.O. 63/20 (Record Office).

7. A ROMANTIC AMONG THE PHILISTINES
Robert Southey
[January-April 1796.   April 1800-May 1801]

IN October, 1795, young Southey, aged twenty-one, his head intoxicated with the fumes of the French Revolution and the delightful vision of pantisocracy, in trouble with his disapproving relations, desired by his mother and by his uncle Hill, English chaplain at Lisbon, to take orders, and quite determined that he would pass through no such 'gate of perjury', wrote to his friend Grosvenor Bedford, 'And where do you suppose the fates have condemned me for the next six months? — to Spain and Portugal! I would have refused, but I was weary of incessantly refusing all my mother's wishes. . . .'

So, despondent at the prospect of exile, the revolutionary youth married Edith Fricker, his tedious and adored betrothed, in the New Year, left her at the church door, and proceeded with his uncle Hill to Falmouth to wait for a wind. From thence he wrote commending his Edith to a friend. 'Her virtues are of the domestic order . . . I hate your daffydowndilly women; the violet is ungaudy in the appearance, though a sweeter flower perfumes not the evening gale.' Edith, though handsome, lacked, it seems, elegance.

Waiting for the wind, Southey felt those apprehensions natural in inexperienced voyagers. 'Grosvenor, I half shudder to think that a plank only will divide the husband of Edith from the unfathomed ocean!' However, the plank held, and they arrived safe, though sick, at Corunna, and journeyed uncomfortably to Madrid, and thence, still more uncomfortably, to the Portuguese frontier, in the wake of King Carlos of Spain and his all-devouring court, who seized all the food on the way and left behind them only dead mules.

It was then that he registered his life-long impression of the greed, corruption, incompetence and cruelty of the Peninsula monarchical regimes. Royalty had even reserved for its exclusive use the only good bridge across the frontier river; lesser mortals had to cross elsewhere. Cross at last they did, on January 21st, 1796. Southey, glad to get out of Spain, was only glad to be in Portugal in that he was getting nearer an English parsonage and saw an end to the horrors of Iberian inns. For a youth of twenty-one, afire with republican principles and dreams of founding a Utopia in an American wilderness, he was definitely fussy about discomfort, dirt, hard beds, insects, and smells. As to the Portuguese custom-house, he compared it, as many travellers have, with the infernal regions, describing it, with the ponderous irony of his period, as 'these agreeable establishments'. Most of his road to Lisbon was similarly labelled. It rained heavily; the inns were extremely comfortless; vermin abounded; everywhere he encountered 'small and miserable towns', or 'large and miserable villages', detestable landlords and landladies. His travelling was sadly different from that of Mr. William Beckford (also on one of his Portuguese visits, just then: the two did not, however, meet). The fortunate millionaire, travelling about this land of hard beds, poor fare, and wretched inns, took with him his own bed, a retinue of servants to put it up for him, a cortège of mules to transport all the delicacies he might fancy, and a chef to prepare them; besides which, he never put up at inns. The simple and unmoneyed chaplain and his nephew had to make the best of such accommodation as they found. It seems doubtful whether Robert did make the best of it; here is the final stanza of a poem he addressed to Edith from one of these inns:

> When late arriving at our inn of rest,
> Whose roof, exposed to many a winter's sky,
> Half shelters from the wind the shiv'ring guest;
> By the lamp's melancholy gloom
> I mark the miserable room,
> And gazing with indignant eye
> On the hard lot of honest Poverty,
> I sicken at the monster brood
> Who fill with wretchedness a world so good,
> And wish, retired in some secluded glen,
> To dwell with PEACE and EDITH, far from men.

And so at last to the Tagus, and across it to Lisbon and his uncle's house. By the time he reached it, he had 'learned to thank God that I am an Englishman; for, though things are not so well there as in Eldorado, they are better than anywhere else'. Certainly English earth seemed firmer; the Lisbon earth quaked during his first night at his uncle's, which was just what he had feared; fortunately it did not prove serious, though these earth-quakes alarm 'the Portuguese dreadfully'.

He began to inspect Lisbon, finding most aspects of it what he called 'very agreeable'. Very agreeable were the filth, the slops emptied from windows, the fierce and scavenging dogs, the deformed and diseased beggars who solicited him in the streets. 'I am at Lisbon,' he wrote, 'and therefore all my friends expect some account of Portugal, but it is not pleasant to reiterate terms of abuse, and continually to present to my mind objects of filth and deformity.' He wrote with sneering contempt of the government, with shocked disgust of the Church, towards which his attitude was one of indignant dismay, with boredom of the English society round him. 'The English here are the most indefatigable dancers and the most inveterate casino players in Europe. I have now almost run the gauntlet through all my introductions, and passed through the purgatory of my first visits.'

'Here I am,' he wrote to Joseph Cottle at Bristol, 'among the Philistines, spending my mornings so pleasantly as books, only books, can make them, and sitting at evening the silent spectator of card-playing and dancing. The English here unite the spirit of commerce with the frivolous amusements of high life.' They played every night, Sundays not excepted. 'This is a comfortless place, and the only pleasure I find in it is in looking on to my departure.' Three years back, he might, he said, have found a friend in Count Leopold Berchold, who used to come and read in his uncle's library, but now there was no one. He had seen through the Lisbon English in the first few days; he had not been there a week before he wrote, 'The society of this place is very irksome: the men have no ideas but of business, and though the women are accomplished, yet their company only renders the absence of one woman more painful. I cannot play with a lady's fan and talk nonsense to her; and this is all the men here are capable of doing ... Gladly would I exchange the golden Tagus with the olive and orange groves of Portugal for the mud-encumbered tide of Avon and a glimpse of Bristol smoke'.

He liked his company no better as time went on. 'Here is much visiting', he complained three weeks later, 'and as little society as you can wish ... I read very hard, and spend every evening in company ... The round of company here is irksome to me, and a select circle of intimate friends is the *summum bonum* I propose to myself.' Heading a letter, 'Lisbon, from which God grant me a speedy deliverance', he sought consolation in books. His uncle had a good library; indeed, this excellent clergyman seems to have been all that was kind to his refractory nephew, who wrote, 'My uncle and I never molest each other by our different principles'. He does not say whether or not he attended his uncle's church; nor whom he met in Lisbon. Were these dancing, card-playing, irksome people all members of the English Factory circle, or did they include diplomatic and military society, and those invalids staying in the hotels of Buenos Ayres whom Mr. William Hickey had, a few years before, watched with kindly apprehension daily sinking into the grave? One gathers that Southey was at least introduced to Mr. Walpole, the British envoy, who had refused to know Beckford and been so hospitable to Hickey. But, whoever his acquaintances were, they were no use to the young revolutionary from Oxford, torn from his friends, his bride, and his just about to be published epic, *Joan of Arc*. One can see the shy, humourless, high-nosed young man sitting awkward and dumb among the genial Philistines who were his uncle's main associates. 'They know much of their own business', he wrote of them later, 'very little of the country they live in, and nothing of anything else except cards.' Their parties bored him. 'I am now going out to dinner,' he wrote; 'then to see a procession, then to talk French, then to a huge assembly, from whence there is no returning before one o'clock.' However, he liked the wines, and found consolation in industrious reading, in learning the language (soon he could converse with Portuguese dogs and cats), and in finding out all he could about the life, history, literature and legends of Portugal, for the book he meant to publish on his return. Indeed, the letters home from which this book was expanded are admirably full of information, erudition and translations of Spanish and Portuguese verse and prose. No one could call Southey an unintelligent traveller, though he lacked that urbane acceptance of other people's ways which marked Beckford, Hickey, and Joseph Baretti.

Sometimes he went to the opera, which he found very absurd. The queen, out of modesty, jealousy and apprehension (for her husband was an opera fan, and he was no less amorous than other Portuguese gentlemen) allowed no women on the stage. Southey thought it strange that she should relax her prohibition in favour of a female dancer who exhibited herself at the theatre and drew large crowds. Where was the queen's regard to public morals in this case? 'No amusement should be tolerated which cannot benefit the spectator and must vitiate the performer.' Both the young man and his uncle seem to have had an unreasonable objection to female dancers; Beckford records a conversation he had in 1794 with the mother of a young lady, in which she reminded him how 'the English Padre' had once said 'it was shameful how very rapturously my poor dear girl rattled her castanets and threw back her head and put forward every other part of her dear little person, at the Factory ball'.

As to Southey, he was a natural disapprover. He disapproved of the Portuguese, of most of their literature, of the Lisbon English, of 'all the mummery of a Catholic Lent', and, in fact, of Roman Catholicism *en bloc*, finding it foolish, superstitious, bigoted, reactionary, cruel, and obsessed with 'the diabolical belief in eternal punishment'. Above all he disapproved of monastic institutions, and these met his eyes everywhere in this benighted land. 'The sight of a Monastery or a Monk always fills me with mingled emotions of pity and disgust: foul and filthy men, without accomplishments or virtues or affections, it is yet the system they are subject to that has made them what they are . . . The monastic life is not however wholly without its allurements. The indolent who is content to vegetate through existence without experiencing more pleasure or more pain than vegetables probably feel, the bigot whose mind is rendered dark and sullen by the dread of a gloomy and severe God, and the man who is wearied and disgusted with mankind because he knows them, will alike love the tranquillity of the Convent . . . If there is nothing to move to rapture, there is nothing to excite anguish.' A few weeks in the cheerful and impassioned atmosphere of a convent might have taught the ignorant young protestant better than this. But he got no nearer to the inside of a convent than the grille of the English Brigittine nuns, where so many of his countrymen, civil, military and nautical, were wont to drop in for a chat and a cup of tea with their sociable and confined countrywomen, who made delicious cakes and were eager for news from home. In spite of the cakes and the tea and the chat, Southey took a poor view of this convent. 'It has been constantly supplied from England with victims to this wretched superstition; but it is now several years since a novice has arrived, and I hope our country will not long be disgraced by this institution. They gave us the history of each day's employment, a melancholy record of prayer and silence, undiversified by one solitary pleasure ... They talked much at the grate of the happiness they enjoyed; yet from the account they gave of their manner of life, and the eagerness with which they appeared to seize the opportunity of conversation, I went away fully convinced that a nun is as miserable in herself as she is useless to society. The delirium of devotion may supply comfort to a few monastics, where warmth of disposition has been thus perverted: these, however, must necessarily be few, and there is too much reason to believe that the greater number, precluded from the exertions of active benevolence, seek to relieve the dreadful taedium of such an existence by the stimulations of vice.'

He concludes his musings with a story of an English wine merchant who kept his cellars beneath the chapel of a nunnery, and, very naturally, observed that his stock diminished....

But he was shaken out of his disapproval by the sight of the convent at Arrabida, so gloriously situated on the mountains above the sea that it evoked from him a poem in which he permitted himself the ejaculation 'Happy the dwellers in this holy house!' The Arrabida mountains and his visit to Cintra, where his uncle had a little house among the hills, shut away from sight by lemon trees and laurels, with a little stream singing at its door, woke in Southey all the enthusiasm suitable and customary among romantic English tourists. Cintra had long received English tributes; its lush and cool verdures and grandiose battlements on wild hills that are more like the Lake country than Lisbon is, its dampness, chill and mists after Lisbon summer glare, have always been apt to suggest the garden of Eden to a people well-read in Genesis and *Paradise Lost* but less familiar with Mesopotamian climate and landscape. To Southey it was enchanting — 'the little green lanes over whose bordering lemon gardens the evening wind blows so cool, so rich! ... I shall always love to think of the lonely house, and the stream that runs beside it, whose murmurs were the last sounds I heard at night and the first that woke my attention in the morning.' He was 'informed that Cintra has been celebrated in song by Captain Jeremiah Thompson of the *Polly* schooner', and quotes some of the captain's song from memory, for 'the genuine beauty of its thoughts'.

Oh tell me what Goddess, what Muse, or what Grace
Could ever have formed such a beautiful place?
Here are Flora's best flowers in full bloom, and here is
The work of Vertumnus, Pomona and Ceres.

'Cintra is remarkably damp,' said Southey, 'but I am told the damps are not unwholesome.'

The landscape was sprinkled with the houses of wealthy Lisbonians, British and Portuguese, who spent there as much of the summer as they could. Among these, three miles from Cintra, stood the famous Montserrate, Beckford's magnificent quinta; but he was not there that April. An encounter between these two uncongenials was not to occur; their circles did not touch. It was perhaps a pity. An incongruous pair; the spoiled darling of rich and devout fidalgos and priests, in and out of palaces and churches, and the solemn, gauche, moral and penurious young poet, earnestly intent on his books and the history of Portugal; a conversation between them would have been worth recording. Possibly they would have found a subject in common in the Lisbon English, who bored Southey and would have bored Beckford still more had they given him a chance to be bored. They could have bewailed together the lack of intelligent society in Portugal, one having in mind the British merchants, the other the Portuguese aristocracy.

Southey, as the spring advanced, sighed increasingly for his common and unlettered little bride. 'Heigho! I should be very happy were I now in England with Edith by the fireside.' 'I leave in April,' he wrote, 'and shall cross the seas no more.'

He did leave in April. But with his pleasure a strain of regret mingled. 'I am eager to be again in England, but my heart will be very heavy when I look back upon Lisbon for the last time.' Portugal had laid on him, lightly as yet, and he did not know it, the hand that was to tighten its grasp through his life. Six months later, living with the Avon mud and Bristol smoke for which he had been so homesick in Portugal sunshine, he had occasional hankerings even after Spain, 'for there most pleasant were my wanderings'. And always the sound of a stream singing in a lemon garden by a little lonely house murmured through his dreams.

He did not consciously want Portugal yet. He was settling down to married life in Bristol, writing, reading law, preparing his *Letters from Spain and Portugal* for the press, seeing his friends, patching up his quarrel with Coleridge, beginning, in fact, his life, all eagerness and literary ambition. If his Edith was commonplace and dull, he did not know it yet. An intelligent companion she could not be, but they were in love. Coleridge said of Edith later that she 'loves her husband almost too exclusively, and has a great constancy of affection, such as it is. But she sympathizes with nothing, she enters into none of his peculiar pursuits — she only loves *him*; she is therefore a respectable wife, but not a companion. Dreary, dreary would be the hours passed with her. Amusement, all the detail of whatever cheers or supports the spirits, must be sought elsewhere. Southey finds them in unceasing authorship, never interrupted from morning to night but by sleep and eating.' Coleridge no doubt wrote with feeling, himself suffering under Edith's sister. As Shelley observed, 'Mrs. Southey is very stupid; Mrs. Coleridge worse'.

Edith was not even a merry fool; she was subject to fits of depression, 'miserable depression', which must have made the hours passed with her still drearier. Southey, escaping into 'unceasing authorship', was already on the way, though not yet there, to being a dull young man, so far as any one of his ardent love of literature and imaginative curiosity about a few things could be dull. He dwelt much, like others of his period, in the swooning east; his dreams were peopled with sultans, sultanas, Arabians, magicians, camels, and persons of dark colour and high rank. His uncle at Lisbon wrote of him, during his visit, 'He is a very good scholar, of great reading, of an astonishing memory . . . He is perfectly correct in his behaviour, of the most exemplary morals and the best of hearts . . . To see a young man of such talents as he possesses, by the misapplication of them lost to himself and to his family, is what hurts me sensibly . . . He has everything you could wish a young man to have, excepting common sense or prudence'.

These he gained with years. But Mr. Hill might have added to the exceptions a sense of humour and the power of self-criticism. He laboured among the delusion common among young men that his poetry was immortal. He wrote steadily, industriously and uninspired, and with the firmest conviction of merit. As Byron, many years later, spitefully remarked,

> With eagle pinion soaring to the skies
> Behold the ballad-monger Southey rise!

> To him let Camoens, Milton, Tasso yield,
> Whose annual strains, like armies, take the field ...
> Oh Southey! Southey! cease thy varied song!
> A bard may chant too often and too long.

And later still,

> He'd written much blank verse, and blanker prose,
> And more of both than anybody knows.

This productive career the future laureate steadily pursued, but for a time slightly hampered and interrupted by a little working for the law and by the brief tenure of a secretaryship: neither of these was what he wanted out of life. He wanted to live in the country, preferably by the sea ('my last dip was in the Atlantic Ocean, at the foot of the Arrabida Mountain — a glorious spot. I have no idea of sublimity exceeding it') with Edith and a few friends and his books, and write. By the end of 1799 he began to 'think seriously of going abroad'. He felt ill; he was sick of his legal studies: he was told by 'many medical men' that his complaint was 'wholly a diseased sensibility (mind you, physical sensibility) disordering the functions ... and gradually debilitating me. Climate is the obvious remedy. In my present state, to attempt to undergo the confinement of legal application were actual suicide ... I loathe indolence; but indeed reading law is laborious indolence — it is thrashing straw. I have read and read and read, but the devil a bit can I remember ... Were I an independent man, even on less than I now possess, I should long since have made the blessed bonfire, and rejoiced that I was free and contained'. He felt wretchedly ill; he started from sleep as if death had seized him; he was sensible of every pulsation, and compelled to attend to the motion of his heart. In short, 'I must go abroad, and recruit under better skies. Not to Lisbon: I will see something new, and something better than the Portuguese'.

Having thus induced his body to put up a successful strike, and fortified his strategic position with a posse of obliging medical men, Southey wrote to his uncle Hill, who suggested that he and Edith should come to Portugal. By February, Southey was contemplating this project with delight. 'I have associations with Lisbon that give me a friendship for the place—recollected feelings and hopes, pleasures and anxieties, all now mellowed into remembrances that endear the associated scenes.' He was already working on the history of Portugal which he planned writing, and which was going to be so superb; he longed to visit the field of Ourique, the banks of the Mondego, the grave of Inez. He would 'disturb the spiders of the Necessidades, and leave no convent library unransacked'. Already he felt quite well again, and full of energy and eagerness. His History would be tremendous — 'a long and arduous and interesting undertaking, which I think I can do as it ought to be done'. He hoped, too, to review Spanish and Portuguese books for the *Critical Review*. Not an hour in Portugal would be wasted. 'In Portugal,' he wrote to Coleridge, 'I shall have but little society: with the English there I have no common feeling . . . My uncle has a good library, and I shall not find retirement irksome. Our summer will probably be passed at Cintra.' With emotion he recalled the brook which ran by his uncle's door among the lemon groves. 'I never beheld a spot that invited to so deep tranquillity.' He would work, travel about, perhaps write another volume about his journeys. Edith (as might be imagined) did not care for the expedition; she wanted, but could not have, a female companion. But 'there is at Lisbon a lady of her own age for whom I have a considerable regard', and who (whatever she might feel about Edith) would not be sorry to see again an acquaintance with more brains than most of her circle in Lisbon. This young lady would be their neighbour. His uncle had taken a house for them, near his own. Finally, a plea of ill health would protect him from cards, company and bull-runs.

So, at the end of April, after a five days' voyage of sea-sickness and scares (in which Edith showed herself a sad coward) Southey had his heart's desire, and sailed up the Tagus, beholding once more the incomparable spectacle of the beautiful city on its banks. It seemed to him the most wonderful sight in the world, 'in beauty and richness and grandeur. Convents and quintas, gray olive-yards, green orange-groves, and greener vineyards . . . the river, bright as the blue sky which illuminated it, swarming with boats of every size and shape . . . innumerable ships riding at anchor as far as eye could reach: and the city extending along the shore and covering the hills to the farthest point of sight'.

He felt he had come home: 'four years absence from Lisbon,' he wrote to Coleridge, 'has given everything the varnish of novelty, and this, with the revival of old associations, makes me pleased with everything. It even amused me to renew my acquaintance with the fleas. To-day is a busy day; we are arranging away our things and seeing visitors: these visits must all be returned; there ends the ceremony, and then I may choose retirement. I hurry over my letters for the sake of feeling at leisure to begin my employments ... The work before me is almost of terrifying labour; folio after folio to be gutted ... but I have leisure and inclination ... My uncle's library is admirably stocked with foreign books'. He describes his plan for the history, which 'will be a great work, and worthy of all labour'.

Their little house, 'very small and thoroughly Portuguese, little rooms all doors and windows' was on the hill of Buenos Ayres, and looked over the Tagus — 'a magnificent scene'. He sat and wrote at a window commanding a superb view of the river and of Almada beyond it, all lying in the luxuriant light of a southern sun. He was very happy.

Edith, however, though she too looked out of the windows, did not remark the view, only the people in the streets. 'Edith,' her husband wrote to Coleridge, 'who has been looking half her time out of the window, has just seen "really a decent-looking woman"; this will show you what cattle the passers-by must be'. It seems rather to show what kind of cattle Edith was. For Lisbon, Portugal and views she cared nothing; but she did enjoy (like the natives of the country to which she had come) looking at people and finding fault with their appearance. 'Their heavy coats of thick woollen amuse her in this weather, as much as her clear muslin. would amuse them in an English winter.' In fact, the attitude was very similar. As Southey expressed it in verse to Cottle,

> My Edith here
> Thinks all things queer,
> And some things she likes well;
> But then the street
> She thinks not neat,
> And does not like the smell.
> Nor do the fleas
> Her fancy please,
> Although the fleas like her ...

Edith was only reconciled to Lisbon by green peas and fruit, and perhaps by the callers who were regarded by Southey as the fleas which infest newcomers. 'God,' he had once said, 'never intended that I should make myself agreeable to anybody', and he had no intention of interrupting his important labours to frustrate the divine intention for him. As to Edith, it was improbable that Lisbon society would find her particularly amusing.

As it happened, Lisbon at the turn of the century, and up to the French occupation which drove the English out, had reached its height as a resort of the English *beau monde*. What with the army, the navy, fashionable invalids who declined and expired on the heights of Buenos Ayres and were interred beneath the Estrella cypresses, the smart rich who had followed in the wake of the Dukes of Sussex and Kent, danced and played high every night and wagered on Bonaparte's next move, the more intellectual set which gathered round the British embassy (where John Hookham Frere, with his brother Bartle as Secretary of Legation, succeeded Walpole in 1800) and included as occasional visitors Lord and Lady Holland, Sir Robert Ainslie, and the brilliant Countess of Errol, Frere's future wife, no one could have described English society in Lisbon as dull. The fashionable English consorted mainly with one another, since foreigners mostly bored them (particularly the French émigrés, poor souls, who, however agreeable in themselves, never had any money and always wanted to borrow some). They combined enjoyment of Portuguese pleasures with that intelligent commentary and intercourse which they believed to be mainly found among their own compatriots, and certainly not among the Portuguese. They attended the court at Queluz, they visited the fine quintas of the aristocracy, they made expeditions up the Tagus, to Santarem, Setubal, Palmella, Alcobaça, Batalha and Coimbra, and, of course, stayed at their beloved Cintra. They amused themselves enormously, enjoying even the discomforts of travel. 'So Bartle is going to Batalha too,' Lady Erroll wrote to Frere years later, 'where I was once so gay and so happy, in fact enjoyed it all, and above all the horrible inconveniences we found in our journey, the swearing of General Wemyss, all the Portuguese women sleeping upon the floor without nightcaps in one room, Mrs. Douglas with my monkey and her own, all the men going to her carriage for brandy, she scolding and cursing all the Portuguese. I assure you it was very amusing altogether.' In short, the English formed that gay, luxurious, enjoying, derisive and self-sufficient clique that the

English upper classes contrive to form wherever they sojourn. Not a clique to which the Southeys, or the Reverend Mr. Hill, or most of the English Factory, were likely to belong. In fact, Southey had a tart comment on the ambassador's social proclivities:

'Frere is acting foolishly: he and the consul are slighting the English merchants, and establishing a little aristocracy with the quality-strangers, emigrants, and corps diplomatic. This is very absurd, as it is their policy to hold their countrymen in as high a situation as possible.' Again, 'The Walpoles are regretted. Their *lieutenants* live too much with the emigrants, and observe too rude a retirement towards the English.'

Towards the resident English colony, he no doubt meant, not the gay birds of passage who winged to Portugal to escape the English winter. The earnest historian of Portugal saw little of these bright and bustling beings, nor, probably, did he wish to see more. As to the Factory, he avoided their distractions as best he could, though sometimes he took Edith to 'a great mob — commonly called a private assembly — and she liked them well enough to stay cruelly late'. But 'we live mostly to ourselves, seeing something of everybody, much of no one except my uncle'. They did not even see much of the Hares, acquaintances with whom they had expected to pass much time; it seemed that the Hares lived in a social whirl, and had little time for the Southeys. Many former acquaintances were now in the burying-ground. However, plenty remained; the American ambassador called after supper ('this was somewhat familiar, and I apprehend was meant as civility') and lady friends invited the Southeys to their houses to see processions. These fascinated and shocked Southey almost as much as they had George Whitefield fifty years before. The Corpus Christi procession, which he watched from the window of a Miss Stevens, seemed to him particularly unseemly and foolish. He talked with a lady who remembered the *autos-da-fé*, remarking to her what a dreadful day it must have been for the English when one of these infernal executions took place. 'No,' she replied, 'not at all; it was like the processions, expected as a fine sight, and the English whose houses overlooked the streets through which they passed kept open house as now, and made entertainments.' Southey thought they should, for the honour of their country, have shut up their houses and expressed silent abhorrence. Were such things to happen now, he would shake the dust of Lisbon from his feet, curse the city, and leave it for ever.

He nearly did as much after seeing a bull-feast, where he saw nine bulls killed, while the spectators, men, women and children, clapped at every wound and watched the dying struggles with delight. 'It is a damnable sport! and much to the honour of the English here, they all dislike it', and seldom see it twice.

So May and June passed, in the burning summer heat and dust, alleviated for the Southeys by their airy house and the evening breezes from the Tagus and the orgy of fruit they enjoyed. The perpetual noise got on their nerves; there seemed always to be cannonading, fireworks, goat bells, mule bells, church bells. Near them a Portuguese merchant had a house with a private chapel, whose bells annoyed all the English in Buenos Ayres. The English hotel, full of declining invalids, had requested this gentleman in vain to moderate his belling; he only replied that he had got leave to ring and should do so. Southey looked forward to Cintra, to which they would repair at the end of June, having stayed in Lisbon for the Corpus Christi procession. Unfortunately the Portuguese merchants, growing richer, were discovering Cintra and buying up the houses, 'so that they will one day dispossess the English, and this I do not like. Cintra is too good a place for the Portuguese. It is only fit for us Goths — for Germans or English'.

To this Gothic paradise they repaired at last, and Southey heard once more the brook that murmured among the lemon groves and breathed that cool and scented air. He and Edith were alone, for Mr. Hill was detained in Lisbon, baptizing and burying the infants of the English army, who appeared and disappeared with troublesome frequency. Southey was extremely happy. When not exploring the country on donkeys, he was busy every hour with his history, with *Thalaba*, and with plans for new works of genius. As he explained to his friend Wynn, 'One overwhelming propensity has formed all my destiny, and marred all prospects of rank or wealth; but it has made me happy, and will make me immortal'. His thoughts still played round the east. 'I have some distant view of manufacturing a Hindoo romance, wild as Thalaba, and a nearer one of a Persian story.' He wanted someone to talk to about all this; it is improbable that Edith listened much, or that her comments were apt. He also felt a craving, to which he perpetually recurs in his letters from Cintra, for English bread and butter; it would seem that the Cintra butter was not good; perhaps the wealthy English and Portuguese merchants bought up the fresh butter, or perhaps it all went to market. Anyhow, 'I long to see the face of a friend, and hunger after the bread and butter comforts and green fields of England'. Yet he felt so strongly the benefits of the climate that he wished his lot had been cast in the south. Cintra was the most beautiful spot he had ever seen or imagined; he rode a jackass, with a boy to beat it. 'I eat oranges, figs, and delicious pears, drink Colares wine, a sort of half-way excellence between port and claret, dream of poem after poem and play after play, take a siesta of two hours, and am as happy as if life were but one everlasting to-day, and to-morrow not to be provided for.'

They rode their asses about the country with 'a Miss Barker, brimful of everything that was good', who was staying at Cintra. With Miss Barker and some cold beef they took happy rambles on their animals for hours on end. Miss Barker's departure for England quite saddened Southey; she was obviously a good companion. He wrote to Cottle of 'the unforeseen and unlucky departure of my only friend. She is a woman of uncommon talents, with whom we have been wandering over these magnificent mountains, till she made the greatest enjoyment of the place. I feel a heavier depression of spirits at losing her than I have known since Tom left me at Liskard . . . I long to be among you. If I could bring this climate to Bristol, it would make me a new being: but I am in utter solitude of all rational society: in a state of mental famine, save that I feed on rocks and woods, and the richest banquet nature can possibly offer to her worshippers'. He was also finishing the eleventh book of Thalaba.

Miss Barker's departure and his mental famine set him hankering again after 'fresh butter and genial society', which two things would make Cintra an earthly paradise. Most of the Cintra society would not make it this at all. Even those of them who were Goths were also bores. Fortunately the Southeys were far from the town, so did not meet many of them. 'Half a mile up and down half a dozen stony hills in hot weather operates well upon people who do not half like me and whom I do not like at all.' As for the natives, for whom Cintra was too good, the richest of the

Portuguese Lisbon merchants came down to Cintra one day with a number of friends to a hotel; they played cards from breakfast to supper for a fortnight, then returned to Lisbon; the host's tavern bill was over £200. No doubt he and his friends enjoyed themselves very much, and got nicely rested in the cool atmosphere before returning to their hot and dusty businesses. But Southey was annoyed with them because they had neither gone expeditions nor read books. 'Read they will not. Indeed, if they would, they have scarcely a book in their own language fit to be read. I would our novel-mongers ... were transported here, and ordered to manufacture trash for the Portuguese. Anything that would teach them to read!' The Academy, he complained bitterly, had not even been able to get beyond A in the huge dictionary it had begun six years ago. People usually fell asleep directly they ceased from physical action, and so deeply that they could scarcely be awakened. This agreeable and sensible habit seemed to Southey deplorable. It is obvious that he was feeling increasingly starved of intelligent and conversable company, as well as of butter. 'Of course,' he wrote to his mother, 'I go among these people no oftener than absolute decorum requires ... I want Danvers here, and Davy, and Rickman, and Cottle, and you, and some fresh butter, and the newspaper: howbeit, I am very comfortable and very lazy.' There were melons and grapes — 'Oh what grapes! Our desserts are magnificent ... I wish I could settle here; the climate suits me so well that I could give up society, and live like a bear by sucking my own paws.'

There is noticeably no hint that the bear's mate could supply any spiritual or mental need. Indeed, this close confinement alone with his beloved Edith was producing some interesting results. One of these was intense and growing irritation with the Portuguese, who, in his view, would not read, who had no mental life, who spent their time in indolence gazing out of their windows, and with the English, with whom he had no interests in common. This image of the Portuguese and of the Lisbon English *en bloc* took ever firmer hold of his chafing mind, as he passed his days with his window-gazing, vacant-minded wife, who was always going to bed for a siesta, and who, even when awake and active, had no conversation worth calling so. Had he been John Milton, he would have written pamphlets about the intolerableness of living with a wife with 'a mind to all other than bodily conversation inaccessible, and to all the more estimable purposes of matrimony useless and almost lifeless', and perhaps tried to get a divorce and marry Miss Barker. Had he been Coleridge, he would, more simply and with less fuss, have left her. Coleridge, married to a similar Miss Fricker, did so. Being Robert Southey, a young man of a good heart and loyal affections, who was devoted to his Edith throughout their married life, he took it out of, so to speak, her reflection in the tiresome people round him, whom he moulded ever more into her image.

'Like beasts and savages', he wrote impatiently to John Rickman, 'these people can bear total indolence. Their delight is to look into the street, put somebody to hunt their heads at the same time, and it is happiness! Even in their garden walls they have grates to look into the road. I lack society sadly. The people here know much of their own business, very little of the country they live in, and nothing of anything else except cards. My uncle indeed is a man of extensive knowledge; and here is one family of whom the master is a man of some science, and to whom I can open my floodgates. I want you and Davy and a newspaper and bread and butter, and a green field for me and the horse . . . But I have ample and pleasant employment: curiosity forever on the hunt — a situation the most beautiful that I have ever seen, and a climate for which Nature seems to have destined me, only, blessed be God, she dropt me the other side of the bay.'

He returns again and again to the lack of intelligent society. 'The wealthier English are all here; still, however, I lack society, and were it not for a self-sufficiency (like the bear when the snow shuts him up in his den) should be in a state of mental famine. My uncle is little here; people will die, and must be buried . . . The English here know very little of the country they live in, and nothing of the literature. Of Camoens they have heard, and only of Camoens. By the help of my uncle I have acquired an extensive knowledge, and am almost as well acquainted with Portuguese literature as with that of my own country. It is not worth much . . .' He described the scenery, adding that it wanted only society to become a paradise. 'Could I but colonize Cintra with half a dozen familiars, I should wish never to leave it. As it is, I am comfortable, my health establishing itself, my spirits everlastingly partaking the sunshine of the climate; yet I *do* hunger after the bread and butter, and the fireside comforts, and the intellect of England.' Literature, he added, was almost dead in Portugal, though 'bad poetry I find in abundance'.

A psychologist might read into these letters a state of mental and domestic tension, and even connect the repeated insistence on butter with the need of some emollient for jangled nerves; though as to that, it seems simpler to conclude that he was fond of butter.

He was a sensitive creature: blind though he was to much of the beauty of art (Italian opera seemed to him 'only high treason against common sense', and 'very absurd', and he quite missed the element of beauty in the gaudy religious processions and the corrupt monastic clericalism that he so detested, and that so intrigued Beckford) he was acutely sensible of the beauty of nature, and his descriptions of the hills and woods of Cintra, the flowers, trees, fireflies, the shapes and colour of the mountains, are not only enthusiastic but sharply perceptive. In natural beauty he was an artist, sensuous and alive. His sense of beauty, defective in art, uneven in literature, here found full scope. When he brought it to bear on his own work, it lit it meretriciously, and about Thalaba and his history of Portugal he had nothing but good to say. He found Thalaba fit to take its place with Samson Agonistes and Ariosto — 'perhaps, were I to speak out, I should not dread a trial with Ariosto. My proportion of ore to dross is greater'. As to his history of Portugal, 'You will find my style plain as a Doric building, and, I trust, of eternal durability. I have no doubt of making a work by which I shall be honourably remembered'. In his application to these immortal works, and his delighted ramblings about the exquisite land, he found his refuge and content.

The Southeys returned to Lisbon from Cintra in the autumn. There was yellow fever in Spain, and Edith, alarmed, was for leaving the peninsula for England. But Southey would have none of this, nor would he take alarm at the prospect of a French invasion. He would not return until the year's tenure of his house was run out. He was happy in Lisbon, collecting materials for his history and making excursions. They went an expedition, with friends, to Coimbra, Alcobaça, Batalha. 'I shall laugh', he wrote to his mother, 'to see Edith among the dirt and fleas, who I suspect will be more amused with her than she will with them.' But Edith came out of it better than might have been expected.

They visited the tomb of Inez, and Southey recalled the famous passage by Camoens on this subject — 'it is very bad, and therefore very much admired by all poetry-dabblers, being a complete specimen of fake taste . . . I, who have long planned a tragedy upon the subject, stand upon my own scene'. It is needless to say that the hackneyed and conventional subject deeply stirred his imagination. At Coimbra the students followed the English party about in mobs, with impudent jeers, as was their custom. Southey would have liked to knock them down, but abstained. With four ladies in the party, nothing else but such jeering curiosity was to be expected — 'we were everywhere the sight of the neighbourhood'. The party consisted of eight, and it was an inconvenient size, as the rooms available at the inns were seldom more than two. Edith bore the hardships of travel well, though she objected when her mule rolled with her, which it did three times, 'to our merriment. She did not like it'.

They returned to Lisbon to find the international situation discouraging: the English expected to be expelled any time, to appease the French, and Mr. Hill was packing his books. Southey did not at all want to leave. He made another tour, this time through the Algarve, and without Edith. He wrote in May that he would like another six months, and to visit the north; but Edith wanted to get back, and indeed, the situation seemed unfavourable for staying. Mr. Hill, just returned after a visit to England, thought more of his nephew than before, after hearing of his reputation in his own country. 'He was not perhaps aware of the literary rank which I hold in the world, till he there learnt it.' An exemplary uncle, he was now helpful in every way, and particularly encouraging to the history of Portugal. Had it not been for Edith, Southey would have risked the war and the French and the expulsion of the English, and stayed on to explore the north, the most beautiful part of Portugal. He was ever more deeply in love with the country, its beauty, its climate, its peasantry, who, sunk in superstition though they might be, were (unlike the urban classes) fine, hard-working, handsome and admirable people. He had 'no pleasant anticipation of English taxes, English climate and small beer, after this blessed sun and the wines of Portugal'. And, to Coleridge, 'I would gladly live and die here. Our unkindly climate will blight me, as it does the myrtle and oranges of this better land'. He has formed strong local, though not personal, attachments, and is in love with the mountains, the glorious river, the sun, the summer paradise of Cintra. He must, he says, return one day, and wants Coleridge to return with him. 'One head full of brains, and I should ask England nothing else.' Not even butter. But, threatened with invasion and expulsion, he must leave this paradise. So had Portugal become metamorphosed to him since that first visit when he had found it difficult to write letters home because 'it is not pleasant to reiterate terms of abuse'. The repentant lover was now to be exiled from paradise, and it assumed for him, and was to wear throughout his life, the more than earthly hues of an enchanted land. To come back to it was for long his supreme aim. Coleridge and he, at Cintra, would tire the sun with talking and send him down the sky; they would, presumably, have the tiresome Fricker women with them, to see to the housekeeping, go to bed with, and provide a little female relaxation, but for society they would be sufficient to one another; and what works they would produce! Southey had almost forgotten his life at Bristol with Coleridge; he did not now envisage how his friend would certainly leave him to pay all bills, would burn holes in his uncle's sheets at Cintra, would perhaps propose himself to give lectures on philosophy at Coimbra and would not turn up.

But it was not to be. Southey and Edith returned to England in June, 1801, leaving Mr. Hill still packing his books and doubtful whether to stay or go.

Southey was never to see Portugal again. He pulled all possible strings to get a job there; his ambition was the Lisbon consulship, over which so many eager and quarrelsome rivals had fought for two centuries; he would have been a poor consul, with his total lack of interest in the merchants and their concerns and his enthusiasm for passing the summer at Cintra and trapesing about the country on a mule, but he did not think about that; he would be in Portugal under the blessed sun, drinking the blessed wine, rooting among libraries for materials for his history, and that was all he wanted. Wisely, he was never offered this post. He visited Keswick, and found the climate deplorably damp and chilly, while for beauty all English scenery must yield to Cintra. 'These lakes are like rivers; but oh for the Mondego and the Tagus! And these mountains, beautifully indeed are they shaped and grouped; but oh for the great Montchique! and for Cintra, my paradise! —

the heaven on earth of my hopes; and if ever I should have a house at Cintra, as in earnest sincerity I do hope I shall, will not you give me one twelvemonth, and eat grapes, and ride donkeys, and be very happy? In truth, Grosvenor, I have lived abroad too long to be contented in England: I miss southern luxuries — the fruits, the wines; I miss the sun in heaven, having been upon a short allowance of sunbeams these last ten days ... My dreams incline to Lisbon as a resting-place; I am really attached to the country, and, odd as it may seem, to the people. In Lisbon they are, like all metropolitans, roguish enough, but in the country I have found them hospitable, even to kindness, when I was a stranger and in want. The consulship at Lisbon would, of all possible situations, best delight me ... 'tis a good thousand a year.'

He could do nothing about it. He had to resign himself to exile, and to the English climate, which he found very grim. 'What an effect must these vile dark rainy clouds have upon a poor nervous fellow whose brain has been in a state of high illumination for the last fifteen months!' He was at first doubtful of Coleridge's proposal that he should live at Keswick, with its 'horrid latitude and incessant rains'. Gradually he learned to endure the latitude and rains for the sake of the beauty of mountains and lakes. But he still longed to exchange it for Portugal. 'Society, connections, native language — all these are weighty things; but what are they to the permanent and perpetual exhilaration of a climate that not merely prolongs life, but gives you double the life while it lasts? I have actually felt a positive pleasure in breathing there; and even here, in this magnificent spot, the recollection of the Tagus, and the Serra de Ossa, of Coimbra, and its cypresses and orange groves and olives, its hills and mountains, its venerable buildings, and its dear river, of the Vale of Algarve, the little islands of beauty amid the desert of Alemtejo, and, above all, of Cintra, the most blessed spot in the habitable globe, will almost bring tears into my eyes.'

Thirty years later he was still hankering. 'If I had Aladdin's lamp, the genius should transport me, my household and my books to Cintra.' But he had no Aladdin's lamp; in vain he sought after the consulship, an embassy secretaryship, some civil employment in Wellington's army, anything. He had to fall back on writing his History, never to be finished or published, and on making himself the interpreter of Portuguese literature to his countrymen. He was not a great interpreter, or even a good critic, but he was an eager and assiduous translator, and, it has been said, more than any other one man, made Portugal an English literary fashion, as it had for a century been a resort for English tourists and invalids. He was made a member of the Lisbon Academy; he boasted more than once that he knew more of Portuguese literature and history than any other foreigner, and than nearly all the Portuguese themselves. He could ill endure rivals; Lord Strangford's translation of Camoens's lyrics into Moore-like quatrains drew from him angry (but just) condemnation, and he did not approve of any would-be lusophile experts among his contemporaries. He himself worked diligently away, guiding the tide of romantic lusophilism that had for some years been rising in England and was to ebb before the middle of the century. There was undoubtedly a note sentimentally unrobust in the gush of Cintra-worship, Inez-worship, Camoens-worship, that flowed at this time; possibly it was the consumptive note. Southey gave it his sane and pedestrian solidity.

He worked intermittently at the History of Portugal which was to endure for ever. The only part of it which ever appeared was the history of Brazil, published in 1817. Alas, it bore every mark of the indigestion of those who have grappled to themselves the Portuguese chroniclers without proportion or selection. It was savagely attacked in *Blackwood's* as the most indigestible book of our days. Every little colonel, captain, bishop or monk discussed it as if he were a Cromwell or a Loyola, and all because Mr. Southey had a good Portuguese library and must show off his knowledge of Portuguese.

It was not the kind of reception to encourage Southey to persevere with his life-work. But he did persevere, whenever his more urgent employments left him time. In 1832 he was still hopefully writing at it and rejoicing in its merits. 'I believe no history has ever yet been composed that presents such a continuous interest of one kind or another as this would do, if I should live to complete it. The chivalrous portion is of the very highest beauty; much of what succeeds has a deep tragic interest; and then comes the gradual destruction of a noble national character brought on by the cancer of Romish superstition.' He lived until 1843, but not to complete the work at which he had been labouring for forty-three years. To-day it seems that no one knows where it is. It was perhaps happier for its author that it was not published while he lived. Most critics would doubtless have complained (and complained angrily and rudely, in that savage age) that the work was ill-digested, voluminous, showing off. It would now be more kindly received. Should it ever turn up, and should there ever be a very great quantity of paper, perhaps someone will publish it. Or perhaps not.

Going to Portugal had given Southey an ardent enthusiasm, a life-long interest and occupation, and no great achievement or reward but these. Unless we are to count an exquisitely happy year, heightened sensibilities, a gauge by which to measure British weather and landscape, and a nostalgic dream of a little stream singing among lemon-groves outside a house on a hill-side.

BIBLIOGRAPHY

Letters from Spain and Portugal, ROBERT SOUTHEY (1797).
Life and Correspondence of Robert Southey, C. C. SOUTHEY (1849).
Selections from letters of Southey, J. W. WARTER (1856).
Early life of Robert Southey, W. HALLER (1917).
Reminiscences of Coleridge and Southey, JOSEPH COTTLE (1847).
Southey, JACK SIMMONS (1945).
La Littérature Portugaise en Angleterre à l'époque romantique, FÉLIX WALTER (1927).
John Hookham Frere and his friends, GABRIELLE FESTING (1899).
Recollections of an Excursion to Alcobaça and Batalha, WILLIAM BECKFORD (1835).
Blackwood's Magazine (1817).

8. THE REGRETTABLE DISCOVERY
Lord Byron
[July 1809]

BYRON made what has been called by a Frenchman 'sa regrettable découverte du Portugal' on his way to Greece in 1809. He was twenty-one, and had left Cambridge last year. The Portugal trip was a casual decision. 'The Malta vessel not sailing for some weeks', he wrote, 'we have determined to go by sea by way of Lisbon, and, as my servants term it, to see "that there Portingale" — thence to Cadiz and Gibraltar, and so on our old route to Malta and Constantinople.' So the end of June found him and his Cambridge friend John Hobhouse at Falmouth, waiting for the Lisbon packet. With Byron were three or four servants — his valet, Fletcher, faithful and ill-humoured, his old butler, Murray, one Bob Rushton, and a nameless German. The last three accompanied him only to Gibraltar. It was not a retinue on the scale of Beckford's, but must all the same have made travelling expensive. Hobhouse intended a book describing their travels; actually he omitted the Peninsula and began with Albania; his only account of the Portuguese tour is to be found in the diary in his *Recollections*. And there is nothing in that to explain Byron's anger with the inhabitants of Portugal *en masse*.

Of this anger, patriotic and indignant Portuguese have put forward one explanation — a legend of unknown origin and no traceable authenticity — and impartial Frenchmen another, and the affair remains a mystery. On the side of the legend, it has to be kept in mind that, though Byron had a ready supply of venom, he usually only discharged it when his vanity or jealousy was touched. But there is no indication of offence in his only extant letter from Lisbon (written the day before he had planned to leave it), or in his letter from Gibraltar to his mother, with its brief account of Lisbon, Cintra and Mafra, or in Hobhouse's more sober diary of sight-seeing. To be sure, Hobhouse reports a rough passage (he makes it twelve days, Byron four and a half; Hobhouse is obviously wrong about the date of leaving Falmouth); says they were charged at their Buenos Ayres hotel 13 per cent on the exchange of their money, mentions many street murders, and found the theatres 'much addicted to Iberian dances of a lascivious character', which must have been distressing to the young gentlemen. He makes the usual British complaints — the monks know no Latin (Byron found they did, but it was perhaps too barbarous for Hobhouse to understand), their manners displayed levity, particularly with regard to women, there are too many of them, about 50,000 in Lisbon, the convents are supported by begging, the people still in bondage to an ignorant and tyrannical priesthood, the Inquisition still arresting its victims, there is no justice, all is done by bribery, still too many murders and dogs, in spite of ten thousand of the latter having been killed by the French. He has a note on Junot, who 'seems to have been much liked in Lisbon', and had kept a liberal table that cost him from £170 to £200 a day; when he left Lisbon, the citizens took to murdering the French left behind. Hobhouse says he and

Byron went to Cintra on July 12th, and left Lisbon for the Spanish frontier on the 21st.

There seems nothing here for tears. Still less in Byron's letter to Francis Hodgson, dated Lisbon, July 16th, presumably after their return there from Cintra. It is good-humoured, nonsensical, and not in the least anti-Portuguese.

'Thus far have we pursued our route, and seen all sorts of marvellous sights, palaces, convents, etc. — which, being to be heard in my friend Hobhouse's Book of Travels, I shall not anticipate by smuggling any account whatsoever to you in a private and clandestine manner. I must just observe that the village of Cintra in Estramadura is the most beautiful, perhaps, in the world.

'I am very happy here, because I loves oranges, and talks bad Latin to the monks' (this apparently was at the Mafra convent) 'who understand it, as it is like their own, and I goes into society (with my pocket pistols) and I swims in the Tagus all across at once, and I rides on an ass or a mule, and swears Portuguese, and have got a diarrhoea and bites from the mosquitoes. But what of that? Comfort must not be expected by folks that go a-pleasuring.

'When the Portuguese are pertinacious, I say *Carracho!* — the great oath of the grandees, that very well supplies the place of "Damme" — and when dissatisfied with a neighbour I pronounce him *Ambra di merdo*. With these two phrases, and with a third, *Avra Bouro*, which signifieth "Get an ass", I am universally understood to be a person of degree and a master of languages.' (All his Portuguese is, of course, quite wrong.) 'How merrily we live that travellers be! if we had food and raiment. But, in sober sadness, anything is better than England, and I am infinitely amused with my pilgrimage as far as it has gone. To-morrow we start to ride near 400 miles as far as Gibraltar, where we embark for Melita and Byzantium.'

So far, apparently, so good. Unless this gay letter was bravado, Byron felt at peace with Portugal on the day before he meant to leave it. Hobhouse, however, gives the 21st as the day of departure; did they change their plans and spend four days more in Portugal? And, during those days, did anything occur to enrage Byron against its inhabitants? The legend, repeated by Herculano, Alberto Telles, João de Lemos, Dalgado and others (wherever they got it from) is that he was struck outside the S. Carlos theatre by an angry husband for making advances to his wife, and never forgave Portugal. It seems improbable: there is no evidence for it, and, even if it occurred, it is the kind of incident that might occur anywhere, and is too slight a basis for the grand edifice of hate that Byron reared. Was his excessive Lusophobia born on the long and no doubt comfortless ride from Lisbon to the frontier? We know little of this ride from Byron or Hobhouse; except that they bathed in the stream dividing Portugal from Spain. Local tradition at Estremoz says that they spent a night there, and points to the pond in a quinta outside the Portalegre gate where Byron had another bathe. He wrote to his mother from Gibraltar that he had had an excellent journey through Spain, 'orders from the government, and every possible accommodation on the road, as an English nobleman, in English uniform, is a very respectable personage in Spain at present'. The Spanish ladies too had been forthcoming and lovely: in short, 'I like the Spaniards much'. (It was the fashion in England just then to like our Spanish allies.)

Nothing about Portuguese accommodation, which was certainly bad, or orders from the Portuguese government, which was suspicious and anglophobe, or Portuguese respect for an English nobleman, or kindness from Portuguese senhoras; they possibly tittered and stared at his club foot. The feeling between the two allies was no better than feeling between allies may be expected to be; the British felt that the Portuguese had let them down by not resisting Junot; the Portuguese were not at all confident that the British were not about to betray and abandon them. In any case, even now that '*os inglezes vindicarem dos francezes o trono de Beresford I°, occupado pelo usurpador Junot I°*' (the English had conquered from the French the throne of Beresford the First, occupied by the usurper Junot the First) the situation was not soothing to Portuguese pride. All the voluminous outpourings of the British officers stationed, to their disgust, in Portugal about this time show extremely imperfect sympathies on both sides. Byron was in Portugal at a bad moment; in spite of the oranges and Cintra and swimming across the Tagus, he conceived for the Portuguese one of his black rages, and spat at them in *Childe Harold* (and elsewhere) malevolent, contemptuous sneers. They were a nation swollen with ignorance and pride, who lick yet loathe the hand that waves the sword; they were dirty, both high and low, both palaces and huts; they were poor paltry creatures, unworthy of the beauties of their land; they were Lusian slaves, the lowest of the low, on whom the Spanish hind looked with scorn. When it was suggested that he should modify some of this, he wrote in a note, 'As I have found the Portuguese, so I have written of them'. He did, however, modify a few lines, substituting in stanza XV 'Gaul's locust host' for 'the Lusian brutes' as suitable subjects for the Almighty's purge, thus writing in a more seemly manner both of our foes and of our allies. But his notes on this canto of *Childe Harold*, some of which were suppressed, outdo the stanzas in venom. He mentions in stanza XXI some crosses on the paths up the Cintra mountains, alleging them to be memorials of assassinations committed all the way up; a Portuguese writer has pointed out that they were nothing of the kind, but erected to appeal to the wayfarers' feelings of piety. In a note Byron says it was a well-known fact that in the year 1809 Englishmen were daily butchered in Lisbon and its vicinity and the murderers got off scot free. According to Wellington and others, many of the British, and particularly the Irish, soldiery deserved what they got; long used to wandering about the Peninsula after capture by the French and before rejoining their own army, they had developed a habit of living on plunder and violence, were as likely to start a quarrel as to be victims, and to knock a Portuguese on the head as to get their own throats cut. Byron, outraged by himself having been held up one evening in the streets of Lisbon, was outrageously biased. It must be admitted that most English travellers just then were.

They were also for the most part (with the honourable exception of young Captain Moyle Sherer) in agreement with him about Lisbon, which they found beautiful from far but dirty near, forgetting that London too was nothing to boast of in the way of cleanliness.

> But whoso entereth within this town
> That, sheening far, celestial seems to be,
> Disconsolate will wander up and down,
> Mid many things unsightly to strange ee;
> For hut and palace show like filthily,
> The dingy denizens are rear'd in dirt. . . .

About Cintra too they were of a mind; Byron fell in love with it, and so did his countrymen. (Time has avenged Lisbon: to-day it is that fascinating city with which we fall in love, surveying Cintra's more obvious rural beauties with calmer eyes.) Byron was the originator of the improbable phrase 'glorious Eden', that has clung to this beauty-spot ever since; though indeed Southey had called it a paradise years before, and Gil Vicente, in 1529, 'um jardin do paraiso terreal'. Too good for anyone but Goths, Southey had said; and Byron 'Why, Nature, waste thy wonders on such men?' The English could not admit that the Portuguese had a right to their own fine scenery.

Byron and Hobhouse spent a few days there, staying at what later became Lawrence's hotel; Mrs. Dyson, the landlady, years later showed the poet's bedroom, a large room with three windows and a fine view. A bust of him had been put up in the room, and tradition had it that an American tourist had bought and taken away a window-pane on which he had scratched his name with a diamond ring. He deserved this notoriety in Cintra, for he wrote of its scenery with unstinted applause, though unfair about the Convention, which was prepared and signed at Torres Vedras many miles away. In his Gibraltar letter to his mother he expatiated on Cintra's beauties: 'Except the view from the Tagus, which is beautiful, and some fine churches and convents, Lisbon contains little but filthy streets and more filthy inhabitants. To make amends for this, the village of Cintra, about fifteen miles from the capital, is, perhaps in every respect, the most delightful in Europe: it contains beauties of every description natural and artificial. Palaces and gardens rising in the midst of rocks, cataracts and precipices; convents on stupendous heights — a distant view of the sea and the Tagus; and besides (though that is a secondary consideration) is remarkable as the scene of Sir Hew Dalrymple's Convention. It unites in itself all the wildness of the Western Highlands with the verdure of the south of France. Near this place, about ten miles to the right, is the palace of Mafra, the boast of Portugal, as it might be of any other country, in point of magnificence without elegance. There is a convent annexed; the monks, who possess large revenues, are courteous enough, and understand Latin, so that we had a long conversation; they have a large library, and asked me if the *English* had *any books* in their country?'

The young men rambled about, climbed up to the Cork Convent and Nossa Senhora da Pena (which he took to mean

Our Lady of Pain), and apostrophized the quinta of Montserrate, now fallen into ruin, and its one-time tenant William Beckford, also regarded by Byron as fallen into ruin, in two impudent stanzas, and a third, suppressed in the printed edition and more impudent still. Byron, always inclined to damn the sins he (possibly) had no mind to, and to moralize over ostracized men of genius, admired Beckford's gifts excessively, but deplored his habits. The suppressed stanza (published later by itself, but scarcely worth it), ran, priggishly,

> Unhappy Dives! in an evil hour
> 'Gainst Nature's voice seduced to deeds accurst!
> Once Fortune's minion, now thou feel'st her power;
> Wrath's vial on thy lofty head hath burst;
> In Wit, in Genius, as in Wealth the first,
> How wondrous bright thy blooming morn arose!
> But thou were smitten with th' unhallow'd thirst
> Of Crime unnamed, and thy sad noon must close
> In scorn and solitude unsought, the worst of woes.

Thinking this might annoy Beckford, he omitted it from *Childe Harold*, and slightly altered the last line of stanza XXII, leaving out 'pollution's lure', but leaving in the next stanza the lines

> But now, as if a thing unblest by man,
> Thy fairy dwelling is as lone as thou!

It is perhaps not odd that Beckford later declined to meet the poet, in spite of his whole-hearted admiration of *Vathek*.

After dealing thus firmly with England's wealthiest son, Byron took the Childe to the Marquis of Marialva's quinta, 'Oh! dome displeasing unto British eye!' where he believed the hated Convention to have been signed, and wrote three furious stanzas about this unfortunate agreement, culminating in 'Britannia sickens, Cintra! at thy name'.

Then, conducting the disapproving Childe over the mountains towards Spain,

> O'er vales that teem with fruits, romantic hills,
> (Oh that such hills upheld a freeborn race!)

he allows his attention to be detained for a stanza by Mafra, where 'the Babylonian whore hath built a dome' (though it is not clear why poor John V, who spent on the building of Mafra millions of pounds belonging not to Rome but to the state of Portugal, whose secular needs went all unmet because of it, should be called the Babylonian whore). Having thus registered protestant disapproval, the dissipated prig rides on towards the nobler land of Spain. He 'seeks not now the harlot and the bowl', but enjoys the scenery and mountain air, musing on the superior merits of Spanish hind over Lusian slave.

Spain shone the brighter against Lusian darkness. Byron enjoyed everything about it, from the cities and the accommodation to the bull-fights, and above all the ladies, who received him with embarrassing warmth. Spaniards of both sexes showed him a very proper respect; he sunned himself in their admiration and returned it. 'Reserve is not the characteristic of the Spanish belles, who are in general very handsome.'

> Oh never talk again to me
> Of northern climes and British ladies:
> It has not been your lot to see
> Like me, the lovely Girls of Cadiz.

And what, ask Portuguese critics, about Portuguese ladies, who have been called 'infinitely the finest that Men can imagine'? What indeed? If we knew that, we might come nearer to understanding the tone of *Childe Harold* about Portugal. Or so say the Portuguese.

But the Portuguese, in so insistently *cherchant la femme*, overlook a few relevant facts in the case. One of these is that Byron left England in an extremely sulky temper; disappointed of literary success, abused in the press, in financial straits, crossed in love, coldly treated by a friend, he took up a pose of cynical and friendless misanthropy, writing to his boyhood's love, Mary Musters, that

> As some lone bird without a mate,
> My weary heart is desolate;
> I look around, and cannot trace
> One friendly smile, or welcome face
> And ev'n in crowds am still alone . . .

> The poorest, veriest wretch on earth
> Still finds some hospitable hearth,

> Where friendship's or love's softer glow
> May smile in joy or soothe in woe;
> But friend or leman I have none,
> Because I cannot love but one

And so on. To be sure, there was also the cheerful doggerel he wrote to Francis Hodgson from the Lisbon packet, beginning 'Huzza! Hodgson, we are going', and grumbling at seasickness —

> But, since life at most a jest is,
> As philosophers allow,
> Still to laugh by far the best is,
> Then laugh on, as I do now —

nevertheless, his watchful friend and mentor Mr. Dallas remarked that 'Resentment, anger, hatred held full sway over him, and his gratification at that time was in overcharging his pen with gall that flowed in every direction'. 'I leave England without regret', he wrote; 'I shall return to it without pleasure. I am like Adam, the first convict sentenced to transportation, but I have no Eve, and have eaten no apple but what was as sour as a crab.'

It was half an adolescent pose; but it shows him scarcely in a mood to like the people he encountered. And the first of these were the luckless Portuguese whom it was at the moment the English habit to despise, in spite of the example set by Wellington. As has been said earlier, the Portuguese were themselves anti-British, and not at their most agreeable; it must be remembered that Hobhouse did not like them either, though he was a calmer and more judicial prig. 'Avarice and immorality', he observed sweepingly, 'appears to be the reigning passions of the Portuguese.' Herculano complains with bitter sarcasm of the British attitude, which was in truth a good deal milder than his own towards the British, whom he hated furiously, allowing them not a single quality; protestantism, he said, drove them to gin-palaces and drunkenness; he was obviously little familiar with English history and our notorious pre-Reformation intemperance. These intolerable sots, he thought, had no right to dislike the Portuguese, so much nicer, more religious, more virtuous and more intelligent, than themselves. He was, of course, particularly angry with Byron, who, on account of buffets which he had been given outside S. Carlos, wrote as he did.

This theory, upheld by so many patriotic Portuguese, may be accurate, but would be more interesting if substantiated by contemporary evidence. At least as likely as an incident of this kind is the natural ill humour, ill manners and callow prejudice of a vulgar adolescent in a temper with life. Having vented his spleen on the Portuguese, he approached Spain in a better temper, and made angels of them by contrast. But it must be admitted that we lack the data for an explanation; and, lacking it, all we can say is that 'Lisbonne lui a déplu, Seville et Cadiz l'ont charmé, et il avait bien le droit de le dire'.

BIBLIOGRAPHY

Childe Harold's Pilgrimage (1809).
Letters and Journals of Lord Byron, ed. R. E. PROTHERO (1898).
Lord Byron's Childe Harold's Pilgrimage to Portugal critically examined, D. G. DALGADO (1919).
Works of Byron, ed. E. H. COLERIDGE (1898-1904).
Correspondence and Recollections of Lord Byron, R. C. DALLAS (1835).
Recollections of a long life, JOHN CAM HOBHOUSE (1865).
O Parocho de Aldeia, ALEXANDRE HERCULANO (1851).
Cancioneiro, JOÃO DE LEMOS (1859).
Lord Byron em Portugal, ALBERTO TELLES (1879).
Byron, PETER QUENNELL (1934).
La Littérature Portugaise en Angleterre à l'Époque Romantique, FÉLIX WALTER (1927).

A VERY RUM CHAP

George Borrow

[1835]

MANY missionaries have been pretty odd, but George Borrow was probably about the oddest. He seems to have performed his task — that of dropping the Bible, or the New Testament (suitably translated into the language required), about among foreigners, with opprobious comments on their religion — with immense zest and from various motives: he needed a job, he enjoyed roving about foreign parts, he liked using and displaying his gift for foreign tongues, and he dearly liked to annoy Roman Catholics. Neither of the two motives which have often moved missionaries, the love of God and of humanity, came his way. He did not even love the Bible, his 'precious little tracts'; but he did love his own discourses on how benighted it was not to read it, how wicked were those who forbade it. He hurled it at the Spanish and the Portuguese like bombs, charged with explosive hate against the church to which they belonged. Fortunately his discourses were, anyhow by the Portuguese, not fully understood. That enthusiastic faith which immolates in the missionary embarrassment and self-distrust he did not need, for he had a flaming natural conceit which served this purpose; if conceit be not too mild a word for that fiery vanity and pride which smouldered in him sullenly or triumphantly blazed, those delusions of grandeur which so fantasticated him to others and to himself. Was he a Christian by belief? He apparently believed himself to be so when he fell in with the Bible Society at the age of thirty, nine years after he had written to a friend, with adolescent grandeur, 'I intend to write plays, poetry, etc., and abuse religion'. He had passed out of this stage, and out of the influence of old William Taylor of Norwich. 'One of his chief favourites', wrote Harriet Martineau spitefully of Mr. Taylor, 'was George Borrow. When this polyglot gentleman appeared before the public as a devout agent of the Bible Society, there was one burst of laughter from all who remembered the old Norwich days.' But Borrow himself, we can be sure, did not laugh; he seldom did, and it is obvious that, however his views may have lacked profundity, he took them seriously. Devout he was not; and few people can have taken less account of the distinctively Christian precepts; Christianity was for him a kind of Robinson Crusoe-like dependence on Providence to bring him good luck and to punish the wicked, and a violent ninety per cent hatred of Roman Catholicism, combined with a firm determination to make its benighted practitioners read the Bible and realize the errors of the Pope. Anyhow, this was the religion adopted by him when he became the employee of the British and Foreign Bible Society. He was offered the chance to do the one thing he greatly enjoyed — go vagabonding about the world, expenses paid, and talk to its inhabitants in their own tongue. While he could do this, the black melancholia that dogged him, that, in less degree, dogged so many of his epoch and of the epoch before, and in his case verged at times on madness, was kept at bay: it seemed his form of opium, and a better form than most, for it stimulated without the subsequent reaction into lethargy, despair, headache or remorse, and he could look back on a task well done, and even write a book about it. A queer chap, said Mr. Ford, the writer of Murray's *Handbook to Spain*; a very rum chap indeed. Scarcely an amiable chap; few had ever liked him much, or for long; an unpopular child, only his mother had cherished him. He believed as a rule that he had been ill-treated; he nursed all manner of hates, malices and revenges; he libelled and pursued his foes without respite. He was of Celtic descent (Cornish), with some French through his mother; this all makes for bitterness, and for exaggeration. He posed to himself and others as a gipsy; he concealed the monotonous eight years, from twenty-two to thirty, that he had spent ingloriously and penuriously in London and Norwich, dressing them up all through his later life as adventurously roving the world, throwing out continual hints of the exciting and romantic encounters they had brought him; he called himself Olaus, Don Jorge, and other outlandish names; he lied persistently about his age; he was a humbug on the grand scale. He recorded the most improbable conversations between himself and those he encountered in the Iberian peninsula; dazzled by his own inordinate gift for languages, he sometimes believed himself to be better understood in them than he probably was. He went to Russia to edit for the Bible Society a Manchu translation of the New Testament; from St. Petersburg he wrote to his employers telling them that they ought to have an agent to distribute Bibles about the country. 'I am a person of few words, and will therefore state without circumlocution that I am willing to become that agent. I speak Russ, Mandchou, and the Tartar or broken Turkish of the Russian steppes, and have also some knowledge of Chinese, which I might easily improve at Kiatcha. I am therefore not altogether unqualified for such an adventure.' The Reverend Joseph Jowett of the Bible Society had warned him before that there was 'occasionally a note of confidence in speaking of yourself which has alarmed some of the excellent members of our Committee'.

Borrow enjoyed himself enormously for two years in Russia; returning to England in September 1835, he reacted into melancholy. 'I hope the Bible Society', he had written to his mother from St. Petersburg, 'will employ me on something new, for I have of late led an active life, and dread the thought of having nothing to do except studying, as formerly, and I am by no means certain that I could sit down to study now.'

He did not have to. A month after his return, the Bible Society proposed, with some doubt and hesitation on account of the formidable difficulties of the enterprise, that he should go and investigate Bible possibilities in Portugal. He jumped at the suggestion; it was just what he would have wished, and he proposed to extend the expedition into Spain also. 'I wish it to be clearly understood that I am perfectly willing to undertake the expedition, nay, to extend it into Spain, to visit the town and country, to discourse with the people, especially those connected with institutions for infantine education, and to learn what ways and opportunities present themselves for conveying the Gospel into those benighted countries. I will, moreover, undertake, with the blessing of God, to draw up a small volume of what I shall have seen and heard there which cannot fail to be interesting, and if patronized by the Society will probably help to cover the expenses of the expedition.'

A week later, the committee passed a resolution 'that Mr. Borrow be requested to proceed forthwith to Lisbon and Oporto for the purpose of visiting the Society's correspondents there, and of making further inquiries respecting the means and channels which may offer for promoting the circulation of the Holy Scripture in Portugal'.

Only Portugal was mentioned, but the Society had Spain also in mind, as its secretary explained in a letter introducing their agent to the Reverend E. Whiteley, English chaplain at Oporto, who kept a stock of their Portuguese Bibles. Mr. Borrow, wrote the secretary, had great tact and enterprise, and already spoke Portuguese; Mr. Whiteley would certainly like to be acquainted with him, but was warned not to form a judgment too soon. An introductory letter was also sent to Mr. John Wilby, a Lisbon merchant, the other depositary of the Society's Bibles.

Thus equipped, Borrow sailed for Portugal, which he seems to have looked on mainly as a prelude to 'the adventure of Spain', the country of his boyhood's day-dreams. He seems to have indicated to his employers that he already knew Portugal and spoke Portuguese; it is obvious, however, from his own story that this was his first visit. He was annoyed by the customs officials, who were 'exceedingly uncivil' and apparently over-charged him; he heartily wished himself back in Russia, took a dirty and expensive lodging, and engaged a Portuguese servant in order that he might perfect himself in Portuguese. In about a fortnight he found himself conversing with considerable fluency and much noise and vociferation and apparently not very intelligibly.

The first few days he devoted to looking at Lisbon, which he greatly admired, particularly the aqueduct, finding it superior to any work of man in Rome; he was also much moved by Fielding's fine new tomb, which he kissed, noting that Doddridge, the Nonconformist hymn-writer, who was also buried in the English cemetery, was an author of a different stamp, but justly admired and esteemed.

Then he set to work on his mission. He had meant not to spend long in Portugal, but to pass quickly into Spain, which was adamant against the Bible; Portugal, since the defeat of Miguelism (the civil war was just over), had allowed it to circulate, so was a less exciting field of campaign. But, though allowed, it had not got about much, and Borrow was doubtful as to whether the majority could or would read it. Mr. Wilby, the Bible Society's representative in Lisbon, was away; he determined to investigate conditions for himself.

So, in his usual spirited manner, he went about Lisbon accosting the residents, asking 'many of the lower orders' (apparently even his prodigious nerve failed before the higher orders) 'whether they ever confessed themselves, whereupon they laughed in my face and said that they had not done so for years, demanding what good would result to them for so doing, and whether I was fool enough to suppose that a priest could forgive sins for a sum of money'. Of a muleteer he inquired whether he reverenced a stone cross that he pointed out on a gate; 'he instantly flew into a rage, stamped violently, and spitting on the ground said it was a piece of stone, and that he should have no more objection to spit upon it than the stones on which he trod. I believe that there is a God, he added, but as for the nonsense which the priests tell us, I believe no part of it'. All very satisfactory: it was apparent that clericalism was routed in Lisbon, and that Dom Pedro and the Constitution had prevailed. A soil ripe for the Biblical seed. But in no one questioned had it yet been sown, or even heard of. Borrow would take from his pocket a Portuguese New Testament and show it to these patient people; many of them could read it, but they knew not what it was, nor had they met it before. Some of them, however, had read much of their own literature and history; or so they agreed when asked. He explored to San Jeronimo, and found that, since the expulsion of its monks, it had been filled with five hundred orphans, being educated 'upon the Lancastrian system'. An orphan informed him that they read the *Santa Escritura*, but he could not produce a copy, and probably meant not the Bible but 'the vile papistical book called *Christian Doctrine*, in which the office of the mass is expounded'. Borrow saw that he must visit the Jeronimos again and learn more.

But at present he decided to explore the country round Lisbon, and made an excursion to Cintra, which enthralled him, as it enthralled all the English of his generation, by its mountainous and bosky beauties, its imposing ancient structures, and its romantic historical associations, from the Moors' ruined castle on one peak to, on another, 'the ruined halls of the English Millionaire'. (not yet rebuilt by the Visconde Cooke) 'who there nursed the wayward fancies of a mind as wild, rich, and variegated as the scenes around. Yes, wonderful are the objects which meet the eye at Cintra, and wonderful are the recollections attached to them'.

So unconnected were these objects and recollections with the Bible, that Borrow might have been in danger of forgetting his task, had he not been recalled to it by encountering, as he was about to climb to the Moorish ruins, a priest. Thus reminded, he drew him out on the subject of the state of education in his parish. Poor, said the priest, very poor. There was, said he, a school at Colhares, a league away, that might be worth a visit. Nothing loath, Borrow made off for Colhares, entered the school uninvited with the confidence of an Inspector, was welcomed civilly by their teacher, and found that the books in use were a spelling manual and 'Christian Doctrine'. No, they did not read the Scriptures, they were too young to understand them. Yes, the teacher himself had a New Testament; but it turned out to be only the Epistles, in Pereira's version, with long Popish notes. Without notes, he explained, the Bible would be unintelligible to simple people. Borrow left him, remarking that the Almighty would never have inspired his saints with a desire to write what was unintelligible to the great mass of mankind.

His next excursion was across the mountains to the great convent of Mafra, whence the monks had been expelled, to get their living as best they could; some, Borrow was told, begged, some had turned banditti, some served Don Carlos in the Carlist wars. One, disguised in blue jerkin and grey trousers and greatly embittered by his distasteful task and impoverished life, had been given the job of schoolmaster in the village school. At first angry at the stranger's intrusion, he thawed enough to offer snuff, but would answer no questions about the school, a topic repugnant to him. Neither could any information be had about local Bible-reading from the lad who had offered his services as guide. Like his fellow-Portuguese of the lower orders, he had never heard of the book. Excellent conversationalists as Borrow found them (so much better than the English peasantry, who were coarse, dull and ungrammatical), on this one subject they showed no comprehension. Confident that, could they but have the book in their possession, they would read it with avidity, Borrow discussed at Lisbon with Mr. Wilby how to proceed in the campaign. Four hundred Bibles or New Testaments had arrived; it was agreed to hand over some to the booksellers and the rest to colporteurs to hawk about Lisbon on commission, but not, Mr. Wilby advised, in the villages outside, as the rural priests, being very fanatical, might have the colporteurs assassinated.

This arranged, Borrow asked Mr. Wilby which was the most ignorant and benighted province of Portugal; he replied, the Alemtejo, which was full of heaths, gloomy dingles, swamps, stunted forests, banditti, and several horrible murders every week at least. Borrow therefore decided to go to Evora, the capital of this disagreeable district, where had flourished a peculiarly malignant branch of the Inquisition, worse than that of Lisbon, and to establish a Bible depôt there, in the very heart of the enemy's country. So armed with Testaments and tracts, he set forth, braving the perils and discomforts of the December journey across the wild Tagus and the wilder Alemtejo with some trepidation but dauntless resolve.

As they rode across the blasted Alemtejo heath, his muleteer entertained him with hair-raising tales of the local bandits; in their strongholds (fortunately empty except for bottles) he deposited a few tracts, and hastened away. He fell in with a Portuguese gentleman, a follower of the late Dom Pedro, riding to Evora; they talked in English of politics, literature, life; the Bible did not so much intrude when the conversation was with the upper classes. When Borrow stopped to ask a goat-herd, carrying otters and wolf-cubs, if he believed in Jesus Christ, the Portuguese gentleman, allowing for English mania, tactfully rode on ahead. The goat-herd also allowed for it; nodding to himself, he stared on the strange fellow and said nothing. Borrow took silence for assent; he reflected on the greater religiousness of rustics than urbans.

His experience of Evora confirmed this view. He strolled about the streets, entering into conversation with the people he met; if Evora inquisitiveness was at all what it is to-day, he must very soon have had half the town trailing after him in delight. Those he talked to had very little to say, 'except a few commonplace remarks on the way of living of the friars, their hypocrisy and laziness'. This subject was apt to turn up whenever Borrow conversed with the Portuguese; whether it was he or they who first mentioned it, he does not say. But 'when I spoke of religion, they exhibited the utmost apathy, and making their bows left me as soon as possible'. He had an introduction to a shopkeeper in the market place, a man much persecuted under the old clericalist régime; with him he left a stock of Testaments, telling him that if he were desirous to lay the axe to the root of super-stition and tyranny, this was the way to do it. Returning to his inn, he tried to talk to some low-class smugglers there, but found them unresponsive and disagreeable. A Portuguese corn-dealer who was also present avenged insults to his country and religion by saying that he hated the English, for they were not baptized and had not the law of God. Having got the best of the ensuing argument, Borrow went out again and seated himself by the stone fountain for two hours, opening conversation with everyone who came there, and one can imagine that they were many, as the news spread. He did this every afternoon during his stay at Evora, and believed that he spoke to two hundred citizens. Most of them seemed to be 'bigoted Papists and Miguelists at heart. I therefore, when they told me they were Christians, denied the possibility of their being so, as they were ignorant of Christ and his commandments, and placed their hope of salvation on outward forms and superstitious observances which were the invention of Satan. I said repeatedly that the Pope, whom they revered, was an arch deceiver, and the head minister of Satan here on earth, and that the monks and friars . . . were his subordinate agents'.

Borrow wondered later that he received no insult nor ill treatment while thus attacking the beliefs of his hearers. He put it down to the 'utter fearlessness' which he displayed. An explanation which did not, apparently, occur to him is that very little of what he said was understood. Even his gift of tongues cannot have enabled him, after a few days in Portugal, to talk Portuguese as the Portuguese talk it; he probably pronounced it rather as if it were Spanish. His servant Antonio told Dom Geronimo Azveto, the gentleman who had met them on the road to Evora, that his master did not speak Portuguese very well, and there are ,signs here and there throughout his account of misunderstanding. Insufficient Portuguese and a lively and efflorescent imagination combined to build up in his fancy and memory many very strange conversations. One can picture the daily scene by the fountain: the odd tall Englishman of six foot three sitting on the stone edge, with his queer brown face, flaxen, almost white hair, brilliant piercing eyes, pockets stuffed with volumes which he kept taking out to distribute among the crowd, chattering away in foreign Portuguese, of which only a phrase here and there was comprehensible. No doubt the foreigner was mad; they summoned one another to come to the fountain and enjoy the sight and sound; they stood all the afternoon, as the Portuguese love to stand, gazing and enthralled. They were apparently polite; there was none of the 'lapidation' of which Baretti and other foreigners have complained; they scarcely even laughed; Borrow was a very large and rather formidable man. He was an excellent show: Evora has scarcely forgotten him yet. As he noticed, many of them departed musing and pensive; he believed and hoped that the words of his mouth had sunk deep into their hearts.

Meanwhile, he went to see Dom Geronimo, and enlisted him in the campaign. He found in this courteous and cultivated gentleman very proper feelings about the deplorable state of education in his country; he and the Governor were thinking of establishing a school in an empty convent. Borrow urged him to see that knowledge of the Bible was the basis of the education given there, and pressed on him half his stock he had with him. He then gave Dom Geronimo a brief exposition of the effect the translated Bible had had on English history; he told him how, before the days of Tyndal, Britain had been the seat of ignorance, oppression and cruelty, and how the last persecutor of the Bible, the bloody and infamous Mary, was the last tyrant who had sat on the throne of England, since when all had been reason, freedom and light. Dom Geronimo agreed politely that, in that case, the Bible should by all means be tried in Portugal. Next morning Borrow sent him the books, in the confident hope that a bright and glorious morning was about to rise over the benighted Alemtejo.

An interesting light is shed on Borrow's attitude towards reason, liberalism, culture and freedom of thought by his condemnation of Volney's *Les Ruines*, which he was shown by his landlady's daughter, 'the fine girl Geronima', she having been presented with it by 'a young man, a great constitutionalist', who had told her it was one of the best books in the world. 'I replied that the author of it was an emissary of Satan, and an enemy of Jesus Christ and the souls of mankind; that it was written with the sole aim of bringing all religion into contempt, and that it inculcated the doctrine that there was no future state, nor reward for the righteous nor punishment for the wicked.' Whereupon Geronima, (apparently, though a fine girl, a rather stupid one), made up the fire and burnt the book without a word, telling her beads till it was consumed. Borrow was as pleased by this *auto-da-fé* as by his daily eloquence beside the fountain, and by his conversations with smugglers from Spain who 'spoke of priestcraft and the monkish system with the utmost abhorrence' and said 'they cared as little for the Pope and his monks as they did for Don Carlos'. Altogether, he felt that he had been a success in Evora; and, having got rid of most of his tracts by dropping them about to be picked up (for they were not always accepted when offered in person), he left for Lisbon.

In Lisbon he spent his last fortnight before starting for Spain.

One visit he paid there, taken by his servant Antonio, was to the English College of the Inglesinhos — the college, as he oddly calls it, of the English ****; throughout his account of his call there and his conversation with the Rector, he substitutes asterisks every time for the word Catholics; it is one of the several occasions when his love of mystery and dark hints leads him into silliness. Apart from alluding to 'the Virgin' without her correct adjective, which gave away his heretical status to his hosts, he conducted himself with tact and discretion, praising the view from the roof, the activity of the sporting seminarists, the respectability and loyalty of English **** in general (even refraining from contradicting the Rector's ingenuous assertion that none of them had ever really been engaged in any plots or conspiracies) and breaking into a paean of praise of Ignatius Loyola and the Jesuits. He did not, apparently, press the Bible on his hosts; in fact, it seems to have been one of the occasions when he toadied.

Having thus politely interviewed the Inglesinhos, to his own satisfaction and apparently to theirs (though their impressions of their effusive visitor are lacking), Borrow had a look at the Lisbon Jews, who gathered each day round the arcades at the ends of Aurea and Prata streets. He introduced himself by uttering a blessing in Hebrew, and passed himself off as a rabbi. 'I have lived in different parts of the world, much amongst the Hebrew race, and am well acquainted with their ways and phraseology . . . in a few days I knew all that related to them and their traffic in Lisbon', he characteristically says. Unfortunately he found that they were 'a vile and infamous rabble', given over to robbery, black marketings, preying on one another and the Portuguese. Since he was posing as a rabbi, he could not distribute New Testaments among them, and had to leave them unreformed.

It was time to leave Portugal for the greater adventure of Spain. Before he started, it struck him that he had not got introductions to the right people in either country, and he wrote to Dr. Bowring in England asking him for these. He would like, he said, a Foreign Office letter of recommendation to Lord Howard de Walden, the British Minister to Portugal. And he was not to be described as an agent of the Bible Society, but as 'a person who has plans for the mental improvement of the Portuguese'; this, he thought, would attract the sympathies of all broad-minded persons in Portugal. Having dispatched this request, he started for Badajoz and Spain on New Year's Day. He made the usual troublesome, uncomfortable and dangerous journey which seemed his only way of getting about Portugal, or indeed anywhere else; no one felt inconveniences more sharply or exposed himself to them more constantly. It was bitterly cold; the crossing of the Tagus was intolerably tedious; he paid 'mercilessly dear' for everything; his muleteer and sole companion was an idiot; he was attacked by a huge and savage dog which he quelled with 'the calm reproving glance of reason'; he was fired at and narrowly missed by xenophobe Portuguese soldiers, impervious to reason; he met a gibbering deaf and dumb maniac; he heard his country insulted by a Portuguese officer. But these were the usual contretemps of travel, and, to make up, he met in Elvas a respectable tradesman who expressed great abhorrence of the papal system and took some Testaments, and at Montemor (which he believed to be named after the Moors) he got into a convent. An unseen nun asked him what he required. He replied that he was going to Spain to introduce the gospel of Christ into a country where it was not known, whereupon there was a stifled titter. Undeterred, he inquired if there were in the convent any copies of the Holy Scriptures, but, as usual, the question was not understood. Changing the subject, he asked if the nuns did not find that time hung heavy on their hands; the voice replied, no, they made cheesecakes. Thanking the speaker, Borrow walked away. Outside the house, he heard louder tittering from the windows above him, and looked up at windows crowded with dusky faces and black waving hair; the nuns were all peeping out to gaze at the peculiar stranger; unembarrassed, he kissed his hand to them repeatedly. Then he walked on to look for Moorish remains. At the inn he ate some of the nuns' cheesecakes, which were most delicious.

It was at the Elvas inn that the Portuguese officer insulted Britain and roused Borrow's patriotic fury by calling her selfish and mercenary. 'I could not command myself when I heard my own glorious land traduced in this unmerited manner. By whom? A Portuguese! A native of a country which has been twice liberated from horrid and detestable thraldom by the hands of Englishmen. But for Wellington and his heroes, Portugal would have been French at this day; but for Napier and his mariners, Miguel would now be lording it in Lisbon.' He talked the officer down with lofty irony, till he presently went worsted away.

It was soothing next day to meet the respectable tradesman who abhorred the papal system and took the testaments. But his last experience of Portugal was yet another outrage, for he was turned away from the fort he wished to visit, on the grounds that he was a foreigner and an Englishman. At this Borrow thoroughly lost his temper; he thunders for two paragraphs over Portuguese ingratitude; the English were unpopular in Portugal because it is man's nature to hate his benefactors. They have fought for Portuguese independence, 'forced themselves by a treaty of commerce to drink its coarse and filthy wines, which no other nation cares to taste', and yet are the most unpopular people who visit Portugal, even when they come Bible in hand.

Shaking the dust of the ungrateful country off his feet, Borrow spurred his mule over the frontier stream, joyfully leaving behind 'the squeaking dialect of Portugal' for 'the magnificent language of Spain'.

But Spain, alas, was to disillusion him, for the Spanish too proved ungrateful — 'a stupid, ungrateful set of ruffians ... No one has a greater right to say so than myself'. And he began at Badajoz by finding 'among the many deeply rooted prejudices of these people, the strange idea that no foreigner can speak their language'. Borrow was easily annoyed, but few things annoyed him more than this strange idea.

Whatever he felt about the Peninsula, it had given him a remarkable book. Written in an appalling style, pompous, portentous, stuck-up, full of egotism, prejudice and hate, crude and uncivilized, it would have shocked and disgusted the English millionaire whose 'ruined halls' had inspired in him romantic thoughts at Cintra. It has none of that other famous tourist's elegance, rich imagination, sharp sense of character, sensitive appreciation of a whole world of art closed for ever to the untrained Philistine who saw no beauty except that of nature. Yet the two tourists, so antipathetic, had something in common: both were magnificent humbugs and poseurs; both lied freely, and have placed between us and themselves a tantalizing jungle of deception and self-flattery wherein they move only half discerned. There is this important difference — of Beckford we wish we knew the whole, of Borrow we feel we know enough. He is, to say the truth, a repellent figure among travellers; he cannot be liked. All the same, he has a zest, a vividness, a ridiculous picaresque absurdity, that sets him in the category of works of art; he is tremendously alive. Across a century we see him sitting by the Evora stone fountain abusing the Pope, gesticulating, vociferating, fluent and mispronouncing, his pockets bulging with testaments and tracts, his dark eyes flashing over the crowd of staring, smiling Portuguese, into whose hearts he believed that his words sank deep. We see him pushing his way into schools, bothering the teachers by incomprehensible inquiries after the *Santa Escritura*, into the college of the Inglesinhos, blandly conversing about the

Virgin and flattering St. Ignatius, stopping muleteers in the streets of Lisbon for a chat about the Papacy, kissing his hands to tittering nuns, lying about his age to ancient crones, braving savage dogs and savage men, galloping his mule over the river into Spain. A rum chap, as Mr. Ford called him: but with a bravura and zest, a sheer, unashamed self-love, a boisterous, inelegant rush of words and imaginations, that are a kind of substitute for genius.

BIBLIOGRAPHY

The Bible in Spain, GEORGE BORROW (1842).
Letters of George Borrow to the British and Foreign Bible Society, edited T. H. DARLOW (1911).
Life, writings and correspondence of George Borrow (1899).
Life of George Borrow, H. G. JENKINS (1912).
George Borrow, the man and his work, R. A. J. WALLING (1908).

10. THE LAUREATE IN THE HEAT

Alfred Tennyson and F. T. Palgrave

[1859]

IT was the wrong time of year: the two poets, with Mr. Crawford Grove, and all three with long thick beards, arrived in Lisbon on August 21st, and put up at the Braganza. It was hot. 'We shall go to Cintra either to-morrow or next day,' Tennyson wrote in his diary. 'It is said to be Lisbon's Richmond, and rather cockney, though high and cool ... I cannot say whether we shall stick at Cintra or go further on. Brookfield gives a good account of the cleanliness of Seville.' They spent a day driving about Lisbon 'in a blazing heat' and seeing churches and the Botanical Gardens, but failed to get inside the English cemetery to see Fielding's grave. Then they drove on to Cintra. 'Cintra disappointed me at first sight, and perhaps will continue to disappoint, though to southern eyes, from its ever green groves in contrast to the parched barren look of the landscape, it must look very lovely.' Tennyson and Grove climbed to Penha, 'a Moorish-looking castle on the top of the hill', which is being repaired. Palgrave too was disappointed in Cintra. 'From Byron and

Beckford we had expected a region little touched by man but rich in nature. But it was a larger Malvern, or Bois de Boulogne', and full of polite parties sauntering or riding about. After a few excursions, they returned to Lisbon. On the whole, Portugal was not fulfilling the expectations aroused in Palgrave by the first sight of its northern hills and valleys from the sea. 'There at last', he had reflected, 'life might be gliding as in some charming old-world fashion; — no club scandal, no scientific bluster, no one to quote the *Times* to you, or believe in Lord Palmerston; no niaiseries about art and the opera. What with handsome shepherd boys and peasant girls with immense brown eyes, there one might find the Golden Age.'

But not in Lisbon; it was too hot, and there were flies, fleas and mosquitoes. Also Tennyson had a toothache, and this ruins any place. They decided to remove to Cadiz, Gibraltar, Malaga, Granada, and possibly Tangiers. Before they left Lisbon, Tennyson's name got about, and the Duke of Saldanha called on him in the *salle à manger* at the Braganza, said he had fought under the great Duke, had been in two and forty combats and been successful in all, and had married two English wives, both perfect women. 'He ended with seizing my hand and crying out, "Who does not know England's Poet Laureate? I am the Duke of Saldanha". I continue pretty well except for toothache.'

But Palgrave said it was the wrong season, the fields were brown and burnt, the mosquitoes afflicting. Tennyson slept in a large bag, which terrified the waiter when he was summoned to light a match for his pipe. More serious than the mosquitoes was the sun. 'This so wrought upon and disturbed Tennyson, in a manner with which many English travellers to Italy during the heat will be unpleasantly familiar, that he now began gravely to talk about leaving his bones by the side of the great novelist Fielding.'

It was time to leave. The travellers abandoned the idea of Cadiz, Gibraltar, Malaga, Granada, and possibly Tangiers; even Seville, of whose cleanliness Brookfield gave so good an account, was renounced. 'The heat and the flies and the fleas and one thing and another have decided us to return by the boat to Southampton which starts on the 7th. We propose on arriving at Southampton to pass on to Lyndhurst to spend two or three days in the New Forest.'

THE LAUREATE IN THE HEAT

So they never saw the hills and valleys of the north, or found the Golden Age. The Iberian peninsula in summer-time was too much: they could not take it. The New Forest was safer.

BIBLIOGRAPHY

Memoir of Alfred Lord Tennyson, HALLAM TENNYSON (1898).
Francis Turner Palgrave, G. F. PALGRAVE (1899).
Article by Palgrave in *Under the Crown* (1869).

CLERGYMEN

I. JESUIT
Father Henry Floyd S. J.
[1592-1597. 1603-1611]

THERE are figures of which it is not easy to get a clear view, less because they are obscured by the mists of the past than because, Janus-like, they present to us two faces (or more) according to who speaks of them. When the tide of religious, political or national feeling has stormed high about them during their lives, they become more than usually enigmatic in retrospect: they are heroes, martyrs, bullies, traitors, offensive noseyparkers, faithful, loyal or faithless men: all these they have seemed to their contemporaries; we cannot judge.

One of these unresolved beings is the Jesuit priest Henry Floyd (alias Fludd, Rivers, Rogers, Symonds, and Francis Smith, but it seems most correctly Floyd, for his brother John, also a Jesuit, was so called). The facts of his life are known: born in Cambridgeshire in 1563, he was educated at the English seminary at Rheims, was sent thence to Valladolid at twenty-six, was at Seville, where he defended universal theology with great distinction, and was installed by Father Parsons as rector of the new English Residency at Lisbon in 1592 or 1593, his charge being the care of the English, Irish and Scots (both Catholic and Protestant) in the city. After a few years he went to England (succeeded in the Residency by Father Nicholas Aston) and lived with the Southcote family till captured, when he did two years in Newgate. He was admitted to the Society of Jesus in 1599; about 1603 he was expelled from England and returned to Lisbon, 'and there worked among the English traders, reducing as many as he could to the bosom of the Church'. He became, in fact, chief visitor for the Inquisition for the English Residence, which then had its quarters with the Jesuits at San Roque.

The history of the Residence is a little tangled and obscure, but it would seem that when Floyd returned to Lisbon its rector was Nicholas Aston, who had also the job of visitor, which meant interviewing the British traders, apprentices, factors and other residents, and the sailors and passengers on the arriving ships, discovering their religious status, taking such steps to amend it as might seem feasible or useful, and anyhow warning them that in Lisbon they must not, if they were (as most were) heretics, obtrude it. When Floyd was on the job, it meant a great deal more than this; an earnest clergyman, his pursuit of souls, and more particularly those of the young factors and apprentices, was indefatigable; he gained many of them, denounced many others to the Inquisition for indiscretions, together with their Portuguese friends, kept a firm hold on those who had by inadvertence got themselves into gaol, labouring continually to convert them, and generally made himself what his superiors called a most valuable instrument for religion, and what the English consul called a public nuisance. When he returned to Lisbon he superseded Nicholas Aston as visitor. He was in Lisbon until 1611, when to the consul's relief, he left. For some years he was occupied with the English mission, where he won a great reputation for the saving of souls, and was more than once in prison. He died in London in 1641.

So much for the facts. His personality and character are more difficult to discern. Generally speaking, there seem to have been two views taken of him, the Roman Catholic and the Protestant (though there are indications that even his own superiors could have on occasion enough of him). A highly successful converter he undoubtedly was; Lisbon became full of his English converts, mostly young factors and apprentices sent out, as the consul frequently complained, too raw and ingenuous to withstand his experienced assaults on their unfledged protestantism. In London he was known to Thomas Killigrew as 'a Jesuit dangerous both for transporting and seducing of young persons'; there is a longish list of the young persons transported or seduced. Undoubtedly he was good at this business, which argues certain qualities. He was much praised by his superiors in the Society. Father Gerard wrote to Parsons of 'Father Henry Fludd, whose zeal and practical proceedings I think would be very profitable'; Father Garnett, in 1599, said that all who knew him liked him very well.

This, however, was not quite the case. The most vivid portrait of Floyd that we have — in fact, the only real portrait — is to be found in the letters to the Privy Council in London of Hugh Lee, English

consul in Lisbon from 1605 to 1617. Lee did not care about
Roman Catholics, or at least about English ones; he did not trust
their loyalty or patriotism an inch, and always knew they were up
to no good, so had a natural bias against a priest whose business
it was to make more of them. But he was not wholesale in his
dislike for them; he liked Father Aston very much, and spoke
amiably enough of many priests and friars. It was Floyd who got
under his skin. Through the difficult years of his consulship,
Floyd, his schemes, his conversions and his spyings, were an
obsession with him; everything irritating about the often extremely tiresome English merchants he attributed to this priest's
machinations. Floyd's official duty of going about among the
English, sounding them for information and persuading them
towards the faith, the consul regarded as mere wanton imperti-
ence. 'I am sorry,' he writes, soon after his appointment, 'there
is no means yet taken for restraining of His Majesty's subjects
from conversing with Henry Fludd; it is a thing too common.
This Fludd ... is the most dangerous man to the state of England that is in these parts, for we cannot rest in quiet but still
he will intrude himself to our companies; and all such as will
profess themselves enemies to England with him they are in
best esteem, and letteth not by all means to labour to convert
those that come rawly and unscathed into these parts. So that it
were to be wished some good cause might be taken for removing
him hence, and when not that, yet that he might be commanded
not to meddle with any His Majesty's subjects to win them or to
persuade them from the true obedience and allegiance to their
sovereign. For he hath done much hurt, and daily doth increase
the same. He came from Madrid to this place. I doubt not but
with your good means this remedy may be had; so shall you make
a great number bound unto you to requite so good a turn. And
for my own part, to my power your worship shall command me.
This man labours what he can to cross me in my place, and
maintains that the King of Spain is to appoint consuls here for the
English nation.'

This attitude on the part of Fludd naturally would, by itself,
cause resentment in a consul. We hear soon of 'the sinister proceedings of our old malicious enemy, Henry Fludd, the English
Jesuit of this place, who now by his practice pretending to work
extraordinary actions upon such youth as shall come out of

England, hath procured himself to be the chief visitor of all the English ships and Scottish that shall come into this port, and hath prevailed so much with the Inquisadores as to remove the former visitor, who was also an Englishman, but not maliciously bent, but rather very forward to do any pleasure to his countrymen, who is called Father Nycholas, and is a priest'. With Father Nicholas Aston the consul couples for favourable mention as a good Englishman Father Joseph Foster, the confessor of the Bridgettine nuns. But as for Floyd. . . . 'This Fludd hath purchased an entrance into his desired purpose, for thereby will he have the first conférence with both master and mariners upon their arrival out of England, for he was always very desirous to hear what news from thence; his intrusion betrayeth his intentions, and therefore requireth prevention'. A postscript hopefully adds, 'There is means made to cross Fludd in his purpose, and promise is made that if he cannot be hindered therein, yet Father Nych[s] shall notwithstanding continue his place as before, but jointly'. In December Floyd is again at his anti-consul schemes, labouring much that the consul for the English should be 'a Subject of the king of Spain'. In February (1607), 'The Fludd, wherewith we are often annoyed, is still offensive — we cannot free ourselves from his visits, neither shall, for he will intrude himself where he knoweth he is slenderly welcome, presuming upon his vain hopes, not forbearing to persecute those of the best stayed in religion, he hath lately drawn two youths to take upon them the profession of friars, and hath placed them in a Monastery, the one of London, whose name I cannot yet learn, the other . . . of Chard in Somersetshire, called Thomas Sparke, who has lately given it out to some of his familiars that he purposes to leave his habit and to return for England; this is a lusty youth without beard, near 20 years of age, and sayeth that Fludd will get leave for him to go for England'. There is another youth just come out, who vaunts himself a Catholic, for whom Fludd has procured an allowance from the majordomo of St. George's Chapel (the traditional centre for Englishmen in Lisbon).

In the following June, Fludd was putting about some miracle, undescribed except that it was connected with a straw, and by its fame seeking 'to suppress and to put out of memory their most foul and horrible Powder Action, stirring up these people in hatred both against His Majesty and his loyal subjects', and labouring to convert 'such English as are prisoners in the galleys, whom for that they will not be converted by him he hath caused them to be very cruelly beaten, and continually are put unto the greatest and most toilsome labour in the said galleys, as themselves daily do complain thereof that it is lamentable to hear'.

From Fludd's victims, Lee passes to his disciples — John Howe, a jeweller, brother to Howe the goldsmith in London, one Williams, and Tho. Jennynges — 'these are daily frequenters of that College' (San Roque) and objects of distaste and suspicion to their consul. According to him, Floyd had a great following; one cannot help suspecting that he was becoming over-strained with the constant annoyance of his enemy in Lisbon, and exaggerated a little when he declared 'Here are daily too many that come out of England for these parts who are altogether the disciples of Henry Fludd, who also are instruments for him in his secret actions'. He was getting to see Jesuits everywhere, 'It is very apparently known', he writes in November 1607, 'that the English Jesuits have been the plotters of all the former treacheries pretended towards His Majesty and State, as here is one Henry Fludd, an English Jesuit, who hath not spared to maintain the great Powder Action at Westminster to be a very lawful thing, such is his insolency; who laboureth to animate the Spaniard against our Nation that will not yield to his conformity, that he is a very offensive neighbour to all His Majesty's subjects that frequent this place, and now lately hath he prevailed to remove unto their College Mr. Hugh Gurgany after fourteen months' imprisonment in the Inquisition, only to labour him from his religion towards God and his obedience to His Majesty, which is an evil and dangerous proceeding; if it be not remedied by removing him from hence, His Majesty's subjects shall so long as he remaineth be subject to his malice.'

About Floyd's anti-English designs (he apparently belonged to the violent hispaniolized section of Jesuits led by Parsons) no one had any doubts. To the English government he was known as a plotter and traitor. Early in 1608, soon after Lee had complained of his praise of the Powder Action, the informer priest, Francis Tillotson, wrote to Lord Danvers of 'an oath of conspiracy lately taken by those English arch-Jesuits, viz. Parsons at Rome, Cresswell at Madrid, Henry Flood at Lisbourne, and Baldwyne in the Low Countries, the tenor whereof' is that five seminarists should be sent to England sworn 'to leave no way unattempted to revenge the death of their Principal, Garnett, and that not to be otherwise done than upon the sacred person of His Majesty' and of the Prince. If they failed, 'it is resolved by these Arch Jesuits that every half year the like number of five shall be sent to continue this damnable conspiracy'.

An unlikely tale; endorsed by Lord Danvers 'A conspiracy lately discovered by one Tillotson', and by Lord Salisbury, 'This is the most unlikely and absurd discovery, and yet all the persons named are arch traitors; but I know this priest is a knave'.

Hugh Lee would have been prepared to believe in any conspiracy attributed to Floyd, watching at close quarters his conspiracies for the reform of the English consulate, and the protection he gave to the more tiresome of his countrymen. 'His Majesty's subjects, that daily come over in most disordered manner . . . many ungoverned youths that think there is no government but in themselves, who misbehave themselves more than is befitting to write of, and if any exception be taken, then they fly to Father Fludd, who is their protector'. Father Fludd obviously had a way with young men. He was, Lee complained, also the protector of thieves and swindlers. These evil-disposed Englishmen, whether merchants or mariners, being discovered in their practices, 'shroud themselves under the protection of Henry Fludd, giving themselves out to be Catholics, wherewith they prevail'.

Fludd also 'haunted' English prisoners, labouring to win them to himself, and preventing others from access to them. He had ingenuity in his conversions, aiming often at those who had influence with their fellows. A notable success in this line was the 'fowling away into the Church of Rome' of Robert Draper, of whom Lee wrote in annoyance in September 1610. Draper, a merchant of London, of the Company of Merchant Tailors, residing in Lisbon, 'a man near forty years of age, who, till his last coming over, made always show of an earnest and serious Protestant, is within these two months, little more or less, by Henry Fludd brought to be a Roman Catholic, with whom he hath been confessed and hath received the Sacrament in their kind, but it is kept very secret of his partners . . . This man, if he be not recalled hence, will prove more dangerous than Fludd, by seducing His Majesty's subjects, for he doth so please the younger sort that frequent this place that they hold him the most wisest fellow that useth this place, whereby they are very prompt to be led by him'. Together with the dangerous Draper, Fludd worked 'to divert the government from all good order'; less ambitiously, he spared no pains to seduce the callow youths 'sent out from the west of England to learn the language' and placed in Portuguese houses only to attend the women of this country daily to the hearing of Mass and the visitations of saints' (the ladies' male relatives lacked, apparently, time or inclination to accompany them to these duties), 'and which is more dangerous, they are nourished up in religion by Henry Fludd, who has free access to them in the Portingales houses, and spareth neither travail nor means to win them to his purpose'.

Interesting confirmation of this branch of Father Floyd's pastoral activities, and of the extreme youth of some of his converts, is given by a statement made by young Emmanuel Lobb (later Father Joseph Simeon) on entering the English College at Rome in 1616. He was, he said, brought up at Portsmouth. 'My parents were of the lower class, and poor, and, alas! heretics ... When I was barely eleven years old, by order of my mother, I passed over into Portugal, to learn that language, with a view to the mercantile life. Here I was soon after converted to the Catholic faith by Father Henry Floyd S.J., at that time living in the Professed House at Lisbon. The same Father Floyd persuaded me to lay aside other pursuits and take to study, and after a while I was sent to St. Omer's College.'

However he appeared to the loyal English consul against whom he so diligently worked, and to those of his countrymen against whom he lodged information, there must have been something winning about Father Floyd when he chose to persuade; his conquests were too many and too various to be dismissed as mere appeals to self-interest. Homesick little boys in Portuguese houses may have been easy game; so may malefactors and prisoners, who saw in him protection; but hard-headed grown-up merchants were another matter. To win these, wrote the irritated Lee, he and Robert Draper arranged a plot to have the book recording the merchants' privileges, commonly kept by the consul, taken out of his hands and kept in the Chapel of St. George in the church of S. Domingos — 'an excellent plot devised to draw all such as be desirous to see them, or such as shall have cause to use them, to come to the chapel to hear a mass, and then shall have a sight of them. This is like to be a plot of Henry Fludd.'

In December 1610, Fludd was occupied with a plot still more offensive to the unfortunate consul — helping 'the mutinous faction' among the English merchants to get rid of Lee and put Richard Cullymore in his place. A petition against Lee was drawn up and sent to the 'Corregedore' of the city, 'and in this business their chief solicitor is Henry Fludd'. Cullymore 'to further his suit, in his petition nameth himself to be a Catholic, which is the principal means to get favour here'. Lee, stung beyond bearing by Fludd's actions and charges against him, put in a complaint of him to 'the Proposito of the House of Jesuits, unto whom I made relation of the said Fludd, his unnatural malice towards His Majesty and the State of his native country'.

Floyd appears to have successfully disposed of these charges, and no abatement of his endeavours to dislodge the consul seems to have occurred. He loomed in Lee's eyes ever more sinister, the power behind every mischief. Anyone who associated with him and his faction was suspect. There was, among others, a ship master, Samuel Dove, to whom the consul had to speak severely, for 'he hath carried himself very forgetfully and suspiciously of his loyalty, in that he hath here componed himself with the associates of Fludd. I, out of my good affection towards him, for his good declared unto him my opinion of such as I hold here to be dangerous people, to the end he might beware of them'. Mr. Dove, rejoining his crew, 'delivered unto them much more than I spoke, and in a more disordered manner than I had spoken, whereupon in their mutinous manner to their ghostly father, Henry Fludd, go they presently, complaining against me, and what trouble I may come to thereby I know not. Wherefore I pray you that he may be sent for and caused . . .' The rest of this letter is torn away; it is not quite clear whether it is Fludd who is to be sent for, or Samuel Dove, nor what Lee would wish to be done to him, though in the case of Fludd it may be surmised.

In his next letter, Lee warns the Secretary to be secret as to what he (Lee) reports from Lisbon of the misbehaviour of His Majesty's subjects, or he may 'incur peril', for Fludd has his own means of getting information of such matters; 'I do insure you there passeth not, neither is intended, any matter touching the

Papists, whereof he hath not the first advices, which is (by all likelihood) by the conveyance of some merchants, which may be prevented. I am very sorry that His Majesty's subjects live in such subjection in these kingdoms that the public enemies, both of His Majesty's person and State of England (such as are natural English born), do carry a hand over them, threatening the authority of the Inquisition to take hold of them if it may be proved that any shall use any exhortation or persuasion unto such as are unstaid in religion or inclining unto Papistry. And yet they hold it very lawful for Henry Fludd to put himself with any of His Majesty's subjects that cometh newly over and freely to labour and allure him from his allegiance to His Majesty by all the means he can make; and yet one of us to another may not be allowed to use persuasion to continue in our loyalty. . . .' It is possible that the Council, perusing these worried letters from the Lisbon consul, may have got a little weary of the recurrent name of his hated foe, which crops up in each topic mentioned, a many-tentacled octopus stretched to achieve all evil. 'For here' — the complaint comes in almost mechanically — 'is not a malefactor of our Nation, but repairing to Henry Fludd he will protect him; wherein is high time that remedy be put.' Once a man has been got hold of by Fludd, the consul may expect no gratitude from him, whatever services he has rendered to him; as in the cases of Francis Buck and Anthony Marlow, brought prisoners from the Indies and subsequently released; Lee had taken trouble and gone to expense to alleviate their captivity and procure their liberty, bribing the Viceroy with gifts at his own charge, but 'they are both very ungrateful men . . . I know it springeth from the Fludd, which never wished me good, for I could never come to the prison where they were but always I found Henry Fludd with them, exhorting them, till he made them firm of his flock'. The door of a Portuguese prison for English captives was so much more easily opened to Fludd's flock than to others that the priest's exhortations were apt to fall on good ground.

It would seem that some young gentlemen of Catholic families were sent over to Lisbon to be put in the charge of Father Floyd, who arranged (either with the majordomo of St. George's chapel or with the Jesuits) for their maintenance. There was, for instance, young Mr. Vause (Vaux), a youth of eighteen, who grew discontented with the amount of his allowance. 'He hath altogether been governed here by Henry Fludd, who keepeth him very short in his allowance, so that the young gent is not well pleased therewith, and hath not let to break out in speeches that the old Lady Vause his mother hath been one of the best friends the Jesuits have had in England, for she hath harboured them and hid them in stone walls and furnished them with money, taking it very unkindly that they esteem no more of him here. And doubtless what I have heard from himself, he taketh small liking of the life of sundry sorts of the churchmen, neither in Spain nor here, so that if he do go in this passage [home] I am in mind he would easily be brought to alter his opinion, for he will often speak of their disordered lives with much dislike thereof.'

It is to be noted that no one, not even the consul, a just if angry man, ever spoke of the 'disordered life' of Henry Floyd; his was a life ordered and devoted, with single-minded zeal, to his cause, to which he was prepared to sacrifice all other causes and people, including himself. To win England, by any means that offered or could be devised, to the faith, even if it entailed mass murder, civil war, and subjugation to a foreign yoke — that was his unswerving, fantastic, and not ignoble aim. An aim, of course, that could never be approved by the consular service of his country. His efforts to amend this service by pushing out Lee and substituting one of his own faith were untiring. He stirred up discontent against Lee, collected witnesses to accuse him of this and that, instigated petitions against him to the Viceroy — 'but I hope', writes the badgered consul, 'God will not permit him to prevail against me'.

'I cannot think,' he wrote on April 23rd, 1611, 'there liveth a more hateful enemy unto His Majesty and State of England than Henry Fludd . . . for he is not at quiet with himself when he is not practising some evil against his Nation. He began with myself, informing the Viceroy and Council that I was a heretic . . . and no Christian, therefore not capable of any office amongst Christians, whereby one Edward Baynes, a confederate of his, was appointed by the Viceroy to be Consul to His Majesty's subjects here in my place'. Lee, however, has put embargoes to delay the matter, and awaits the visit of the English ambassador from Madrid.

'The said Baynes is a venomous branch issuing from that poisoned Fludd . . . The world may judge of the purpose of Fludd in preferring him to be consul. Further, the said Fludd hath possessed the Justices here that it is unfit any English should live here at liberty, but should give account of their lives, whereupon the Justices called divers of the meaner sort into question by imprisoning of them; and proceeded against them in this sort, that they should lodge in Portingales' houses according to the laws of this land, or within fifteen days to avoid the country. After they had banished two or three of the meaner sort, they began by imprisoning one of the principal merchants, without accepting of any bail, but to prison he must go, at which time the Viceroy being at his house in the country, there could no present remedy be had till the day following', when the Viceroy, being appealed to, immediately ordered the prisoner's release.

Further, the Inquisition had ordained that Floyd should be the only priest to converse with the young English bachelors who came and went; 'though there are sundry others that profess religious lives, Englishmen in this city, yet no friends to him', none of them might have to do with any English youth touching church matters, 'but only Fludd, so that he having gotten an entrance, if in time he be not curbed, he will grow very headstrong. All which shall be signified unto the Lord Ambassador at his arrival at Madrid'.

Floyd was in a strong position for getting the ear of authority, for the Father Proposito of the Jesuit house in Lisbon was the Viceroy's confessor, and could pass on suggestions to him. The Lisbon Jesuits showed the usual skill of their Order in securing influence in high places. Floyd worked it vigorously: 'he laboureth all he may to vex and disquiet those that profess to be the loyal subjects of His Majesty our sovereign, and spareth not to say that there shall no Consul be admitted here but such as shall be known to be a Roman Catholic, and he with some others of his confederates have informed against me that I am not such, but rather say I am no Christian, wherein credit is given to their reports'.

Floyd was working also to destroy or to bring into oblivion 'the Articles of the Peace', by which the English in Portugal believed they had been promised liberty to worship in their own way so long as they did it strictly in private; as the Portuguese, or anyhow the Inquisition, never seem to have taken in this clause in the Articles, misunderstandings were apt to arise. 'And further, some of the civil magistrates have in an upbraiding manner taken exception to the testimonies of Englishmen, saying that being heretics their testimony is not to be allowed of in course of justice; all which are stirred up by Henry Fludd to bring us in odio with these people.' Fludd, in short, is 'A 1 public enemy unto the State of England' (an unexpectedly early use of this phrase, but it seems to bear no other reading).

But on July 6th, 1611, just a month later, the consul had good tidings to give. 'Henry Fludd, the mortal enemy to His Majesty's person and the State of England is gone from hence, it is said unto the Bath' (Caldas?) 'for to seek his health, but I hope he shall not return hither. His absence will breed our quiet, for he was a very busy body in the time of his abode here.' 'I rather suspect him', Lee wrote in another letter, 'to be gone for England, or mindeth speedily so to do, and my reason I have from himself, who hath often said that he hopeth to live to be hanged, drawn and quartered, whose vile intention I leave to your Lordship's wisdom to censure. He is a man of a mean stature, his visage and nose somewhat long and thin, his hair of a dark red colour, he is of a slow speech, aged about 35 years.' (Floyd was actually forty-eight.)

Whether to achieve his vile intention to get himself hanged, drawn and quartered, or for any other purpose, the A1 public enemy to England and to the English consul was gone, and Lisbon was free of him and his schemes. His young men continued to arrive in Lisbon, hoping for maintenance from him, but, finding him departed, did not linger. He was succeeded as visitor for the Inquisition by William Newman, whom Lee found pretty harmless; he was a secular priest, not one of those cursed Jesuits for ever plotting against England, and not given to denouncing his countrymen.

Lee has one more allusion to Floyd, in June 1617 — 'Henry Fludd, a Jesuit I hear to be in the Gatehouse at Westminster'.

Floyd was, indeed, for the next many years of his life continually in and out of the Gatehouse, the Fleet, Newgate and the Clink. He never achieved his 'vile intention', but he took every risk of it. He worked under several aliases, became familiar to pursuivants and informers, was skilful in escape, got to know the private hiding-holes in many a Catholic house, and was famed as a converter and transporter overseas of young persons of both sexes, including his nephews and nieces. He seems to have been convincingly plausible in denying his priesthood when brought before justices; he was in favour with fashionable lady converts in the palmy days of Queen Henrietta Maria, and was, when imprisoned for the last time in 1637, released by the queen's order on grounds of age and infirmity. He died in 1641.

His was a life lived with a single aim, the service of his Church, and the winning of his country back to the fold. He was a believer in the violent way when other ways failed; he approved of the great Powder Action, of torture and the stake for obstinate recalcitrants; he could be cruel, as to his protestant countrymen in the galleys. He was an intriguer, a plotter, an informer, when to inform was to get rid of enemies of the faith; he knew no loyalty but to his Church, his Order, and his God. His country was to him not a sovereign state to be served, but a lapsed land to be won back by persuasion or force. He was intrusive, impudent, for ever busy with other men's affairs, prying, persuading, slandering, denouncing, said Hugh Lee; in short, a most intolerable nuisance and enemy to all loyal men. To set against this, he was liked and frequented by many of his fellow countrymen in Lisbon; he had the art of conversion in a high degree, which he practised on young and old, men and women, in England and abroad. He could persuade young people into the religious life, and shipped them overseas with untiring zeal. Himself he never spared.

He was brave, with the cool dauntlessness of those who face a dreadful risk with open eyes and take it, not on one occasion, but for long years on end. He left the safety of Lisbon for the peril of England, from which he had been banished eight years before. William Newman, ten years after Floyd left Lisbon, refused to go on the English Mission when ordered by his superior at Rome, on the grounds that it would be too dangerous, for he was 'visitor for the Inquisition of all the strangers' ships that come into the port', and so well known to merchants and sailors and other travellers that he would inevitably be recognized in England; also, his being a servant of the Inquisition had made him odious there. Father Floyd and other divines, he said, had decided long since that they could not send him into 'such singular and certain dangers'. 'It is yet without any example that ever any was sent into England after that he had once served in that place.' Newman did serve the Inquisition more closely and domestically than Floyd, for he was employed by it as censor of the English books that came in, and apparently had an office in the Inquisition House; but Floyd too worked for it, and was probably better known as its visitor on the ships and quays; he certainly played a more notorious part in Lisbon life and politics, openly applauded the Gunpowder Plot, championed any action against the State of England, and, worst of all, was a Jesuit, and *ipso facto* a traitor. 'These men are in subjection to a foreign power, and disclaim our sovereign': it was simple, conclusive, and undenied.

Yet Henry Floyd calmly braved everything, left his successful and comfortable, if quarrelsome, Lisbon job, his following of obedient convert apprentices, his influential position in the congenial society of San Roque (where he had the ear of the Viceroy's confessor), all the cosy and sunny pleasures of that rich world mart, that lovely capital of a Spanish province, where he was a citizen of the only State worth serving, and crossed the intimidating seas into the murky and perilous gloom, the furtive fugitivism, the angry anti-popery, the shifting from alias to alias, the midnight alarms, the secret lurking-holes between chimney and wall, the sharp, greedy stare of pursuivants, flaring suddenly into confirmed suspicion, the damp cells of Newgate, the gruelling questions, the long, insupportable strain, the hurdles to Tyburn waiting at the prison gates. Floyd must be accorded the honour given to his fellows on that valiant, romantic, improbable mission, even though he came to it after the worst years.

Lisbon did not seduce or hold him, as it had seduced and held many of his co-religionists and compatriots. 'Ulissiponto mittitur, ut inde in Angliam discederet', Parsons had written of him long since: and, for once, it worked out like that.

BIBLIOGRAPHY

State Papers, Portugal 89/3 (1605-11) (Record Office).
Records of the English Province of the Society of Jesus, H. FOLEY (1871).
Cal. S.P., Domestic, James I (1608).
Anatomy of the English Nunnery at Lisbon, THOMAS ROBINSON (1622).
Memoirs of Missionary Priests, RICHARD CHALLONER (1924).

2. METHODIST IN LISBON

The Rev. George Whitefield

[1754]

THE Reverend George Whitefield, busily crossing and re-crossing the Atlantic on his errands of converting America, Scotland, Wales, and London to Calvinistic Methodism, quarrelling with the brothers Wesley, chaplaining Lady Huntingdon, and founding orphanages, crossed to America in April 1754, on the ship *Success*, which was to touch at Lisbon to drop a cargo of wheat. Mr. Whitefield, at first dubious about this delay, hesitated to sail by her, but on second thoughts 'believing it might be serviceable to me, as a preacher and Protestant, to see something of the superstitions of the Church of Rome', took his passage, and in due course reached Lisbon.

From this city he wrote four letters home to a friend, which were printed in periodicals and later published in a tract, under the title *A brief account of some Lent and other Extraordinary Processions and Ecclesiastical Entertainments seen last year at Lisbon*. The tract achieved several editions; the last, in 1851, was bound up with an excellent account of the earthquake by an English merchant, and entitled *Whitefield at Lisbon. Being a detailed account of the Blasphemy and Idolatry of Popery, as witnessed by the late servant of God, George Whitefield, at the city of Lisbon during his stay there. Also a Narrative of the Dreadful Earthquake that totally destroyed the above city a few months after Mr. Whitefield's visit. With Mr. Whitefield's remarks thereon.*

The little volume is prefaced by one who distrusts Popery. In England, he observes, chary of betraying its true character to English eyes, it wears a mask; would we know what Papal superstition is in its free, unchecked development, we must see it in thoroughly Popish lands. 'Shortly after Mr. Whitefield had witnessed unmasked Popery in the streets of Lisbon, a calamity befell her ... It has been thought desirable to append a lively description of this dreadful scene by an eye-witness, as a striking comment upon the superstitions witnessed by Mr. Whitefield. Idolatry and its punishment soon succeeded each other. The proceeds of the publication will be given to the Aged Pilgrims' Friend Society.' The tract was cheap at twopence.

Mr. Whitefield, it will be seen, was not disappointed in his search for superstition. It met him immediately on landing at Belem. 'Providence had so ordered it that a gentleman of the Factory, who had heard me himself, and whose brother had been wakened under my ministry several years ago' invited him to stay. On the road from Belem to Lisbon he looked about him, and what he saw was not the Tagus, nor the Jeronimos, nor palaces, orange gardens, churches and gaily coloured houses, nor even the

Portuguese women going about their business driving donkeys and carrying loads on their heads; what Mr. Whitefield saw in the streets all the way from Belem to Lisbon was wayside shrines with crucifixes and images of saints, and people bowing to them and singing. 'This seemed to me very odd, and gave me an idea of what further ecclesiastical curiosities would probably fall in my way, if I should be detained here any time.'

He was detained there twelve days — Passion Week and Holy Week — and each day was full of ecclesiastical curiosities. He mentions nothing else; there is no indication that he went about sight-seeing, felt any interest in Lisbon, or any admiration for the country round it, crossed the Tagus, explored to Cintra, or even saw the aqueduct, that joy of British tourists. It was superstition he enjoyed, and superstition he found. Very soon after his arrival he saw a procession of priests and friars attended by people very commendably carrying provisions to the prison; a mixed multitude followed after, 'addressing the Virgin Mary in their usual strain, "Ora pro nobis" '. It was the first of the many superstitious processions that edified Mr. Whitefield that last fortnight of Lent. There was one for rain; another for St. Francis, showing the events of his career; this sounds, as described by Mr. Whitefield with great detail and zest, very charming. Another, more shocking, occurred late the same evening. Mr. Whitefield was talking with his host when in came an Englishman and told him in great haste that he had seen a train of near two hundred penitents passing along, 'and that in all probability I might be gratified with the same sight if I hastened'. Mr. Whitefield did hasten, and was gratified. He caught up with the penitents, who were clad in white, with holes for their eyes and chains for their ankles; they carried immense loads, such as great stones, bones and skulls, and heavy crucifixes; most of them whipped themselves with great severity (and surely, considering their loads, with considerable difficulty). 'Had my dear friend been there, he would have joined with me in saying that the whole scene was horrible . . . I know you would have joined with me in praising and adoring the Lord of all lords, for the great wonder of the Reformation, and also for that glorious deliverance wrought out for us a few years past in defeating the unnatural rebellion . . . To have had a papist for our king . . . But, blessed be God, the snare is broken and we are delivered. O for Protestant practices to be added to

Protestant principles! . . . Pardon me, my dear friend, I stop to weep. . . .'

On Good Friday he wrote 'Providence still detains us at Lisbon, and I know you will be inquiring — what more news from thence? Truly as extraordinary as ever, for I have now seen the solemnities of a Holy Thursday.' These he admirably describes, and in the next letter those of Good Friday, when there was performed in a church a play representing the Crucifixion, which shocked him inexpressibly. By this time his emotional Calvinist-Methodist imagination was quite captured and enthralled; no detail is too trivial for him to describe, with the eloquent vividness for which he was justly famed. Alas that he could not stop over Easter; but the *Success* had finished her business and on Saturday she sailed, carrying Mr. Whitefield to the Protestant mission fields of America. It was perhaps none too soon: his imagination thus intrigued, his faith might have been captured too; he was of the stuff of which converts are made.

'Let us comfort ourselves with this thought, that there is a season approaching when the Lord God of Elijah will himself come and destroy this and every other species of Antichrist', he wrote, pleased to think that he had seen it before this occurred.

As a foretaste of this final destruction, the earthquake crashed down on the idolatrous and superstitious city next year. The account of it appended is a grim and vivid piece of writing by an English merchant who only barely escaped with his life. A comment by Mr. Whitefield concludes the little volume. 'Poor Lisbon, how soon are all thy riches and superstitious pageantry swallowed up! . . . O to lay up treasure in heaven! . . .'

Less than twenty years later Mr. Whitefield's own Bethesda College was destroyed by fire. No doubt this visitation was regarded by Roman Catholics, Anglicans, Wesleyan Methodists, and American Indians as a judgment on the shocking superstitions of Calvinistic Methodism.

BIBLIOGRAPHY

A brief account of some Lent and other Extraordinary Processions and Ecclesiastical Entertainments seen last year at Lisbon, GEORGE WHITEFIELD (1755).
Whitefield at Lisbon. Being a detailed account of the Blasphemy and Idolatry of Popery as witnessed by the late servant of God, George Whitefield, at the city of Lisbon during his stay there (1851).

3. TRACTARIANS

J. M. Neale   Joseph Oldknow
[1853-1854]   [1854]

THERE is here some overlapping of categories, for the Reverend J. M. Neale, besides being a clergyman, was also a writer, a celebrated hymnologist, and pre-eminently (as regards Portugal) a tourist; indeed, he was a guide to all subsequent tourists. Still, a clergyman he was, and among the noble company of clerical tourists he must take his place.

He went first to Portugal in May 1853, to practise ecclesiology (as he called looking closely at churches) and to write a book for a publisher. The expedition, however physically comfortless, must have been a pleasant change from his struggles, as Warden of Sackville College, East Grinstead, with a tiresome bishop, who inhibited him for being High and 'debasing the minds of these poor people with spiritual haberdashery'. His travelling companions were Bishop Forbes of Brechin, Canon H. L. Jenner, and Dr. J. H. Rogers; their society was congenial, and they were probably all High too; anyhow the bishop was to be censured a few years later for proclaiming the Real Presence, and was to endeavour to explain away the Thirty-nine Articles. High in another sense they were, and must have been much stared at by the Portuguese, a nation of gazers, for all but Dr. Neale were over six feet, and he only just under.

Portugal was excessively uncomfortable in the 1850s. 'The tourist in Portugal,' Neale wrote in his book, 'must be prepared for the worst accommodation, the worst food, the greatest fatigue, and he must not expect much that can interest in the way of architecture, ecclesiology, or fine art.' Getting about was extravagantly difficult. The railways were, in nearly every case, still only 'designed'; there were scarcely any diligences; the roads were mere tracks; one had to trust to horses and mules, make one's way over rough mountain country, often in the rain, and sleep at inns which remain in the primitive barbarity which was their characteristic when there were convents to shelter the tourist. The labour of travel was scarcely to be conceived; there were extremes of heat and cold, and 'you lie at night on the boards of inns to which you would hesitate in England to consign a favourite dog'. Vermin and smells of course abounded; and 'when in a passion the Portuguese becomes dangerous'. Sometimes the bishop could endure no more, and left the party for a time, presumably to stay in the nearest large town in comparative comfort. But Neale (one can see it in his hymns) was made of sterner stuff. He had not wrestled with persecuting bishops in Sussex to be overthrown by vermin and bad lodging in Portugal. He was an ascetic; 'O happy if ye labour', he wrote, 'O happy if ye hunger', and 'The trials that beset you, the sorrows ye endure, what are they but his jewels, of right celestial worth, what are they but the ladder, set up to heaven on earth?' However weary, however languid, however sore distressed, he would always struggle on until his task was accomplished; he knew that sorrow, care and brief life were our portion here, and weighed them lightly against spiritual achievement, aesthetic joy, and the fulfilment of his aims, which were, in Portugal, to write his book and some articles on churches for the *Ecclesiologist*. And the scenery was truly magnificent; any fatigues and bodily anguish were turned to joy by the mountain views of the Minho and Tras-os-Montes, even on muleback in the rain. As to the mules, they sometimes crushed your feet, and often kicked you off. But their behaviour mattered little when, descending from Miranda, you looked down on the Douro from the steep mountain's side and saw 'the black foaming river dashing from a ravine on the left, the confusion in which the wild peaks are tossed together, the abrupt rocks towering up all round'. Neale had the poet's eye and word; such sights as this, and the rarer pleasures of ecclesiology and missal-hunting, enabled him to endure sleepless nights, dirt, and uneatable food, before which the more worldly bishop quailed and fled.

Neale liked the people, too, finding them kind, courteous, and as inquisitive as children, though with a bad habit of staring, and, as has been mentioned, dangerous when in a passion. Once he was lucky enough to find a lost sequence by the author of the Dies Irae in a Franciscan convent at Lisbon; it seems from his letter to a friend that he took it away with him. Indeed, he was little hampered by too scrupulous a legality; Anglo-Catholic priests in the mid-nineteenth century soon trained themselves out of that. On one occasion during his second visit to Portugal he and his companion, a Mr. Oldknow, ('a very tolerable companion, though he minds roughing it a great deal more than a traveller in Portugal ought') boldly defied the quarantine laws which forbade entry into Portugal from Spain during a cholera epidemic, enlisted a local smuggler, 'the principal smuggler on the Minho, a very clever fellow', in their cause, crossed the river in a boat, braving possible shots, bribed the guards on the Portuguese side, and got into Portugal, riding twenty-five miles from the frontier to Viana in a storm.

An energetic and thorough man, Dr. Neale covered an immense amount of ground, taking a fifteen hours' ride over mountains to see a church or cathedral, riding up the Estrella range and lodging in a little pilgrimage house in scenery that reminded him of Theocritus, spending the next three days piloting his course through wild untravelled country, sleeping in verminous cottages (this was perhaps where Mr. Oldknow minded roughing it more than he ought), finally, 'half starved and eaten up with vermin', descending on Thomar, where they rested a day and saw the Convent of Christ. Thence to Batalha, Santarem and Lisbon, where he enjoyed the society of the English College. 'On Sunday I was at the English College most of the day, and found them very well up in English matters. They were more than civil and we had a most pleasant dinner. The contrast of their High Mass and the slovenly Portuguese services was very striking'. Both he and Mr. Oldknow, but particularly Mr. Oldknow, felt, like other Tractarians, attracted and repelled by, inferior and superior to, and irresistibly impelled to argue with, Roman Catholics, so they had a most interesting Sunday.

It must have been, after all these pleasurable adventures, rather chilling to come home and find that he was being accused of appropriating the funds of Sackville College to his own uses. It is to be hoped that he found solace in writing his book on Portugal; it is one of the best that exists, and ran into many editions; every wise traveller to Portugal has taken it with him ever since. It abounds in useful and interesting, and occasionally acid, information, such as that 'The English consul is Mr. Smith, the Vice-Consul Mr. Meyler. From the latter gentleman, every kind of courtesy will be experienced'. It contains a list of the main dates in Portuguese history, written in a good terse style, and conveys in brief words the glory and decline of the empire and the remarkable line the Portuguese were able to show in sovereigns. '1497: Vasco da Gama discovers India. 1501: Pedro Alvares Cabral discovers Brazil. 1513: Conquests in Africa. 1665: The King, from indulging his passions, loses his sense and is deposed.' And so on.

The book contains also a conversation vocabulary, which is chiefly noteworthy for the continual intrusion of the horse among the usual remarks about how far it is to Batalha, does Mr. R. live in this street, wash the linen carefully, I am dressing, undressing, not at home, don't come in, I want more light and air, must I make a bargain, I shall take a bath ninety degrees, he is faint, bring the salts, throw water in his face, etc. No conversation in Dr. Neale's book can get far without breaking into 'Does the horse kick, shy, rear? Put the horse under shelter. Give him a feed of maize. Wash his hoofs. They are still dirty. Give him fresh straw. The saddle must be stuffed. You have not cleaned the horse, the stable. He is lazy, hard in the mouth, kicks, shies, rears, stumbles, limps. His back is sore. He is a tricky horse. He is broken-winded. He is blind of an eye. He is a jibber. He won't go.'

This unsatisfactory animal has unfortunately disappeared from the more modern editions of the book, which has marched with the times and made the suitable adjustments. Its last edition was over thirty years ago; in it there remained unaltered Dr. Neale's favourable opinion of the neo-Gothic castle of Penha, the Portuguese Balmoral, built on a Cintra mountain top by Prince Ferdinand of Saxe-Coburg-Gotha, consort of Queen Maria da Gloria and cousin to Queen Victoria, 'By him,' wrote Dr. Neale, 'it was restored with much taste, and has assumed the appearance of a feudal castle.' Modern guide-books do not encourage their readers to admire Penha except as an oddity.

The name of the book was *A Handbook for Travellers in Portugal*; its publisher John Murray.

As to the Reverend Joseph Oldknow, who shared the second trip and also wrote a book about it (but not so good a one) one would infer him a touch Higher Church even than Dr. Neale. Or possibly only more combative about it. Neale complained that his companion was sea-sick all the time when on the ocean; but directly he landed he threw off his malaise and entered with fire into ecclesiastical controversy. The English church at Oporto shocked him, for, having no churches of their own sects, the British dissenters all attended it, and all got on together perfectly well in the discussions on church affairs. 'I should fear,' said Mr. Oldknow, gravely, 'that such an amalgamation must stand in the way both of a clear inculcation of the distinctive doctrines of the Church of England, and of a full development of her ritual . . . so desirable that she should appear in her true character, not as a Protestant sect, but as a reformed portion of the Catholic Church'. She should, he said, be known abroad as she really is, as much distinguished, *to say the very least*, from all Protestant bodies, as from the Churches of the Greek and Roman communions. When foreigners see Presbyterians, Independents and Wesleyans permitted to unite with Church of England members and have a voice in her concerns, worship brought down as nearly as possible to the meagreness of the conventicle, chaplains removed and appointed by the Foreign Office, bishops playing no part, 'who can wonder if they consider her but as one of the many sects which arose at the so-called Reformation', and stand aloof, refusing Christian communion?

Deeply interested in all convents and churches, Mr. Oldknow regretted their spoliation and decline, and hankered after the good old days. In Lisbon (they stayed at the Braganza hotel) he lamented the unrestored ruin of the Carmo church, which harboured a chemist's shop and bats.

The mutual misunderstandings between Roman Catholics and Anglicans also depressed him. He did his best to remove them, calling both at the Irish Dominican and the English College; at the latter he and Dr. Neale had a controversy on Church differences of the kind that Tractarians enjoyed, discussing such matters as unity, the authority of the Pope, Anglican orders, and so forth. Mr. Oldknow left with his hosts a French tract on the doctrine of the sacraments and Dr. Cosin's Latin tract on the Church of England; Dr. Cosin could be trusted to keep up Anglican prestige against 'that erred Church', and to take down the pride of Rome. 'They all sound sensible,' said Mr. Oldknow, 'of the inefficient condition of the Church in Portugal.'

He came away feeling that he had clarified and justified Ecclesia Anglicana before his erred countrymen abroad. It was his mission. Dr. Neale, engrossed with ecclesiology and *Murray's Handbook*, had less time while in Portugal to give to these important matters; he wrote, however, several poems for the *Churchman's Companion*.

BIBLIOGRAPHY

Murray's Handbook for Travellers in Portugal, J. M. NEALE (1855).
John Mason Neale: A Memoir, ELEANOR A. TOWLE (1906).
Letters of John Mason Neale, edited by his daughter (1910).
A Month in Portugal, JOSEPH OLDKNOW (1855).

CLERGYMEN

4. ECCLESIA ANGLICANA

The Reverend John Colbatch
[1693-1700]

THE position of chaplain to the British Factory in Lisbon was, taking it all round, for a good many years a rather uneasy post. Protestant clergy in an uncompromisingly Roman Catholic country, disliked and spied upon by the Inquisition, which resented and disputed their right to be there, impatiently tolerated (up to a point) by king and ministers, in distasteful fulfilment of an agreement, continually embroiled in disputes with everyone, never certain as to the limits of their religious rights, always grudged their stipend by their congregation, who had to pay it, these excellent clergymen picked their way dubiously yet firmly among the most disconcerting difficulties, finding life among their unruly flock in Lisbon dauntingly different from anything one might have expected. The first chaplain was appointed after the Cromwellian treaty of 1654, which stipulated for a moderate freedom of worship for the English in Portugal; he was a Mr. Cradock, who arrived in Lisbon in 1657, and soon found himself involved in the perennial wrangle with the Inquisition about the right to hold services in any house but the ambassador's. According to the articles of the treaty, services might be held, unobtrusively, in any private house. But the Inquisition blandly denied it; they had never heard, they said, of any such article. The right to worship in houses and on ships was claimed by the British to have been granted so long as no scandal was caused: but then, what was scandal? The Inquisition thought it scandal if any Portuguese noticed, or even guessed, what these heretics were up to. It was certainly scandal if a Protestant mentioned his religion to a Roman Catholic, whether English or Portuguese. As to the idea that Protestants might be allowed to build a church, it was unthinkable; even a burial ground was frowned on. The Inquisition carried on a patient, unwearying fight, breaking into open skirmishes at intervals, with chaplains, envoys and consuls, on the chaplain question. One enterprising envoy, in the 1680s, called on the Portuguese ministry armed with the Anglican Book of Common Prayer, pointing out to them all the religious duties mentioned in it which could not be performed without a priest — the sacraments, the absolution, private confession if required, and so forth; it was no use; the government still maintained that, for Protestants, leave for private worship without benefit of clergy was more than enough, and that when and where there was no British ambassador there could be no British assembly for worship. There was something touching in the stubborn and repeated efforts of the Holy Office to crush this alien scandal that raised its head in the devout land of Portugal, a scandal that had to be partially endured on account of the advantages of foreign commerce and foreign military aid, but which could never be really tolerated or accepted: every little while the Inquisition, tired of pretending to look the other way, would pounce, and make a gallant effort to scotch the viper, which would retaliate with envenomed hissings and writhings and, though it might be put out of action for a time, it was never slain, and in the end it had its way.

It was scotched for a while by the diplomatic hiatus which followed 1688, the Portuguese taking but a poor view of our glorious revolution. But in 1692 or so we had an envoy in Lisbon again — Mr. John Methuen; and soon after him followed a chaplain, the Reverend John Colbatch, a learned, earnestly moral, but heated and passionate clergyman, later notorious as a quarrelsome enemy of the great Dr. Bentley's. Quarrels, indeed, seem to have been his speciality throughout his life. While in Lisbon he quarrelled with nearly everyone, but most particularly with the British envoy. His quarrels and his grievances he related to his patron Bishop Burnet of Salisbury, in one of the longest, wordiest and most pained epistles that can ever have been inflicted on those tough, enduring, seasoned prelates, the bishops of the Christian churches. He wrote it in October 1696, the differences between the envoy and himself having by then raged for at least two years and a half. He had written other letters, describing and deploring the conduct and lives of members of the English Factory; he was by no means a tolerant, live-and-let-live kind of clergyman, and no doubt Bishop Burnet had had occasion before to regret his censorious temper; but it was more embarrassing that he should complain of the immoral life and unchristian doctrines of His Majesty's envoy.

He began his letter with apologies for troubling his Lordship, but it was 'indispensably necessary'. He must give his Lordship an account of his past conduct towards Mr. Methuen, and beg his directions as to how to behave towards him in future, 'matters having come to the pass that I can no longer act of my own Head'. Apparently Mr. Methuen had taken against his appointment from the first, but the bishop had made himself responsible for it, and from his first coming to the envoy's house he had tried to fulfil, if not to exceed, what his Lordship had promised for him. But alas, nothing had gone as it should between him and His Majesty's envoy. He himself had shown the greatest respect and deference, exceeding that of any of his predecessors towards gentlemen in his place; he had undergone many inconveniences in order to assist the envoy's son in his studies, 'notwithstanding the little hopes I had of success upon one so abandoned to himself as that unfortunate young man was'. He had not been discouraged by Mr. Methuen's manner towards him; he had not wanted to leave his house; it was to his interest to continue there. But he had had to make up his mind to leave it, for reasons which would have made any decent man of his profession do so, for 'it appeared to me that this gentleman had his mind totally corrupted with such Notions as directly tend to the Subversion of all Religion and Morality'. The trouble was that Hobbes's *Leviathan* had, apparently, become Mr. Methuen's chief study and the standard of his notions, so that 'in any serious discussion anyone who knows Mr. Hobbes his System will know beforehand what Mr. Methuen will say'. He showed a sad contempt for religion. Mr. Colbatch, himself anti-Hobbes, could not without grief see His Majesty's representative 'thus deluded by so wretched an Imposter'. Indeed, Mr. Methuen must have been something of a bore about Hobbes, for he 'seemed no more able to forbear harping upon that string than other people can help talking of the Trade or Business'. He seemed to the clergyman to be striving to make infidels, 'as if he thought himself sent hither on no other errand'. The chaplain had 'a difficult task on't to behave myself without giving offence or scandal'. He had either to be perpetually contradicting or opposing a gentleman in his own house, or see young people debauched in their principles and consent to it by his silence. He chose the first alternative, which annoyed Mr. Methuen, but did not cramp his style. Whenever the news was heavy, which no doubt it often was, a European war being on, the envoy had recourse to such topics to entertain his guests. The chaplain began to feel that he must leave the house, and a more than usually shocking occasion finally determined him. But he was careful that his leaving should not give offence, and he regularly visited the envoy afterwards. He 'observed with astonishment that he was constant at the Holy Sacrament, which seemed apt to augment rather than abate the Scandals given by his Discourses at other times'. Mr. Colbatch made up his mind that he must Speak. So on Good Friday he stayed behind at the envoy's house after divine service, in order to do so. While he waited there, a message came to him from Mr. Methuen that the consul and his lady were to dine there that day, and would he join them. 'I was somewhat surprised: the Envoy was giving me to understand he was throwing off all Common Decency and the very appearance of things; so I returned home, after saying it was not my Custom, as the Envoy knew, to dine on those days, nor indeed did I before observe it to be the Envoy's.'

After this episode, Mr. Colbatch decided to speak his mind in a letter. He let the envoy have it straight. 'The Notions you have entertained,' said he, 'concerning Religion, and endeavoured to spread, are such as (if anything can) do incapacitate any Person from the Receiving the Holy Sacrament; And therefore my Humble Advice is that you do Abstain for the Present. The Rubric which I am bound to follow shows that there are cases where the Curate is obliged to offer Advice of this Nature . . . What I now say is by way of Request only, as supposing that you would not that I should make my Reasons public, which I acknowledge you have a right to demand of me.'

To this firm intimation the envoy returned a short note expressing his surprise, and promised a letter next day. The letter said that he had given serious consideration to the matter, examined his heart, and 'could not find he entertained a Belief of anything in Religion that is not conformable to the Holy Scriptures and the Doctrine of the Church of England'. It had never been his intention to spread irreligion, and if he had done so he was heartily sorry for it, would avoid it for the future, satisfy all with whom he conversed of the sincerity of his religion, and, if Mr. Colbatch thought it necessary, would make an open declaration. If the chaplain was satisfied with this, he was to read no further; if he was not, but still intended to refuse him the Holy Sacrament, he was to read the second page, which was sealed up. About this page (which no doubt contained Mr. Methuen's plans of action in case of the clergyman's obduracy), Mr. Colbatch 'was not solicitous at all'; he wrote that he was satisfied. 'I doubted not,' he told the bishop, 'but it would presently appear in his Conversation, which would be the easiest way to take off the Scandal he might have given.'

But he soon learnt that the envoy had 'resented it as a very High Presumption in me for daring to write to him, that had I anything to say to him he thought it my duty to wait upon him in Person . . . that being his Chaplain and his Servant, had I observed any faults in him it was not for me to take notice of them; that his Notions were more orthodox than my own, he understanding those things better than myself . . . I could not help wondering what the Gentleman should mean by his Orthodox notions'. The notions complained of by Mr. Colbatch were the Hobbist denials of the fundamental articles of religion concerning good and evil, conscience, immortality, and such.

But there was worse to come. The envoy did not content himself with theory; he proceeded to put his tenets into practice. There had lately arrived in Lisbon a young English gentlewoman 'to marry an eminent person in the Factory' (actually Mr. Earle the consul, though Colbatch does not say so), a person very friendly with the envoy, who became shortly very friendly with his wife. They became 'cousins'. 'Summer coming on, the Envoy takes a small Quinta, saying the air of the town did not agree with his Cousin, and therefore he designed she should live with him there the following Summer. This was a matter which the Envoy, who had had sufficient experience of the humour of our English here, could not suppose would be concealed long . . . The Design went on and the Talk of People increased accordingly. Nor could it be decent for me supposing I were able to express what sport it made among people whose grand concern it is to make descants upon what their neighbours do.' Thinking how strange the affair must seem to the people of the country (possibly Mr. Colbatch overrated the unfamiliarity of the Portuguese with the spectacle of gentlemen of consequence thus disporting themselves), and remembering the censorious humour that reigned among those of his own nation (and this could scarcely be overrated), the chaplain resolved once again to speak. After what had recently passed between them, he naturally felt some hesitation in addressing the envoy on the subject, so he broached it to the lady, 'in the most easy and inoffensive Manner'. No doubt she meant, he told her, nothing but what was altogether innocent, 'yet I thought advisable in her to consider what a Country we were in, and what People we conversed with; that those Innocent Liberties that are taken in England are not accounted such here, and that if our own People were so ill-natured in their reflections already, it was not to be expected they would be otherwise did she persist in her Design ... that we had to do with a People that spared none'. To this effect he discoursed twice with the lady, warning her of the 'great inconveniences attending sinister Reports of this kind. She agreed with me that the inconveniences I mentioned were to be carefully avoided', but it was now too late to get out of her engagement without offending the envoy, and indeed she seemed to think it so fine a thing to be in favour with him that she could never do enough to deserve it. As to the gossip, she said it sprang from malice and envy, and, knowing her own innocence, she did not mind it. Mr. Colbatch told her that one should be concerned not only to be innocent but to seem so. She repeated that she could not draw back, but said she was greatly obliged all the same.

It is not clear what part the lady's husband played in this affair, why the chaplain never, apparently, discussed it with him, nor whether he felt any objections himself to his wife's staying at the envoy's quinta. Nor does it emerge what Mr. Methuen's household consisted of. Presumably a widower (or there could scarcely have been a scandal), he seems to have had at this time one son with him, the abandoned young man whom Mr. Colbatch had tried to assist with his studies, and who later this summer, after a drinking-party given by one of the merchants ('a noble treat', some one called it) 'went a-serenading, which occasioned a quarrel with the natives', in which he was killed. The elder son, Paul, an intelligent young man with a future, and a niche in Westminster Abbey to reward him for his assistance to his father in the matter of the port wine treaty, was already in the diplomatic service; he may or may not have been now in Lisbon. For the rest, there was Mr. Methuen himself, a tall, dark, suave, plausible man, aged about forty-five, 'in his complexion and manners much of a Spaniard', wrote John Macky of him; 'a man of intrigue, but very muddy in his conceptions, and not greatly understood in anything'. Dean Swift's verdict was 'a profligate rogue without religion or morals; but cunning enough; yet without abilities of any kind'; it should be remembered that most Whigs were rogues to the Dean.

Some one more kindly disposed towards Mr. Methuen described him as 'a man of great parts ... his manly yet easy eloquence shined in the House of Commons on many important and nice occasions'.

Such as he was, his man-of-the-world attentions turned the head of young Mrs. Earle. She repeated to him forthwith the chaplain's warning; she may or not have told her husband also; but he is an enigmatic background figure in the drama.

Mr. Methuen was definitely annoyed by this fresh piece of impertinence on the part of the young clergyman whom he insisted on regarding as his private chaplain. He took his revenge, or so the clergyman thought, by spreading slanders against him. 'It is incredible, my Lord, what little Tricks I have observed him condescending to use, in order to lessen me in the Esteem of our People and Prejudice them against me.' Colbatch resented the reflections made on him by the Factory, who regarded him as a tale-teller to the envoy of their malicious remarks about his affair with Mrs. Earle. Particularly he incurred the enmity of Mr. Milner, the chief English merchant in Lisbon, and so 'I came to be universally condemned'.

At this point Mrs. Earle got smallpox, so her visit to the envoy's quinta was deferred for a time. But he took a still larger quinta, where he spent the summer, and invited her to stay there to get fresh air after her illness, and there they lived together for the rest of the summer and much of the winter following, 'giving such scandal to all sorts of People as infinitely exceeded what I had foretold ... I refer myself for proof of the Scandal to any Englishman that hath set foot in Lisbon for any time these two years past'. The scandal was increased by the envoy's boasting; to his friends he read aloud a congratulatory letter on the affair from the Marquis of Halifax, and generally showed off.

Before Christmas he paid a visit to England. It was soon after his return to Lisbon that Mr. Colbatch 'found people's minds alienated from me in the strangest manner imaginable'. Puzzled, he was presently told that this was because, 'I had made it my business to send Characters in to England of All in General, and of each of them in Particular'. One merchant told him that he had for some time abstained from church for this reason, 'I having said in my letters that our Factory consisted of such a Horrid Crew that I fancied myself to be in Hell while I was amongst them'. These unkind reports had been made, according to the Factory, both to their business principals and to bishops. One bishop had been so much concerned that he had called on Mr. Methuen when he was in London to ask him 'what sort of people we had here'. People began to draw comparisons between Mr. Colbatch and his predecessor, Mr. Geddes, who when asked by a bishop 'to give an account of his thoughts concerning our Factory, instead of those Black Characters that I had given them, reported that indeed they Led none of the Strictest Lives, but yet they were just like other men'. It being very true that for the most part they did not lead the strictest lives, Mr. Colbatch could see no harm in his reports of them, but nevertheless these reports 'put people into a Strange Commotion'. That he had written such a letter, Paul Methuen testified; and his father let the Factory know that if they would signify their dislike of the chaplain to him, he would have him removed.

He had two special enemies in the Factory, one whom he had refused to marry to a papist (having been warned by the Inquisition not to do so); the other 'is very often Quite Distracted and Raving Mad, and well were it for him had he no Lucid Intervals, it having been his custom at such times as he was himself to send for Prostitutes to his House for the entertainment of all comers, and the lewdness committed there used to be a subject of our People's Diversion upon the Public Place'. The chaplain had once preached a sermon on the topic of men who glory in their wickedness, 'and the poor man thought it all aimed at him, and that was enough to enrage him against me'. These two and another wrote to the envoy requesting the chaplain's removal 'that he may have the satisfaction elsewhere which as things are can't well be had here, and we a Minister with whom we may have a friendly Correspondence'. The envoy, a most insincere man, was all this time hypocritically friendly, paying Mr. Colbatch visits and asking him to dine, and meanwhile 'he and the Lady cohabit at the Quinta, in the most scandalous manner imaginable'. They were generally observed to show evident marks of affection, 'playing those fooleries which they say are usual between folks that are in Love'. Colbatch remonstrated several times again with Mr. Methuen, the envoy replied impatiently that people were so malicious they would say anything; and even were it true, the manners of people were such in this age that he could not believe it would cause scandal; anyhow it was unlikely anything criminal should pass between him and the Lady, since they lived so openly together, and were he to be monarch of the universe, he would not attempt anything to dishonour this lady or her husband. Colbatch again repeated his piece, that much scandal was occasioned, not only among the English but among the other nations here, 'in so much that, as I had heard, the very Friars in the neighbourhood pretended to be Scandalized at his Conduct'. The envoy promised to inquire among his acquaintances about the scandal, and if he found any scandalized, would remove the occasion. 'What inquiries he made I know not'; but the occasion was not removed. Next Good Friday (his day for moral protests) Colbatch sent another of his letters. The envoy answered that 'no one ought to know better than yourself the Malicious Impertinent talking Humour of the Greater Part of this Factory', and went on to administer a threat. 'I own no quality that you either are or can be in here save that of my domestic chaplain while I have the honour to serve His Majesty in this Court ... Whenever you shall totally disown that character, I will immediately furnish myself with some other Person, and leave you to pursue your Pretensions in England to any other character or qualification here.' When, soon afterwards, he called on Colbatch, he said he did not believe he had become the talk of the other nations in Lisbon. Of this, said Colbatch, the late Dutch Resident and the Spanish envoy could have told him, and 'it is said the King himself has heard of it' (which is certain, since King Pedro's favourite occupation, after sport, bull-fighting, and indulgence in 'certain pleasures that are too much allowed in Portugal', was hearing gossip of the intrigues of the town).

Soon after this interchange, Mrs. Earle settled at the quinta for all her time, staying there even when the poor consul lay sick in Lisbon.

So matters continued for a year. After the following Easter (1696) the envoy gave notice that he had to leave his Lisbon house, owing to the moving into its proximity of the French ambassador, which might lead to brawls between the servants, since the two countries were at war. So, until he had another house, he intended to move his household into the country, and church services must therefore be suspended. This raised the old issue as to whether English services could be held in some other house than the envoy's.

Mr. Colbatch told Mr. Methuen that the articles of the Treaty had arranged for this; Mr. Methuen, taking a leaf out of the Inquisition's book, declared that they arranged for nothing of the kind. He tried, said Colbatch indignantly, to put us on a level with the Dutch, who had no such privilege. The quarrel became acute; in the middle of it Mr. Methuen departed to England, probably to take another post, leaving his countrymen to fight out their rights of worship with the Portuguese. The chaplain shook his head over the insincerity of this man. 'If ever any one arrived to that perfection in Hobbism as to be able to wear out of his mind the Distinguishing Sense of things Vile and Honourable, I am persuaded this Gentleman is the person.'

As to the church matter, the question Cui Bono raised itself. Why was the envoy so set on having the Factory prevented from worshipping in the house of the consul? He no doubt wished to ingratiate himself with the Portuguese court, and he also liked the chaplain to be completely dependent on him. But the grand reason of all Mr. Colbatch took to be connected with the lady: if the consul her husband were obliged to provide a convenient room for church services, he would have to move to another house; 'he lives now in one so situated that the Lady cannot endure it, and is sickish whenever she comes near it, but if a better should be taken, then this, the only Pretence for her living at the Quinta, would be removed, and she probably be obliged to remain at home, and the Envoy thereby be deprived of her Conversation in a great measure at least, which is a thing he is so taken with that in all Appearance there is nothing in the World he would not rather undergo the Loss of, he daily discovering more Evident signs of a more Desperate Passion, and it is the general opinion of such as know him that he is so much in love with the Air of this Country that he will never totally abandon it, and is resolved to return hither whether with or without the Character of Envoy, and the Lady for her part has declared it before Company that whenever he leaves the Country she Hopes she shall not remain in it an Hour after him'.

Turning from this grand scandal, the clergyman gave the bishop an account of the contentious Article 14 of the Treaty of 1654, giving the English leave to meet for worship in private houses. The King of Portugal had demurred to this at first, pleading that the power of the Inquisition was above his. But 'Cromwell returns word that if the King of Portugal was no King in his Own

Dominion, he would send a Power sufficient to make him so. And Blake is sent with a Squadron to Cruise before the River in order to intercept the Brazil Fleet. Hereupon King John signs the Treaty, and the Church is immediately held at the Consul's'. Colbatch ran through the history of the various suspensions of the Church by the Inquisition, 'who, as your Lordship knows, may at any time pretend ignorance of what the Civil Power does where Religion is concerned'. There was no difficulty about the case, he maintained, except that of prevailing with Mr. Methuen for his consent to our rights.

He ended his extremely long letter by asking for directions how to behave if the scandals should continue, and (should Mr. Methuen not return) for a gentleman to succeed him whose regard to religion and morality might prove exemplary, for there is 'no other remedy for these Deplorable Mischiefs occasioned by the Irregular Lives of former Envoys, and increased I am afraid by this Gentleman to a far higher degree . . . I am sure they are much greater than I am either able or willing to express'.

As to himself, he owned himself not exempt from faults and follies, or from 'the railleries of our people here' — indeed, no one had ever been that. But his bitterest enemies had not accused him of any immorality. He had been so unhappy as to become uneasy to Mr. Methuen, but all from a sense of duty. Finally, he apologized to his Lordship if he had let fall in his letter some unbecoming expressions, and so closed.

It must have taken Bishop Burnet, a busy man, some time to read all this. Having done so, he was, apparently, not sure how to answer it, and was rather loath to do so, for he did not reply until March. He then sent a kind but slightly repressive letter to the zealous young clergyman, telling him that he valued his courage and just strictness, and that, according to his apprehensions, he had done his duty and hazarded his own interests for the sake of a cause that ought to be dearer to us than our lives. The Methuen affair was, however, over, since the envoy had left Lisbon. Further, the bishop had made inquiries among those who knew him, and found nothing but commendations. He had talked with him; the envoy had thanked him, and had admitted that he might, in the course of discussion, have maintained some things that he did not believe, but as a matter of fact he abhorred Hobbes's views on religion and policy, firmly believed the Christian religion, and made it the business of his life to conform himself to it. 'Many', the bishop observed, 'have delighted mightily to shew their wit in the venting of paradoxes, and passed for Atheists, yet I am sure were not so.'

As to Mr. Methuen and that gentlewoman, what he said was that, having lived a long time at the consul's house, he had invited him and his wife to his quinta. He was not surprised that the Portuguese should pass remarks, but he was sure none of his own servants, who had watched him and the lady together, did so. Anyhow, 'his taking pains to be fixed here does not look like a strong passion to return, so whatsoever may be with the matter, I must leave it to God'. This, said the bishop, was the substance of his two long conversations with Mr. Methuen, and 'I could not press things further after such plausible answers delivered with great calmness. When I had done, he began to recriminate. He said you were a man of unblameable life, of good learning, of great firmness against Popery, and was a very good Preacher, but he said you had let your temper sour you extremely; you had many narrow notions, and were apt to take things ill and to judge hardly, and had too much of a roughness of spirit that he thought was much in your constitution, had been heightened at the University, and did not wear of being abroad in the World ... To tell you truly what I think, I am afraid somewhat of this may be true, for there is an eagerness of style that runs through your letter which disposes me to believe you may be a little heated'. Now that this business was over, however, Mr. Methuen would write to his son, who was to succeed him, telling him to live with the chaplain in friendship and confidence. 'I do very earnestly beg of you', the bishop admonished, 'that you will study to bring yourself to as towardly and tractable a temper as you possibly can, make the best of things you can, discharge your duty, but with discretion and tenderness, and bear with many things, though you cannot help them, for so we must live unless we would go out of the world, for if you cannot procure yourself quiet and satisfaction where you are, you had best think of coming home.'

This is the longest letter, he added, 'that I have writ of a great while, though it is but a short billet in comparison with yours'.

It is unlikely that Mr. Colbatch was pleased with this letter. The plausible Mr. Methuen had had the last word and the ear of authority; the affair of the young gentlewoman, though apparently over, was still a matter for gossip among Lisbonians. Bishop Burnet, who little knew Lisbon, set it aside as a storm in a tea-cup, and anyhow now done with. Was the chaplain then to look the other way and disregard notorious scandals among His Majesty's representatives? Was he, out of 'discretion and tenderness', to leave (like the bishop) such matters to God?

We have, unfortunately, no information as to how Mr. Colbatch got on during his remaining two or three years in Lisbon. Did he live in the house with Paul Methuen? Were they on friendly terms? What were his relations with the consul and his wife, and did these two settle down domestically together now that the tempter had gone his way? We know little of Mr. Earle beyond his brief, dull, legibly written, business-like letters to Whitehall; we do not know whether he was a complaisant husband, an indignant husband, or whether the whole affair was a mare's nest built up in the heated mind of the chaplain and the wagging tongues of Lisbon. This, however, in the light of John Methuen's reputation, and of normal human habits, seems unlikely.

However this was, Mr. Colbatch was left to bring himself to a towardly and tractable temper as best he could. His contentious later career seems to indicate that at no time did he become very towardly or tractable.

While in Lisbon he wisely threw himself into the study of Portuguese life and history. He was an intelligent observer and recorder, with a good acquaintance with affairs; his *Account of the Court of Portugal in the Reign of Pedro II*, which he published in 1700, after his return to England, is well put together and shows shrewd observation. He took a diplomatically optimistic view of Pedro, whom he liked, in spite of his over-indulgence in those pleasures which Colbatch had regarded so severely in Mr. Methuen; as King Pedro was not a British envoy, his habits could be observed more objectively. 'I never heard that he had any favourite of the sex, unless it were one Frenchwoman . . . Those he hath had his commerce with are said to be of the lowest rank, and very many, and not all of the same colour. He hath not as yet acknowledged any unlawful issue, save one daughter, whose mother was a mean person'. But the king was withal a modest man, of grave and comely aspect, melancholy and devout, and loved to convert heretics, and so sober that he frowned on wine; he was illiterate, but could sign his name, and enjoyed sport, gossip and bull-fighting; a good ruler, Mr. Colbatch on the whole admired him. About the Portuguese people, too, he is very fair; no people less addicted to drunkenness, but they bore a mortal hatred to foreigners; they had been most ungrateful, too, to the English, who had been with such frequency their saviours. Colbatch felt it very tiresome of them to remain neutral in the present fight against the common Tyrant (Louis XIV), 'if on no other account but the conveniency of their harbours, which in a war at sea must have been of mighty advantage to the side they adhered to. But they thought it was their interest all along to continue neuters, and our Princes have not thought fit to oblige them to declare, though in defence of the common liberty, in which they had as great a concern as others'. In consequence, Portuguese ports had become nests of French privateers and Irish pirates.

But our British virtues, Mr. Colbatch patriotically explained, had endeared our countrymen to the Portugueses. True that in the country parts the horrid ideas that the people had of heretics made them look on us as strange sorts of monsters and try to do us mischief; but they soon learned how honourable, peaceable and gentle were English soldiers, and how admirably they spent their time in serving and helping the people on whom they were quartered, so now they were welcomed and caressed, while Frenchmen were apt to be knocked on the head. Neither in the cities did the people insult the English for their religion, for they were a humane people, and their government forbade opprobrious treatment of foreigners. Only last year a lawyer who had described the English as Heretics, Lutherans, Schismatics, and Excommunicated persons, whose oath could not be taken in a court of law, had been complained of to the king and his arrest ordered; he took sanctuary in a church, but it had been decided that his crime was of such a nature that the Church could not protect him; unfortunately he had died before an example could be made of him.

Colbatch has an interesting note on the image of the national patron saint, St. George, who was carried in processions — 'a fat, burly image, dressed up, as I take it, in the habit worn by the English at the time of the Saint's first coming into the country. He was brought into request here, as some think, by John of Gaunt; others are of opinion that Edward de Langley, Earl of Cambridge, brought him in a little before; but about this time it was that the Portuguese began to call upon St. George in their battles instead of St. Jago; and ever since he has been the patron of the kingdom and hath had his place in the procession accordingly, wherein he, whilst other saints are carried upon pageants, rides on a horse that is kept on purpose for him, a boy for his page following on another horse to carry his lance'.

These comments on Portuguese customs and character show an interested and friendly observation of the people among whom he lived which is one of Mr. Colbatch's more amiable sides. Bishop Burnet was pleased with the book, so was Queen Mary; both promised its author preferment for it. Preferment, however, was a thing Colbatch seldom got, since he had the misfortune not to be very likeable. One need not take as literal the character given him by his enemy the learned Dr. Bentley, that Master of Trinity whom Colbatch and other Fellows of his college spent half a life-time trying vainly to unseat; the Master wrote in a violent passion, in language as unrestrained as befitted a learned scholar of his period; he called his victim 'violent and malignant', 'a pious calumniator'; 'he never broaches a piece of mere knavery without a preface about his *conscience*, nor even offers us downright nonsense without eyes, muscles and shoulders wrought up into the most solemn posture of gravity'; he 'roars, bellows, and calls the mob together, as if the whole Church was in flames'; he lies sleepless whole nights out of anguish when things are quiet and flourishing about him; when there was some squabble in the College to keep up his spirits, 'he would look something gay among us, smile horrible, like Satan in Milton, and extend his wide jaws with an agreeable yawn'; he 'bawls and bellows against a phantom of his own making'; 'was there ever such haughty sufficiency, accompanied with such gross stupidity?'

Unfair, even unkind, as this was, there is in it a faintly familiar suggestion; these are not words that would have commended themselves to the suave and diplomatic Mr. Methuen, but it is possible that he might have been not ill-pleased to hear them from the splenetic Master; they might have expressed for him, with, indeed, some violence and excess, something that he too had more mildly felt about Mr. Colbatch when that zealous and moral clergyman was speaking to him for his good in Lisbon. Even his friends said that 'his virtue was by some thought too severe', and that 'that virtue seemed to have something of the disagreeable'.

It seems certain that the roughness of spirit which Mr. Methuen had told Bishop Burnet was in his constitution and had been heightened at the University, was further heightened by his residence there as Fellow of Trinity and Doctor of Casuistry and his long feud with the malevolent and invincible Dr. Bentley. There were too many occasions in his career when the bishop might have been again 'disposed to believe that you may be a little heated'. As at Lisbon, he often had cause for heat. Of nearly all his encounters he got the worst; there must indeed, even in his virtue, have been 'something of the disagreeable'. The Lisbon Factory had felt it; his Majesty's envoy in that place had felt it; Bishop Burnet, and the youthful noblemen whom he had tutored, had felt it; Cambridge felt it, and no doubt the village of Orewell, where, as its incumbent, he ended his days. It could not be helped. Dr. Bentley died Master of Trinity, triumphant, undislodged; John Methuen and his son Paul were both buried in Westminster Abbey (a tribute to the blessings of port wine); Dr. Colbatch, their foe, keen scholar, upright moralist, zealous reformer, pertinacious patron-seeker, conscientious, contentious clergyman, suffered defeat and died obscure.

Lisbon chaplains have now been tamed. It is scarcely now worth while to be at the pains of investigating their careers; they have become too peaceable, too far removed from their stormy beginnings, when the Inquisition watched them with grim impatience waiting to pounce, when the long-drawn feud perpetually simmered and at intervals boiled over. All is now toleration, amity, brotherly co-operation; *odium theologicum*, which used to keep so many tempers, clergymen and faggots briskly a-flame, is turned to ashes in a cold grate; stir them, and you may get a sulky smoulder, but never a spark. Nor do consul and merchants now grudge their pastor the milreis they contribute to his support. And nor (so far as I know, but of course I do not know) have recent chaplains felt it their duty to lecture and excommunicate ambassadors for their moral conduct or their irreligious views, even should the latter be Hobbesian and the former incline envoys to live in quintas with the consul's wife. It would seem that the chaplains have taken to heart Bishop Burnet's admonishments, have learnt to bear with many things, and have acquired a towardly and tractable temper. It seems likely also that their flocks have improved, and are no more the Horrid

Crew that made Mr. Colbatch fancy himself in Hell when he was among them.

BIBLIOGRAPHY

State Papers, Portugal, 89/16, 17 (Record Office).
B.M. Add. MSS 22908 (transcribed by A. R. WALFORD in 2nd Annual Report of Lisbon Branch of Historical Association 1938).
Memoirs of the Secret Service, JOHN MACKY (1733).
Brief Historical Relation of State Affairs, 1678-1714, NARCISSUS LUTTREL.
Works, JONATHAN SWIFT (vol. 10, 1814 ed.).
Life of Richard Bentley, J. H. MONK (1830).
Essay on Richard Bentley, THOMAS DE QUINCEY (1830).
Answer to pamphlet criticizing his proposed Greek Testament, RICHARD BENTLEY (1721).
An account of the Court of Portugal under Pedro II, JOHN COLBATCH (1700).
Memoirs, WILLIAM WHISTON (1713).
Dictionary of National Biography.

PORT WINE

The Portuguese and the English have
always been the best of friends because
we can't get no Port Wine anywhere else.
Peter Simple, CAPTAIN MARRYAT
1834

THE British wine-shipping colony of Oporto is one of the
more romantic phenomena in the history of settlers abroad.
Its members might mostly themselves repudiate the adjective:
but it is nevertheless apt. The romance lies largely in their trade,
and the circumstances which surround it; the culture of vines in
the magnificent country of the Upper Douro, the beauty of the
mountain quintas of the wine firms, the gathering of the grapes
and the making of the wine, its shipping down the great wild
reaches of the Douro to the picturesque wine lodges of Vila Nova
de Gaia, the processes of coopering, piping, maturing, bottling
and shipping to England, the rich hues and bouquet of the port
itself, the part it has played for two and a half centuries in English
life, since it emerged from the acid sourness of its *vinho verde*
adolescence and the muddy impurity of its early eighteenth-century career.

> Mark how it smells, methinks a real pain
> Is by its odour thrown upon my brain.
> I've tasted it — 'tis spiritless and flat,
> And has as many different tastes
> As can be found in compound pastes . . .
> But fetch us a pint of any sort,
> Navarre, Galicia, anything but Port,

wrote an anti-port poet in 1693. Though port had then been
imported from Portugal for many years, it was not yet worthy of
the name; its great days were still to come. It was a common
habit in taverns, even under Queen Anne, to 'crack a bottle of
claret, dashed with port'.

Apart from the wine itself and its handling, the romance of the
British Portonian wine firms lies in the unique character of their
long colonization. They captured and occupied Oporto in a
sense in which the British Factory at Lisbon never captured and

occupied the capital; these have remained, after all the centuries, a foreign colony, varying in character and personnel from generation to generation. The Oporto families, some of them established in Oporto or Viana do Castelo since the seventeenth century, have the air of owning the city, so Britannically, so unconsciously arrogantly, they walk its mountainy streets, play cricket and football in their own playing grounds, hold rowing regattas on the river, meet for business and entertainment in their magnificent eighteenth-century granite Factory House, conduct their business across the Douro in their ancient and beautiful wine lodges, and superintend the vintage from their quintas far up the river. Their fine houses and gardens stand on the noble eminences of the city, looking down the Douro to the bar and the sea beyond; they have their summer houses and bathing beaches at Foz, their own society, entertainments, sports and church parade. Less touched by continual influxes from the outer world than Lisbon, and lacking the stir and sophistication brought by the Corps Diplomatique, they have lived for centuries a jolly, self-contained British life, friendly with their Portuguese neighbours (except during periods of anger, resentment and feud), more familiar with them, some eighteenth-century tourists remarked, than were the Lisbon English, but still a close colony. Probably they have always been so, since the first west-country cloth merchants put their factors there to see after their business in the fourteenth and fifteenth centuries. The earliest English merchants trading to Portugal were what were later called rag merchants; they shipped cloth and cotton to Lisbon and Oporto and the other ports, and took back in exchange wine, fruit, sugar, salt, wax, cork, honey and spices. The wines of Portugal (Lisbon wines were then the best) thus became well known in Britain. Indeed, they had been well known before; English crusaders calling in to help Lisbon to get rid of the Moors, and the army taken over by John of Gaunt, had enjoyed them so much that they were seldom seen sober. The British soldier and trader, finding himself in a land where he could get cheap wine and plenty of it, made the most of his opportunities; he earned a name for tipsiness among the temperate Portuguese, and the memory of that copious drinking was perhaps one of the few happy recollections he took home with him.

Most of the wine shipped to Britain from Portugal was at first from Viana do Castelo, and grown in the Minho country; they called it Red Portugal, and it was rather like Burgundy. The first English to come into the trade ran it, apparently, in connection with the sale of Newfoundland cod to the Portuguese; the cod was bartered for wine; the wine was shipped to Newfoundland, and some of it sent on from there for sale in England; it was soon found that the process improved its quality, and 'matured in Newfoundland' became a boast. But the wine was for some time more or less of a side line; the merchants concerned were primarily cloth merchants or Newfoundland fish merchants, who took the wines of Minho in exchange for their goods. During the second half of the seventeenth century more and more factors of British firms resided at Viana, Monção and Oporto, and made it part of their business to select wines suitable for shipping home. The firms owned their ships; they did not, as they later did, themselves go up into the wine country to inspect the vines; the growers brought the wine to them at Viana and Oporto. Many of the best vineyards were owned by the monasteries, and the best wine was called 'priest port'. Some firms flourishing to-day can trace back their history to these seventeenth-century merchants and agents; Hunt, Roope & Company, for instance, who had premises at Oporto and Viana about 1654, shipping dried cod-fish and oil from Newfoundland, wheat and wool from England, and wine, cork, fruit, etc., from Portugal to England. Their Mr. Page got into trouble in 1661 for shipping money out of the country; his son or grandson is mentioned as living in Oporto forty years later and having a house also at Viana. But the shipping of wine in exchange for cod and cloth had been going on since the fifteenth century at least; interrupted by the Spanish annexation of Portugal and the English war with Spain, it had revived again with the peace of 1603, when the Company of English merchants trading with Spain and Portugal had renewed their charter and were given a consul. The treaty of 1654 gave them fresh privileges and their trade a fresh impetus. The British colony in Oporto developed vigorously; it had its own consul, its Factory, its chaplain (during the intervals when he was not suppressed and chased out of Portugal by the Inquisition), its religious persecutions, and its full tale of oppressions and grievances.

The Factory, in fact, was by then about as vocal as its Lisbon brothers, and even more vigorous in its revolts against Mr. Maynard, the consul-general, who tried in vain to tyrannize over them from Lisbon. They were obviously men of spirit; even Maynard's son-in-law wrote him sharp and firm letters upholding the Factory's independence. They stood up to the consul-general, they stood up to the Inquisition in the matter of their right to worship Church of England and have a chaplain and not to have their children kidnapped, and they stood up to the Portuguese government and their own government in London. Like Lisbon, they were 'a jolly free Factory', and their energy and initiative were such that they soon succeeded in beating their Portuguese commercial rivals out of the field and getting most of the wine trade into their hands. Long before the Methuen Treaty of 1703 English agents in Oporto had been pleading with London for a reduction of the duties on Portugal wines, foreseeing that if they were allowed to compete with French wines on equal terms they would soon beat them, and their increased import would add considerably to His Majesty's revenues, besides improving our cloth trade with Portugal. The Methuen Treaty lowered the duty to less than that on French wines, and demand gradually increased, though, owing to the poor quality of the wines imported, and their inexperienced treatment, it was at first disappointing to the British merchants, who had thrown their energies into encouraging the Douro farmers to grow more vines, and had begun to travel into the wine country to see for themselves.

There are some interesting letters in the early years of the eighteenth century from young Thomas Woodmass, sent out by his father to north Portugal at the end of 1703. He arrived at Viana on Christmas day, met Mr. Job Bearsley, an English merchant trading in corn, oil and iron, other English merchants, the consul, and the English clergyman, who took a service on the following Sunday in the house of Mr. Bradley (of Phayre & Bradley); 'after dinner some Portugal cockerels did engage in battle, the Minister directing, and then the older gentlemen did play at cards and sip wine'. Soon afterwards, Woodmass was taken by his friends to see the wine country at 'Monson' (Monção), and reported intelligently on crops, pipes, prices, and quality. English coopers had been brought over to show the Portuguese how to make casks; they were a 'drunken lot, but the natives now know how to make casks'. In September he went from Viana to Oporto, where 'after many troubles' (which included highway robbery on the journey, apparently from Lord Galwey's British soldiery, a wild and disreputable horde, and, like the coopers, a drunken lot) 'I am now with your friend Mister Page in the Ruo Nuovo' (Thomas's Portuguese was still rudimentary). 'O Porto is much larger than Viana, and here are more English and Scotch families. The wine of the Duro is much praised by Mr. Harris and others. Of the language I know but little, the servants being mostly blacks from America who speak English.' In November he wrote, still from Oporto, 'I have seen Mr. Lee, our consul, at a small tavern in the Ruo Nuovo, with regard to the way in which the authorities would deal with our trade. Mr. Lee says there is bad feeling against us, inasmuch as the principal trade of the country is in our hands, but that the treaties of commerce are in our favour. Among the Portuguese there is a desire to have control of our lodges, so that we should have to bribe the officials in order to do business. The farmers seem honest enough, but the Customs men are a bad class, and I fear me would soon destroy our trade. There is much talk about the Government raising a heavy tax on us, and by all accounts they will not be satisfied until they have driven us out of the country. With this I send you my diary'.

The diary is interesting, as giving a vivid picture of local life, travel and inns (so insect-infested that the travellers preferred to sleep on the tables). Various English merchants crossed the young man's path: Mr. Clark, Mr. Phayre and Mr. Pratt, for instance, who had thought to evade the company on the road of Mr. Woodmass and his companion Mr. Stert, but, says Thomas complacently, they failed because one of their horses cast a shoe. The firms of some of these gentlemen are still extant and famous; Phayre & Bradley became later Messrs. Croft & Co. At the end of September, 'the heat is so great that breathing is difficult. Wine is at 13 millreas the pipe, but of this vintage there will not be abundance . . . Letters from O Porto; I regret our apprentice is dead and was buried in the sand at low tide'. Heretic corpses were not allowed the use of the local burial grounds, nor to have one of their own; our early merchants, factors and apprentices were shovelled underground anywhere, usually on the shore of sea or river, and no stone marks their graves, which, for historians of the English in Portugal, is a pity.

Woodmass describes Viana and its life, where the English used the quay as their 'Change street. The main business of the Viana British was to import Newfoundland cod; but it was also from Viana that most of the wine was shipped; factors living at Monção bought it from the growers. English ships trading with the American colonies called at Viana on their way back and traded negro slaves for wine; as Thomas Woodmass remarked, the servants of the British merchants in Oporto in 1704 were 'mostly blacks from America'; their names survive in the baptismal and marriage registers of the Factory.

The British wine trade shifted gradually from Viana to Oporto; by the middle of the century only about half a dozen British families were left in Viana. More firms began to sell only wine; the Douro valley vineyards increased, and the technique of viticulture improved. The sale of the wine in England was an uneven, up-and-down business; there were bad periods, when both merchants and farmers suffered heavy loss, and bitter quarrels raged between them, and between both and the Portuguese government who tried to tax the English trade out of existence. But, in spite of setbacks, the wine trade was soon established as the aristocrat among Anglo-Portuguese trades, and the Douro and Corgo valley as its unchallenged soil. The vine-growers grew rich; after a good year, said John Croft, they have 'come down to the city and bought cloths of the richest brocades of France, and strutted with them in the streets like so many peacocks, and thus vied with each other in the gaudiness of apparel'. The wealth and importance of the British shippers in Oporto grew steadily; no doubt they too strutted like peacocks. Each year after the vintage they went up the Douro to Regoa, where they met the growers with their samples and bought their wines. New experiments were tried in fermenting, fortifying and maturing. Adulteration with elderberries became a habit; according to John Croft this was originated by Peter Bearsley of Viana, who one day at an inn expressed elderberry juice into his wine and found it improved the colour and taste. The results were not always happy, and British demand sometimes slumped with alarming capriciousness.

The trade became increasingly a British monopoly; in 1727 an association of shippers was formed to regulate and improve it and keep down the prices paid to the growers. The war between shippers and growers sharpened; each accused the other of cheating and trying to ruin them; Portuguese discontent with the British monopoly in the produce of their country became acute; it came to a head in 1755, when the shippers printed a letter to the growers complaining of adulteration, the poor quality of grapes, and the high prices, and fixed the price at £2 a pipe. Retaliation came swiftly, with the foundation by Pombal, in response to the complaints of the Douro farmers and as part of his campaign against British trade, of the Companhia Geral, the Alto Douro Wine Company, which made the sale of Douro wines practically a government monopoly; British shippers had to buy from the Company, at the Company's prices. No more would the vine-growers be bullied by British firms; no more would their daughters be sacrificed, as their parents complained they were, to Oporto Britons who insisted on them as a condition of the purchase of their fathers' wine. The Company was Pombal's darling scheme against the overbearing, importunate British merchants whom he so disliked. Nominally, it was formed to save the vine-growers from ruin, and to secure steady prices and greater purity of quality in the wines, which the English were accused of colouring and adulterating; actually, its main object was to break the British monopoly.

The British shippers were furious. It seemed to them a gross infringement of their treaties and of their right of free buying and selling. In future only wine passed by the Company's tasters might be exported; the British might only export to Britain; the Company alone might distil and sell brandy; the wine zone was strictly limited; and prices were kept high. Also, no elder trees might be grown in the vine country, so that their berries could not be used for colouring. Except to the vine growers and the government, the new company was a disaster. The British Factory felt it bitterly; they spent several years sending complaints to Pitt and deputations to Pombal. Pitt took little notice and Pombal none, beyond remarking that he presumed the king could dispose of the growths of his country as he thought proper, and that if British merchants were really, as they stated, faced with ruin, they could go. The Company's prices hit the tavern-keepers too; Oporto rioted; twenty-six rioters were executed. Pombal might have relished executing at least twenty-six of the British Factory also; this not being feasible, he merely went on annoying them, and looking blandly the other way when their ambassador called to protest. Pitt looked the other way too, his attention being engaged by the Seven Years War. The Factory went on vainly complaining, the Wine Company triumphantly functioning. The arbitrary classing of wines as fit or unfit for export naturally led to great expense in corrupting the judges, and the price to the British buyer went up by about £6 a pipe. It says much for the hold of port on the British consumer that it held its own at all.

The British, faced with ruin though they might be, had no intention of taking Pombal's advice and leaving Portugal. They made the best of it, managed to evade the laws against importing dry goods and cloth, sold wine surreptitiously in the country, adulterating it as before, prospered sufficiently, and complained bitterly all the time. As some one proudly observed, the Alto Douro Company 'threatened to be a stumbling-block in the way of the English, but the latter are still the *beati possidentes*'.

Gradually the Wine Company became less tyrannical in practice; bribery oiled its juggernaut wheels; British shippers had to come to terms with it, and some even became members of it. The wine firms prospered. By the second half of the eighteenth century port had become the accepted English upper and middle class drink; as John Croft remarked, in 1788, 'an Englishman of any descent, condition or circumstances cannot dispense with it after his good dinner, in the same manner as he uses a piece of Cheshire cheese for pretended digestion-sake'.

The Oporto wine firms increased in numbers rapidly. Those which had been represented in the seventeenth century by a factor at Viana, Monção or Oporto, dealing in corn, cloth, iron or Newfoundland cod, taking a little wine in exchange for goods, like Job Bearsley, Phayre & Bradley, Peter Dowker, Mr. Page, Thomas Woodmass and the rest, had grown into great wine firms; others had come in under Anne and the Georges. By the 1780s, the shippers of Oporto were a cheerful, hospitable, quarrelsome, jovial and opulent society, closely intermarried and connected, living on excellent terms with their Portuguese neighbours and rivals, in the main patriotically British, protestant and loyal. We get pleasant accounts of their lavish and kindly entertainment of visitors to Oporto from contemporary writers, such as Captain Costigan, and Richard Muller, the author of that improbable melodrama, *The Memoirs of Lord Cherington*. The young English doctor who is the hero of these memoirs arrived in Oporto to be doctor to the English Factory one evening when the Factory was giving a grand ball and supper in honour of some victory of the King of Prussia's; the consul took him across the Douro in his barge to the house prepared for him, where he was waited on by all the principal merchants, who took him to the ball and a very elegant supper in an illuminated garden; he was delighted with the sprightly conversation and sumptuous repast, and thought he had entered into the regions of bliss. Next morning his apartments were crowded with fat turkeys, hams and hampers of wine, presents from the British merchants, and, until ruined and betrayed by a false Portuguese cleric, his life was all pleasure. This was some time in the 1770s; the hospitable merchants might have included the representatives of the present firms of Croft, Hunt Roope & Co., Morgan Brothers, Butler, Offley Forrester, Warre, Kopke, Taylor, Fladgate & Yeatman (descended from Job Bearsley of Viana), and many others then flourishing.

In 1786, under the direction of Consul Whitehead, the present Factory House began building. It stands magnificently at the corner of what was then the Rua Nova dos Inglezes (now, more patriotically, the Rua do Infante Dom Henrique) and the Rua de S. João Novo; a fine, granite, three-storied house, seventy feet by ninety, with arcaded front, spacious vestibule, massive stone stairway, library, sitting-rooms, billiard and smoking-rooms, and large, beautifully proportioned dining-room, dessert room and ballroom — worthy setting for the scenes of revelry by night and business by day that occupied the attention of its patrons. As the enthusiastic Mr. Charles Sellers put it, 'in its earlier days it resounded daily and nightly to the festive carousals of men who were making for their posterity names to conjure with in the wine trade ... The severity of its architecture savours of the proverbial rectitude of our pioneers of commerce'. It was admirably adapted to festive carousals on the grand scale; in its banqueting and ballrooms distinguished visitors of all nations have been entertained for a century and a half. Through the Peninsular War British officers danced, dined and wined there, and the visitors' book is a register of famous names. The ballroom proved also useful for church services before an English church was allowed in the city.

The new Factory House had only been finished a few years when the wine trade was disturbed by war. French invasion threatened; the British Factories of both Lisbon and Oporto were warned to move their property to safety; many did so, and much wine was shipped off and sold at ruinous prices. But most Oporto firms continued their business so far as was possible under war conditions, until Soult captured the city in March 1809. Two months later Wellington, brilliantly crossing the Douro, drove Soult and his army out. Portonians went mad with delight; they revelled and celebrated for days and nights on end; the British Factory entertained Wellington's officers, made them honorary members of the Factory (their names are entered in the Factory House book), and gave wine (quite too much) to the troops. Business was resumed, under difficulties; wine exports had heavily slumped, and did not recover for many years.

Nevertheless British firms throve, and new ones were established — Cockburn, Graham, Smith Woodhouse and others; and it is a pleasant interlude in military activities to hear of Mr. George Sandeman (who had established his firm in 1790, with £300; since then it had become one of the great firms) staying with Wellington at Torres Vedras in 1810 and discussing vintages with the mess. 'Mr. Sandeman said he thought the vintage of 1797 was the finest Port Wine known . . . General Calvert, as a great favour, asked him to send two Pipes of this celebrated wine to England. Mr. Sandeman did so . . . Two generations later it was minutely examined. It was in curious old-fashioned bottles, was of a beautiful colour — a light ruby, not tawny — and perfectly sound.' George Sandeman, a generous man, like most wine shippers (their hearts seem warmed by their vintages) sent presents of port to various officers stationed about the country; 'the best I ever drank', wrote a grateful Colonel O'Toole in 1815; his friends had 'found it so good that I could hardly get them out of my house yesterday'.

Meanwhile, the cheerful, energetic British mercantile life in Oporto revived and flourished again after the war. It had its quarrels: there was, for instance, the feud about the ownership of the Factory House, that came to a head in 1825, when twenty prominent merchants who were not wine shippers sent a memorial to the British Foreign Secretary, complaining that 'the few individuals who assumed the exclusive management of the Contribution Fund, having formed into a Club under the title of "The British Association", appropriated to themselves the exclusive use of the great National Building called the Factory House.' They refused to admit merchants lately established unless they belonged to wine or fish houses; 'so that your Memorialists who are chiefly engaged in the importation of British manufactures have become the objects of a most marked and offensive distinction. As a consequence, your Memorialists suffer under the daily mortification of their feelings, and a deprivation of that consideration in Society which the respectability of their connections and paramount extent of their establishments entitle them to'. Worse, the Association often affixed public stigmas on individuals against whom they happened to have a grudge, by leaving them out of otherwise general invitations to Factory entertainments. 'In a small community of rival traders such an ordeal cannot be submitted to . . . Such a combination as the British Association should no longer be allowed to thwart the interests and affect the happiness of Your Memorialists'.

Whether or not through the Foreign Secretary's intervention, the Association seems to have been brought in time to a better mind in this matter. But the wine shippers might be excused for being above themselves in 1825, for the British export duty had just been halved, and shipments had increased by forty per cent. They fell next year owing to trade depression, and the pride of the shippers no doubt also declined.

Portugal in the nineteenth century went through stormy times of revolutions, counter-revolutions, tyrannies, a plague of constitutions, reigns of terror, and civil war. In Oporto, boasted by Portonians as the cradle of liberty (a cradle which rocked many abortive and ill-fated infants), there were spirited insurrections, usually cheered on by the sporting and liberty-loving British residents, who entered into the events with sympathetic zest fanned by self-interest (since arbitrary and reactionary governments never liked the British), juntas which seized power for a brief hour, the proclamation of noble and infatuated constitutions, subsequent mass imprisonments and executions, and persecutions and insultings of the British. To most anti-tyranny movements our Oporto countrymen lent their cordial co-operation. The exception was the revolution of 1820, which had for one of its objects the removal of Marshal Beresford from Portugal, British officers from the army, and British influence from the government; three admirable aims in which British subjects could scarcely be expected wholly to concur, though some of the more enthusiastic liberals did so. When no such patriotic considerations complicated the issue, the British helped the governor to barricade the streets.

But such upsets seem to have made little difference, by and large, to the wine trade. The British maintained through these Portuguese ups and downs their calm British annoyance, but mostly continued in business, going up into the wine country at the vintage to buy wines, shipping them down to their lodges, maturing them, and exporting them to England. They kept up meanwhile their cheerful and solid social life, entertaining one another and their Portuguese friends, holding assemblies, balls and dinners in the Factory House, playing cricket on Saturday afternoons in silk hats or beavers on their field by the Carrancas palace, as they had played it since the eighteenth century, going for summer holidays to their houses at Foz, bathing there from the praia dos Ingleses, their national beach, and watching the Portuguese, attired in Turkish trousers and long hanging caps, more ceremonially bathe from theirs.

But even British calm was disturbed by the war of the two brothers, and Dom Miguel's siege of Oporto in 1832 and 1833. The British residents, liberal by tradition and instinct, were solidly against Miguel, that troublesome and un-English tyrant. who seized the Alto Douro and prevented access to the wine country; they energetically helped in the defence of the city, and formed a volunteer corps to man the batteries when attack seemed imminent. The dramatic story of the siege belongs to another section of this book. To balance its bloodshed and privations, it brought to the residents much excitement, and a new circle of friends, including the ex-emperor Pedro and his entourage, and his hordes of assistants from Britain — valiant and quarrelsome army officers eager to break a lance and win glory for themselves and liberty for Portugal, naval officers from the volunteer squadron and also from the official British squadron which, painstakingly neutral, somewhat cynically looked on at their countrymen's activities from their stations in the Douro, only intervening to guard British lives and property, offer asylum on their decks to British subjects in case of need, and (the outstanding feat of their commander Captain Glascock) land with seamen and marines to fight the flames which threatened British wine lodges when the Miguelites blew up the Old Wine Company's stores.

The raising of the siege in August 1833 left Oporto exhausted but triumphant, to resume gradually its normal life. There were, of course, more revolutions; as a placid English engineer, incurious, unsurprised and resigned, put it in 1846, accepting Portuguese revolutions as acts of fate, like thunderstorms, 'We got to Vigo, where we found the whole of the Portuguese fleet anchored and learnt that a revolution had broken out and had been going on for some time. It appeared the Insurgents had the upper hand, it was called the revolution of Maria da Fonte'. It upset Oporto a good deal. The issues seem, looked at from a century after, singularly complicated and involved, but British Portonians apparently grasped them and supported the right side.

Between such interruptions, Oporto life ran prosperously on. There is a snobbish, picturesque account of it written in 1844 by W. H. G. Kingston, the adventure-story writer. Brought up in Oporto, the son of a partner in a wine firm who was also a banker, he returned there in 1843 for a visit, his bitter regrets for the London season tempered by his pleasure in mixing with the best Portuguese society, to which not all his Oporto countrymen had access. On his return he wrote a book about north Portugal. Mixed with smug moralizings, he has some vivid pictures of Oporto and the country round it, and enthusiastic accounts of Portuguese high society. 'Many English residents, not mixing in the more select circles, have been unable to form a correct opinion on the subject; indeed, I know of few writers on the country who have enjoyed opportunities of observing the higher classes correctly.' Lord Carnarvon, some years before, had had this opportunity, and so had Mr. Kingston now. Society was not, of course, what it had been before the present democratical tendency had gained so much ground, but Mr. Kingston hoped that when the bitter animosity between the two parties had died away, and as the present generation of noblemen grew up, accustomed to mix with their less aristocratic countrymen, society might become more polished and harmonious. It was extremely pleasing to him even now. As to the British, 'in speaking of Oporto they must not be forgotten, for though forming but a small portion of society, they are tolerably conspicuous. There are about fifty families, a part only of whom move in the higher circles, and are much respected by the Portuguese, living on the most friendly terms with them, in the constant interchange of all the courtesies of life. They inhabit some of the best houses in the most airy parts of the city; there is no city in the Peninsula where an English family can enjoy so much comfort and independence. I must observe, that I believe there are not a more honourable set of men than the gentlemen representing the long-established British mercantile houses in Oporto; nor can I resist the satisfaction of paying a just tribute to the name of my friend Mr. John Graham, who from his liberal and amiable disposition, and noble generosity on all occasions, is an honour to his profession. However, there are several other British merchants to whom the same encomiums would apply'. He also commends the amiable chaplain, Mr. Whiteley, and the two English physicians. It is probable that many of his countrymen, who had known him as a boy, thought that Willie Kingston had had his head turned by London society and literary success. All the same, he gives a lively account of his visit, of the bathing season at S. João da Foz, with its club-house, assembly rooms, balls, billiards and bathing (many of the English used to have houses there and spend the summer in them), of social life among his friends the fidalgos and particularly the fidalgas, of Oporto and its streets and buildings, and of his rides into the Douro country and the towns of the north. He was there during the period before the railway connected Oporto with the wine country, and before the British shippers had their own quintas there; later the great British firms, like the Portuguese, had their country houses up in the Douro mountains, and stayed there each year for the vintage, as well as often for shooting in the summer. Before that, the buyers used to go up to the wine country after the vintage (usually in January or February) on mules, accompanied by large staffs of clerks, servants and attendants, visit the different farms, taste the wine from a silver saucer, and buy what they wanted. A little later, they used Regoa, the chief town of the wine country, as clearing house, made an annual expedition there in parties, and met the farmers with their samples; during the week they spent there, the crop was entirely sold. The railway, making the journey easier and quicker, turned many shippers from mere buyers, blenders and maturers, into *vignerons*; they began having quintas in the vine country, and took up viticulture themselves.

After the sale of the wine, it was drawn off into pipes, taken down to the river, and embarked in flat-bottomed wine-boats for the voyage down to Oporto — a wild and magnificent journey down sweeping curves and gorges bordered by terraced mountains, vineyards, olive groves, great and small quintas, straggling, white-washed towns and villages. The Douro runs through some of the finest scenery in the world; for sheer magnificence, there is nothing to beat that swirling river cascading from gorge to gorge through the mountains down to the pastoral country above Oporto, and so under the great bridges to the white precipitous city and the red-roofed wine lodges of Vila Nova on the south shore.

In the middle of the nineteenth century, there was an air, among the British wine shippers, of adventurous prosperity. All the most famous firms were by then established; their representatives, top-hatted, white-trousered and elegantly dignified, may be seen standing and chatting in the Rua dos Inglezes outside their Factory House in Baron de Forrester's painting of 1834—Cock-burn, Croft, Graham, Hunt Roope & Co., Morgan, Sandeman, Offley Forrester, Taylor Fladgate & Yeatman, Guimaraens, Warre & Co., Lambert Kingston & Co., Smith Woodhouse and the rest. Typically British gentlemen of business; against a background of hazardous Portuguese civil dissension, romantic mountain vineyards and swirling Douro rapids, they pursued their trade, bought, matured and shipped their port, played their cricket on Saturdays, attended their church on Sundays, got up rowing clubs and regattas, went to Foz for bathing, lived in beautiful old houses on the steep city hill and looked out at the Douro flowing broadly golden out into a silver sea, went down each morning to do their business at the Factory House, met there for cards, billiards, newspaper-reading, dinner and conversation, married the daughters of other British wine shippers, sent their sons, when the transport became easy, to English public schools. (This custom began some time in the nineteenth century; in the earlier years of the century English boys went to school at Mr. Whiteley's in Oporto.)

Among the Oporto British, as among any other collection of British, there were many eccentrics; such as, for instance, Mr. Richard Noble, who, when he saw a mob fighting with the military in the streets for any reason, would leave his office and join them, leading the crowd with his walking-stick and remarking, 'I like to see *men*! Come on!' There were eccentrics, and there may have been geniuses: but on the whole the air of Portugal is not apt to breed these. In the year 1831, however, a young man of genius did arrive in Oporto, to join the wine firm of his uncle

Forrester. He was Joseph James Forrester, aged twenty-two. He learned quickly to talk Portuguese well (this was unusual among the British, even those who lived in Oporto for years); he went about and made friends with everyone, foreigners and natives, high and low; he went up country and got to know every mile of the wine country, every bend of the Douro, and every vineyard on its shores; he produced a most detailed, exquisite and remarkable map of the river, all down its course from the Spanish frontier to the Atlantic, another of the wine district, a third of the bed and margins of the Douro, showing the rapids and the geological formations, a fourth of *Oidium Tuckeri*, the peculiar and loathsome disease contracted by Douro vines. Besides being a brilliant cartographer and vine specialist, he was a landscape and portrait painter of immense fecundity and charm. His gallery of portraits included most of the distinguished Portuguese and British in the Portugal of his day; he was popular with everyone and moved about among opposing parties, succeeding in keeping on terms with them all. Through the siege of 1832-33 he kept guard over his firm's wine lodge at Vila Nova, among the Miguelites, sending daily reports across the river to his uncle in the city. It was an alarming life—lodges were broken open and wine commandeered by the Miguelite troops; it was planned to blow up the stores of the Old Wine Company; all military guards were removed from the lodges, and those in charge of them assaulted; every Portuguese lodge ran up a British flag for protection. 'Vila Nova is in such a state of anarchy and confusion that I find I cannot remain in the lodges nor go to them with any degree of safety. Officers have no longer command over their soldiers, and soldiers have no command over themselves. My life has been twice threatened, and it was with considerable difficulty that I escaped yesterday from seven exasperated soldiers who were inveighing against the English, their Government, and their flag, which is now so grossly abused and flying over the doors of many armazems ... Can no measures be taken for the saving of British property; cannot the Consul interfere? *N.B.* The fire took place this very p.m.' Next day he reported 'the awful scene of yesterday', the blowing up of the Company's stores, the fight to save the English lodges from the flames. For his part, unlike most of the Oporto British, he went as near as may be to taking no side in the civil war; he was an artist, a cartographer, a vine doctor, not a politician.

He had other wars to fight, in which he showed no such bland impartiality; he fought almost the whole British wine trade in Oporto and London on the subject of the adulteration of port. In the early forties port slumped; it accumulated in Oporto and could not be sold. Forrester accused his countrymen of shipping inferior wines, of adulterating them with too much brandy, elderberry and sugar, in order to make a wine 'black, strong and sweet', fit, Forrester protested, only for the lowest classes. His pamphlet *A Word or Two on Port Wine, shewing how and why it is adulterated and affording some means of checking its adulterations* was fired like a rocket at his fellow wine shippers in 1844, and exploded with a bang that resounded through the Alto Douro, Oporto and London. 'It is proposed', he began, 'to show from what causes Port has fallen in the estimation of persons really capable of judging of wine.' Port, he lamented, had come to be 'a nauseous, fiery compound of sweets, colours and alcohol; consequently Port at the tables of private gentlemen soon began to appear less frequently, and it is to be feared that it is gradually falling into total disuse'. It was the old complaint made against the British Factory nearly a century ago — too much brandy, too much elderberry, too much sugar — and had been one of Pombal's pretexts for the Wine Company; Forrester must have been the first Englishman to say a good word for the old Companhia Geral. Since its abolition, he thought, there had, for all its abuses, been a change for the worse.

Forrester's accusations, whether right or wrong, made enemies of all the wine shippers and merchants, and a war of recriminations, vindications, denials, protests and pamphlets opened. He had a large following among the Alto Douro vine-growers; he gave a dinner to enthusiastic land-owners and agriculturists at his firm's quinta near Regoa, at which he was toasted by the Visconde Santa Martha (once commander-in-chief of Dom Miguel's besieging army) as 'the friend of the Alto Douro', and replied with a long and eloquent speech explaining what port wine ought to be and what it was not. The Portuguese *vignerons*, delighted with the idea that their sales could be improved by such simple and negative methods, wrote ardent supporting letters in praise of 'pure wine' and against the 'diabolical process of suspending fermentation by large doses of alcohol combined with sugar and elderberry'. The topic becomes in Portuguese hands enthusiastically verbose and magnificent; adulteration is 'diabolical';

one expects every moment that Freemasonry will come marching in; chambers of agriculture congratulated Senhor Forrester for his brave stand, aged generals thanked him in the name of Portugal, bishops and the Cardinal Patriarch in the name of religion, applauding the luminous ideas advanced by the noble Englishman. The Cardinal Patriarch deplored the 'intemperate opposition' which had formed itself against him. The opposition was, in fact, as intemperate as the attack. Twenty-two British houses of Oporto combined indignantly against their accuser; insults and counter-insults shot to and fro; the firm of Offley, Forrester & Co. defended their brilliant *enfant terrible* with a dignified cannonade. J. J. Forrester, with all his countrymen in Oporto aligned against him, remained cheerful and truculent, and gave as good as he got.

The storm went by, and port wine remained pretty much what it had been; that is to say, it never became the light, thin, dry, unportlike drink that Forrester thought it should be. He had practically the whole trade against him, and, backing the trade, the taste of the consumers. He turned his attention again to mapping the Douro, painting, viticulture, and vine diseases. He recovered the favour of his countrymen, was beloved by the Portuguese, wrote more books, was a member of many learned societies, received many medals and decorations from royalty of all nations and the Pope, painted everyone's portrait, and was made Baron de Forrester by the King of Portugal. In 1861 his boat capsized on the Douro and he was drowned in the Cachão da Valeria.

Forrester's views on port were extreme, but have had some support, even in his own time. T. G. Shaw, brother of General Sir Charles Shaw, who had fought for Queen Maria da Gloria, and a member of a Leith wine firm, believed him largely right. He compared most of the port exported for the British market unfavourably with 'the fine, highly flavoured, light old port that the English merchants kept for their own use; most excellent it is'. He put down the faults of most port to the Wine Company, which would only pass strong, dark, rich wines, and to the fine vintage of 1820, which started a taste for sweet wine, so that subsequent vintages had to be adulterated. 'The talented Baron Forrester, who was drowned in the Douro two years ago, struck out right and left against all his neighbours and fellow countrymen, who had hitherto lived an easy-going life, undisturbed by intestine discords.' It must be remembered that Mr. Shaw's firm dealt mainly in French wines, and he appears to have been biased. Port, he declared, 'is now generally regarded as an intoxicating vulgar wine. Whether it will regain its prestige is very doubtful ... Port is losing caste, and is seldom seen on the tables of the higher classes; and we all know that when anything in this country has become vulgar, its fate is sealed'. He lamented the good old days when six friends at dinner would easily drink twelve bottles, when gentlemen seldom left the table before eleven o'clock, and were generally tipsy. There used to be four, five, or even six bottle men, drinking slowly, out of small glasses, for hours on end, experiencing 'that class of cordiality which frequently wanders into stupefaction'. As to the port trade, it could be resuscitated and brought back to its pre-1820 state if the wine was properly treated, racked and fined.

But the port wine merchants and shippers did not take this depressed view of their business. They did not see much wrong with the tradé, which indeed was very flourishing through the second half of the century, except for the ravages of the phylloxera, a disagreeable insect who arrived from America into the European vineyards about 1868, finding American vines unpalatable, and gnawed at their roots. All that could be done was to replant the vineyards with American vines, which, nothing daunted, the cultivators did.

In good years the Oporto wine shippers in the nineteenth and twentieth centuries led as fine a life as could be wished. Forty-five miles up the Douro began the Eldorado of the port vineyards, climbing the mountains in terraces, from the rich valley soil to the heights where the thinner wines grow. At Regoa the river Corgo meets the Douro; and beyond the Corgo the finest wines are grown. The hot summers, the cold winters, the slight rainfall, the nature of the soil, the soft schist rocks, combine to make the perfect port country; there is no other such in the known world. From this country the British port shippers and the Douro vine growers have drawn their sustenance for two centuries and a half. Some shippers learn viticulture and grow their own wine; most still leave it to the farmers, coming up or sending agents for the vintage and contracting with a grower for those of his grapes of which they like the look and taste (a job for experts); the farmers hire the labour, the buyers supervise the picking and wine-making and supply the brandy. They stay at their firms' quintas, which lie all up the Douro on the steep hillsides, among vineyards, olive gardens, cork woods, chestnuts, plantations of almonds, figs, orange groves and canes, green and silver-gray against pasture land and forest, terracing down to the yellow river in its deep bed. Pleasant country houses, with wine stores attached, the quintas, English and Portuguese, stand among white peasants' cottages, straggling villages with their goats and pigs and clanging church belfries, like seignorial manors. Many English use their quintas (equipped with *conforts modernes*) as shooting-lodges and for summer holidays; more stay in them for the vintage. The date of this annual crisis is chosen by the anxious growers, who know that a wrong choice or wrong weather may ruin the whole affair; they gamble as a rule on the first days of October. Then, with song and dance, guitars and immense zest, the vintage workers swarm in, a gay invasion from the mountains and valleys of the Douro and Minho, Trás-os-Montes and Galicia, eager for their laborious annual festival. Whoever does not enjoy the vintage (and the pleasure of buyers and growers is often flawed by anxiety or mischance) the vintage workers do.

But, if all goes well, the buyers too enjoy the occasion. All the processes of wine-making have a kind of festal bacchic beauty; no other business is like it. Crushing the grapes in the stone tanks, fermenting the juice, drawing off the must, adding the brandy, running into great tonels, racking off after the winter into casks, sending the casks down to Oporto — every stage has grace. The old Douro voyage in wine boats, wild, lovely and perilous down the swirling gorges of the river, was delightful for the boatmen, who drank of the casks and topped them up with river water, sometimes containing fishes; the journey is now made by rail, and the wine reaches the lodges quicker, safer, and fishless. The lodges, which line the river's left bank at Vila Nova de Gaia, are cool, spacious, smelling darkly and sweetly of wine. They employ a great army of workers — lodgemen, tasters, blenders, bottlers, coopers, labellers, porters and office staff. It has been said that the economy of all north Portugal hangs on port wine; and when one considers the great army of those, from farmers to bottle-makers, who labour so long and diligently that London wine merchants may receive their port, one must agree.

The British wine-shippers have dug themselves deeply for generations into Portuguese industry and life. Many Portuguese, and many envious foreigners, say too deeply, and that they have robbed the Portuguese of the greater part of their own wine trade. German and French visitors to Oporto have grumbled at British influence, which has made this patriotic Portuguese city, this cradle of Portuguese liberties (such as they are), with its large and rich British colony, its fine British houses on the heights above the lower town and stretching all the way down the river to Foz, its British shops, club, church, London newspapers, Factory house, cricket ground, wine-lodges, quintas up the Douro and bathing-villas down it, almost 'une ville anglo-portugaise'.

However this may be, the British shippers have a place in Oporto life which is unlike that of any other foreign colony anywhere, so intimately are they bound up with the history and economy of the place, so known and familiar and yet so detached. Insular by tradition and taste, they consort mainly with one another, and the hierarchy of status within their close society suggests that of an English country town. This genial, unconsciously arrogant Britishness, easy, hospitable, lavish, Pro-testant, assured, descending from generation to generation with the historic continuity of the great port houses, has a not un-charming piquancy, when set in the precipitous ancient capital of northern Portugal, teeming with its native life, against the back-ground of the distant mountainy vineyards up the golden river which provide their so romantic sustenance. They seem, to the onlooker who is not of them, to be poised between poetry and prose, half unconscious of the beauty for which they stand. Their attitude towards their Portuguese neighbours is kindly and friendly rather than intimate; the language of the country is not perfectly acquired by most even of those born in it; pursuits, out-look and amusements are different. The British have always, it seems, gone in for athletics, games and sports, perhaps kept in training by the steepness of the Oporto streets. As to that, the Lisbon British, with streets equally precipitous, ought to be able to rival them; but the Lisbon climate is less bracing, and British Lisbonians have never been able to hold their own against their rivals in the north. They used once to put up a four to row against the Oporto rowing club; they never won, and after a few years ceased to try. As a Lisbonian wrote to a Portonian in 1877, apropos of the Oporto regatta, 'Very difficult to get fellows to row against you, for they say Lisbon is sure to be drubbed . . . I don't think many of our fellows will go in for Athletics, there being too much of the muff in their composition'. This regatta was watched with immense interest by the whole British colony in Oporto and by the Portuguese, themselves not an athletic people, but prepared to take a sympathetic interest in any spectacle. As the *Commercio* reported, 'the result of the struggle was the victory of the boat rowed by the gentlemen resident in this city. The winners were greeted with urrahs'. The regattas of the Oporto Boat Club went on till 1939, and will no doubt be resumed. The power of the British wine shippers to enjoy life has never been in doubt. How they have been, on the whole, regarded by the Portuguese, is perhaps more doubtful. Envy and patriotism have played some part here; and not all the Oporto British have had those ceremonious and amiable manners so desirable abroad. Ramalho Ortigão (whose anglo-phobia could on occasion break out into a kind of bitter, jeering near-hysteria) wrote sixty years ago of the British merchant in Oporto and in the wine country as he saw him: strolling up and down the Rua Nova dos Inglezes, dressed like a travelling jockey, complete with monocle and cane, saying 'Aoh! Vossemece! . . . all right!' looking with disapproval on those of his countrymen who dressed like foreigners, smoked cheroots in the street, curled their moustaches, trilled their 'r's like the Portuguese. Up in the wine country, said Ortigão, the Englishman's attitude was so signorial, so dominating, so full of conviction, that he himself had believed as a child that these lordly beings were the owners of everything between the Pedrões de Teixeira and the Cima-Corgo. In vintage time, the meals of the wine-grower's family would be interrupted by a factotum carrying his employer's suit-case and calling, 'The Englishman! Here is the Englishman!' The farmer would jump up in a hurry, because the Englishman did not like to be kept waiting, and, Ortigão apostrophizes the visitor, 'Your grand majestic air during those interviews is a thing which I shall never forget'. Clad in chamois-leather riding-breeches, your hat over your eyes, your legs wide apart, flicking the vines with your whip, you begin your off-hand inquiries, spitting out horizontally the skins of the grapes that you deign to try. 'How much produce? How much the pipe?' You take notes in your note-book; you go from quinta to quinta, dismissing the farmer with a brief gesture of glove or whip. Two or three days later you call again, to fix the price and clinch the deal. The transaction is conducted in the Portuguese that you use, interpolated with plebeianisms picked up from the boatmen of Massarellos and the warehousemen of Vila Nova de Gaia. It is signed only with a hand-shake and a pencilled scrawl in your pocket-book. Thus simply you buy in the Douro the wines you sell abroad (before having paid the grower), under the names of *London legitimate, London Special, London Superfine*. I find you sublime, says the sarcastic Senhor Ortigão, I begin to venerate you. Because, in short, this simple citizen of Porto, this poor farmer of the Douro, whom you so lucratively exploit and treat with the same scorn with which you would treat a dog, is a human being of a race incomparably finer, more beautiful, more intellectual and more noble than you. He is Portuguese. His family, in the sixteenth century, when your ancestors (according to Drapper), were as barbarous as Mexican Indians, were illustrious all over the world for intelligence, courage, science, commerce, letters, and the arts . . . To be sure, you have more money, but he is happier, making verses and playing the guitar under a blue sky, than you, with your millions and your spleen. You are both decadent, he from three centuries of Jesuit education, you from insular egotism and mercantile interests. England will cease to exist for civilization as anything but the indigestible island which disgust has prevented the ocean from swallowing.

Senhor Ortigão's patriotism was, no doubt, well enough known to the British wine shippers of the eighteen-eighties who were the targets of his discourse to prevent their profiting much by it; it is probable that they thought, if they read it, that a critic who compared Shakespeare, Spenser, Sidney, Raleigh and Sir Thomas More to barbarous Mexican Indians (even on the authority of one Drapper) need not be taken seriously when he criticized themselves; their withers were unwrung. Whatever anyone might think of them, they proceeded cheerfully, impassively, on their way, buying and shipping their wines, complete with millions, spleen, eye-glass, cane, binoculars, arrogance, and ungrammatical Portuguese.

They are, by and large, conservative in outlook today; unlike their great-grandparents in the Miguelite war, they are inclined to back the anti-liberal side in peninsular civil conflicts, and most of them supported, in moderation, General Franco's rising against his government. Capitalist by tradition and interest, their dominant principle and instinct in European affairs is, nevertheless, true-blue British patriotism; their country's interests are set unquestioningly before their own.

However hard hit by war, no vicissitudes can get them down for long. They know, as we do, and as Portugal knows, that 'we can't get no port wine anywhere else'. Wars, political tensions, economic depressions, criticisms and disagreements between ancient allies, may come and go; port wine remains.

BIBLIOGRAPHY

Oporto Old and New, CHARLES SELLERS (1899).
A Treatise on the Wine Trade, JOHN CROFT (1788).
State Papers, Portugal 89/50 (Record Office).
Letters on Portugal and its Commerce, MERCATOR (1754).
Institution of the General Company for the Culture of the Vineyards of Alto Douro, MERCATOR (1758).
Wine Trade of Portugal: Proceedings at the meeting of the Nobility, Wine Proprietors and Public Authorities of the Wine District of the Alto Douro, held at the Quinta of Messrs. Offley, Webber & Forrester October 1844 at the invitation of Joseph James Forrester (1845).
A Word or Two on Port Wine, J. J. FORRESTER (1844).
The Past, Present and probably the Future of the State of the Wine Trade, JAMES WARRE (1923).
Port, ANDRÉ L. SIMON (1934).
Port, from the Vine to the Glass, GEOFREY MURAT TAIT (1936).
From Grape to Glass, G. G. SANDEMAN SONS & Co. LTD. (1935).
The Story of Hunt, Roope & Co., Oporto and London.
Wine, the vine and the cellar, T. G. SHAW (1864).
The Memoirs of Lord Cherington, RICHARD MULLER (1782).
Farrington Diary (August 1796).
Recollections of old country life, JOHN FOWLER (1894).
Farewell to Wine, RICHARD AMES (1693).
Sir John Bull, RAMALHO ORTIGÃO (1887).
Lusitanian Sketches, W. H. G. KINGSTON (1845)

TOURISTS

William Hickey
[1782]

WHEREVER chance placed Mr. William Hickey, he managed to put in a cheerful time. Even when stranded for a fortnight, through just missing the Lisbon packet, at Falmouth, 'the most despicable town in His Majesty's dominions', he made himself at home, taking neat lodgings at a turner's shop for himself and his 'amiable partner' Charlotte Barry, who was to accompany him to India under the title of Mrs. Hickey, and at once, through introductions, getting to know hospitable neighbours, who were so delighted with the pair as to be for ever entertaining them. They passed a pleasant fortnight enjoying company and Cornish beauty spots, and sailed for Lisbon on February 11th, 1782.

Hickey, then a dashing young man of two and thirty, was bound for India, where he was to be a Bengal attorney. His Charlotte, an estimable young woman and the best of companions, who had lived a free-lance life in London under various protectors, had thrown in her lot with his, and the strongest and most constant affection linked them. Hickey even proposed that they should get married, but this seemed to Charlotte superfluous, and 'from that hour I considered myself as much her husband as the strictest forms and ceremonies of the Church could have made me'. Indeed, for the remainder of Charlotte's short life, she filled the wifely office with great credit to herself and to Mr. Hickey, becoming the admiration of all who knew her. The behaviour of this admirable young woman in a shipwreck reveals her as a being of remarkable self-control and calm. When Hickey told her above the raving of wind and waves that the ship could stand the storm no longer and must soon break in pieces, so that they would all be lost, 'the dear woman, with a composure and serenity that struck me most forcibly, mildly replied, "God's will be done, to that I bend with humble resignation, blessing a benevolent providence for permitting me, my dearest William, to expire with you, whose fate I am content to share, but oh! my dearest love, let us in the agonies of death be not separated".' If Charlotte really said all that in such a tempestuous moment, she was no ordinary creature, and Hickey was indeed fortunate.

The Hickeys had an excellent run before the wind to Lisbon, which they made in four days and a half. Hickey makes, in his *Memoirs*, none of the usual English whines about sea-sickness, the insolence of the customs, the miserable filth of Lisbon. They had a pleasant and useful companion on the voyage, a Lisbon resident, who got accommodation for them at 'a noble mansion standing upon the point of a lofty hill called 'Buenos Ayres', which has been identified by one local historian as the present British Embassy. It commanded a noble view of the city and river, and was kept by an old Irish widow named Williams. The Hickeys had a suite of spacious rooms, including servants' chambers and a private staircase; nothing could be more commodious or elegant, 'but the expense was enormous', as indeed Hickey's expenses always were; no wonder that he often complained of shortness of means.

The hotel was full of distinguished British invalids, mostly consumptive, including the Earl of Winchilsea, just recovered from what the physicians had pronounced a confirmed decline, and Mrs. Mundy (whose health improved at Lisbon but when she went to the south of France next winter she relapsed and died) and several male invalids. Each morning the kind-hearted Hickey would spend an hour or two in the coffee-room, reading the papers and admiring the magnificent view; 'it was, however, a great drawback to my amusement to observe several of the invalids daily sinking into the grave, yet notwithstanding this was too evident to every person who looked at them, the victims themselves seemed unconscious of their danger'. There was, in particular, one very elegant young man of twenty-two, a Mr. Richardson, the owner of large estates in Devonshire, who had become an absolute skeleton; Hickey used to watch him with the most anxious alarm, expecting every moment to behold him fall from his chair a corpse. This actual spectacle Hickey missed, as poor Mr. Richardson died one morning in bed.

From these interesting and melancholy happenings at Mrs. Williams's, the Hickeys sallied frequently forth into Lisbon social gaieties. Unlike Southey, they enjoyed society; unlike Beckford, they were received into it with immediate welcome; there must have been something genial and pleasing about Hickey that opened all doors to him. He had introductory letters, and at once received at least a dozen invitations to dinners, 'commencing with a sumptuous one at His Excellency the Honourable Mr. Walpole's. The next was an equally splendid one at Sir John Hort's' (the consul), and so it went on, with never a dull moment. It was worth while entertaining Hickey, for he appreciated a good evening with enthusiasm, even as, if offered poor entertainment or a mean dinner, he would make no bones about showing his disgust by walking out on it. But no such thing occurred in hospitable Lisbon, where the embassy and the mercantile colony rivalled each other in agreeable hospitality. One of his hosts was Mr. Koster, whom Southey later found the only conversable Englishman in Lisbon; Hickey found them all conversable; they liked the Hickeys and the Hickeys liked them. They hired a chaise and drove about Lisbon seeing the sights, which they greatly admired; they went to high Mass and saw the royal family at their devotions; they went delightful expeditions to Cintra and other beautiful spots, in spite of the weather, which actually included a fall of snow, the first for forty years ('the Catholic clergy, with their usual bigotry, declared this phenomenon portended some dire calamity to the kingdom, to avert which and appease the wrath of an offended God every church in the city was immediately opened and prayers offered for pardon and for mercy'). They had several very pleasant parties with the English merchant, Mr. De Visme, at Montserrate, his beautiful quinta near Cintra, 'where he entertained in a manner never surpassed and seldom equalled'. From Hickey's description of the grounds and the rareness of their exotic plants, it would seem that Beckford, acquiring them twelve years later, can have found little to be done to improve them. De Visme had even peopled his woods with nightingales that sang for eight months of each year.

Hickey found nearly everything delightful, though he condemned as blasphemous balderdash the religious puppet and miracle play they saw in Lent, which ended with 'the Virgin Mary bedizened with jewels and a profusion of gold and silver ornaments, dancing a fandango with our Saviour, his head being covered with an immense full-bottomed periwig well powdered'. This, Hickey felt, was going too far, and not at all the thing. Nor did he approve of the inconstant conduct of Commodore Johnston, who landed in Lisbon from a frigate to marry the dashing Miss

Dee, when he already owned a very respectable, accomplished and worthy mistress who had borne him two sons and conducted herself in the most irreproachable manner, being also an exemplary mother. Hickey had his own humane, generous and merciful code: he would never have treated a mistress ill himself, and could not esteem a man who did so.

Meanwhile, and in spite of Lisbon air and gaieties, his Charlotte's health began to decline; it seems likely enough that she had contracted lung disease from the invalids at Mrs. Williams's hotel. Dr. Hare, the English physician, advised that she should leave Lisbon. Mr. De Visme offered the Hickeys the use of a country seat of his by the sea; they accepted the polite offer, and spent ten days there, after which Charlotte seemed recovered, and they returned to Lisbon in time to see the Easter celebrations in 'the richest church in Lisbon'. These moved the congregation, including Mr. and Mrs. Hickey, so deeply that Hickey's blood thrilled, many burst into tears, and several ladies fainted. Charlotte escaped with a good fit of crying, 'afterwards telling me she never could have had an idea of anything so awfully grand and affecting'. But in spite of these stimulants, Mrs. Hickey continued to decline, and Dr. Hare told Hickey confidentially that he was convinced the climate of Lisbon was so hostile to her that she would fall a sacrifice if she remained there, and also that India would never suit her. Hickey, though much depressed by this, broke it to Charlotte, who was at first extremely hurt, declaring that all she desired was to expire under his protection, but after a time she yielded, and consented to return to England on the *King George* packet, with her maid Harriet, who was also so unfortunate as to be in a decline. Hickey had both his and Charlotte's portraits painted in oils, and on May 5th took a fond and melancholy, and, as he believed, last farewell of his beloved and watched her carried, insensible from grief, on to the boat. He himself was so lost in despair as to be saved from a severe illness only by the unremitting attentions of Dr. Hare and the solacing exertions of a number of friends, who forced him into society, till by slow degrees he became reconciled. He heard from Falmouth from Charlotte that the eight days' voyage had quite restored her once more to health (she was a quick rallyer), and was waiting for the first ship for India, as without Hickey life was not worth living.

On June 4th, Hickey was dining at the ambassador's; the ladies had left the table, and the gentlemen had been at the bottle about an hour, when a servant came and whispered to Hickey that Mrs. Walpole would like to speak to him. He was conducted upstairs to a dressing-room, 'opening the door of which what was my amazement and agitation at my loved Charlotte's rushing into my arms, bursting into tears, and the next moment insensible in a fainting-fit'. Mrs. Walpole, who had been waiting in readiness with hartshorn and other remedies for such an emergency, came to the rescue, and Charlotte was soon enough restored to utter one of her admirable speeches. 'My dearest William,' she said, 'if I am doomed to die an early death, oh do at least, I beseech you, let me have the consolation of knowing that I shall draw my last breath and heave my last sad sigh in your loved arms. Without you I cannot exist. Besides, my William, I can confidently assure you that my health is entirely restored; I am as well as ever I was in my life.' William, though alarmed for her life, was too happy at being able to press her once more to his bosom to reproach her, and they passed a gay and cheerful evening, with supper and dancing, to celebrate His Majesty's birthday, before returning to their hotel.

Charlotte was certainly better, though Harriet, whom she had brought out again, was definitely worse, and Dr. Hare held out little hope of her recovery. The weather became oppressively hot, but the Hickeys enjoyed a number of agreeable country house parties at Mr. De Visme's, Sir John Hort's and others, before embarking on the *Raynha de Portugal* on June 23rd. By this time Hickey was deeply in debt, his Lisbon expenses having been prodigious, and had to raise eight hundred pounds, to be repaid in Bengal. The last ten days in Lisbon were a round of entertainments and farewells, and on the last night the Walpoles threw a large dinner-party and dance where all the principal English residents assembled to bid the popular pair adieu. The lovely Mrs. Walpole, Hickey regretted to record, soon after this fell into a decline, from neglecting a cold, and expired.

From the ambassador's party the Hickeys went straight on board, and sailed next morning, leaving with regret the magnificent capital where they had been treated with so much hospitality and kindness by so many estimable persons.

It is pleasant to read of visitors to Lisbon who had such a good time, had no word to say either against Portugal or its inhabitants, were so much liked, and so hugely enjoyed everything, from parties of pleasure to Easter High Masses. These pleasant, good-natured, affectionate people, of generous feelings, humane sensibilities and unlimited sympathies, went through the world as if through a non-stop party, where they got on with everybody, and which they never wanted to leave. Poor Charlotte, alas, had to leave the party all too early.

BIBLIOGRAPHY

Memoirs, WILLIAM HICKEY (1928).

2. SOI-DISANTE MARGRAVINE

Lady Craven

[June-November, 1791]

SPRIGHTLY, unrespectable, faded, self-confident, rather smug, and still handsome at forty-one, Elizabeth, the faithless and many-years' separated wife of the dull, also faithless, drunken and now (Lady Craven hoped) dying Lord Craven, arrived in Lisbon in June, 1791, with her *cher ami* (who had once bidden her regard him as a brother, but now no more), the Margrave of Anspach. Already they had undergone a nuptial ceremony in Germany, but it had not generally been considered satisfactory, in view of Lord Craven and the Margravine. Still, it definitely asserted the new unfraternal relationship, and Lady Craven's travelling tours with Mr. Henry Vernon and the Margrave's domestic relations with Mrs. Burne and the elderly French actress Mlle Clairon were superseded.

The affair had never been favourably regarded, either in Germany or England. It passed the understanding of Gräfin Sophia Marie von Voss that such a person as Lady Craven should be received at the Prussian court. 'She is faded, must have intelligence, but is extremely conceited', she wrote. 'She converses only with the Margrave, who is bewitched by her.' That was in 1790. In the spring and summer of next year they visited England. They stayed with William Beckford at Fonthill. 'The Margrave and Lady Craven are here,' he wrote to Sir William Hamilton. 'The Margrave all goodness, meekness and resignation, my lady all eyes, nose, fire and fury, exclaiming against relations who will not allow her to live as she likes, and against beastly Germans who accuse her of leading their gentle sovereign out of his senses and out of his Dominions . . . I believe they intend taking their departure for Lisbon in a few days, where it is to be hoped no drunken husbands or boring brothers will disturb their felicity.'

Beckford no doubt warned them that his Majesty's envoy, the Honourable Robert Walpole, who had cold-shouldered him in Lisbon four years ago, on directions from the English court, would probably do the same to them and for the same kind of reasons; when it occurred, Lady Craven wrote of it without surprise; she bore it more philosophically than Beckford had. She set out for Lisbon in great spirits.

Horace Walpole wrote meanwhile to Miss Mary Berry, of 'the new *soi-disante* Margravine. She has been in England with her foolish Prince, and not only notified the marriage to the Earl her brother [Lord Berkeley] but His Highness informed his Lordship by a letter, that they have an usage in his country of taking a wife with the left hand; that he had espoused his Lordship's sister in that manner; and intends, as soon as she shall be a widow, to marry her with his right hand also. The Earl replied, that he knew she was married to an English peer, a most respectable man, and can know nothing of her marrying any other man; and so they are gone to Lisbon.'

Said the *Bon Ton Magazine* for August, 'The Margrave of Anspach and his *chère amie*, Lady Craven, intend making a tour of Portugal, Spain and Italy previous to their return home. They have by this time probably reached Lisbon'.

They had; to the embarrassment of Mr. Walpole and his chaplain Mr. Hill, Robert Southey's uncle and a most respectable man, who reprobated even castanet dancing, let alone left-handed marriages. The ambassador was not, probably, on his own account, fussy about that kind of thing, but Queen Charlotte disapproved of the frail *soi-disante* Margravine, and desired him to turn the light of his countenance from her. So, says Lady Craven in her memoirs (that matchlessly complacent manipulation of facts), all the foreign ministers except Mr. Walpole 'paid their respects to me'. Poor Mr. Walpole was put in a difficult position, for the Queen of

Portugal, an excessively pious and moral woman, though not strong in the head, extended to her persecuted sister her especial favour, saying that the Queen of England, as a mother, ought to protect and not persecute her. So two parties formed in Lisbon; 'all the good and spirited people', Lady Craven decided, 'with the party attached to the Queen of Portugal, were for me; while the base and corrupted levelled the shafts of their malice against me'. (That was the manner in which all her life she found society was divided about her.) The queen, as a mark of her favour and protection, gave orders that Lady Craven's letters were to be delivered at the post office only to her ladyship personally, which made it awkward when she had not time to call for them; it has already been mentioned that intelligence was not the kind queen's strong point. All sorts of spiteful gossip circulated, as that Lord Craven was by no means dying at Lausanne, as his wife claimed, but was in perfect health, and 'that I artfully would say that I expected news of his death every day, in order to live as I pleased ... I had refused balls and large parties, saying that I did expect such news, and, as I was not parted from Lord Craven, I thought it would be highly reprehensible in me to lead a gay and dissipated life, when expecting by every post to hear of the death of my husband. But envy soon amused itself at my expense ...'—in brief, be thou chaste as ice and pure as snow, thou shalt not escape calumny.

So Lisbon, like other places, had its annoyances; and there was always the discouraging reflection voiced by Lady Craven a year ago — 'I am told the Ogre is declining, but I can never believe it, because with his manner of living he should have been dead long ago.'

She wrote to her friend Beckford bright complaints of diplomatic slights and self-gratulating reports of kind civilities shown her by all outside the horrid British embassy circles. At Falmouth she had seen 'an express' given to the captain just before the packet sailed, for delivery into Mr. Walpole's hands on arrival; she was sure it contained his orders for the boycotting of herself and the Margrave, for 'Walpole has not given the M. a sign of life'. However, things went gaily enough; 'Marialva gives us a dinner Monday, the French Minister's wife and all the People are mighty civil, and I only wait to be better lodged to get things in a mighty good train. The Prussian Minister has told the truth here, which is that I am only waiting for a piece of news, to become autre chose, and that, having overturned the Project of that abominable woman you know', (Mlle Clairon?) 'makes her now pursue both the M. and I as much as she can . . . I suppose one day or other she will have it all come home to her, as 'tis vulgarly said.

'As to you, the more I see of the People here, and the more I wish you to *be* here . . . I do not think you would like to be rooted here.

'I like Franchy most amazingly, and I hope you will do something friendly and proper by him. . . .

'*Dust, Stinks, horrid faces, Bells,* contents of Chamberpots, fleas, vile Curs, horrid Blacks, trees burnt to a Coal, badish water, no good wine — such are the delights of this place.'

Cintra was better. They made up parties for Colares, dined the Dukes of Luxembourg and Cadaval on venison dressed English fashion and 'so good that I really never eat anything like it'. The queen had sent a whole buck and a whole stag, so they made presents to right and left and gave the rest to the poor. 'People are civil to a degree here — all Parties, all Ranks, except Walpole and Sir J. Hort, who I suppose have private orders not to wait on the M. I confess the air and climate are super-excellent — but the country and people centuries behind-hand . . . and then the people will not talk French, tho' they can . . . De Visme is building further on at a Place called Montserrate. Beautiful situation, but a Vile Planned house' ('perfectly true', Beckford inserted into the letter). The M., Lady Craven continued, had a fine prancing grey horse, and she a humble mule, 'but these perpendicular pavements and ugly narrow roads are sad things to crawl about. . . .

'I hope you are making plans with Sir W. Hamilton, for much as I wish to see you here this winter, I cannot, as your friend wish to see you *settle* here. I know by experience the Jealousy of Natives to a stranger — who desired nothing and refused everything, and I know what you . . . would suffer. No, no; stand firm on your liberty and independence, and make yourself a nest of amiable friends; but alas, you are incomprehensible. Stupid people . . . I should pay to keep *out* of my house — and pay others to keep wit going round me.'

As the summer wore by, she became almost hysterically anti-Portuguese. The climate, she wrote to Beckford, was perhaps the healthiest in the world; but the People, and the Noise! She described with horror an evening of what sounds very like modern crooning and dance-music — 'horrid negro airs, miawling of cats

— door-hinges, or anything horrible, is preferable to such a diabolical noise. Why, how can you suppose that these people . . . will do anything for you (digne de vous) if England or who governs it frown? . . . I can conceive that your Cuisine may tempt the Royalties and Nobilities to court you when here — for their Cuisine is detestable — but — and then, would you ally yourself with Jewish-Moorish blood . . . Do anything for God sake but misally yourself thus — use them to your Purposes, but never *tie* yourself to negro land'.

The Margrave informed Mr. Hill the chaplain that he would require to be married by him shortly. The clergyman was somewhat disconcerted by this anticipatory order, and consulted the ambassador about it. There was nothing Mr. Walpole could do; he no doubt hoped that Lord Craven would die as soon as he could manage it, and that this dubious pair would marry and betake themselves elsewhere. But Lady Craven complained that the ambassador learned of her husband's death five days before she did, 'but which, like a base sycophant, he kept from me' — or possibly it was the chaplain who kept it from her; her style is confused. In any case, she omitted to call at the post office for her letters for five days, the weather being bad, and when she did so 'I found five letters apprising me of the death of Lord Craven. The climate of Lisbon made my hair grow very long and extremely thick; and the salubrity of the air refreshed and invigorated my constitution'. After this bland change of subject, her Ladyship writes a few pages on the history of Portugal, then remarks that 'the Opera house at Lisbon is very good: we frequently visited it, and were seated in the Royal Box'. They also attended the bull-feasts on Sundays. Then, 'as by the death of Lord Craven I felt myself released from all ties, and at liberty to act as I thought proper, I accepted the hand of the Margrave without fear or remorse. We were married in the presence of one hundred persons, and attended by all the English naval officers, who were quite delighted to act as witnesses'.

They were married by Mr. Hill on October 30th, in the chapel of the British Embassy, and no doubt 'all the good and spirited people' came to the wedding. But the ambassador and his wife, being of the base and corrupted party, did not attend it. Horace Walpole's account (to Lady Ossory) is:

'Lady Craven received the news of her Lord's death on a

Friday, went into weeds on Saturday, and into white satin and *many* diamonds on Sunday, and in that vestal trim was married to the Margrave of Anspach by my cousin's chaplain, though he and Mrs. Walpole excused themselves from being present. The bride excused herself for having so *few* diamonds; they had been the late Margravine's, but she is to have many more, and will soon set out for England, where they shall astound the public by living in a style of magnificence unusual, as they are richer than any one in this country. The Dukes of Bedford, Marlborough and Northumberland may hide their diminished rays.'

As Horace predicted, Brandenburgh House became a centre of lavish opulence, grand theatricals, and brilliant social festivities. But the Margravine had to be content, in London as in Lisbon, with 'the good and spirited people'; the base and corrupted, who included the highest society, stayed away, and she was never presented to the queen, any more than she had been able to induce His Majesty's envoy in Lisbon to wait on her. When she and William Beckford foregathered, they no doubt raged together against the hypocritical and malicious English.

BIBLIOGRAPHY

Memoirs of the Margravine of Anspach (1826).
The beautiful Lady Craven: edited with introduction by A. M. BROADLY and LEWIS
    MELVILLE (1914).
Horace Walpole's Letters, PAGET TOYNBEE (1903, etc.).
Hamilton Papers (Register House, Edinburgh).

3. THE CONSUMPTIVE VIEW

Henry Matthews

[1817]

MOST of the British invalids who sought, but seldom found, health in Portugal were afflicted with lung trouble; Mr. Henry Matthews does not tell us how he ailed, but, from the morose depression and lack of *joie de vivre* with which he approached all he saw, one is inclined to diagnose this lowering complaint, though it may have been jaundice, and a reviewer in *Blackwood's* said it was the colic. Anyhow, his travels did his spirits no good. He was an Etonian, a Fellow of King's, and a barrister; born in 1789, he was twenty-eight when, in September

1817, he 'set out on a wild-goose chase after health, and to try to run away from death'. He could scarcely hope, he thought, to see his home again; he was very sick on the voyage to Lisbon. On September 13th, he sailed up the Tagus; but he did not echo the usual rhapsodies about the view seen from thence; he thought it over-rated. 'He who has 'seen London from Greenwich Park may survey without any great astonishment the capital of Portugal.' Still, the river was fine, and there was no smoke to spoil it. After a broiling walk through the 'indescribable nastiness of the town', he fetched up, as most Britons did, at Reeves's hotel in the Rua de Prior, and here found his first satisfaction, for it was an excellent house kept by an Englishman, full of cleanliness and comfort, 'qualities one appreciates after a walk through Lisbon'. For 'the gay and glittering city proves to be a painted sepulchre. Filth and beastliness assault you at every turn, in their most loathsome and disgusting shapes . . . The abominations of Lisbon are incapable of exaggeration'. Further, there was a scorching sun and a cold wind, and something in the appearance of Lisbon seemed to portend an earthquake. 'To an earthquake it may look as its natural death'; the indolence of the people had not cleared away the remains of the last one; its daily preservation was a standing miracle.

About this precariously poised and disagreeable city, Mr. Matthews drove in a clumsy carriage that jolted him, since, for an invalid, it was impossible to walk. He went, of course, to stay at Cintra, that paradise of good English. 'I should compare it', he observed tepidly, 'with Malvern . . . Cintra is not cheaper than Cheltenham . . . A wolf sometimes makes its appearance here, and one has lately been very mischievous' — it had devoured an old woman in the mountains. The views from Cintra were less pleasing than most from Malvern; instead of the fertile valleys of Worcestershire, the eye had nothing to repose on but a dreary and barren waste. However, he was fortunate in encountering our chargé d'affaires, Mr. Ward, whom he had known at Cambridge, and also two old Etonians; with one of these, a Colonel Ross of the Portuguese service, he passed a pleasant evening. He returned to Lisbon on October 1st, and at once put on foot inquiries for a vessel bound for Italy, for 'to contemplate residence here for the winter would be enough to make a healthy man sick'. There were no fires in the hotel, so even Reeves's lost its good marks. 'So much for comfort; then the disposition of the people towards us offers no inducement to stay. There is no doubt of the fact that neither the generosity and good faith of the British, nor the blood profusely shed in defence of this country, have endeared us to our Portuguese allies. They dislike us mortally. How is this to be explained? Is it that malicious sentiment of envy, which seems to have overspread the whole Continent, at the prodigious elevation to which England has arisen; or is it the repulsive unaccommodating manners which an Englishman is too apt to carry with him into all countries?'

It was, as any Portuguese or his friend Mr. Ward could have told him, our most unpopular hour: the hour of Marshal Beresford and the British domination of the army and much of civil life; Portuguese officers ousted from promotion by British ones, Beresford reigning like a viceroy at the Patéo Saldanha, the patriotic conspiracy of Gomes Freire to get rid of the English crushed and broken, its leaders under sentence of death. Mr. Matthews did not seem fully to realize this situation; but he perceived that his countrymen were disliked, and that the Portuguese were full of discontent, 'abandoned as they are by their sovereign, who has converted the mother country into a province from which men and money are drawn for support of his transatlantic dominions; whilst the command of the national army and the principal situations of power and profit are in the hands of foreigners'. The Inquisition too, though no longer active, was still, he believed, a depressing thought, of which people were reminded when they and their friends disappeared suddenly and were never heard of again, for that was what the present government and police caused to occur daily. Then of course there was Superstition, which Mr. Matthews of Eton and King's found, probably, a good deal more depressing than the Portuguese did. Classically reared, he preferred Greek and Roman mythology, which was 'as amusing as Mother Bunch, illustrated and adorned too as it was by such divine statues', so much superior to the tawdry images to which these poor creatures bowed down with such humble prostrations. Everyone was sadly indolent, too. Arts, sciences, literature, everything languished in Lisbon. The monasteries were castles of indolence filled with portly monks; their stoutness gave credibility to the tales of their sloth, good cheer and debaucheries. The nunneries had a better reputation, and were said to be filled with sincerely pious women, who had been led, from perhaps a mistaken sense of religion, to bury themselves in the unprofitable seclusion of a convent.

On October 2nd he attended the funeral of one of the Regents, a very anti-British man. The streets at night were dark, the lower orders carried large clasp-knives, and assassinations freely occurred. Dogs and priests were numerous. The French used to bayonet the dogs and make the monks sweep the streets; but the French went, and the monks and the dogs came back. The Portuguese were worthy of better things, but 'they are bowed down by a despotic government and hoodwinked by a besotted superstition'. The suppression of the late conspiracy had strengthened the government's hands, but a change must take place sooner or later.

Depression deepened. On October 6th, 'Everything warns me to depart. I have to-day been attending as pall-bearer at the funeral of one of my fellow passengers from England. He was in the last stage of a decline . . . It may be my turn next — *mea res agitur paries cum proximus ardet*. He lodged next door. The English burying ground is pleasantly situated and well shaded with fine cypresses'. He looked in vain for Fielding's grave, and found no stone; a pity Mr. Canning had not, during his embassy, been solicited to prepare a suitable inscription.

October 7th — impatient to leave. The flies were a plague; he sympathized with Domitian. On Sunday he went to Mass, where he liked nothing but the music. On the 14th he found a ship for Leghorn. 'And so much for the Lusitanian — or, as it might with more propriety be called, the Lousytanian Metropolis . . . I shall quit it without one feeling of regret. In fact, to remain is impossible: I am fairly stunk out.'

So off he sailed for Italy, where he felt a little better; it was the cultivated Englishman's mecca. He travelled for three years; on returning to England he published his travel diaries, under the title *Diary of an Invalid in Pursuit of Health, in 1817, 1818, and 1819*. It would seem that the pursuit was vain; eight years later the sad traveller died, a judge in Ceylon.

BIBLIOGRAPHY

Diary of an Invalid in Pursuit of Health, in 1817, 1818, and 1819, HENRY MATTHEWS (1820).
Dictionary of National Biography.

EARTHQUAKE

I. A NUN
Sister Catherine Witham
[1755]

IT may be remembered that one of the things that Joseph Baretti enjoyed most on his visit to Lisbon in 1760 was calling at 'the English Nunnery'. He found the nuns charming company; 'all their visitors', said he, 'are used by them with such an endearing kindness, that their parlatory is in a manner never empty from morning till night. The poor things are liberal to every body of chocolate, cakes and sweetmeats . . . I will positively see them as often as I can while I stay here'.

Baretti was only one of many who felt this. British sailors frequented the convent grille, for sweetmeats and chat, with such assiduity that, in 1735, when the British fleet lay in the Tagus for a year, the lady abbess had to ration their visits; and during the Peninsular War a group of English protestant sailors, having observed that the Syon Convent monstrance was inferior to others in Lisbon churches, 'exclaimed with an oath that their countrywomen should have as fine a house for their God as the Portuguese', and subscribed among themselves for a very handsome monstrance, which the sisters use to this day. A less approving visitor was Robert Southey; the cakes and the tea did not mitigate his disapproval of such an institution; he went away convinced that a nun is as miserable in herself as she is useless to society.

These miserable beings, whom Baretti found so charming, and Mr. Richard Twiss, in 1772, 'very chatty and entertaining' (he regretted the grille), had become, since their arrival in Lisbon in 1594, deeply rooted in its life. Founded in 1415 at Isleworth, as a mixed community of monks and nuns according to the Bridgettine contemplative order, they had fled from the Reformation and spent thirty-five uneasy years wandering from one continental resort to another, finding each in turn unsatisfactory, for Zeeland was unwholesome and exposed to pirates, Mishagen was exposed to Calvinists and Lutherans, Mechlin to religious wars, Antwerp to Protestant reprisals for Spanish atrocities, Rouen to Henry of

Navarre, to whom their confessor, a staunch member of the Catholic League, could not think it right to submit, even after his discreet conversion. So, in 1594, off the Bridgettines went to Portugal, to live, they hoped, safely in the domains of His Most Catholic Majesty of Spain. They settled in a pleasant Lisbon suburb, and led their quiet, enclosed life among the friendly Lisboans, receiving supplies from time to time of young English gentlewomen who managed to slip out of their native land and join them, to the mild scandal of the English consul in Lisbon. 'Here arrived lately', he wrote in July 1607, 'the *Seaflower*, of London, master Luke Whetstone, who brought into his ship two gentlewomen, whom the first night of arrival were privily conveyed unto the Monastery of English Nuns . . . but what their names are is kept very close; the one is thought to be a Catesby . . .' And so on. All the same, the Bridgettines did not get enough young English gentlewomen, and, as to young gentlemen, by the end of the seventeenth century the last monk was gone. Baretti explained their flattering manners in 1760 by their desire to enlist novices and keep up their numbers.

By that time, the convent had been entirely destroyed by the earthquake, and rebuilt. The nuns, who escaped into the garden, were all unhurt. Here is the story as told by one of them in a letter to her mamma in England. Kitty Witham's spelling was not good, but I have preserved it.

Jan. 27th, 1756.
Poor Sion Houes.

My dearest Mama

The Agreable favour of my Dearest Mama I received on the 9th Instant which gave me the greatest Pleasure to hear you was all well, which I pray God to Continue. I don'te in the least doubt of the great Concarne and trouble you was in aboute me, but that itt was Sincear, to be shure we was all in great danger; but Allmighty God's goodness spaird us, sweet Jesus make me and us all grateful to his devine Majesty for the great favour he has done us; Now I will give you a little description how we all mett together in our little valley; that Morning we had all been att Communion, and had done the quire and then went to gett our Breakfasts which is tea and bread and butter when 'tis not fasting time; we was all in different places in the Convent, some in the Refectory, some in there Cells, others here and there; my Lady Abbys her two neces Sister Clark and myself was att Breakfast in a little Room by the Common, which when they had done they went to prepair for Hye Mass, which was to begin at ten a Clock. I was washing up the tea things, when the Dreadfull afair hapned. itt began like the rattleing of Coaches, and the things befor me danst up and downe upon the table, I look about me and see the Walls a shakeing and a falling down then I up and took to my heells, with Jesus in my mouth, and to the quire I run, thinking to be safe there, but there was no Entranc but all falling rownd us, and the lime and dust so thick there was no seeing. I mett with some of the good Nuns they Cryed Outt run to the low garden, I ask where the rest was, they sayde there, so Blessed be his holy Name we all mett together, and run no further, we was all as glad to see one another alive and well as can be exprest. We spent the day in prayers, but with a great deal of fear and aprehension, as we had shakes and trembles all that day and night, and in fine ever since, only God knows how and when itt will end, last night we had a vere sharp one which renewd our fright vere much. We layde under a pair tree, covered over with a Carpett, for Eight days, I and some others being so vere frighted every time the wind blode the tree, I thought we was a going, so could not possible rest there, so we went into the Open air and slept there with much Pleasure, then the good fathers made us anothr little place with sticks and Coverd with Matts, where we some of us rested there a few Nights with the two fathers who came to us that Morning and glad to see us all alive as we was to see them. We have got a Wooden houes made in the garden, where the two good fathers and aboute half of us lives and lays there, but we lye in our Cloes I have never lain without my Cloes since All Saints. Which I finde vere Uncomfortable but I beg God to accept it as a small Pennance. There is a bell that is rung att five a clock by them that has Currage to lay above, for those that has a mind to go to Mattins, if we have no fright in the Night by any Shock which we have some times then we dar not go and iff not we go, our Covent stands so hye that we have two and thirty stone steps to goe up to itt, Out of five and thirty Cells we have not One that we can lye in, till they are Repaird, the Church Door has never been Opend Nor Mass sayde in itt since, tis so full of Rubish, as also the Quire and Refectory and the Kitchen

entirely downe, so we must dow as well as we can till itt pleases
All mighty God to send us a forturn, for I heard say we can take
no more without. Them that has seen Lisbon before this dreadful
Calammity and to see itt now would be greatly shockt the Citty
is Nothing but a heep of Stones caused by the Great fier tis Call-
culated above forty thousand was destroyed and one of the most
terrible things that hapened was this, that many poor Souls
Inclosed in the Ruings not Killd, but Could not gett out so some
was burnt alive and Others dyed of humger: The poor Presedent
of the English College was Killd as he was prepairing for Mass.
tis thought he lived aboute four and twenty hours in that Misery
for when they found him he was nowhere Brused by reason he
was under a bench. A Gentleman of my Acquaintance tould me
the other day he was two hours under the Ruing, and did not
know how to gett out att last he spyed a light through a little
crack, he thought if he Meddled he might throw downe more and
so kill him, so he trusted in Allmighty God's Provedence, a while
after he felt the heat of the fire and then he made the best of his
way Out, There was a Nother man lived under the Ruings for
some days, he was in his Shope, so helped himself to live, att last
he was dug Out and found harty and well, the same thing hapend
to an Old woman that was in her Pantry that help her, a poor
Gentleman was going to gett Out of his Window and offered a
hundred Moyders to anybody thatt woude give him a lader,
everebody desire to save there own Lives none durst Ventur so the
poor Soule was Killd. Sir Henry Franklen an acquaintance of
Mr. Killinghale was going in his shayz and percevd the houses to
fall, he Jump out and a house fell upon him, he gett out throu
some little hole and see a good many alive in a Nother street, he
had Portugues to say Vene, that is Come hear, so saved them all,
he left his shaze in the street broake, his Servants and horses killd.
. . . We was all glad Mr. Killinghale had the good fortune not to
come to Lisbon this year, as we have had such a dreadfull Callamity amongst us which is a Nufe to shock anybody to see, but God's
holy Name be praised for spairing us, for there is some toons in
Portugaull that is quite swallowd up. this youll Read in the Newspapers, as allso a present from the good King of England to
the King of Portugaull, God bless him for itt, for tis Cartainly
Necessary for his subjects. The fleet is not yett come in but tis
expected dayly. I wish an Oportunity would offer for I have

something to send you, for only God knows how long we have to live for I believe this world will not last long. happy are those that has gon well out of itt. My Dear Cosn Harry dyed a happy Death thank God. Good father Confessor Buryed him in his Own Voult which is under Our Hye Altar, so was Carryd in att the little door as there was no going in att the other. his Widdow desires to be Rememberd to all frends, indeed poor thing she is vere Kinde to me if he had lived she would have been my Lady for the King Would have Knighted him, but poor thing he being so vere ill would not Receve his title. We have account of some Earthquakes you have had in some parts of England but itt was some days after All Saints. The towo fathers with my Lady Abbyss desires there best Complements to Dear Papa and your Dear Self. The same with myself and all other Acquaintance desire Our best Complements to Mr. Killinghale. Pleas to Remember me to all frends and lett them know Im alive and well, to admiration. if the Earthquake had hapend in the Night as itt did not thank God, we should all or most of us been Killd in Our Beds. Or if we had been att Hye Mass which we would have been att ten a Clock God knows how it would have been the quire falling might have knock us all dead befor we had all got Out so thanks be to God for his great favour. so now must conclude with my Duty to Dear Papa with many thanks for his kinde Rememberrance of me, and I hope not to be so troublesom as I have been. My Duty to Dear Aunt William and Dear Unkle Paul and to my Dear Sisters and Kinde Rememberrance to Mr. and Mrs. Fermor and Others of my Dear frends and acquaintances .. and belive me my Dearest Mama to be Your Ever dutyfull and Obedient Childe

KITTY WITHAM.

P.S. I wish some good frend in England that has itt and Can afoard itt would send us a Brace of hundred Pounds to help to Buyld up the Convent Im just going downe to my Logeings which is the Cabana in the garden few in Lisbon sleeps in aney place Else now a days they send them over from other Countrys ready made. hear in the feeld youll see little Els so Dearest Mama adew till the Next.

With this letter is another, very pious, to an aunt.

EARTHQUAKE

My dearst Aunt

I Recevd the favour of my Dear Aunts Kinde lines, and am sorre you are in such a bad state of health but I hope the great God of all goodness will preserve you yett many years. I am vere sorre for Dear Cosen Bette being so ill butt I hope to hear of her Recovery . . . Dear Aunt what is all this World Nothing in itt to be Admired seeing Allmighty God can destroy us all in so little a time if his Devine Majesty had not stopt his Mercefull hand, thank God for Spairing us this time that we may be better Prepaird. My Dear Aunt will hear by Dear Mamas letter what danger we was in and how Almighty God throug his great goodness Spaird us I hope for a better End. Youll hear the Newspapers: what they say of this Callamity hear and in Other Countrys which God knows tis too true: my Duty to my Dear Unkle. Dear Aunt tis thought this World will not last long so itt behoves us to prepair for the Other for my part Im going to prepair for a General Confession pray for poor Kitty for she allways prays for you all. which is all from your ever loveing and Affectionat Nece

KITTY WITHAM.

The world lasted longer than Kitty expected, and Syon House built itself up again. Ruined and homeless, the nuns petitioned 'the nobility, ladies and gentlemen of our dear country' for help; these played up well, and by 1760 the convent was rebuilt and prosperous. It stayed in Lisbon through all troubles and disturbances, such as French invasions and Portuguese anti-convent campaigns, until 1861. To-day Syon Abbey keeps, after five travelled but unbroken centuries, its ancient order among the Dartmoor hills.

BIBLIOGRAPHY

MS Letter in the possession of Syon House.
History and Antiquities of Syon Monastery, C. J. AUNGIER (1840).
Story of the English Bridgettines, CANON J. R. FLETCHER (1933).
Journey from London to Genoa, JOSEPH BARETTI (1762).
State Papers, Portugal, 89/3 (Record Office).
Letters from Spain and Portugal, ROBERT SOUTHEY (1797).

2. A MERCHANT

Thomas Jacomb

[1755]

THOMAS JACOMB was a merchant in the woollen trade in Lisbon; he was the son of the member of parliament for Thetford. In the midst of the horrors of earthquake, he had enough presence of mind and methodical habit to set down, though with a little incoherence here and there, his experiences and impressions, apparently for the benefit of his family, who have had his manuscript ever since. It here appears through the kindness of his descendant, Mr. S. Jacomb-Hood. As I have not meddled with the spelling of Sister Kitty Witham, I have also left Mr. Jacomb's untouched; his is very much better.

Portugall.
November 1st 1755.
At about 10 o'clock in the morning I, Thos. Jacomb in my Country House in the Prazio in Lisbon felt the commencement of the Earthquake and immediately ran to Mr. Montgomery, who without delay desired me to follow him from the House into the Yard; when had no sooner got than saw the Inquisition, Senate House, the Duke de Cadavalls, and my own House falling: the Earth shaking so much cd hardly stand and making so great a noise that imagined must be the day of Judgmt. This continued about 3 or 5 minutes during which time from the falling of Houses arise so great Dust that thought shod have been suffocated, but on ceasing went into the Prazio which was almost full of people who had escaped from their houses, on enquiring found all the City within my view almost all demolished: the Castle, St. Domingos St Roch's etc.

In about 15 minutes was repeated another shock and Half an Hour after another — and about 12 another but none so violent as the first. By this time the Prazio was so full has hardly to hold the People who now assembled. Old, Young, Male and Female seeking their Parents, Children, Relations and Friends many sick, many maimed and wounded from the fall of the Houses, some dead and most part especially Women half naked so dismal a sight was never seen, neither can thought imagine or fancy describe the various scenes of misery, the Fryars and Priests as many as now saved giving Absolution Confessing and Praying with everyone; when unhappily a Fire broke out at the Marquis de Louvicalls at about half an hour after 12 at S. Domingos when the Smoke was great and the Concourse of People was so great in the Prazio that fearing to be suffocated, many strangers, among the rest myself, imagining my House to be quite down resolved with Mr. Freeman to proceed to Campo Grande to a friend of his, but finding himself afflicted and his House down resolved to go about two leagues from Lisbon, when met Mr. Holford and Mr. Larkins and hired a boat to remain in the water that Night, and during the Night felt sevl small shocks. The Distresses on the Road are not to be described. Everyone in Tears and Knowing not whether to fly, or to remain and almost all the Houses on the Road having met the same fate and no one place remaining entire except the Grand Aqueduct which seemed to have no damage.

In the streets of Lisbon . . . saw many coaches, chaises, carts, Horses, Mules, Oxen etc, some entirely some half buried under Ground, many People under the Ruins begging for assistance and none able to get nigh them, many groaning under ground, many old and hardly able to walk, now without shoes and stockings and still hurrying to save life, but now no distinction of Sexes, Ages, Birth or Fortune are regarded . . . The Custom House part sunk into the River with the new stone quays, the other part was burnt and no goods saved, which is an immense loss to Trade as also all the Sugar warehouses. My former apprentice Mr. Sale was killed, as was Mr. Parminster's English serv^t who followed me into the Yard by the falling of one of the Pillars of the Balcony. A sickness is dreaded . . .

Most People have lost all their cash, no Bills can or will be paid and must be returned Protested: which will be a dreadful consquence in England Holland France etc and cause many Bankrupts. The Portuguese will never be able to pay their obligations or debts, as all the Shopkeepers have lost all their goods and effects.

3rd. Several Shocks and at 12 last night a very large one — the Distress of the People increasing many Thousands still continuing to fly, all in tears, Misery and Want, the Nobility, Fryars etc burying the dead in Lisbon and the King giving as prudent orders as possible in the great calamity. All prisoners set free and a General Pardon, but incredible the Barbarity caused by Superstition, Enthusiasm and Bigotry. The Jews who were in the Inquisition and in a few days an Act of Faith was to have been published for them so suffer now tyed on Horses and sent with a guard to Coimbra, several of whom I saw pass the Ferry Boat at Sacavem.

4th. I saved some Linen and woolens before the Fire got to the House at Montagues; Lucas Houses with whom I had left my Household Furniture Plate and Linen were all burnt. To my great Joy I found Mr. Lucas was aboard the Packet for one of my servants had assured me he and all his Family was killed: Mr. Lucas was up to the head in Ruins and was got out by the Resolution and Courage of his cousin Mrs. Spillar. This day not so many on the roads, tho' met old and young Women who had lost their Parents Friends etc and were seldom used to walk begging to supply Nature, all in tears lifting up their hands to Almighty God to assist them in their Distress, who I doubt not will hear their Prayers and save us all. This is a lesson to the Proud and Ambitious and makes us reflect what is this world who to trust in but God, what are Kingdoms, Kings, Nobility, etc. without his Guidance. One moment has reduced one of the largest Trading Cities to ashes and Killed Maimed and reduced to Poverty and Misery above five hundred Thousand Souls without a House to shelter themselves in, it is said near Fifty Thousand Portuguese are killed and not above twenty English in the Factory which is very few as for so large a number as are in Lisbon. The weather has been very fine, which a great mercy, as everyone is obliged to stay in the Fields or Tents or Ruins.

Houses some distance from the City, the Opera House the Pride of the Royal Family was demolished in a moment, but that does not grieve the King, so good a man as he certainly is beholds the Misery of himself and People with great Pity and Compassion and is endeavouring to assist them and begs many with Tears not to quit and depopulate the City. This night lay in a Tent in the Fields and there has been no shock since eight this morning, so hope it will please God shall have no more.

5th. ... All Publick and Private Papers are burnt or lost. The flying of the Portuguese may be compared in one respect to the burning of Troy, when the Trojans took such care of their Household Gods, but now hardly to be seen on the road but with an Image of our Saviour on the Cross, the Virgin Mary, St. Anthony, and many other Wooden and Brick Images which they embraced and prayed to save them and took them to their Beds, but setting that aside, which is contrary to our Notions, they behaved with great decency and Religion.

7th. Waited on Mr. Castres the English Envoy, much confusion still in the Town.

8th. At 5 this morning a most dismal Shock, very loud and terrible last ½ an hour but did no great damage: was so frightened that resolved with Mr. Holford to go on Board the ship, and immediately took Boat, and about ½ an hour after I got on Board the Theodorick Capn. John Hale of Scarborough, a worthy Humane man who was willing to receive all in Distress . . . The Ruins of the City from the Water terrible to behold, especially where the Merchants resided. Neither Church Convent Palace or any other Building left standing except the Mint and the Arsenal but little damage towards Belem . . .

11th . . . from Porto and Coimbra it had been but slightly felt. Several accounts of Eruptions in the Earth especially at Cintra near the Rock where much Flames and Supher were seen to evaporate. Lay this night at a Home at Sacavem.

12th. Remained at Sacavem to examine what things I had saved, found many things stolen particularly my Linnen, some pieces of fine cloth long ells etc. . .

13th. Yesterday several were hanged in Lisbon for Robbing and Plundering, in Particular a Frenchman an Italian or Spaniard who confessed at the Gallows had set fire to the city in 4 different parts that they might plunder and rob the easier . . .

14th . . . Greatly fear it has reached England. Letters from Cork mention the same . . . Now computed about 10 or 15000 Portuguese buried in Ruins. Many of the Factory returning to England.

18th. Another Shock.

BIBLIOGRAPHY

MS Letter in the possession of Mr. S. Jacomb-Hood.

3. ENVOY AND CONSUL

Mr. Castres and Mr. Hay

[1755]

IN Whitehall they thought for some time that Abraham Castres, his Majesty's envoy at Lisbon, must have perished in the earthquake; on December 1st, a month after the melancholy occurrence, instructions were issued to Charles Townshend, who had been secretary to the Legation at Madrid, to go to Lisbon and take charge of affairs there. He was to convey sympathy to his most Faithful Majesty and inform him that Britain was sending for the relief of sufferers fifty thousand pounds in money and as much more in kind. If, as seemed likely, Edward Hay, the consul, should be dead too, Townshend was to send a report of British affairs and the number of British dead. Two days later, however, news had been received through Sir Benjamin Keene, ambassador at Madrid and Castres's intimate friend, of the envoy's safety.

Castres had himself written to London on November 6th his account of the affair. His own house, Santa Martha in Buenos Ayres, had stood the shock, though a good deal damaged; in fact, it tottered dangerously. As it was beyond reach of the flames, many of his compatriots, themselves burnt out, took refuge with him; he accommodated them in tents in his large garden, as no one but himself, Lord Charles Douglas, and Mr. Williamson the chaplain, dared to sleep in the house. He also had the Dutch minister and his lady and three children and seven or eight servants of theirs; the rest of the company 'of the better sort' were merchants of the Factory, who had for the most part lost all they had, though some had saved a little of their cash. Of the Dutch visitation Castres must have written to his friend Keene with an exasperation he concealed in his official dispatches; Keene responds with sympathy, 'I enrage at your Dutch guests'; and later, 'I assure you it never came into my imagination that the Dutch family should have the Dutch conscience to stay with you above a day or two till they could turn themselves elsewhere, instead of which they are become sojourners in your land. I lose all patience with them. There is no bearing with imposition. The Dutch consul has gotten a reputation here for his performing miracles and feeding hundreds; why does he not feed his Chief?

Indeed my friend, I would, after all this humanity on your part, send them and the horses of the Factory that are eating you up all together agrazing. Take care of yourself and poor Williamson and company . . .'

But Castres, a humane and conscientious envoy, would send no one agrazing, not even the Dutch. His letter goes on to report that the Factory had 'escaped pretty well, considering the number of houses we have here', and to give some account of the disasters that had befallen others. The Spanish ambassador, for instance, had been crushed under his door as he ran into the street. This, with all the other sad accidents to his acquaintances among the nobility, had greatly affected poor Mr. Castres; 'but in particular' (and here all members of the Corps Diplomatique will, out of bitter experience, sympathize) 'the miserable objects among the lower sort of His Majesty's subjects, who all fly to me for bread and lie scattered up and down in my garden with their wives and children. I have helped them all hitherto, and shall continue to do so, as long as provisions do not fail us, which I hope will not be the case, by the good order M. de Carvalho [Pombal] has issued in that respect'. The envoy's house was tottering, and if the rains began and the people in the garden had to come indoors, the floors would probably give way.

Directly the road was passable, he had waited on the king and royal family at Belem; they were encamped in a garden, none of the royal palaces being fit to shelter them. The king received him with more serenity than might have been expected; the queen and princesses begged to be excused, as they were in their tents and in little else.

Most of the chief Factory families had secured their passages to England. When Castres should be rather less fatigued and troubled he would, he said, be considering some way of putting the poorer sort on to a Portuguese hulk or British vessel until they could be shipped to England or Ireland; but many of them wanted to stay and look for their cash among their ruins. Rapine and murder were all about, though being firmly dealt with; the envoy was nervous about his house, which contained the money rescued by some of the English Factory, and was surrounded last night by ruffians; he had asked for a guard.

'We are to have in a day or two a meeting of the scattered Factory at my house, to consider of what is best to be done in our present wretched circumstances. I am determined to stay within call of the distressed, as long as I can remain on shore with the least appearance of security, and the same Mr. Hay seemed resolved to do the last time I conferred with him.'

The consul wrote a week later, from Marvilla, a few miles out of Lisbon, describing the shocks, the fire, and the ruin caused. It has pleased God, he said, to spare most of His Majesty's subjects residing here, but their fortunes are sunk in the common ruin. Several merchants of the Factory had offered the king 'such provisions as they had by them, which was very well taken'. On Sunday he had gone with Mr. Castres to see the king in his garden at Belem and presented an address of condolence from the Factory, which His Majesty said he would read at his leisure. Care was being taken to ensure provisions, but no steps for the re-establishment of commerce, except the fixing of a new custom house. The only immediate distress was the want of habitations. Many of the Factory were going home; others would stay and see to their affairs; so long as there was a Factory in Lisbon, the consul thought it his duty to stay with it.

In the matter of the re-establishment of commerce, Mr. Hay and his merchants seem to have been rather inopportunely persistent. The consul wrote four days later that he had seen M. Carvalho about this, asking his leave to draw up proposals. The minister replied that 'it could not be yet, that I could but see the distressed condition they were in, all the court encamped under canvas tents in the garden, and no other habitations, nor even places of devotion', and that the kingdom was threatened with plague and famine; the first step must be to provide against these evils, 'and then I might be assured that commerce would be taken care of'. The merchants complained that their cargoes of Newfoundland fish arriving at Lisbon were detained and unloaded, though destined for sale elsewhere; their strictly commercial approach in this crisis strikes one, and no doubt struck the Portuguese government, as a little narrow and unadaptable. They could not bear that trade should suffer such annihilation; as Mr. Hay observed, 'the unsettled state of commerce seems to have dampened the spirits of the Factory more than their losses'. There were no warehouses for housing the goods that arrived for them, no arrangements made about the custom house; in short, they could not stir a step.

One of Castres's chief worries was that he had run out of cash, having had all these people to feed. As to the Factory, 'our poor Factory, from a very opulent one, is totally ruined, at least for the major part'. The trading quarters had been the worst hit, and hardly one merchant in a hundred of any nation had saved anything, except some little cash which they had raked for among the ruins. 'As to their goods, their houses being burned to ashes, as well as the India house and custom house, not one of them that I hear of has been able to save a rag, nor can the Portuguese, who are all greatly indebted to our merchants, pay one single shilling of what they owe them.' The only bright spot to the envoy was that he had escaped with whole bones, after having had to jump out of a window from a second story; also that his servants had been able to get bread and rice to supply the wants of the vast concourse of people.

Hay, on December 11th, now in Lisbon again, at S. Joseph da Arriba near Belem, complains again of the merchants' grievances — the searching of ships before they could sail, the fixing of prices of provisions, no warehouses allowed to be built on the river towards Belem, which was very inconvenient. More annoying still (particularly for Castres), after it had been resolved by the Factory that 'the poor of our nation' must really be sent away, and a lot of them had been put on a boat for Ireland, the government had shilly-shallied in their procrastinating Portuguese way about granting them passes, so that they had all had to be landed again. The consuls of the various nations met to confer on the situation at Castres's house, as being most convenient for all the gentlemen. But the French ambassador, 'in consideration of the present posture of affairs between England and France' (the posture was the customary one) 'thought proper to direct M. Grenier, the French consul, not to attend'.

Meanwhile, shocks continued, and few people dared to sleep in buildings; instead, they caught colds and worse from lying in the open. The English Factory kept themselves warm with expostulating about their grievances and entreating the government for a custom house and warehouses in which to do business.

Castres had, on Christmas Eve, the pleasure of conveying to Carvalho and their Majesties the promise of generous help from Britain; the king and queen were much gratified and moved, and 'the company gathered about their tent expressed their most agreeable surprise that I had not been charged with empty compliments only, but with such proofs of real grandeur and dignity as would confer eternal honour on our gracious sovereign and the whole British nation'.

By the end of the year it was possible to send home a list of the British dead. They were thought to number seventy-eight altogether — twenty-nine men and forty-nine women. Fortunately, it seemed that they did not all matter much; there were only two prominent members of the Factory — Mr. Churchill, a young gentleman, and Mr. Casamajor, an ancient one, and only two Englishwomen 'of any note', Mrs. Hake and Mrs. Perochon. Keene wrote to Castres of the former of these, 'Tell Kit Hake how really sorry I condole with him upon the loss of that poor creature his wife'; and of the latter, more moderately, 'Mrs. Perochon's life was as dear to her as that of another, and I would not be wanting to her husband on such an occasion'. Having been envoy at Lisbon for two years, he knew all the Factory personally, and was (unlike many envoys and many consuls in Lisbon) fond of most of them; he had found pleasant and congenial company among them, and missed 'the jolly free Factory' society sadly at the formal Madrid court, where the British merchants were mostly Irish Catholics.

The Lisbon Irish, reported Castres, who were 'extremely numerous, particularly of the poorer sort', had suffered more heavily than the English; many of them were missing; it did not greatly matter, since most were 'so obscure as not to be known to any but the Irish friars'.

On the whole, British subjects had come well out of the affair, as regards life and limb, which led them to concentrate bitterly on their financial ruin. They strongly objected to the import duty of four per cent which was levied as a contribution towards the rebuilding of Lisbon; Hay interviewed Carvalho about it in vain; he advised the Factory to put up with it without further protest, but it rankled.

The common disaster, and the gratification at the lordly present from Britain, had only temporarily sweetened the relations between the British Factory and the firmly anti-British Pombal; there were too many causes of strain on both sides. When the promised money and goods arrived, the strain was eased for a brief moment; the minister asked the British envoy what proportion should be allotted to the needs of King George's subjects; the envoy suggested one-thirtieth, and so it was arranged.

By May, Hay was able to record 'Our affairs are upon no bad footing. We have the *pas* of all other nations in point of trade'. All the same, the Factory never recovered from the earthquake; its days of golden opulence were over.

BIBLIOGRAPHY

State Papers, Portugal, 89/50 (November 1755-May 1756). (Record Office).
The Private Correspondence of Sir Benjamin Keene, edited by SIR RICHARD LODGE (1933).

THE WAR OF THE TWO BROTHERS

Interventionists

[1832-1834]

I

IBERIAN civil war follows, in recent centuries, a pattern. It is war between constitutionalism and absolutism, liberty and tyranny, liberalism (often with a little Freemasonry thrown in) and clericalism; in brief, between Left and Right. Carlist wars, Miguelist wars, legitimist wars, uncles against nieces, dictators against republicans: whatever form they assume, their basis is the same. The same too is the cleavage of opinion about them abroad: liberals support one side, conservatives the other.

This was so with Dom Miguel's war against his elder brother Pedro and his young niece Maria, in whose favour Pedro resigned the Portuguese throne in 1826. As Greville remarked, the Tories were for Miguel, the Whigs for Pedro. Wellington thought Pedro a ruffian and the Constitution 'odious'; so did Lords Aberdeen, Londonderry, Eldon and Beresford, and all other Tories, though they were not moved by any particular esteem for Miguel; they had not taken to the young fellow when he visited England on his way back to Portugal after his four years exile, at the beginning of 1828. He had disgusted everyone in Paris by his boorish manners; he came to England to be instructed in his behaviour as Regent, pledged to observe a constitution that Britain was pledged to support. Wellington found him unbusinesslike; he had him to stay at Strathfieldsaye, together with the Marquis of Palmella; while Wellington and Palmella discussed the form of the oath he was to take, the backward young man (who no doubt had no intention of taking or keeping an oath at all) paid no attention, but sat flirting with Princess Thérèse Esterhazy. 'This will never do,' said the duke to Palmella. 'If he is so careless in an affair of such moment, he will never do his duty.' To which Palmella had answered, 'Oh, leave him to us, we will manage him'. Wellington explained afterwards to Greville that his protégé had no notion then of playing false; he was persuaded into it by his mother and terrified by the lengths to which the constitutionalists seemed prepared to go.

On the same visit, Dom Miguel stayed with the king at Windsor, and was received with great magnificence; he was reported to behave well enough, but to be farouche and shy; he went out stag-hunting in a red coat and full hunting costume, and 'rode over the fences like anybody else'. In fact, together with Wellington and Prince Esterhazy, he led the field. He must therefore, in spite of appearances, and of his outrageous behaviour to his father four years ago, and of some pretty queer stories about him, be a decent enough fellow at bottom; a sportsman and a sound Tory, at least, and a good bulwark against Jacobinism, that ever present peril on the Continent. The king gave him a fine horse (which his mother, an ardent anglophobe, later killed) and lent him his private box for Drury Lane; Maria Fitzgerald wrote in her diary that it was expected that he would be hissed there: 'I hope not', the kind girl added. He was not. His entrance was greeted with loud shouts of welcome from the audience, to which he made repeated obeisance. When God save the King was sung from the stage, an extra verse, complimentary to the royal guest, was added. To be sure, he did not seem quite to enter into the spirit of the pantomime, but he enjoyed the rope-dancing, and the evening was a great success. Indeed, his whole visit was a round of festivities, banquets, receptions and reviews; his particular cicerones were Wellington, Sir Charles Stuart (the godfather of the Charter: did he guess its fate?) and the sinister Lord Beresford, who may have seen in the blank, stupid, handsome Bourbon face the green light that might again open the forbidden road for him into Portugal after all. Even the *Times*, that sturdy organ of liberty, wrote of him now in an almost cordial tone, hoping (without probability) that the young despot's long sojourn in Europe with older despots might have improved him. Having bestowed some money on charities, he departed for Portugal early in February, together with Sir Frederick Lamb, our new ambassador, amid general acclamations, virtuously to assume the Regency in the name of his brother and niece and govern through the Charter of the Constitution so kindly brought by Sir Charles Stuart from Dom Pedro in Brazil.

Who would have guessed that by the end of March he would have become in the *Times* 'the wretched Miguel', 'the ungrateful and contemptible young despot', about to usurp the crown, only held in check by the firmness of Sir Frederick Lamb and by the presence of our troops, only waiting his opportunity to tear the constitution to tatters? 'So loathsome a spectacle of barefaced treachery and profligate absurdity was never presented to the civilized world.' Miguel had, in fact, wasted little time in revealing his purposes. He had taken the oath to the Constitution, but no one had heard his mumbled words, and it was not believed to be the Missal which he kissed; soon afterwards he had allowed himself to be proclaimed king by shouting mobs in Lisbon and the provinces. The English papers published letters from Lisbon giving desperate accounts of the situation, which it was said only energetic British measures could check. Acts of terrorism had at once begun. One was against Count Villa Real, the Foreign Minister, who had come with Miguel to England and shared in the banquetings there; being loyal to his master, Dom Pedro, he resigned office; when he went to take leave of the Regent and kiss his hand, the angry prince slapped his nose and mouth with the back of his hand; he was lucky, onlookers said, not to have all his bones smashed by Miguel's gang of palace ruffians.

A furious campaign of hate against the English began. Miguel was angry that English brigs off Oporto had fired a salute when Pedro was proclaimed there, and that English ships in the Tagus not only refrained from saluting him when he was rowed by, but sang the constitutional hymn. Besides, the English were well known to be all Freemasons, and to Freemasons Miguel and his party had a quite peculiar dislike; they thought them irreligious. There was a sermon preached at mass in the Santos church about Miguel's recent visit to England. 'Behold', said the preacher, 'our beloved Miguel approaching the English soil, where thousands of furious devils — for all the English, besides being heretics and damned to all eternity, are Freemasons — behold, I say, our angel landing among them, and merely by the power of his saintship and the heavenly sweetness of his adorable countenance imposing submission, respect and admiration on the hellish concourse!'

Gangs were hired to abuse and insult and throw stones at British merchants as they came from the Exchange; some were arrested. Even the pro-Miguelite Lord Beresford was abused for having made false promises of British support; he was defended by Mrs. Rochfort, *née* Harriette Wilson, who was in Lisbon at this time, whether in order to blackmail Sir Frederick Lamb (who, she had complained years back, had never paid her anything, either during or since his protectorate of her) we do not know, for Harriette's life lapsed into some obscurity after her marriage to the handsome Colonel Rochfort; it is tempting to think that she may even have flown as high as the Usurper himself. Anyhow, she championed Lord Beresford; she told Miguel that the marshal intended all that was good towards him, but had been let down by his colleagues in Britain, who were largely Freemasons and Jacobins. Certainly Lord Beresford did what he could for his protégé; he was openly accused of receiving pay, and of employing agents to work for the cause in Lisbon.

Meanwhile the foreign ministers, finding their protests unavailing, departed, which left their countrymen more than ever unprotected. Sir John Millay Doyle languished furiously in a dungeon in St. George's Castle; so also did Mr. William Young, of Leiria, who was accused of being an Englishman, a republican and a Freemason; both were miserably confined in gaol for about three months, and but for the unremitting efforts of the British consul they would be there still.

The attitude of the British government seemed to the English in Portugal, and to the *Times* in London, disgraceful. On September 13th the *Times* printed an open letter from Lisbon, signed 'A', to the Duke of Wellington, accusing him and his cabinet of favouring the usurper, of having made the British troops, till they were withdrawn from Portugal, stand supinely by watching 'the flagitious conduct of the Apostolical faction'; and, in fact, of connivance. The *Times* in a leader pitched into Wellington, spoke bitterly of the 'infatuated' pro-Miguel speech of Lord Aberdeen on the crisis, and complained that one word of encouragement to the constitutionalists from our ambassador would have checked 'the wretch on whom such absurd attentions were lavished' so short a time ago. King George had, indeed, declared in parliament that he disapproved of Miguel's behaviour, and affirmed loyalty to Pedro; he had also sent for Lords Wellington and Aberdeen and told them that the nine-year-old queen Maria, shortly to visit England from Brazil, was to be well received. The plump little girl arrived, was given the royal salute as her ship sailed into Falmouth, and spent the winter in England, treated coldly by the Tory ministers, but received, after a longish delay (on account, he said, of gout) by the good-natured king, with the ceremoniousness due to royalty and the kindness due to an exile child. But her position was awkward in a country which had no intention of actively supporting her claims, and whose non-interventionist policy was used in favour of her usurping uncle, as when Saldanha and a company of Pedroists were prevented by a British squadron from landing on Terceira from Plymouth. Little Maria was presently removed to France.

But in the summer of 1829 the political wheel turned, and more liberal counsels began to prevail. Palmerston, in a debate in June, made one of his thundering opposition speeches; the kind of speech that many liberal M.P.s would have liked to make in 1936 and 1937, but were restrained by caution. 'The civilized world rings with execrations upon Miguel; and yet this destroyer of constitutional freedom, this breaker of solemn oaths, this faithless usurper, this enslaver of his country, etc. . . . is, in the opinion of Europe, mainly indebted for the success which has hitherto attended him to a belief . . . that the Cabinet of England look upon his usurpation with no unfriendly eye . . . It is said that they have displayed a very patient forbearance under indignities offered to England in the persons of British residents in Portugal; while their steady refusal to interfere in cases in which their interference would have been prejudicial to Don Miguel has been contrasted with their promptitude and vigour to interfere when their interference was subservient to his projects. All these things, it is said, seem to show that they look upon his conduct with very different eyes from the rest of mankind, and appear to countenance the supposition that they have attempted by negotiation to give a legitimate sanction and permanent existence to his usurpation. . . .'

Wellington and the Tories fell next year; but even under a Liberal government non-intervention was maintained. When French subjects were ill-treated in Lisbon, a French naval division arrived in the Tagus, bombarded the forts, captured the Portuguese fleet, and terrified Miguel into submission to their demands, sailing back to Brest with Portuguese ships as hostages for good behaviour. The British lion, even under the truculent Palmerston, did nothing of the sort; and the old Duke protested indignantly in the Lords that it 'went to his heart to see the French dictate peace under the walls of Lisbon'.

London filled up with Portuguese liberal refugees fleeing from the terror. The diaries of those years are sprinkled with these charming exiles; they lived in Upper Baker Street, in Portman Square, everywhere; some were so little fortunate that they had to live in Newcastle, Bristol or Plymouth, or even Liverpool, and these never got over it; they included many literary men. There were two cousins of the Palmellas, very pleasing and gentleman-like young men, who called on the Fitzgeralds and the Trants and sang the constitutional hymn composed by their leader the Emperor of Brazil; there were the two rival Portuguese ministers and their wives, the minister to Pedro and the one to Miguel, who sometimes met at parties; there were pretty young Portuguese ladies who had married their uncles and shrank from the English habit of walking in the streets alone; the climate they all found dreadful, but nowhere had they, they said, found such good and interesting society. 'Foreigners', wrote Maria Fitzgerald, 'are always good-humoured and civil.'

Such was the friendly attitude of the British public. But when, in 1831, the Emperor sailed for Europe (bringing his child, the twelve-year-old queen) and prepared for armed expedition against his brother, enrolling volunteers, raising a loan, and equipping a fleet in England under the English Captain Sartorius, the Foreign Enlistment Act was held up against volunteers. Colonel Lloyd Hodges, an old Peninsular officer enthusiastic in the cause, who later commanded the British battalion of the constitutionalist army for over a year, before retiring in dudgeon amid the usual quarrels and grievances which hamper Iberian military service, complained that Miguelist agents in England, while the fleet was being fitted out, plotted with Lords Aberdeen and Beresford and other high Tories as to means for hindering an undertaking 'so hostile in principle to their own particular modes of thinking and feeling'. The rallying-point for Miguelite intrigues was the Portuguese consul-general, Sampayo; he was surrounded by English 'admirers of the modern Nero', as the colonel brusquely put it, and 'held forth the terrors of the Foreign Enlistment Bill against all who might feel disposed to disturb the exemplary reign of the royal object of their devotion'. They warned people that the Whigs would soon fall, and that officers and men who enlisted would then be ruined. 'Such, however, was the generous military ardour of those foremost to engage, the desire amongst many of fame, the impatience of an inglorious activity . . .

amongst all, moreover, such the ardour of a zeal which sought to promote the cause of freedom and the restoration of a constitutional monarchy ... that all these representations, however insidiously and industriously circulated, failed of effect.'

These lofty sentiments no doubt obtained in the breasts of Colonel Hodges's volunteers, mostly ex-officers in need of adventure. Another side of recruiting, more detailed and more realistic, is given by Sir Charles Shaw, then a Scotch ensign on half pay whose battalion had been disbanded in 1818, and who had led a restless, disgruntled life ever since, unsatisfied by roaming over the continent, fishing, and commanding volunteer sharpshooters at Leith. He arrived in England after a long continental tour in September 1831, a restless, turbulent, caustic-tongued, red-headed free-lance of thirty six, ripe for adventure, with 'the more lark the better' to it. Adventure was waiting for him. He fell in with that unpractical and hare-brained schemer Sir John Milley Doyle, who was 'commander-in-chief of an expedition to upset that vile vagabond Don Miguel', who had imprisoned him so rudely in Portugal in 1828. Shaw was easily persuaded to become his adjutant, though slightly disappointed to learn that the only force so far collected was a young Mr. Walsh, Sir John's aide-de-camp, 'but as the whole adventure was somewhat odd, I was not very much astonished'. Odd indeed it was. Shaw was told that recruits used to assemble in a tavern in Windmill Street, but had been dispersed by the police. The men, said Sir John, were engaged as 'labourers for Brazil', but it was generally known that it was for fighting. The captain of the schooner *Jack O'Lantern* and a Mr. Johnston, a smuggler, were engaged to find out the cost of taking this imaginary army to Terceira. But Sir John would do nothing definite until money was lodged for them in the Bank of England by the Portuguese Regency. Shaw wrote to a friend in Scotland for 'about a thousand Mull Highlanders'. Sir John said the late King John VI had presented him with a tract on the banks of the Tagus, where the Highlanders could live by fishing after the fighting was over, thus saving the expense of their passage home. The Highlanders, wisely, remained in Mull. Sir John made Shaw the lieutenant-colonel of a battalion, with a gratuity of twelve thousand acres on the banks of the Tagus, where he too, presumably, was to live by fishing when the fighting was over. Shaw thought he had better be introduced to Palmella, the president of the Regency, at this point; Sir John took him to call, but he was not there, and Shaw had a notion he never had been, and that it was the wrong house. They did, however, go and see Mendizabal, Dom Pedro's financial agent; he listened quietly to the expeditionary plans, and Shaw thought he smiled rather oddly; he offered no money, and when Sir John, at Shaw's advice, wrote to him making a firm offer of troops for cash, he returned no answer. After that the Doyle plans evaporated; Shaw began to suspect them pure moonshine and that the Regency was laughing at them; he thought he had better drop his lieutenant-colonelcy and the land on the Tagus and offer himself as an ordinary volunteer. Soon after this he met Colonel Hodges, a more practical organizer, and was given the captaincy of a company of marines in Sartorius's fleet. On December 5th he began recruiting, after meeting with Hodges his fellow-officers of the liberating army, and being 'agreeably surprised to find them gentlemenly young men'. He found a recruiting station in Seven Dials, with a back door exit because of police raids, but the neighbours suspected them for Burkers (very rife just then) and shouted 'Off, you Burkers you!' so they left Seven Dials and settled in George Yard, St. Giles's, which had back doors into Soho. Here they posted a staunch old marine as look-out man, and put up a placard saying 'Wanted, by a Trading & Colonial Co, some active and intelligent men as Settlers for Brazil and elsewhere', adding that they must be prepared to act in any capacity and go anywhere. Everyone knew what it meant; no one might say so. A Scot who said 'I ken y'ere gaan to Portingale. Am ower knowing for you, am a canny chap. A'll gang as a sodger, and that's the plain matter of fact', was turned away. But hundreds came, took their sixpences, and enrolled for this vague settling. The office was raided by police; Shaw escaped by jumping out of a window, and the recruiting office moved to Frith Street. The recruits were of all trades and professions — old soldiers, clergymen, lawyers, medical students, carpenters, weavers, cobblers, labourers, servants, tailors, poets, clerks, prize-fighters, out-of-works, and several who had good reasons for wanting to be out of their native land. 'I may be wrong', says Shaw, 'but I am inclined to state that the most troublesome men as soldiers are tailors, weavers and lawyers.' There were 'not a few adventurers of the most doubtful character', said Colonel

Hodges, and the pure love of freedom was at once stimulated and hampered by the accompanying love of gain.

It had been intended to collect 1200 men; actually 400 were enrolled. Three vessels were equipped, seized at Deal through the machinations of the Portuguese consul, but eventually released through those of Palmella, the Pedroist ambassador; the law-officers decided that they could not legally detain them, since they appeared to be bound for Flushing. Warrants were issued for the arrest of the recruiters, but they evaded observation. Finally, in mid December, the liberating army sneaked in several small detachments and with the utmost caution down to Dartford, where the *Edward* lay off shore. Miguelite agents hopefully watched for them, warrants in hand, but, telling inquiring and sympathetic onlookers that they were going 'hopping to Kent', which, in December, deceived no one, the motley army was somehow got onto the waiting lighters and conveyed out to the *Edward*, having with difficulty shaken off the lady friends who desired to board the lighters and come and liberate Portugal also; 'the conduct of these irregular mates was excessively violent' said Shaw; or, as one of the recruits put it, there was 'a deal of noise with the women'. To a police boat which accosted the lighters as they pulled out, the answer 'hopping to Kent' was given, and evoked cheers even from these officers of the law. The heart of Britain was undoubtedly Pedroist; possibly too the police were relieved to lose the liberators; one of them remarked some time afterwards, 'Sir, we are very quiet now in the St. Giles's district, for most of our greatest scamps are gone a-soldiering to Portugal'.

Once on board the ship *Edward*, the liberators (possibly led by the tailors, weavers and lawyers) behaved in a very troublesome and noisy manner, rioting on the deck and shouting 'Money! Money!' Some deserted at Flushing and got back to England. The Flushing Dutch disliked the look of the lot of them, particularly of Shaw, and suspected them of anarchical designs. However, they got off unarrested, and arrived at Belleisle in the Azores on January 3rd, 1832. The Emperor Pedro looked on his brave British volunteers a little coldly; perhaps he thought they should be more, perhaps he did not want any at all, only ships to transport the Portuguese troops (for some international jealousy obtained) or perhaps he merely, like the Dutch, did not care for their appearance. They spent six months in the Azores, preparing for the expedition, drilling, getting into military shape, enjoying the tropical life, seeing a lot of the nuns in the convents, who were extremely obliging but on the whole plain, and getting excessively drunk. There were continual 'horrid scenes of drunkenness and riot', which the Portuguese inhabitants bore with great patience.

On June 1st the expedition — forty-two ships, with the emperor on the *Amelia* and the royal standard at his mast — sailed for Portugal. It landed unopposed at Mindello, six miles from Oporto, on July 8th, saluted by guns from the flagship of the British navy lying off shore, and marched on Oporto, which Dom Miguel's army evacuated in panic, having been informed that the Pedroists were a force of over 30,000. Actually they were under 8000, of which the English battalion commanded by Colonel Hodges, with Major Shaw leading the advance guard, numbered 300, besides Hodges's supernumeraries, mostly ex-officers from the Peninsular War. There were other foreign volunteers — French, Germans, Dutch, Poles; about 550 altogether. The Miguelite forces round Oporto, immensely larger than Pedro's army, fled across the Douro and left the Pedroists to march on the city unopposed.

There was panic in Oporto among the Miguelites, mostly the fidalgos, the rich Portuguese merchants and the priests. The liberals, the Freemasons, the *negros*, the *malhados*, were upon them, and they feared a rising and massacre; many of them fled out of the city with the army. The general citizenry, easily swayed in any cause, cared little who ruled them; they would shout 'viva the Constitution' and 'death to the Constitution' with equal fervour, according to the way things were going. The liberals, after four years of Miguel, were mostly already executed, fled, or cramming the full prisons. The British merchants and wine shippers, liberal men of commerce who hated the *rei absoluto* and all he stood for and did, were strongly Pedroist, though they discreetly kept in with the Miguelite Portuguese on whom their trade depended; the Wine Company, for instance, was practically entirely in the hands of Miguelites. Ever since the Reign of Terror had begun, the population had been incited by officials, soldiers, and the church, to insult and call them names; they were Freemasons, liberals, English atheists and constitutionalists; angry friars spat at them in the streets. The imperturbable wine shippers, going about their business in the Rua dos Inglezes and the Vila Nova da Gaia where their wine lodges stood, did not bother much about this. But they felt the arrival of Pedro a relief, and that their existence and business would be much safer and more prosperous if that blackguard Miguel were expelled. The news of the landing had already sent up their stock, and they were now viva'd in the streets by enthusiasts, who burnt the gallows in the square, shot the hangman (an unpopular fellow), opened the prison doors to let out Miguel's prisoners, and changed the Miguelite banners all about the city to the liberal blue and white, shouting 'Viva a Constituição! Viva o exercito liberatador!' with the greatest empressement. The known Miguelists who had not fled cowered behind their shuttered doors; they felt like Paris aristocrats in 1789.

Next day the liberating army marched into Oporto, with the Duke of Bragança on a farm horse, and his motley army of Portuguese and foreigners. Among the former were the usual band of *academicos* who are to the fore in any revolution — Coimbra students and young intellectuals, among whom was the poet Almeida Garrett, returned from exile together with the Portuguese liberal leaders. The crowd cheered; or 'some of them', as Corporal Knight put it; even the cheerers thought the army disappointingly small. The English residents thought so; nervous about the outcome, they got ready to seek, if necessary, refuge on the British naval ships in the port. Captain Shaw, however, felt no doubts at all; he agreed with some brother officers not to shave until they marched into Lisbon; the others weakened on this, but Shaw grew his red beard until it swept his breast.

The British quartered in the convent of S. Lazareto. 'We were quartered,' said Corporal Knight, 'in the convent of St. Lazarus, receiving strict orders not to molest the monks, who lived in fine style, but the temptations were too much for us poor men'. So the poor men too lived in fine style, stealing salted pigs' heads, vegetables from the monks' garden, pigs and poultry, so that well supplied with pork, fowl and aguadente, they lived famously. Meanwhile Dom Pedro began to put the city into defence, throwing up barricades and breastworks and digging trenches across the streets, helped by sympathetic citizens, both Portuguese and British, and hindered by the unsympathetic monks of the four and twenty convents in the town, who, when opportunity offered, set fire to the barracks or blew up the defences. A peculiar dislike was felt for monks by the Pedroist Portuguese soldiers; it appears to have been mutual, and more than once the clergy made vigorous attempts to burn the troops in their beds, which exacerbated relations further.

So the siege of Oporto began, and lasted over a year. This is not the place to tell its story, which belongs to Portuguese history; our concern is with the British actors in the scene, who were, taking them all round, of a most vigorous activity. Whether one gets the story from Colonel Hodges, Captain (later General) Shaw, Colonel Hugh Owen, Colonel Lovell Badcock, Corporal Knight, Mr. William Bollaert, or the letters of Mrs. Dorothy Proctor of Entre Quintas, they all tell a tale of British dash, vitality, effective fighting in the field, drinking (among the soldiers) of a truly staggering immensity, and feuds and quarrels on much the same scale. Knight said '3000 British could have forced the lines'. But there never were more than a few hundred British, and a few hundred French. Except for one or two famous Caçadores regiments, said the corporal, you could not depend on the Portuguese; their best troops, anyhow, were with the Migs (as Knight usually called them).

Colonel Hodges trained what a fellow officer called his three hundred ragamuffin infantry with great skill and firmness, turning them into soldiers who fought with dash and tenacity, but were, the Portuguese complained to Dom Pedro with truth, apt to be drunk in the field. Hodges, a martinet of the old school, had them ferociously flogged for very little; how men survived two hundred lashes has ceased to be clear to us; it is one of the mysteries of man's tough and inhumane history. Hodges was not a colonel of easy temper; he had many grievances, about pay, about command, about the negligent treatment of his wounded in hospital — for he really cared for his men — and his complaints were ignored. The Portuguese commanders were jealous of the British and French officers, and made some trouble between them and the emperor (as everyone still called him). Hodges considered that he was caught in an 'odious net of intrigue'. He complained of a hotbed of 'gossipomania', and of continual conclaves 'where at every word a reputation dies or is born'. He resented the supersession of Captain Sartorius by Napier as commander of the navy, and the sudden arrival of the complacent, comic-opera figure of Sir John Milley Doyle in Oporto and his immediate capture of Dom Pedro's capricious favour, by dint, said Hodges sarcastically, of his convivial habits of whistling and singing, which got him a high post on Dom Pedro's staff and for a short time the command of the British forces, whereupon the officers threw up their commissions and said they would not serve under him. They were put under arrest, but reinstated by the emperor, and Doyle quietly removed from the command. Characteristically, Sir John talked of a regiment of five hundred men he had waiting in England to come over; they never did so, and 'Doyle's regiment' became a name for such airy fantasies. Hodges, disgusted by the ignoring of his complaints and the factions and intrigues around him, finally sent Pedro his resignation, which was taken so calmly that he then, in a huff, sent back also the order of the Tower and Sword conferred on him; this was taken calmly too, but gave, as he had intended, offence. Shaw thought it a mistake. He sailed for England in umbrage; a valiant soldier and popular officer, he took with him British sympathy, the scars of a wound and of a hundred quarrels, the honour of several successful engagements with the enemy, and a large debt for arrears of pay which he never got. He wrote a well-informed and acrimonious book about the expedition directly he got home. 'A most excellent fellow in every sense of the word', wrote Captain Shaw early in their acquaintance. 'I suspect he troubles the Portuguese diplomatists much. I go all lengths with him as to reform, liberty, etc., though many do not like to.'

Shaw, who would go all lengths with anybody as to reform, liberty, etc., might be described as a sympathetic, sensitive and egotistical tough. First-class in the field, sharp of temper, a good disciplinarian, rebellious and impatient of humbug, corruption, and red tape in high places, he did not know fear, and his men would follow him anywhere. He grumbled acrimoniously, but made the best of circumstances. The six months at Terceira, for instance, bored and wearied him, but he took such alleviations as offered. 'This is a horrid place', he wrote home to his brother, 'although we have oranges, lemons and figs . . . Nothing like a lady is to be seen, so we amuse ourselves with the nuns, who keep open house when it is dark, but are quite correct during the day. We have astonished them by our band, and four of us danced a Scotch reel in the *parloir*, such doings were never heard of. They are very ugly, dirty and slipshod, and spit about abominably'. He also attended 'a feast and ball of the Holy Ghost', where he made friends with 'ruffian-looking peasants'. But, though these may have been his nocturnal entertainments, he was very busy by day licking his raw recruits into shape, and trying to put some discipline across them. He wrote to his mother that he believed in making friends with his men and winning their confidence; he rather preferred the wild young fellows, and hoped to get them under control by a system of reasoning and kindness. They got terribly drunk, and often disgraced the British before the somewhat chilly eyes of the emperor and the patient politeness of the Portuguese islanders, who would resignedly lead the intoxicated warriors home, aware from long experience of the habits of their ancient allies.

Shaw had no illusions about his men, but he esteemed their qualities, drilled them into an army, and championed them against injustice. They proved themselves when they landed in Portugal to be dare-devil fighting men. 'Captain Shaw, we'll follow you anywhere', one of his corporals said to him in the thick of a battle. He kept good discipline, without much flogging; he preferred to stop pay, or to devise punishments to make culprits feel fools, such as shaving their heads and blacking their noses. When they mutinied and fought on the voyage from England, he joined in and got both his eyes closed. 'A Reform meeting is a joke to it', he wrote home from Flushing. When he came on a sleeping sentry by night, he knocked him down. Unconventional methods, but they worked. When his men, after an action in which they had fought with desperate valour on no food, were falsely accused by the Portuguese officers of having been drunk in action, he was furiously hurt for them. 'Yes, my Lord', he retorted to the Duke of Terceira's inquiry, 'they were drunk, drunk as I myself was with the rations this day served out, I mean no drink, no food, but lots of ammunition . . . It is a shameful thing to say. Oh, it is a shame!' The Duke said he knew it was false, and would tell the emperor so, and was very complimentary, but Shaw was bitterly hurt, and refused an invitation to be the emperor's guest at dinner. He was indignant, too, about the hospital conditions and the neglect of British wounded, and at the reported remark of the emperor's that the British must not be amputated, as they expected pensions for it and it came expensive.

He wrote himself to London for medical requirements, which were stolen when they arrived. It was a heartbreaking business for a commander who cared for his men. As for himself, he was always in the hottest part of a skirmish, was wounded more than once, and once pretty badly.

'A queer figure he was', said Corporal Knight, 'with his shaggy red whiskers and beard, his blue jacket, red cloth cap with blue tassel, and long pole in his hand'. He had no illusions about the lofty motives inspiring most of the volunteers; of the ruffianly-looking crowd of Scots who arrived, six months after the earlier volunteers, and were handed over to him for training, he remarked that he 'suspected they had thought it prudent to leave their Glasgow looms and to try what effect the liberating air of Portugal might have on the memory of the police officers in their native towns'. 'I never beheld', wrote Colonel Lovell Badcock, himself something of a dandy, 'such a motley crew . . . mostly in rags and tatters . . . with something of the devil's daring in their eyes.' The day after they landed, five of them presented Shaw with a paper containing their conditions as to terms; they demanded five shillings more a month than the English soldiers got, 'which if you don't agree we shan't serve, and Donna Maria may gang to hell'. Shaw turned their terms down, telling them they might all 'gang where they wanted to send Donna Maria'. This caused a great hubbub. The five leaders said they were 'a Comitea. A wheen of us join together and ca' ourselves the Comitea, and we gar a' the others dae what we like'. 'I see', said Shaw, 'a Comitea is a Colonel. Call me either the one or the other, as I shall gar ye dae what I like'. After some more haggling, the men gave in, and the row ended with shouts of 'Hurrah for Cornel Shaw and Dony Maree!' Thus were formed Shaw's famous Scotch Fusiliers. They were at first so raw that their commander dared not let them practise loading and firing; many had not learnt the use of arms, and many were drunk. So they were set to do bayonet practice, upon which they charged with such furore as to put all the spectators to flight, including Marshal Solignac, the commander of the French battalion. 'Mon brave Colonel', he exclaimed to Shaw, 'voilà des loups!' Wolves they proved, both in fierceness of attack and in hunger, for rations were short and the troops seldom got enough to eat. 'We'll make that damned John Macdougal (the Scots' name for Dom Miguel) 'pay for this some fine day', they would growl. The Migs, outside the city and therefore well supplied, would sometimes hold up a fine white loaf or a nice piece of beef on their bayonets, which never failed to draw fire from the Scots. All the latter could do was to drink, and to steal and eat Shaw's greyhound and terrier, and fight the Irish for having in their possession the skin of his fat pointer. As to the cats, the French ate all these.

In spite of everything, Shaw's Fusiliers became one of the best units in the army; they had three pipers, and sported tartan in their bonnets, which Shaw pulled out when they disgraced themselves by drunkenness. Shaw's organizing capacity and energy were immense; he galvanized officers and men with his fiery Highland vitality. He had strong views on the Cause, and thought those with Miguelite sympathies despicable, 'supporting a man who had been, and was, inflicting so many unheard-of cruelties on his fellow creatures'. He had little patience either with Mr. Crispin, the British consul (recalled soon) who would not let English soldiers be buried in the British burial ground, or with Captain Glascock, R.N., of the *Orestes*, commander of the British naval squadron which, pledged to strict neutrality, was mounting guard over British interests in the river between Vila Nova and Oporto. Glascock did not feel or talk neutral; like many naval officers, he was a good Tory, and was obviously for Miguel. He asked officers from both sides to meet and dine on the *Orestes*; Shaw always refused to do this. 'I may be wrong in my views, but I pride myself in being able to say that, during the whole active war in Portugal, I never met an officer of Don Miguel's army except in the field. Many of our countrymen's politics in Donna Maria's service were not those of liberals, and many drank more wine than the Miguelites,' which gave the enemy they met at dinner an excellent chance to pick their brains. Besides, 'I thought it indelicate to dine with them' when on returning to the town one saw innocent women and children the victims of their shelling and their starvation blockade. These dinners, Shaw thought, did infinite harm to the cause. For he, whatever other British might feel, took the cause *au grand sérieux*. He disliked the Miguelites. They stood for despotism, tyranny and bigotry; they were worse than Tories (if anyone could be that). Besides, 'they are savages. They cut our dead in the most horrid manner', and killed the wounded too. In revenge, the French and Portuguese were apt to give no quarter; the British (in theory, whatever Shaw's wolves may have done in practice) forbade such lawless massacre. But, 'this is a war like no other war: if you don't kill them, they will kill you. All the old prejudices as to their being fellow creatures evaporates. You see to what perpetual exposure to shot brings a man'.

Shaw was highly prized as a commander and strategist by the emperor and his commander-in-chief; and, indeed, his conduct of the defence, his sorties, observations, reconnaissance parties and field actions, if over reckless at times, had a dash, ingenuity and brilliance that put him in a class above the ordinary valiant officer. During the last six months of the siege (February to August 1833) he was stationed with his Fusiliers at the exposed and dangerous battery of Lordello, west of the city, with only a low wall between his camp and that of the enemy. All that deserters had to do to join the Miguelites and their good food was to get over that wall; that scarcely a man did so speaks much for Shaw's influence. The newly-arrived corps who were sent to join his battalion at Lordello felt at once complimented and slightly alarmed; 'we well knew that Shaw had a peculiar way of his own of leading his friends on to glory'. Shaw declared himself glad to be at Lordello, a little out of the way of the factions and intrigues that buzzed at headquarters. 'I never enter Oporto', he wrote, 'as there are such intrigues with the English about who are to be commanding officers, etc.'

Sir John Doyle came out, bland and fantastic as ever, in October, 1832, with 'young men in officers' uniforms sufficient for two regiments'. Shaw called on him, 'and I could scarcely keep my gravity when he mentioned that he had left 400 men on board the steamers ready to sail the night he left Falmouth'. 'I had not forgotten the lieutenant-colonelcy and the 12,000 acres he gave me in Lisbon.' He refused flatly to serve under Doyle, who placed him under arrest. However, Doyle was soon got rid of; the emperor perceived that his smiling, whistling favourite did not go down with the British army. 'He is a queer mixture', Shaw wrote to his mother, 'of — and —' (the editor of Shaw's letters was apt to be cautious), 'but has done an infinity of harm among our soldiers. I have been obliged to shew him up in his true colours. . . .' Dom Miguel would appear to have been right, for once, when he threw Sir John into a dungeon in 1828. When, soon after the Doyle fracas, Shaw, wounded in both thighs in action and kept in bed for a time, wrote to his mother that his sufferings had done him good, and that 'I think I can now bring my mind to follow all the Christian rules', he added, 'except forgiveness to certain people'.

Among the intrigues, jealousies, corruption, confusion, quarrelling, starvation and disease that made up siege life, Shaw, though disgusted and angry, kept his belief in the cause. Though 'the bright romance of ideal life had vanished, and the only thing that now bound us together was common danger', though they trod 'a dirty road of intrigue and selfishness', and though 'every man must regret deeply that those who are employed in disseminating liberty through the universe are sometimes stained with vices and baseness . . . happily in spite of these impediments the march of liberty continues progressively onward, thus strongly indicating that this chiefest and supremest blessing gathers daily strength over Europe'. Hugging to himself this consoling and pompous thought, Captain Shaw would rally his Scots about him and sally out into the enemy's lines to plant the flag of freedom on a Miguelite battery and a piper to play on the ramparts, with 'Pipe, damn you, pipe!'

For he doted on freedom. As he wrote just before landing in Portugal, 'I am at present madly in favour of liberty. Two days ago we heard the Wellingtons are in power: we all spoke out. Many fellows feel as I do'. He was happy in his adventure at the outset, with the happiness of fulfilment; he felt he had a cause to live and die for, and he was, after long frustration, in his chosen profession once more. 'I am grateful, happy, contented . . . I came naked into the world, and I suppose I shall go naked out of it, as liberty-hunting, I should think, is not a money-making trade . . . I am sure you will be glad to hear how completely I am in my element, no matter what occurs'. And, after two months in Portugal, 'All the old romantic feelings with regard to liberty are now in full force with me'. Ambition, adventure, liberty, and sheer *joie de guerre* combined to keep him in a state of exaltation, from the moment when the fleet, fifty sail strong, sailed for the Portugal coast with bands playing, and he and his men leaped on shore, dashed up a hill in overpowering heat and took and sacked a convent, and were from then on plunged into constant, violent and dangerous action. 'I am happy; the road to honour, not to wealth, is open to me . . . My own situation as commanding officer of a set of unruly determined dogs . . . and the certainty of being daily exposed to shot (consequently to death) keeps the whole inward man in an exalted state, but still as ready to be merry and childlike as to be serious and religious: it is a curious mixture, but still a mixture in which I absolutely delight . . . I shall never die a better man.' Again, 'The Lord forgive me, but I positively like the sport. It is just the same excitement as trying to nick a roe-buck or wild blackcock. The Miguelite officers behave very well'.

But for the Miguelites and their cause he had an almost mystical hatred. He was divided, he said, between the ambition to 'make a name, to show what I really am', love for his family at home, and 'the most venomous and active hatred to oppression and tyranny', in which Dom Miguel and his gang seemed mixed up with the Tories in England and in Edinburgh, a symbol of reactionary darkness.

In the spring of 1833 Shaw heard privately from England that an expedition was being fitted out for Lisbon; he was asked to join it, with five hundred men. He was anxious to go. 'Oporto', he wrote to Hodges in May, 'is such a *sink* of vice and low intrigue that I would dare anything to get out of it . . . The conduct of some of the British here has not been good, and I think they have for a time hurt the English name in Portugal . . . We are supposed a set of adventurers.' In June there called at his rooms at Lordello the organizers of the new expedition from England — Palmella; the emperor's inscrutable, brilliant financier, Mendizabal; and 'a dark-eyed, determined-countenanced man, badly dressed from head to foot' — Admiral Charles Napier, coming out under the name of Carlos de Ponza to supersede Sartorius as commander of the emperor's British naval forces, and to lead the fleet to the Tagus. Shaw remembered that his friend General George Napier had said to him in 1831 that if one man could finish the war it would be his cousin Charles; but at that time he was taken up with his newly-invented frigate paddles, and could not be tempted. Now, having presumably grown used to the novelty of these gadgets, he was tempted and came out, taking Scottish care first to put his services on a secure financial basis (so far as such a basis could exist in Portuguese service; it was, as all foreign volunteers discovered soon, not saying much).

General Napier had been right; his erratic, brilliant, unconventional cousin did finish the war. The news of the victorious expedition to Lisbon of Napier's fleet and Terceira's army meant the raising of the Oporto siege and the march south of Miguel from the Douro to the Tagus. Shaw, to his bitter disappointment, did not go with the expedition; Dom Pedro could not spare him. He stayed in Oporto, and was given the command of the combined Scotch and English battalions, now much dwindled. The siege was raised in August. 'We have got more room', wrote Shaw, 'plenty to eat, and cheap, and the river, I trust, will be opened to-morrow.' So ended the blockade. But, 'I do not think this war is to be over so soon as people imagine; I am a little tired of it, though the soldiers do not think so'. All the same, he was anxious to follow the enemy south. 'I hate a milk and water life.' He was now the only British officer left who had embarked from London a year and a half ago. The British, he said, 'are no great favourites, nor any foreigners'. He added (perhaps to please his mother) that he would shave when he got to Lisbon. He embarked with his men on September 27th, landing two days later north of Lisbon, near Caldas, capturing and sacking Obidos and Peniche (with the French and some Caçadores), knocking down men who said they would march no further without pay, getting to Torres Vedras, where he found a large chest full of shako ornaments and badges left by the Peninsular British twenty years ago, which he distributed to his Fusiliers. They marched on to lie outside Santarem, held by Miguel. Shaw spent four hours in Lisbon *en route*; he felt shabbily dressed there. 'I am now entitled to cut my beard, but it is a comfort in sleeping in open fields.'

His battalion spent a dreary winter in the Santarem country. The Scotch troops were very badly treated, he wrote, and no accounts yet settled. They were entitled to their discharge, pay, and free passage home. There was also airy talk of settling them in a colony on the land, near Setubal. None of these promises materialized. The troops stationed in Lisbon mutinied; Shaw, temporarily in Lisbon, was falsely accused of inciting them, and turned out of the city by his enemy General Zagallo. He had no opportunity, he complained, of seeing anything in Lisbon, except a fine ball given by the Duke of Terceira. After his expulsion, and his protests to Saldanha, the emperor, to repair the injustice and perhaps hoping to keep him quiet, made him a colonel. But nothing could make either Shaw or his Scots quiet while injustice rankled in their breasts. The troops got out of hand, and struck and rioted. Shaw spent the Christmas of 1833, as he wrote in an embittered letter to that good and charitable woman, his mother, in fighting, knocking down and sending to jail those whom she had apparently miscalled 'those wonderfully well-behaved Scotchmen'. 'Such a set of ungrateful blackguards are nowhere to be found. And in the midst of this scene of iniquity, sin and all horrors, I get a letter from my good mother in praise of human nature! Long may you think this ... Just let anyone see this human nature as I have seen it for the last four years of my life, and he will have the same love and respect for it as I intend to prove I have before an hour passes — by giving one of the ringleaders 300 good lashes.' 'Mildness and justice', he bitterly adds, 'have no effect.' From what we know of Shaw, it can be hoped that this was only a threat, to warn the misbehavers and startle his mother; he was no flogger, and three hundred lashes seems more savage, even in that savage age, than suits with his character and usual methods of discipline. Nevertheless, he had grown to think his Scots 'great blackguards', though good soldiers. They had been, owing to his exertions, better treated, better clothed, better cared for in hospital, than the English troops, but they behaved much worse. 'I am sorry for them, but as soldiers, they deserve to be shot, or the officers must resign.' He has a firm word to his mother about the plausible Corporal Knight, now in England badgering the families of all the officers he had known in Oporto. 'I am very sorry your feelings for human nature have made you kind to Corporal Knight. He is a horrid blackguard ... I have given him out of my pocket more money than the pay coming to him. He is a beggar by trade, and a very persevering one.' Later, he read the book his brother had edited, containing Knight's account of the siege and anecdotes of the British officers, taken down pretty much as the corporal had related it. 'He has a good memory — but what a confusion of dates and places!'

The winter passed; drilling, trying to keep the troops from mutiny and the young officers from gambling, took much of Shaw's energies; the rest were expended in vain efforts to get his men paid off. In May, he 'considered the fighting at an end', and that they would soon be disbanded. 'But I have a dreadful labour before me.' The labour was to get justice for his troops, whom he would not desert. With all his native tenacity he attacked the ministry of war, the government, the emperor himself, till they were sick of his name and the sight of his truculent red beard. He spent most of June in Lisbon, where five hundred Scotch Fusiliers landed in Black Horse Square on the 7th, were quartered in a Belem convent, and said they would not go until paid. Shaw got promises for them from headquarters, and induced them to embark for Setubal, where he went himself at the end of the month. Before leaving Lisbon he waited on Dom Pedro at Queluz. Pedro, already in his last illness, said to him, 'Vous avez bien servi la reine; je vous en suis obligé'. Shaw never saw him again. He found that his reputation in Lisbon had been foully attacked by his old enemy, Sir John Milley Doyle, and by various officers he had sacked as useless, who held him up as a savage and a robber. Either for this reason or because of his rather eccentric appearance and clothes, no English resident, he said, called on him; but Admiral Parker, and all the people he respected, were very attentive. Captain James Alexander describes him riding about Lisbon on a great grey galloway, in braided surtout, white trousers, forage cap, and formidable red beard. He was not, apparently, much in with the Embassy, where Lord Howard de Walden had just succeeded Lord William Russell. He was invited to the 'splendid ball' to be given to the Duke of Terceira, but by that time he was in Setubal. There he remained for many months, trying to get the troops' claims paid, dissuading them from departing for England unpaid. There was, they said, no enemy left to fight in Portugal; 'my answer is, no rations and no wine in England'. Meanwhile Shaw was examining the land that he heard it had been proposed to allot to the men in settlement of their claims; it was good rich soil, and he did not think the government would part with it. He was right.

Setubal he found a very Miguelite town; ex-officers there laughed at the funeral of a drowned Scotch sergeant. But those who were not Miguelites were 'very civil'. For amusement, he went spearing fish. 'I never enjoyed anything so much; it is a screaming excitement.' He found time to weave dreams of his future, to visit the ruins of Troy, and to philosophize on life and his own character. 'How my eyes have been opened', he wrote to Hodges, 'in this service. I used to argue against original sin . . . I go to Lisbon to-morrow, to encounter it in its most mawkish shape, in being embraced, flattered with words, by men who dress well and wish me at the devil.' He is 'disgusted by the whole set here'. He found in the 35th Psalm, which he had to read aloud to the men at Sunday service, a true description of himself. 'I not only was astonished, but so were the soldiers . . . Read it, and you have a good picture of my state. I have real pleasure now in reading the Psalms.' Indeed, the author of the 35th Psalm must have been a little like Shaw, with his obsession with persecutors, false witnesses and busy mockers gnashing upon him, and with his eager hope for their destruction. He was tempted to settle in Portugal, whose climate he liked, if steam-boats should be established; but 'there is great risk as long as the Tories are at the head and Don Carlos allowed to show his nose. I must tell you that such is my immense hatred of that class, owing to the individual misery caused by their style of thinking and acting, that I almost feel anxious for employment in Spain; and I know if I were to go home, in the present excited state of the nation, that I should have worse to encounter than a jury trial'. He hopes the Tories may be upset. 'What misery they have caused in Portugal, and how they have disgraced the English name!' 'Of course', he wrote to Hodges, 'you never will permit the old Tory set to rule; and as for —— —— —— [The Duke of Wellington? Shaw's discreet dashes are tantalizing] he is a Don Miguel.'

In February he fought a duel with an unnamed foe who had grossly insulted him; as he was half Shaw's size, he was probably Portuguese. So many people grossly insulted Shaw that one cannot guess. Both duellists missed; Shaw was disappointed. He brooded deeply over life and its horrible injustices.

Sometimes he thought he would 'like to put Spain to rights' and have 'a go at Don Carlos'. 'I am a great enthusiast, and I seriously think that Providence is arranging to destroy in full the horrid remains of the feudal system.'

What neither Providence nor Portugal was arranging was to pay off the Fuzileiros Escoses; and 'the Utopian idea of founding a Glasgow on the ruins and convents of Santarem', or on the alluvial soil round St. Ubes, had faded like an airy vision. On the contrary, the Fusiliers were shipped out of the country as mutineers with no pay at all; it seemed to Dom Pedro's ministry the cheapest, simplest way of disposing of these troublesome foreigners. By the middle of March, they were all embarked. 'They were put on board like convicts, with the muzzles of Belem Castle pointed against them and guarded by Caçadores.' Many of them, said Shaw, were so enraged that if Don Carlos were to recruit, he would make a good thing of it among them. Shaw remained for a while in Lisbon, still fighting the government for money. He had at last shaved his beard and moustaches, 'and was once more Charles Shaw'. He wrote to his mother that he feared she would find him an altered, disagreeable man. He had no object in view, he would be listless, idle, get headaches, indigestion, and fancies. As to intervention in foreign squabbles, he had seen through that. 'I wish to know, if a nation chooses to quarrel among themselves, by what right other nations walk in to meddle. I would not stand such work.'

A week later he was writing to Hodges, in reply to a letter telling him of recruiting for the Queen of Spain in Portsmouth and for Don Carlos in Liverpool, 'I shall be home without delay. I can gather all my own regiment and 4 or 500 of the Irish. Of course I shall be happy to join in the affair . . . if I can get a regiment, and tolerable terms'.

He embarked for England in June 1835. Across the Pyrenees there awaited him another quarrelling nation, more nieces and uncles, more hateful tyranny, more horrid remains of the feudal system that he would arrange with Providence to destroy, more liberty to spread with bayonet and gun, more Iberians to annoy him. It was his destiny. He went off to Spain. His expedition there ended, like that in Portugal, in quarrelling and resignation; like the psalmist, he was ill-treated to the end. He published his account of both affairs in 1837, so near the events that his printed letters had to be full of blanks, and abound in 'the low, ungentlemanlike conduct of — and — ', 'I have never been so completely deceived in a man as in — ', though on what grounds the blanks were selected, is not clear, for names abound too.

Another British officer who wrote his story of the Portuguese affair was Colonel Anthony Bacon of the Lancers. But his book never got beyond the proof stage, and the second half of the proofs got lost. Bacon was a cavalry officer of the Peninsular campaign; like Shaw, he was thirty-six when he came out in November 1832 in command of a cavalry battalion, which he had undertaken at the request of Mendizabal, and rather for love of his profession than of Dom Pedro's cause, though, like most Englishmen who were not firm Tories, he disliked Miguel and his ways. His job —

and a tremendous job it was — was to form a regiment of cavalry lancers out of the recruits who arrived in Oporto from all nations — British, French, Germans, Belgians, Poles, Portuguese (or, as Captain Glascock's tar put it, raw Scotch, wild Irish, Lunnon light-uns, heavy Garmans, long Poles, French hop-kickers, Bulgum butchers, 'and many more o' similar sort I can't this minute remember'). The majority, and the best, were British. Bacon, a cavalry officer of the hard-riding, hard-hunting, hard-swearing school, who had hunted with Wellington's fox-hounds in the Peninsular War, and with the best packs in England in peacetime, was a vigorous martinet, and soon knocked his lancers into shape, assisted by a rather quiet, dejected and gentlemanlike adjutant. 'He used to knock his men about in capital style,' said Captain Glascock, R.N. 'He seemed to be an excellent drill and spared no one.' 'A well-known dashing character', Mrs. John Proctor of Oporto called him, while the emperor observed that he would send his men to the bottomless pit so loudly as to be heard a great way off. Shaw, who was obviously jealous of him, complained that he was allowed to pick out the best men from the other battalions (including Shaw's) and added, rather cattily, that though the Lancers were in very good order and looked smart, they were seldom in contact with the enemy, and that there was some ill feeling about them among the other troops. No one but Shaw thought the Lancers backward in action; if they seldom met the enemy it was, said Bacon, because the enemy fled at sight of them and could only be pursued. Certain it was that the Lancers charged, galloped, lanced, and did whatever else Lancers do, with tremendous *élan*, whenever they got the chance. The emperor made a special favourite of Bacon, which did him no good with Dom Pedro's other servants, such as Saldanha, who called him 'L'enfant gâté de l'Empéreur'. The emperor also made favourites of the colonel's wife, Lady Charlotte, and their two children; the small boy used to ride out with him on an Arab pony in a miniature uniform. Lady Charlotte Bacon with her children joined her husband in Oporto and stayed there with him through the siege; she was a daughter of the Earl of Oxford, an exquisitely lovely creature, the 'Ianthe' to whom, as a child of ten, Byron had written his dedicatory stanzas at the beginning of *Childe Harold*; the 'young Peri of the West' had grown up during the Regency, and had the fashionable aristocratic habit of strong

language, which, with her masculine riding breeches that made
her look, when she rode about with her husband, like a handsome
boy, rather shocked the middle-class respectability of the Oporto
matrons, and must have shocked the Portuguese ladies far more.
'A spirited, dashing woman', said good Mrs. Proctor, who called
on her on her arrival, 'though somewhat too masculine in her
manner for my taste. Mr. Whiteley' (the English chaplain and
schoolmaster) 'admires her amazingly — she is celebrated by Lord
Byron as Ianthe . . .' She used to ride round the lines with her
husband on a spirited bay; a junior officer wrote, 'Her figure was
perfectly sylph-like, and in my young imagination she was the
most beautiful creature I ever beheld'. When the enemy caught
sight of them and opened fire, the Bacons would leap their horses
over a high stone wall and escape, Lady Charlotte, trained in the
hunting-field, laughing at the unskilled attempts of the officers
who followed them. How this lovely and free-spoken aristocrat
from the shires and from Parisian life got on with the female
society of British mercantile Oporto there is, except for Mrs.
Proctor's dry comments, little record; it is probable that all male
creatures fell for her.

Bacon gives a lively picture of social life in the besieged city.
'Notwithstanding the desolation and destruction, amusement was
not lost sight of.' They had steeple-chasing, which he regarded as
an excellent riding school for cavalry officers, lark-shooting (on
the emperor's grounds), a ball from time to time, and a theatre.
And on every fine night, an hour after sunset, conversazioni on
either bank of the Douro, when officers and soldiers assembled to
talk across the river, usually at the Quinta de China. There would
be loud and fluent orations, inquiries after the well-being of
friends and relations on the south bank, and then a vociferation of
mutual abuse. The Miguelites would call 'Send away your
foreigners, and see how soon we'll be in Oporto,' there would be
an exchange of 'Malhados, freemasons', 'corcundas', and other
taunts, a volley of musket fire would wind up the party, and it
would be time to go home. More intimate communications with
the enemy were held at Captain Glascock's dinners on the
Orestes, where Bacon, unlike Shaw, was often a guest. He would
ask the Miguelite officers why they did not go about in a more
scientific manner to reduce the Serra battery, which was the key
to the city. He found them remarkably well informed about

Oporto affairs and movements, and concluded that their espionage was excellent.

Shaw accused Bacon of permitting, even encouraging his troops to 'forage', a thing he himself forbade; no doubt, he said, the colonel's zeal for his horses 'led him into this indiscretion'. It seems that Bacon foraged on occasion for himself too; when Corporal Knight called on his brother, Squire Bacon, in Berkshire, he pleased him with a tale of how, plundering at Vallonga after a battle, he had come on the colonel in a gentleman's house, busy on the same job. The colonel, said Knight, had already cleared most things; still, Knight got hold of a gold crucifix and a few other trifles. Squire Bacon, delighted with this news of his dear brother, gave the corporal five pounds and the address of the brother of Colonel Shaw. One remarks with interest that the occasion for the challenge sent by Bacon to Sir John Milley Doyle in Lisbon a year and more later was Doyle's 'vile calumniation' that he had appropriated to himself his troops' plunder after Vallonga, having it all brought to his quarters to be sold for the common benefit and keeping nearly all the money for himself. A story difficult to sift now, but Bacon was obviously a good plunderer, like his horses, who kept the vines trimmed by eating all the young shoots, devoured the thatch roofs off the houses, and the corn hoarded by the poor peasants, which, thought Bacon, was much more useful at headquarters. In fact, he 'winked at all thefts of provisions or forage'. His private table was pretty well supplied, at a time when to most people 'a slice of dog or cat was a great treat', for Captain Glascock used to bring him food from the *Orestes*.

When the siege was raised, Bacon took his Lancers south; they distinguished themselves in the Estremadura and Alemtejo fighting; Bacon got wounded, and was made a brigadier-general. Lady Charlotte and the children arrived in Lisbon from Oporto in the autumn and settled there, enjoying the gaieties of the new court (which were rather mild and depressed) and of the British Embassy under the William Russells, which were much better. Lisbon was gayer than it had been for five years; it had been a five years of fear, repression, police spying, imprisonment, armed terror, during which families and friends could not trust one another, nor any one a stranger. But the British officers and troops were not very cheerful; they were tired and bored, and beginning to feel that they were not going to get their pay. They quarrelled. They complained. They advanced on the ministry with demands, reproaches, and occasional mutiny. Colonel Shaw lost his temper for good. Colonel Bacon, the emperor's pet, fell out with Saldanha, decided that there was 'a deep-rooted conspiracy' against him (almost like Shaw and his psalmist), and resigned his command in April. Before this, he had a furious row with Sir John Doyle, who sent him a letter accusing him of appropriating the soldiers' plunder and pay. Bacon replied, 'You are a dirty, cowardly, back-biting, infamous scoundrel', made an appointment for a duel, and threatened a horse-whipping if the duel was refused. Here the emperor stepped in, stopped the duel, persuaded Bacon to refrain from the horse-whip, and dismissed Doyle from his post. It was all a great interest to Lisbon society, many of the emperor's ministers and friends were pleased to see Bacon publicly accused; Saldanha, always jealous of him, had him court-martialled for letting his Lancers march on the government demanding pay; he was pronounced guilty. The emperor's friendship for him, which never failed, only made matters worse.

At the end of the year (1834) Bacon sailed for England with his family and lived in Harley Street. His book on the Portuguese adventure was written, but never published. It seems to have been a peppery work, and would have been a lively addition to the literature on the civil war by British military men.

As to Colonel Bacon, the verdict on him by the observant Colonel Owen of Oporto brings him before us — 'as good a soldier as ever gallopped amongst skirmishers ... a dashingly brave, hard-working, swearing fellow; very troublesome to the authorities when he wanted anything for his regiment, much more so to the enemy when he could get at them'.

He did no more fighting. He spent the rest of his life taking an interest in cavalry reform and corresponding with the Portuguese government about the money they owed him. In 1839 he went to live at Cadiz, so as to be near Lisbon and go there often about his pay. He never got it.

11

Captain Nugent Glascock, of His Majesty's Navy, was not a volunteer for Dom Pedro; rather the contrary, some Pedroists thought. He was in command of the British squadron which was ordered to lie in the Douro between Oporto and Vila Nova to keep an eye on British interests during this dangerous Portuguese explosion, and receive on board any British citizens of Oporto who might be endangered. Its instructions were to observe the strictest neutrality, and not to interfere unless British interests demanded it; in brief, to keep the ring. Captain Glascock, a lively Irishman, commanded the *Orestes*. He was himself inclined to be something of a Tory, and had no particular sympathy with the constitutional cause, still less with his countrymen who were swarming officiously out from England to support it. He had his modern counterparts in the young naval officers a century later who cruised off Spain to take off embarrassed Britons, allowed to land in the ports held by General Franco but not in the strongholds of 'the Reds', of whom they spoke with breezy disapprobation. Captain Glascock did not quite take this line; he knew too many British officers in the Liberal army and navy, and saw too much of friendly Oporto British, Liberal almost to a man and woman; he really did try to be neutral, though getting little credit for it; Captain Shaw said he overdid the neutrality, and that the dinners on the *Orestes* where Pedroist officers dined and talked with Miguelites, each side pumping the other, were a grave mistake; but Captain Shaw was a fanatic. All the other officers enjoyed the *Orestes* dinners very much. Captain Glascock, disliked as a suspected Miguelist by most of the Portuguese Pedroist army, was popular with the English, and, as Shaw put it, 'any one in want of a dinner was sure to find it on the *Orestes*'. Shaw thought Glascock was 'led by his political feelings to take Miguel's side of the question', and, to judge from the lively sketch 'Jack at Oporto' that he published when he got home, Shaw was on the whole right; indeed, this cheerful dialogue between tars becomes at times almost a Miguelist pamphlet. Anyhow, he became extremely angry with the Pedroists who slandered his neutrality, accused him of firing on drowning Pedroist troops, and other crimes which, said he, would have disgraced a British sailor. He was also angry when a merchant steamboat with troops and gunpowder for Pedro came in through the bar under the shelter of a British red ensign; he wrote to Santa Martha, the Miguelite commander in chief, hotly disclaiming being party to this fraud, and declaring his determination to pursue a strict and honourable neutrality;

from that time on, the Liberals labelled him a rank Miguelite. 'The fact, Sir, is', he wrote to Captain Markland, 'any officer who observes a strict and honourable neutrality is suspected to be an enemy by the little-minded partisans of Dom Pedro.' He became so much disliked by these little-minded partisans that he was warned not to go about Oporto by night unarmed; so he always took his coxswain with him, and they each carried a stick; the only time his life was attempted, they knocked down the three assassins and walked on. He was however on excellent terms with the British, both military and civilian, and used so far to violate neutrality as to send in food to his friends, particularly to the John Proctors, who had allowed a signal station, used daily by the navy, to be set up in their garden, and with whom he and other naval officers continually dined. 'Almost daily', Mrs. Proctor wrote, 'I have a confab with Captain Glascock, commander of the British squadron in the Douro — he is author of the *Naval Sketch Book*, *Sailors and Saints*, etc. He is a native of the Emerald Isle, and possesses all the quickness and brilliancy for which it is famed, but he is unsteady and inconsistent, acts first and thinks afterwards. I propose plans of attack for taking such and such positions . . . he laughs at me and calls me Generalissima!' Mrs. Proctor liked Glascock, but, with other Oporto Liberals, was apt to fall foul of him for what he called his strict neutrality and they his tenderness for the Miguelites. It was unfair; as he complained, His Majesty's ships conveyed all hospital stores into Oporto, and the surgeons of the British naval squadron attended the wounded Pedroist troops, and there was never the slightest acknowledgment or thanks from Dom Pedro's government; nor had the slanders about firing on the Pedroist soldiers ever been apologized for in the official gazette; 'it is my own opinion', he wrote to Admiral Parker, the Commander of the British fleet in the Tagus, 'that many of the partisans of Dom Pedro use every endeavour to create an anti-British feeling in Oporto'. There was certainly 'a lack of courtesy and amity for neutral British subjects'.

The slander about the firing was a gross injustice. A raiding party of Pedroist soldiers had been sent across the Douro to Vila Nova to bring back some wine from the lodges of the Portuguese Wine Company; they were landed in boats near where the British warships lay, and took the opportunity to burn and loot a convent before returning, while the boatmen loaded up the wine. When

the troops got back to the river the boats had pushed off and refused to return; the soldiers started to swim, were fired on by the
Miguelites, and tried to scramble to refuge on the British ships.
Some succeeded, others were repulsed, the Miguelites fired on the
ships and on the swimming men, wounding some of the English
sailors. Those who succeeded in making the Oporto shore spread
the story that the English had fired on them as they ran to their
boats, and afterwards in the water, and had even struck with
hatchets at the drowning men trying to climb onto their ships. The
Portonians were furious, and began to execrate the English.
Captain Glascock, furious too, wrote a note to the British senior
naval officer of Sartorius's fleet urging him to send boats at once
to remove the wounded men from the two English merchant brigs.
He ended 'Send steady silent hands (Englishmen) and not damned
noisy jabbering Portuguese'. Captain George did so, removed the
wounded, and sent a report to Dom Pedro's Minister of Marine
protesting against the slanders against the English, and enclosing
with his letter by mistake Glascock's note about the damned
jabbering Portuguese. As Glascock complained, there was no
denial published in the gazette; the emperor explained that he had
been 'compelled to give credence to the statements of his own
officers', and unpleasant mutual feeling was left. Glascock wrote
also to Santa Martha protesting against his ships being fired on,
and for a time the *Orestes* dinners for both sides languished. But
Glascock's bitterness was against the Pedroists, with their ingratitude and slanders. When the *Orestes*, *Nautilus* and *Echo* were prepared for the reception of British refugees who might wish to
escape from Oporto in case of a Miguelite victory, he was abused
behind his back for creating a panic. The emperor coldly addressed
him in public, 'I understand you have been advising British merchants to embark, and trying to create panic in the town'. He
replied, 'Your Majesty must not believe all you hear in Oporto'.
Captain Glascock was of those who did not like Dom Pedro. Not
that he thought much of 'Don Mogul', as his sailors called him,
either. 'Somehow or other', said 'Jack at Oporto', 'we was always
in hot water, for interfering 'tween those two thundering Dons
was, for all the world, like interfering 'twixt man and wife; if Bob
don't give you a black eye, Bet's sure to leave the sign of her five
fingers over your face.' And, 'to be peppered by a Portuguee priest
is more nor nature itself could stand'. As to the Mig bombard-

ments, they were like 'a bit of Vauxhall', and when the shelling
was done, both sides would blackguard and abuse each other across
the river through speaking trumpets. But 'Mogul's officers used
often to meet Dom Pedro's gemmen aboard the ships of the
squadron ... they used to bundle below and grub and grease
their moustaches together at the same table', and relations from
opposite camps would meet one another with embraces.

Captain Glascock's finest hour was in August 1833, just before
the raising of the siege, when Miguelite French officers blew up the
Old Wine Company's lodge at Vila Nova. Negotiations between
the two sides as to the disposal of the wine had been going on for
some time; on August 16th two French officers of Miguel's army
mined it, to prevent it falling into their enemy's hands. There was
a terrific report, a dense column of black rose in the air, and a boiling stream of port ran down the streets of Vila Nova into the
Douro, turning it from brown to red. The wind blew the flames
in the direction of the English lodges; Ormerod's was already on
fire. Mr. Sandeman crossed over from Vila Nova to tell the
consul of the danger; Glascock, who was with the consul, returned
to his ship and summoned all officers and men, warning the men
that they were only to put out the fire, and on no account to fight.
They landed and got to work, with the employees of the wine firms,
in time to save Ormerod's lodge. It was a tremendous and terrible sight to port-lovers. 'Wine and brandy in boiling and flaming
torrents were running in rapid streams down the different lanes
leading to the lodges. It was impossible to approach the scalding
vapour floating in the air ... I never had a notion of the infernal
regions before.' In the middle of this shocking scene, arrived the
French general who had caused it, indignant at the sight of armed
British sailors violating neutrality thus. He ordered them away;
Captain Glascock told his men to fix bayonets, and he retreated;
the sailors, helped by the citizens, continued fire-fighting, and all
British property was saved. About 27,000 pipes of port were
destroyed, at something like £20 a pipe. A shocking disaster and
crime, about which there were four slight consolations; it had been
perpetrated by Miguelites, it was mostly Miguelite property, it
would put up the price of port in England, and the Douro tasted
for some time of wine.

Glascock was glad to leave his difficult and thankless post next
year; a hasty-tempered, impatient, hospitable gay sailor, he was

happy to be shut of this 'neutral nonsense', and of 'the rum ways of Jack Portugoose'.

His colleague of the *Nautilus*, Lord George Paulet, was a sailor of more liberal sympathies and greater discretion; he was a trusted friend of Saldanha's and acted as go-between for the general and the Miguelites when Saldanha was trying in vain, by secret conversations with a Miguelite general, to bring about a reconciliation. Paulet was honourably neutral, and was liked, it seems, by all parties.

The unfortunate Sartorius, on the other hand, Dom Pedro's English admiral, was always in hot water. To serve Dom Pedro was no easy task, as every one, British, Portuguese and French, discovered in turn (to serve his brother was even worse). George Sartorius, a half-pay captain, who had conceived an immense distaste for Miguel and his methods while he was commanding one of the ships of the British squadron in the Tagus in 1828 and helping to rescue some of the fleeing victims, was engaged to command the constitutionalist fleet of seven ships in 1831, had blockaded Lisbon, captured a few prizes, successfully engaged part of the enemy fleet, but failed to take it; when he arrived at Oporto he was received coldly by the emperor and his ministers, who thought he should have had more success. He lay off the Douro keeping open the line of supply; his crews were unpaid and ill fed, and mutinied; many officers resigned; one ship was run away with by her crew; Dom Pedro became colder each time his admiral mentioned pay for the fleet; by March 1833, when Sartorius threatened to resign unless his men were paid, the emperor sent Sir John Doyle to arrest this troublesome Englishman; when Sir John boarded the flagship remarking 'Admiral, you are my prisoner', Sartorius's repartee, much applauded by the fleet, was to send him below under arrest.

Sartorius was sick of the whole business. Dom Pedro's government disliked him, the officers of the British naval squadron looked at him slightly askance, his men lived on the edge of mutiny. When, that March, his command was given to a Captain Crosbie, he made little protest.

But Captain Crosbie's command was only temporary. Negotiations had been going on all that winter in London with the naval commander who was to win the war for the queen — the indomitable, dynamic, eccentric Charles Napier. He was a bigoted

Liberal, one of the Napiers of Merchistoun, a cousin of General William Napier, who had said of him once to Shaw that here was the man to win the war, if he could be lured away from his new paddle-steamers. 'Black Charley' was what is called an original: slovenly in dress, bold and clever in action, impetuous in speech, the navy in his blood, generous and loyal to his friends, firm and calculating in striking a bargain, so that, in spite of his adventurous ardour for the cause, he would not stir a foot in it until he had a firm contract made out for pay, prize money and insurance. Charles Shaw wrote of him long after these events, 'Napier was the most egotistical, selfish man I ever knew, but clever and brave. He never wrote or spoke well of any one with whom he served' (this was quite untrue: Napier's letters are full of commendations of his officers); 'I always held my own with him, but pretended not to see when he was fishing me'. (There were few men whom Shaw did not find selfish and egotistical, or with whom he failed to hold his own.) The discussions between Palmella, Mendizabal and Napier that winter in London ended in the offer of the command of the Pedroist fleet to Napier, who accepted it on condition that his friend Sartorius agreed, that good terms should be arranged, and that there should be an immediate expedition on Lisbon. Money was advanced by London capitalists. To evade the Foreign Enlistment Act, Napier took the name of Carlos de Ponza; the four officers with him (who included his twenty-one-year-old son) also took *noms de guerre*; they collected two battalions of soldiers to strengthen the Oporto garrison, and embarked in May.

Croker's version of the enterprise was, 'A strange, wild Navy captain, half mad, of the name of Charles Napier, became a radical in hopes of being returned for Portsmouth. Failing there, he turned his energies towards Portugal, has engaged with Pedro to take Sartorius's place, and has collected and sailed with a large steamer, a couple of transports, and ten thousand men. He calls himself, I am told, Don Alphonso de Leon, or some such thing, and hopes to pass for a native officer. The Duke' (Wellington) 'asked Lord Grey last night if he knew anything of this expedition. Lord Grey said, "no more than he had seen in the newspapers"; the Duke gave notice of an address to the king to maintain a bona-fide neutrality'. Croker's Tory feelings were as much scandalized as Wellington's by such goings-on.

Napier lay for a while in Falmouth road, writing home, 'We

can manage the men very well at sea, but in harbour they are the devil'. With him on the *City of Waterford* were Palmella and Mendizabal, and the voyage was enlivened by Lady Charlotte Bacon, returning to Oporto after a visit to England; 'she made herself very agreeable, and on the whole we got on very well'. They arrived off Foz on June 2nd; Napier, before landing, went to see Sartorius on his flagship, finding him disgusted with everything. Napier gathered that the prospect before him was 'by no means brilliant', in fact, pretty sticky. At Foz they were met by Saldanha, and rode mules into the town. The emperor received them with frigid brusqueness. He had been kept in the dark about the Lisbon expedition, and distrusted its intentions. He 'stood with his hands behind him, looking very angry and speaking as roughly as he looked'. He referred the visitors to Marshal Solignac, his French commander-in-chief, who was discouraging; Napier thought he didn't want an expedition which would deprive him of *la gloire*. Napier had bad neuralgia and his face tied up, and was cross and offended by his reception. Shaw said 'he was so displeased with the entourage of Dom Pedro that it was with the greatest difficulty that the late Mr. Bell and I prevented him from returning to England the day of his arrival in Oporto'. However, Pedro soon became more gracious, and Napier persuaded him that he must either throw up the struggle or send a force south. In spite of intriguing and hampering Portuguese advisers and of Solignac's continued disapproval, the expedition was arranged, and on June 11th Napier, with the titles of vice-admiral and major-general, took over the squadron. On the 20th they sailed, with about 2500 troops from Oporto, and the fleet of ill-equipped little ships. The two dukes were on the flagship; Terceira to lead the land forces, Palmella to set up a provisional government in any territories these might conquer.

'With this force and in this state', said Napier, 'we had to conduct an expedition to rescue Portugal from the tyranny of Dom Miguel and place Donna Maria on the throne against 100,000 men and against the will of the nation, as has been repeatedly asserted and believed by the Tory party in this country.'

The fleet made for the Algarve, and took Faro with ease; the dukes landed, the one to set up a government, the other to march on Tavira. The Algarves turned unanimous for the queen. In Faro Napier, a devoted family man, did not neglect his wife and children; he got 'a monkey for Fanny, and I shall find something for you and Georgie'. Having done this, he met the enemy fleet off Cape St. Vincent, coming from the ,Tagus to crush the squadron half its size. Napier audaciously engaged, promising his crews that they should return to Portsmouth full of prize money. 'I'll give you half an hour to take 'em', he shouted. There followed a brief but bloody action; the Miguelite ships, some after short fighting, some after none, hauled down their colours. Napier, who had himself led a boarding-party, lost five officers and twenty men, with ninety-one wounded, among them his son. The enemy flagship surrendered without a casualty.

After the action, Napier offered reinstatement to all officers who would enter the queen's service; most of them did so; others loyally refused, and were taken prisoner; the seamen transferred their allegiance with as little apparent trouble as had the towns of Algarve. It had been, as Napier said, a remarkable action. 'We had 176 guns against 372, and they were thrashed. It is not for me to comment on this action; I shall leave that to the world, simply observing that at no time was a naval action fought with such disparity of force, and in no naval action was there ever so severe a loss in so short a time.'

Next day the victorious squadron landed at Lagos, and was received with generous Portuguese acclamation for its all-British victory over an all-Portuguese fleet. A deputation from the municipality came to meet the admiral, bearing a large and hand-some wreath of evergreens, which they tried to place on the victor's manly head. Napier had a British distaste for being garlanded; he shook his head, when the wreath approached it, like a bull being roped. The wreath had to be laid on a table, and every officer was given a sprig of it, which disappointed the town councillors. Meanwhile, a corvette had been sent north to carry the good news to Oporto; Colonel Badcock received the signal in the Proctors' garden, and rode off with the news to the emperor. Pedro was delighted, and threw a magnificent party at the Carranças; there was a day and night of bell-ringing, fireworks and rejoicings, watched from across the river with enormous depression. The corvette was returned to Napier laden with thanks, titles and orders; the admiral became the Visconde Cabo de São Vicente. 'All this was very gratifying; but I should have preferred the latter part to have been left alone' — possibly because the title, in its

English form, had already been appropriated by another admiral who had fought off the same cape thirty-six years before.

Napier's cousin the general had predicted truly: Black Charley had won the war for the queen; the spectacular action of July 5th was the turning point. The news of it upset the Miguelites in Lisbon so badly that they quickly marched out, and Terceira marched in. When the queen's flag was hoisted on the Castle, Admiral Parker's squadron, listened for anxiously in Lisbon, fired a salute. The British had come out for the constitution, and Lisbon too went constitutional in an hour. On the 25th Napier and Palmella rowed up the Tagus; they first visited Admiral Parker, on the *Asia*, who, with all the British squadron, their patriotism overcoming their political prejudices, gave them a thundering reception; it had been a great British victory, and the guardian angels sang their customary strain in loud pride. From the flagship Napier and the duke landed at the Arsenal, where they met a tremendous reception; 'the whole population was drunk with joy'. Napier was kissed by everyone, and taken in a gorgeous equipage to the house of Baron Quintella, the richest man in Portugal, in Quintella Square, into which all Lisbon seemed crammed. There followed triumphal days of eating, drinking and rejoicing.

The news was received in England with delight by the Whigs and mortification by the Tories. The latter had been doing their best for Miguel; Captain Elliott, R.N., his naval adviser and admiral elect, who had already embarked on a steamer with five hundred seamen, 'a host of officers', and a band, to join the fleet before it set out from the Tagus, was checked by the news of the defeat, and only got to Gravesend. An encounter between the two British naval commanders and crews would have been dramatic, but it never came off.

On July 28th, Dom Pedro arrived in Lisbon, now wholly in Liberal hands, with the blue and white standard on the Castle. All Lisbon hastened to meet him, tumultuously welcoming. Rockets, fireworks and salutes, Napier remarked, used more powder than would have fought an action. There was an affectionate and enthusiastic meeting between Pedro and the victorious admiral, who was the first to greet him on board his ship; he was 'met on the gangway by the emperor, who fairly pulled me out of the boat and embraced me. He gave me the credit of having placed the

319

queen upon the throne'. Napier went with the emperor to Mass; the latter during the service 'made several remarks on the ceremonies, and asked whether I did not think a man might be a good Catholic and a good Christian without so much mummery'. The admiral, we may presume, replied that he did. Later, after the arrival of the queen, there was a dinner at the Necessidades palace, at which Napier was the most honoured guest; it was plain and cheap, and the wine no good, for Pedro was, unfortunately for his entourage, an ascetic about food, as about clothes.

The first excitement over, Napier, always domestic, took a house in Lisbon and wrote to Mrs. Napier to come out with the children. 'I have got an excellent house', he wrote, 'and have also a box at the opera. I am getting everything ready for you.' They arrived on October 2nd, on the *Superb*. Meanwhile, in England Napier was struck off the navy list 'by the infuriated howlings of an enraged and disappointed party, who by such a step could glut their revenge, but could not save Dom Miguel'. Lord Londonderry, Colonel Hodges wrote, who had 'taken Dom Miguel under his immediate patronage', raised the question of Napier's conduct in the House; and 'as for old Eldon, he (peevish old soul!) thought hanging not good enough for you'. Napier was not much concerned, though he objected to the cancelling of his Greenwich pension. He wrote to the Admiralty to protest, and was addressed in reply as Charles Napier Esq., 'a piece of gratuitous impertinence', to the admiral and commander-in-chief of the Portuguese navy, even if they liked to ignore the Visconde Cabo de São Vicente. He wrote sharply back, giving his rank.

But what bothered him considerably more was his work of reforming the Portuguese navy and the incompetent and corrupt Arsenal. He found himself 'opposed by every species of intrigue', and it seemed that everybody combined to evade his orders. When he was on the spot, 'all was bustle and activity; but no sooner did he turn his back than idleness and sleep descended once more upon the establishment', though, before settling down to siesta or cards, the staff usually posted sentinels to warn them of the approach of this bustling Briton with his quite unnecessary orders and fuss. Like the Rajah of Bhong, the Portuguese thought all this bustle was wrong, and there was much mutual annoyance.

Meanwhile, Napier was on the best of terms with the emperor, and spoke frankly to him about his mistakes. The queen's government had now an accredited British minister, Lord William Russell, a diplomat of tact and known as a friend of liberty. The Lisbon British, subjected to tyranny and odium for five years, enjoyed society, gaiety and popularity again; their government was regarded by the constitutionalists as their stay and support, though British neutrality soon enough scotched this fond hope, and rifts and disillusionment chilled the scene. Meanwhile, the Miguelist army under General Bourmont lay outside Lisbon, and the city was in peril. On September 7th Bourmont attacked and was repulsed. Napier decided that it was time the affair ended; he wrote a bluff letter to the French general to say so, as from one foreigner to another.

'Marshal. You are a foreigner and command D. Miguel's army; I am a foreigner and command D. Maria's navy. You are I believe a decided Royalist: I am a decided Liberal. Is it impossible Marshal to put an end to this unfortunate war in an honourable manner? . . . You will perhaps answer that the greater part of the nobility, the priests, and the peasants, support you. I grant it: more than that, every robber and malefactor in the country is on D. Miguel's side.' His supporters were practising unheard-of cruelties, murdering women and children. The nobles fought for their privileges, the peasants were excited by the priests. 'Are they the intelligent people of Portugal? No!!! They are to be found in the large towns and in the middling classes, who are all for the queen. Ought such a state of things to exist? I put it to your Excellency as an experienced soldier, as an honourable man, and above all as a Frenchman, ought this unnatural war to be prolonged? This letter is dictated by humanity alone.'

Marshal Bourmont replied that he and the Admiral were not in agreement about the desires of the Portuguese. 'Je crois que l'immense majorité des habitans répoussent les institutions novatrices que vous voulez introduire dans le Royaume.' Simple men were often more estimable than the better educated and better off. As to atrocities, the Admiral had been misinformed; his own side had perpetrated many more. What about the confiscations of Miguelist property at Lisbon? And he was surprised at the uncivil expressions about robbers and malefactors. Napier, replying, apologized for these. He added that if the Marshal could see the joy that now reigned in Lisbon, the high honour of a French general would induce him at once to sheathe his sword. Bourmont, tired of the correspondence, answered that peace without victory would never be accepted by D. Miguel.

Soon after this Bourmont and most of the other French officers lost their command and retired to Spain; Bourmont was superseded by the Scottish General Ranald Macdonell of Glengarry, late of the Spanish service; but neither he nor his successor could do anything against Saldanha's army.

Meanwhile Napier, in his character of Portuguese admiral, got rather above himself. He was on the watch for British Miguelists coming out from England on steamers. Captain Elliot, on the *Lord of the Isles*, evaded capture when his packet was taken, and escaped to enemy territory. But his agent, Mr. Williamson, alias Luckraft, a supercargo on the same vessel, was arrested in Belem as a suspicious character corresponding with the enemy, and taken to Napier, who ordered his arrest and sent him to the prison of St. George. Mr. Williamson wrote an embittered protest to the British consul, who passed it to the ambassador. He presumed that 'a Portuguese admiral' had no authority to violate the privileges of a British subject by arresting him without an order from the British Judge Conservator; he protested against these high-handed proceedings by the Viscount Cabo de S. Vicente. Lord William Russell, shocked and indignant at this unconstitutional naval high-handedness on the part of his eccentric countryman, protested to the Foreign Minister, who justified the arrest but released the prisoner and packed him off to England. Admiral Cape St. Vincent, said the ambassador, had no right to commit British subjects to prison. 'Be that as it may,' the admiral airily waives this point, 'he was released a few days after and sent out of the country, not a little satisfied at his escape.' Napier maintained that the ambassador was wrong, 'for it could never have been contemplated by the Methuen Treaty that in the event of Lisbon being besieged it should be necessary to consult the Judge Conservator before a man who had confessed to having been in the enemy's camp could be arrested'. However hazy as to the terms of the Anglo-Portuguese wine and cloth treaty, the admiral was not at all hazy about what do with spies. They should be hanged. To his ambassador, he was something of a diplomatic responsibility.

Napier through that winter grew bored and restless. His seamen, so admirable in action, were less admirable in port; they got cholera, they got drunk, they got mutinous for lack of pay. Napier, himself getting mutinous against the incompetent government and the impossible Arsenal, had a fancy to sail north, do a little land campaigning, and take some towns on his own account. In March he sailed from the Tagus up to the Minho, refusing to notice the emperor's message of recall, landed at Vigo, marched to the Minho (the Spanish-Portuguese frontier), took the fortress town of Caminha by surprise, and sent a message to Dom Pedro 'I have taken the castle and town of Caminha and am marching on Vianna'. He did so, himself riding 'a wicked pony' belonging to the governor, his staff 'on mules and donkeys or anything they could get, with 500 Portuguese, and English marines and sailors as well pleased as the Duke of Wellington at the head of his cavalry'. He took, by sheer bluff, town after town; Fifo fell, then Viana, the Miguelists marching out of one gate as Napier's motley army marched in at another. In the chief square of that pleasant sea town, he halted his force, had the constitutional hymn played, and proclaimed the constitution, then issued a promise to the citizens that no one should be persecuted, and marched on, his force swollen by recruits, to Ponte de Lima and Valença. This, the strongest fort of the north, he had to besiege for some days, marching his troops round and round across a space outside the town to make them look more, and threatening capture by battery. He was visited outside the town by Lord William Russell and Colonel Hare, who had put into Vigo *en route* for England; they inquired how on earth he proposed to take Valença with his little force; he showed them the message he was about to send in to the governor — 'Why, with this piece of paper, to be sure.' The message told the governor that a hundred guns were on their way, and that unless he surrendered the town would be battered down and the defenders killed. He did surrender. The garrison marched out, and Napier marched in.

He was much pleased with himself as a land general. 'I have much enjoyed my campaign', he wrote to his wife in Lisbon, 'and we have done wonders with a handful of sailors and marines.' He described his troops as a motley crowd — 'broken-down weavers, tailors, drapers, man-milliners, poachers, disappointed lovers, resurrection men, a Burker or two'; some had been kidnapped when drunk. Nevertheless, he said, they were generally well behaved. On April 6th he went to Oporto; his reception was tremendous. He went to the theatre; a warrior came on to the stage and recounted his glorious deeds, while two small children entered his box and 'to my utter astonishment and dismay dropped a naval crown on my head, which of course I took off. The whole house resounded with acclamations, the ladies all standing and waving their handkerchiefs'.

After some festive days in Oporto, he returned to Lisbon, where the emperor made him a count and gave Mrs. Napier the Order of Isabella. In May he went campaigning again, taking Figueras and (with Shaw's Scots and some Portuguese Light Infantry) Ourem. He wrote to Mrs. Napier that she had missed a lot by not coming with him. 'This country is more beautiful than anything you can think of. I wish you had seen it! I have good quarters, and you could have ridden with me all the way.'

At the end of May Miguel surrendered at Evora Monte, and the war was over. Napier returned to Lisbon, to find none of his suggestions for improving the navy followed by the Minister of Marine, a dreamy, lazy man, who scarcely even answered letters, and was truly sorry to see this tiresome admiral blow in again. He was relieved of him for a time that summer, when Napier went to England to see about standing for Portsmouth; he had a fine reception there, and was delighted to find that Don Carlos of Spain was lodging opposite his hotel and kept his blinds down against this defeater of absolutism until he could escape to London next day. Napier returned to Lisbon, was one of the three chief mourners, with Saldanha and Terceira, at Dom Pedro's funeral in September, had his navy reform schemes rejected by the ministry, and resigned his post. 'I shall buy a place', he said, 'and rest quiet the remainder of my life.' Buy a place he did; rest quiet he did not. He was back in Lisbon in 1837, during the War of the Marshals (his friends Terceira and Saldanha) and the coming to power of the Septembrists; he was not popular either with these or with the Arsenal, and thought it wiser not to go out at night. He pressed his claims for pay; the government promised he should be paid later, as just then there was nothing in the Treasury and no one had been paid for ages. The highspot of this visit was his attendance by invitation, with forty other visitors, at the palace while the young queen had her first child. Immediately after the birth, the forty guests were all ushered into the royal bedroom, 'where, lo and behold, seated in a chair was the Queen of Portugal, looking as if nothing had happened!'

So ended Napier's Portuguese adventure. Leaving it, he left behind him a name to dazzle his friends and intimidate his foes, and the memory of a sea fight the like of which for audacity had seldom been seen off those coasts.

In 1810 General Napier had written of his cousin from Torres Vedras, 'Black Charles is a queer fellow as ever crossed me, and as honest a one . . . He is the delight of my life, and should live with me, and be trusted with any enterprise, if I were a great man. He being just fit for a sailor, that is, bold decided and active; he will make a figure yet.' The General was right.

Charles Napier was the most successful and spectacular figure among Dom Pedro's British officers. But they were, taking them all round, an engaging and lively set, from the colonels who wrote their accounts of the affair down to Corporal Knight, of Shaw's battalion, who did not write his, because writing was not his strong suit, but related his experiences to a brother of Colonel Shaw's after he returned to England wounded and was cadging everyone for a living (cadging was, as Shaw remarked, his profession, and he indefatigably pursued it). 'We met Corporal Knight', says the preface to the book compiled from the corporal's narrative, 'and were so pleased with his graphic and animated descriptions that we have been led to write them down, to get some money for him.' The editor had been advised to leave out the descriptions of eating, drinking, getting drunk, etc., and to infuse a little sentiment and fine feeling, and polish up the whole. Fortunately he had not done so, but only linked the episodes into a narrative, and avoided 'as much as was consistent with the corporal's style and manner, all disagreeable vulgarisms'. The result was a racy book, however rambling, disconnected and confused. Knight, an old soldier, with the Waterloo medal (usually in pawn) enlisted in the autumn of 1831 as a 'settler for Brazil'. His account of martial life in Oporto is largely concerned with the plundering of food and drink and the 'famous feasts' this enabled him and his friends to have. He met Colonel Bacon, also plundering, in a gentlemen's house after the Vallonga expedition, and divided the swag with him. He was wounded in the battle of September 29th, and laid up in hospital till January; the hospital was a horrid place, from which only those with remarkable constitutions got out. Knight got out, but only to hobble about on crutches and starve, for by this time the blockade was severe, and Oporto 'was but a poor place to live in'. There was little left to steal; the cats and dogs all got killed; the cats were liked by the French, but Knight couldn't fancy them. He found that snails made 'pretty good prog'. It was, in fact, a wretched life; Knight stayed in it, however, until the following October, and gives a lively account of the quarrelling British officers, of Colonel Shaw with his shaggy red beard, blue jacket and red cloth cap, of the arrival and behaviour of Sir John Doyle, 'always currying favour and humbugging the men', of the Migs, who hung their prisoners, and of the French and Portuguese who gave no quarter to the Migs. He landed at last at Bristol without a thing in the world but his clothes, and the Order of the Tower and Sword given him for brave conduct in battle. 'I have always worn it since; with the first seven shillings I can scrape together, I shall take my Waterloo medal out of pledge and wear it above'. He calculated that Dom Pedro owed him £43, but saw no prospect of getting it, and lived chancily but on the whole rewardingly by calling on the families of the officers he had known in Portugal and telling them interesting tales of their brave relatives abroad.

Such was Corporal Knight's excursion into what his editor, quoting Canning, called 'the commencement of that war of opinion now spreading over the earth'.

Outside the war of opinion, whatever they felt about it personally, were Colonels Hare and Badcock, British military commissioners and observers, sent out in June 1832, with Lord William Russell, to find out and report what Dom Miguel was up to; Colonel Badcock was also commissioned to investigate the movements and intentions of the Spanish on the frontier. He put up at Reeves's hotel in Lisbon, and set out to explore the country round, which he found to be hostile and suspicious and shouting 'Viva Dom Miguel!' 'What can Dom Pedro, if he comes, do with 8000 men against 120,000?' they were asking. Badcock stayed with a Mr. Pring, an English merchant; each night the house was serenaded by a mob singing 'Viva Dom Miguel' and patriotic songs, and threatening to break in, for the English were under a cloud, being indicated by the Church as liberal, constitutional, heretic and Freemason, and enemy number two. Badcock felt insecure. His object was to ascertain if a Spanish force had so far entered Portugal, so he rode to Badajos, where he was ill received and sent back by the governor to Elvas. Feeling more insecure still, he took the opportunity of the siesta hour one day, when everyone was asleep indoors, to ride back to Aldea Gallega as quickly as he could, and reached the British consul's in Lisbon in time for dinner. If the country seemed Miguelite, the city seemed full of clerical processions. Dom Miguel was sailing about the Tagus in a red and gold schooner; whenever he passed them the Portuguese and the American squadrons saluted him; the British squadron, however, did not. Fortifications were being thrown up, to defend the Tagus. On Corpus Christi, Miguel walked in the procession, 'with his sisters and the priests'. When, driving to Cintra in a mule carriage, Badcock met Miguel riding with three servants; he bowed; he heard afterwards that the usurper had been angry at his not alighting to pay his respects. He found Lisbon dull, with no amusements or visiting, everyone subdued and frightened, the British unpopular, a great noise all the time from continual salutes, which wasted much gunpowder. He was not sorry to go into Spain early in July; he was there until December, forming official conclusions about Spanish intentions as to Portugal, unofficial ones about the relative merits of Portuguese and Spanish ladies: the Spanish were handsomer, but the Portuguese more pleasing, with most brilliant eyes, very attached, faithful and domestic. 'The danger of bringing the two sexes so near together in so warm a climate' was on the minds of Spanish duennas. Portugal was perhaps less warm, the duennas possibly less conscientious.

Badcock had a rather nervous journey through Miguelite country to Lisbon; arriving there safely, he delivered his report on the military and political condition of Spain to Lord William Russell (his account of the female population was not committed to writing, but Lord William may have enjoyed this also) and was ordered to Oporto, where he was to relieve Colonel Hare as military observer. Calling before he left on the Prings, he found that they had been obliged to fly (flight was frequently advisable for the Lisbon British under Dom Miguel) and that the fright and fatigue had thrown Mrs. Pring into a fever, of which she had died.

Badcock arrived at Oporto in January, and joined the besieged community of British, who found him 'a sensible and unassuming man with whom we are mightily pleased'. He made friends with

Dom Pedro and Saldanha, found the former very affable, and the British consul, Colonel Sorell, 'a gentleman of most amiable manners, who took a very just view of the situation'. He was concerned about the conditions of the siege — starvation, cholera, the unpaid British troops mutinying, the town knocked about by shelling, men women and children killed and wounded in the streets and in their houses, all his doors and windows broken by shells; he found it better to leave them open. 'The effect of the shells was something pantomimic — tables, chairs, and other articles of furniture were snapped to pieces in a moment; as for sleeping, it was next to impossible, the continual growling of the guns, with flashes of light from the explosions, the falling of tiles and ruins, defied repose. Indeed we neutrals . . . were all getting pretty well tired . . . We began to think it time that something should be done towards bringing matters to a conclusion.' Badcock felt fairly neutral about the affair of Portugal, though he liked Dom Pedro and sympathized with the constitutionalists, and, above all, with the sufferings of Oporto. The town, he says, being largely of solid granite, stood its knocking about pretty well; but flesh and blood was less tough, and so were the gardens and trees, about which Badcock was an enthusiast; like Mrs. John Proctor, he was full of the Taylors' enormous magnolia tree and its wounds. There were tragedies all round. '81 grenades fell in my neighbourhood', killing many children and girls; 'a young lady, one of the belles of Porto, whilst sitting at her window lost her arm and part of her face by a cannon shot'. 'An unfortunate lady was killed in the midst of her family party; the rest, falling through with the floor, escaped.' Money was sent from England for relief; a soup shop was started for the poor by British residents. When Oporto was all but starved out, and there was talk of sending Badcock to Braga with terms, more food was landed at Foz, and the town could carry on again. Meanwhile, the British merchants and their wives went regularly on Sundays up the hill to church, and Badcock bought a parrot, which imitated the screams around it. The Proctors were very hospitable to the officers stationed at the signal post in their garden. Badcock was there when the news of Napier's victory over the enemy fleet was signalled; it was he who galloped off to the emperor with the message, and was embraced for joy. Three weeks later came the news of the taking of Lisbon by Terceira, and Pedro left for his capital. In August the siege was raised. Badcock noted that the English could now hear their clergyman's voice in church instead of its being drowned by cannon, and that parties began again, the British Association giving on September 4th in the scarred Factory House their first dinner since the siege began. The Portuguese parties, however, were dull and reserved, with, as usual, the gentlemen sitting on one side of the room, the ladies on the other; perhaps even in Oporto the climate was thought too warm for closer proximity to be safe. In December Badcock went to Lisbon, put up at Reeves's again, paid his respects to Lord William Russell, now ambassador to the queen's court, and to the young queen and her stepmother the empress. Maria appeared amiable, and 'I have no doubt will turn into a fine young woman. She handed me some little pictures with charades on them to look at'.

Till the spring, Badcock stayed in Lisbon, seeing the sights and going to dinners and balls in an English society which, though much diminished, could now breathe freely again. Not that they were popular; in fact, both parties abused them, the one because they were on the Liberal side, the other because they were jealous and because the British troops were tiresome about always wanting pay. On the whole, Badcock did not think that the queen's cause grew more popular; Pedro's ministry did unwise things, there was much privation still, the fidalgos were not conciliated nor the poor fed, and the clergy carried on their bitter campaign, telling people their ancient customs would be taken from them and the Church despoiled, which was too true. The prisons were full of Miguelistas; the Miguelista army lay outside Lisbon still. Badcock rode about with the emperor, advising about the defence of the lines. Most of the country round Lisbon, he decided, was still for Miguel; the nobility, the Church, half the peasantry. There were great sales in the Roçio of the property of ruined fidalgos; one could pick up furniture, pictures, jewellery, at low prices. Had one been setting up house in Lisbon, it would have been excellent. But Badcock was ordered home in April; taking leave of his friends, and of Dom Pedro, who was ill, he bought a few goldfish and some other objects and embarked for Britain on the *Nautilus*. He departed full of good wishes — 'that the Portuguese may still be enabled, under the new government, to repose beneath the shade of their olive and orange trees, in their gardens enlivened by flowering mimosas, pomegranates and oleanders, listening to the charming song of the May nightingales, or observing the handsome storks wandering on the green below and the pretty hoopoe perched on the vine-clustered cottages, whilst the children play in peace, is the sincere desire of the Author'. Which, from this seasoned hussar colonel, with his face scarred from French sabres, is a very pretty and amiable wish. He wrote, when he got home, one of the best accounts of the civil war; unlike the British officers in Dom Pedro's service, he had no personal grievances to embitter his style.

An agreeable contrast to the narratives of these military men is provided by the chatty feminine letters written through the Oporto siege by Dorothy Proctor to her brother in England. Dorothy was the wife of John Proctor, a partner in the wine shipping firm of Knowles, Proctor & Bold; a brisk, lively, vigorous matron, enthusiastically Pedroist, like all the Oporto British, full of charitable energies for the wounded and of interested gossip about her neighbours, the British volunteer fighters, and the progress of the war. She gives a vivid picture of British Oporto, eagerly watching the day to day sway of battle, alternately cheering and illuminating for victory, and making ready to flee to the British ships for refuge. A rumour of a liberal rout sent the Proctors, already packed, down to the river and on board a ship with their trunks; better news next morning brought them back again. Some ladies kept their best clothes on board, which proved inconvenient when they had occasion to wear them. Some, but a minority, left for England. Most ladies stayed at home, and made themselves useful preparing food for the wounded in hospital and giving lavish meals to British officers. Dorothy Proctor rather enjoyed the excitement. She records the disasters that befell their friends — the Jones's house and furniture destroyed by shelling, all the Smiths' best furniture, including two pianos, and the Taylors' magnolia tree, Dr. Rumsey and his wife attacked and robbed by guerillas, another poor lady dead of pleurisy from standing at her open window one night to observe the shelling, the Ormerods driven from their house by three shells in the garden and fleeing to the Proctors for refuge; poor Mrs. Omerod burst a blood vessel every time a shell fell near her; the three highest stories of the Hebblethwaites' magnificent house completely in ruins, every window broken, poor Mr. Wright suffered dreadfully from a cannon ball, which entered his house while he was at dinner, overturned the dinner-table, and hit his left arm, the surgeons found it literally a mass of jelly; he also had a broken jaw and some teeth knocked out by his wineglass. The Proctors themselves were lucky; they had nine 36-pounders in the garden, and one went fairly through the summer-house and made a great dust, and John had three shells in his lodge, one burst three pipes of wine, but 'so far we have been truly fortunate'.

The Proctors saw plenty of society, and had to entertain many visitors at meals, owing to the use by the navy of their summer-house as a signal station; 'we have always a party there from the *Nautilus* from sunrise to sunset . . . and as all are anxious to know what is going on, we have visitors innumerable, more than I like in this time of scarcity — the Commander, Captain Glascock, takes a luncheon with us three days out of four, and Lord George very frequently, besides many others — 6 or 7 at once. Thornton is half employed in making bread and cakes for them . . . I know not what will be the end of all this protracted warfare, but it is become very irksome'. Provisions were scarce and dear, but the Proctors did pretty well. Though sometimes 'puzzled how to make a dinner in such times' for the parties of officers and others who dropped in, Dorothy 'got fish and soup, stewed beef, fricasseed rabbits, ham and patties, for the first course, and afterwards a superb turkey which cost 6 crowns, roasted pork, tarts, custard, sweets, anchovy toast, etc. etc., and so did very well'. It will be seen that British appetites kept their ancient form. Mrs. Proctor made no apology for this feasting amid starvation, at a time when most of the citizenry and troops were thankful for a slice of plump dog and seldom got it. 'The army has had nothing but rice and wine for some weeks past, not a morsel of bread — the English growl dismally: the French have killed and eaten all the cats in the city, and after an engagement they eat all the horses and mules that were shot. They then get drunk . . .' But the navy sent in food secretly to the Proctors, who never got down to mules. They appear to have lived in a social whirl; apart from the navy there came to Entre Quintas Sir John Milley Doyle, the elegant and handsome Colonel Rochfort, 'who married the notorious Harriette Wilson', Saldanha, even the emperor himself, Colonel Hare, Colonel Badcock, who 'came in and said they were firing like h—l and that his groom had been shot dead in the street', the dashing, swearing Colonel Bacon and his handsome sporting wife, Lady Charlotte, and all kinds of stray visitors from England. The Oporto British remained throughout the siege full of courage and spirits; sometimes the emperor would give a ball, a very gay international affair. The fascination which the impact of the war had for the British, whether volunteer fighters, neutral observers, or civilian residents, is shown by the many accounts, published and unpublished, which they wrote of it. One thing must be deplored — that Harriette Wilson was not in Oporto with her husband, the debonair Colonel Rochfort; her account of the British colony and of army society would have made racy reading. If she had been anything near her old form, she would have secured the ex-emperor as protector, and have been at the very centre of army feuds and intrigues.

It was a strange time for the gentlemen of the English Factory, conversing and doing business in the Rua dos Inglezes outside their shell-scarred Factory House, with the babel of foreign tongues from all the nations of Europe clamouring about them, the medley of uniforms (someone counted fifty in one day), the high lilt of voices from the Clyde and the Liffey, the sharper twang from the Thames, broad slurring speech from the shires, incomprehensible attempts at Portuguese, British soldiers confused with Portugal wines reeling in the gutters, often helped to their feet by amiable Portonians (who favoured them above the French), the ladies brought by the French troops, *la belle cantinière*, attending on their patrons with admirable Gallic matter-of-factness. The dignified British wine shippers felt that their city had become something of an international circus. A dangerous, destructive circus, with grenades, cannon balls and shells crashing everywhere, and always the crackle of musketry from across the river. A fantastic, stirring scene, which must have more than satisfied the desire for drama of the English groom who had accompanied General Villa-Flor from England because 'town had grown so dull since the Reform Bill'. He went with his master to Lisbon when the General, now Duke of Terceira, led the campaign in the south; and in Lisbon Captain James Alexander, of the 42nd Highlanders, met him in 1834 when he called on the Duke — 'a sleek, well-bred man,' who remarked of a little girl running about the premises, 'That's the daughter of the lady's maid; she's looked on as one of the family; very different with us at home, sir'. He told Captain Alexander, 'If they don't treat me well here, I'll leave and set up for a veterinary surgeon. They are damned ignorant about horses in Portugal, sir'.

On which noticeably English note we conclude these comments on the British adventurers who served Queen Maria overseas. On the whole, they had not found it rewarding, except in so far as fighting for a liberal constitution in a foreign land is its own reward. They returned home feeling cheated, disillusioned, and embittered. Many of them went off to Spain to serve Don Carlos, hoping that the cause of liberty in that land might prove more profitable.

Those (much fewer) who had lent their swords to Dom Miguel no doubt felt embittered too, but, since they did not publish their experiences, perhaps anticipating a chilly reception, we know less about them. One of them, Captain Elliot of the Royal Navy, may, however, have done well out of the business; some Portuguese historians, anyhow, have so believed. Their story was that Dom Miguel had been left, by his loving and wicked mother who had worked for him with such truly Bourbon cunning and tenacity, a box of precious stones hidden in a secret place, to be used by him only in the greatest emergency. The emergency arrived; the diamonds were unearthed, and passed over to this British Tory naval officer, to be spent on raising and equipping a squadron to defend Lisbon against the enemy. 'We do not know', says a Portuguese writer darkly, 'what was done with those diamonds entrusted to the conscience of an Englishman. We hear nothing more of this officer, or of the squadron he should have taken to Lisbon.'

This is not quite fair. Some of the diamonds, perhaps, went to pay for the steamer with five hundred seamen and a band in which Captain Elliot had just embarked when he was checked at Gravesend by the news of Napier's capture of his employer's fleet off Cape St. Vincent. But the discouragement was only temporary; in September the dauntless captain sailed again, in the steamer *Lord of the Isles*, with General Ranald Macdonell and some other Scottish officers, for Portugal. Dom Miguel's English admiral was 'still sighing', said Napier, 'for opportunity of serving his worthy master's cause'. Exactly how he served it on this visit to Portugal is obscure; his steamer was captured by the enemy, but he escaped and joined Miguel, and presumably talked over the matter of the squadron with him. It never, however, materialized, in spite of Lord Beresford's eagerness that it should do so. Napier was disappointed; in December 1833 he wrote to Colonel Hodges, 'As for Elliot and his squadron, I shall be glad to see him. Tell him to keep an account of what his ships cost — it will facilitate their valuation here'.

The need for valuation never arose. The captain slips from our view, squadron, diamonds and all, and we hear no more news of him.

General Macdonell, on the other hand, we may follow to his end. Ranald Macdonell of Glengarry was one of those hazardous Roman Catholic Highlanders who have always roamed the continent as soldiers of fortune, lending a hand when and where they could against England the ancient foe. They were helping Castile against John I of Portugal and his five hundred English archers at Aljubarrota in 1385; they were in the army of Philip II and of every Spanish army since; as anti-Elizabethans, Jacobites, Bonapartists, Miguelists, Carlists, Franquistas, a sprinkling of these adventurers from the glens have always been there. Ranald Macdonell had fought for Spain in the Peninsular War; at the beginning of 1823, anxious to escape from Cadiz, he made the mistake of embarking in a pirate ship bound for Gibraltar, which was captured by the Portuguese, and its crew, including himself, were imprisoned in St. George's castle at Lisbon. It happened that João Carlos Saldanha at the same time had the misfortune to find himself a political prisoner in St. George's; on his first day he shared quarters with the pirates, and became interested in a prisoner in faded black who held aloof from the others and was addressed as 'general'. He had the stranger to dine with him; in spite of their ideological differences, they made friends; they dined and played chess together daily. When Macdonell was released, Saldanha gave him money for a new suit and for his passage to England. They met again in Paris in 1832, when Macdonell, card-broke, was unable to get home; once more Saldanha, most generous of men, after appealing to the British ambassador for his friend in vain (the ambassador probably knew his man too well) supplied him with his fare to Scotland. And now here he was, cropping up again in Portugal, engaged with other Scots by Dom Miguel to fight for his cause against all the damned constitutionalists and English Whigs, arriving at S. Martinho in the *Lord of the Isles* with several French and Scotch officers and Captain Elliot in September 1833. On the 18th he took over from Bourmont the command of Miguel's forces before Lisbon, and faced his old friend Saldanha from the enemy camp. Driven back on Santarem, he put forth a dispatch bristling with Highland arrogance and vanity, complaining of the position bequeathed him by Bourmont. 'I thought it desirable to retreat to Santarem to establish a base of operations' — but not because of any talent or courage in the opposing army or its general. 'I am thoroughly satisfied that I did right.' He regretted that it had not been feasible to take Lisbon, but he had done his utmost in the circumstances, no one could have done more. He was self-assertive, ungenerous, vain. He continued to fail to take Lisbon; Miguel's Portuguese staff intrigued against him, jealous of all these foreigners that their master preferred to employ; before Christmas he was replaced by a Portuguese general. He retired over the frontier to Don Carlos.

He did not appear publicly in Portugal again until 1846, when he commanded guerilla troops for Miguel in the Maria de Fonte rising. But for some time before this he had been working disguised in Minho and Douro as Miguel's agent, helping to stir up trouble, gathering Miguelistas together, passing intelligence back to his master in Spain. Then, as a Portuguese historian put it, one fine day Macdonell came out of hiding at the head of an army of guerillas on the shores of the Douro; 'it would seem', wrote the British chargé d'affaires in Lisbon, 'that the efforts of General Macdonell and other Miguelite agents have been successful'. Macdonell and his three thousand armed men were received with rejoicings in Guimaraens and Braga and throughout that Miguelist countryside. 'All the Minho, influenced by landowners', wrote a correspondent from Oporto, 'follow the Miguelite banner.' Macdonell's old friend and foe, Marshal Saldanha, leading the queen's forces, must have remembered bitterly that he had twice helped this wrong-headed Scot to safety; and now here was 'the red-trousered Miguelite chief' again interfering in Portuguese affairs in the cause of despotism.

But not for long. Adventurous to the last, he was surprised at Chaves by the queen's cavalry in January 1847, wounded and killed. He lies buried in a chapel in the little mountain town of Sabrosa, one of the many Highlanders who have given their lives for reactionary absolutism, the distaste for liberalism and whiggery hot in their unsoothed hearts.

As to Dom Miguel, who had cost so many lives among so many nations, those who had fought against him thought it a mistake to have turned him loose in Europe after his defeat, to slip back and make more trouble. As Admiral Napier put it in 1834, 'there are several very nice islands in the western ocean'. Instead of inhabiting one of these, the persevering pretender spent his embittered, scheming years in Rome, in Spain, in Baden, where at last he died of an apoplexy at sixty-five.

BIBLIOGRAPHY

F. O. Portugal, 63/ 384, 399, 400, 402 (Record Office).
Portugal Contemporaneo, J. P. OLIVEIRA MARTINS (1881).
Revista Historica de Portugal desde a morte do D. João VI ate o Falecimento do Imperador (Coimbra 1841).
The Wars of Succession in Portugal and Spain, WILLIAM BOLLAERT (1870).
Diary of Maria Fitzgerald (MS. belonging to Mr. Aubrey Bell, printed in 4th Report of Lisbon Branch of the Historical Association, 1940).
Narrative of Expedition to Portugal, G. LLOYD HODGES (1833).
Memoirs, SIR CHARLES SHAW (1837).
The Story of General Bacon, A. J. BOGER (1903).
Naval Sketch Book (2nd Series), W. N. GLASCOCK (1834).
Account of the War in Portugal, SIR CHARLES NAPIER (1836).
Life and Correspondence of Sir Charles Napier, E. H. D. E. NAPIER (1862).
Life and Letters of Sir C. Napier, H. N. WILLIAMS (1917).
Life of Vice-Admiral Sir Charles Napier (1854).
The British Battalion at Oporto, Thomas Knight (1834).
Adventures in Holland and at Waterloo and Expedition to Portugal, THOMAS KNIGHT (1867).
Rough Leaves from a Journal in Spain and Portugal, COLONEL LOVELL BADCOCK (1835).
Sketches in Portugal during the Civil War of 1834, CAPTAIN J. E. ALEXANDER (1835).
The Civil War in Portugal, COLONEL HUGH OWEN (1835).
Letters from Oporto 1832-4, DOROTHY PROCTOR (MS. in possession of British Factory, Oporto).
Siege Lady, C. P. HAWKES and MARION SMITHES (1938).
Oporto Old and New, CHARLES SELLERS (1899).
Diccionario Popular, PINHEIRO CHAGAS (1876-86).
Encyclopedia, OLIVEIRA LEMOS (1910).
Nouvelle Biographie Générale (1851).
Historia do Marechal Saldanha, À. DA COSTA (1879).
Memoirs of the Duke of Saldanha, CONDE DE CARNOTA (1880).
The Times (1826, 1828, 1832, 1833, 1834).
The Greville Memoirs (July 25th, 1832; July 15th, August 24th, 1833).
Croker Papers (May 6th, 1833).

PLOTTERS

I. THE ILLUSTRIOUS JAMES

James Fitzmaurice Fitzgerald

[1577-1579]

IN the great Enterprise of England that occupied the imaginations and intentions of so many earnest English and Irish
Catholic émigrés and foreign potentates and so worried the queen
and her ministers, after the Bull Regnans In Excelsis had deposed
'that servant of infamy Elizabeth' and declared anathema against
all who gave allegiance to her, Portugal was cast by the rest of
the continent for the part of jumping-off ground; but there were
various reasons why she did not play it satisfactorily. The would-
be invaders slipped in and out of Lisbon; they bought and freighted
ships there, waited there, talked there, got such money as they
could there out of the worried papal representatives, schemed
there quite in vain to enlist Portuguese royal help; and sailed
away down the Tagus to anywhere but the British Isles. Until,
anyhow, after the Spanish occupation, the plots were hatched and
financed elsewhere, at the court of Madrid, or in Rome, and,
when sent to Lisbon, drifted away and dissolved. Usually they
were first offered to the thrifty court of Paris, then to the cautious
and procrastinating Philip of Spain (who never quite liked that
wild Bull, though he felt he ought to be King of England), then,
in impatient disgust, taken to the more warmly incubating climate
of Rome. 'Take hold of the Pope', wrote the most determined
and extreme of the Spanish Party among the English émigrés,
Dr. Nicolas Sanders, to his fellow exile, Cardinal Allen, 'for the
King is as fearful of war as a child of fire. The Pope will give you
two thousand . . . If they do not serve to go to England, at least
they will serve to go into Ireland. The state of Christendom
dependeth on the stout assailing of England.'

It was a familiar cry: take hold of the Pope, for the king will do
nothing. His Most Catholic Majesty handed out pensions, indeed,
to the crowd of needy and clamouring British refugees who
besieged his court; he had elaborate and far-reaching designs

drawn up; he had his agents for ever sounding and reporting on his fifth column in England (and in the end as incorrectly as optimistic foreign agents always do); he had his right of succession both to the English and the Portuguese crowns made out by an English genealogist who 'has taken upon himself the task of proving that His Majesty is the legitimate heir to the crown of England'; he furnished one enterprising gentleman after another with sums of money for an assault on England, on Ireland, on Scotland; he sometimes sent them to Lisbon to await further directions and get them out of the way; but the plots seldom hatched; they turned as a rule into addled eggs under this lethargically brooding hen; there would only be an occasional ill-designed expedition, and a thin trickle of hot-headed Irish patriots leaping on to their native soil to raise the Pope's standard and their own relations. To get real enthusiasm and support, the would-be invaders had to go to Rome, where Pius V, and after him Gregory XIII, would enter into their plans with delightful Italian sympathy and religious zeal. Little invasion expeditions would be arranged there, even sometimes mildly financed and equipped. And then the invaders would make the mistake of going off to Lisbon to wait for more help before taking off for Britain, and in that pleasant port, among the easy-going Portuguese and their abstracted, traditionally Anglophile king, invasions were apt to peter out.

There was, for instance, James Fitzmaurice Fitzgerald, that eager Irish patriot — 'the greatest rebel (Shan O'Neill only excepted) in all Ireland', wrote Denis Molan to Walsingham of him in 1578, 'running from one Papist prince to another with the Pope's commendations and his proud letters to his foolish friends in Ireland, comforting them to resist their prince'. Sir Henry Sidney's picture of him, living at St. Malo in 1576, is less restless, more prosperous, but more formidably to be reckoned with — 'James Fitzmaurice lieth still at St. Maloes, and keepeth a great port, himself and family well apparelled and full of money . . . oft visited by men of good countenance. This much I know of certain report, by spiall of my own from thence, the man is subtle, malicious, and hardy, a Papist in extremity, and well esteemed and of good credit among the people . . . If he come, and in show and appearance like a man of war (as I know he will) . . . he may take and do what he will with Kinsale, Cork, Youghall, Kilmallock, and haply this city [Dublin] too, before I shall be able to come to the rescue thereof.'

Fitzmaurice was, indeed, as seen from the British Isles, an alarming figure. He had spent ten years trying to make himself head of the Irish anti-English party, first storming about Ireland in family feuds and nationalist rebellions, then, defeated, taking the oath to the queen (so that unrealized hopes were entertained that he might prove 'a second St. Paul'), then taking to the Continent and plunging into the strange, wishful career of the Catholic refugee, offering the English crown to the King of France and being rewarded by the queen mother Catherine de' Medici with five thousand ducats, then off to Spain, with Ireland on a plate for Don John of Austria, which brought in some more ducats, and finally to Rome, to confer with all the conspirators there, including his English rival, Sir Thomas Stukely, jointly with whom he pressed Ireland on the Pope's son, to be rewarded at last with the promise of an expeditionary force, slightly marred by being shared with the pushing Stukely.

Fitzmaurice was apt to be in and out of Lisbon, where his boy was at school at the Jesuits' college, and he was constantly on the edge of taking off from Lisbon to Ireland. He was there in February, 1577, with a letter from Cardinal Galli, the Papal Secretary, commending him to the Apostolic Collector in Lisbon. 'The bearer of this', the Cardinal discreetly wrote, 'will be James Geraldine, an Irish nobleman, who, having been for some days at Rome to do his devotion in visiting the holy places, is now departing to return to his country. He has chosen to go by way of Portugal, that he may see a little son whom he has at the Jesuits' College at Lisbon. He has been received with favour here, and gladly seen by the Pope as being a very honourable gentleman and very devoted to the Catholic religion.' The collector is to help him to find a ship, and other conveniences for a safe passage to his home, 'which, as you will learn from him, is what he particularly desires'.

But his desire was not gratified. In August he was still (or again) in Lisbon, trying to get his passage. 'James Geraldine is here', the collector wrote to Rome, 'very eager to accomplish what he has promised to his Holiness. I am perpetually at work with the Catholic ambassador to secure him a good passage ... Geraldine has had his son Maurice brought hither, and a mighty comfort it is to him to see the boy.' Again, 'The Catholic ambassador spares no pains to procure for James Geraldine as safe a passage to Ireland as possible, nor do I fail to solicit it; and James manifests the utmost impatience at the delay . . . He hopes to accomplish great things there, as by God's grace we trust he may'. To this letter there is a cipher postscript. 'On two successive days I have brought James Geraldine to kiss, as he desired, the king's hand; but the king has refused an audience, to the great astonishment of everybody.'

Everybody should not have been, and doubtless was not, astonished. King Sebastian's whole mind was obsessed with his forthcoming enterprise against the Moors in Africa; he had no intention of being entangled with expeditions against England. He might and did quarrel with the English queen over her subjects' piracies, and disapprove of the heretic regime, but he had no notion of assisting hostile expeditions against his ancient and valued ally. Fitzmaurice waited in Lisbon in vain; no help was forthcoming from there, nor yet the assistance promised him from Spain, which not all the pushing from Rome could induce his unenthusiastic Catholic Majesty to send. Discouraged tidings of him came through every little while from the Papal Collector in Lisbon to Rome, during the summer and autumn of 1577, and were passed on by Cardinal Galli to the Papal Nuncio at Madrid. 'James Fitzmaurice is still waiting for the promised help.' 'James Geraldine is trying to get a Breton ship for Ireland.'

By the end of October he had got hold of a ship, but it lacked 'comfort'. 'Having got the ship stayed, he has asked for culverins, sakers, arquebuses, powder, soldiers, and so many other things to equip the ship for comfort, without saying whether he will pay for them or no, that I doubt it will be some time before he sails.'

The papal officials began to think he might get off quicker if he really wished. On October 30th he wrote that he had received the Madrid Nuncio's letter bidding him delay no longer; he had, he explained, only just been able to hire a ship, and will sail in it in about a week. He begged the Nuncio to send help after him to Ireland. A week later the Lisbon Collector wrote, 'James Geraldine thinks of departing for Ireland this week'. He had been waiting for the Bishop of Killaloe, who was to have accompanied him, but had been robbed by Rochelle pirates on the seas off Portugal and lost the bulls for his bishopric, without which he did not care to go to Ireland. James himself wrote to Rome on November 5th on a proud and desperate note.

'I came to Lisbon that I might sail to Ireland, where I should have been long since if the Nuncio at Madrid had not delayed me, thinking to procure me some help. But at last he tells me I have nothing to expect. I therefore am resolved to wait no longer, and unarmed, without ships, without men, in the name of our Lord Jesus Christ and supported by apostolic authority, I sail for Ireland, relying much upon your prayers to obtain victory against the enemies of the Church. Having awaited aid and not obtained it, I shall find all my friends who were eagerly expecting me turned lukewarm and faint-hearted, and my enemies will be the more eager and zealous to fight against me when they see me entering the country unarmed and unaided. Therefore I ask your Eminence, in whom I trust, to hasten the promised supplies after me to Ireland.'

It is, on the whole, the letter of a man who does not much want to go to Ireland, though he will do so if he has to, and anyhow feels himself in an increasingly false and uncomfortable position where he is. Indeed, his months in Lisbon had not been satisfactory. The English residents fought shy of him as a traitor; the king would hardly see him; even the Pope's representatives had begun to tire of his never-ending requests for help. 'He has been several times to court, where he found small entertainment, and was few times heard of by the prince', Botulphe Holder, the English merchant who sent intelligence to his government from Lisbon, wrote to Burghley. Holder himself had cold-shouldered him. 'He sent divers times to ask my leave to visit me for country's sake. I did the best I could in going from home . . . but he waited his time and came suddenly upon me. I shook him off, by saying I was sent for abroad, whereby his tarrying was very short, and never before nor since have we had any conversation, nor did I desire it, as I understand he was a mover of differences between princes, and between prince and subject, whereas I wish peace and concord between all princes in Christendom . . . He has freighted a French barque, taken up a hundred tinkers and other rascals for soldiers', and bought or borrowed some arms. He had sailed away on November 17th, giving out that he was going to Brittany to his wife. But, 'as I am informed, he goes to Ireland, with power from Rome to animate all men to assist him against our queen ... It is said that Stukely has gone with him in the ship, but others say he is secretly in the Spanish ambassador's house. ...'

Fontana, the Apostolic Collector, writing to Rome, offered no opinion as to where James had sailed to; his letter seems to assume it was to Ireland, but, having seen a good deal of James during the past year, he may have known better. 'James Geraldine delayed his departure till he had come by munitions for the ship. Don Théotonio of Bragança has given him a culverin and some arquebuses, and the Archbishop of Lisbon some powder. He tried to borrow 500 ducats from the Colettoria, but he had from me a civil refusal. At last, on November 19th, he departed, saying he went in great peril of certain ships of the Queen of England. He has made a fidalgo here his proctor for the receipt of moneys that the good folk here will contribute in aid of his enterprise, and has left here the priest David Wolf who was his interpreter, and the Bishop of Killaloe, that he may go to Madrid to negotiate for him with the king.'

Once out of the Tagus, Fitzmaurice disappeared from the harassed guardianship of the Apostolic Collector into the questionable Atlantic. An account of the voyage that ended in Galicia was written later to Cardinal Galli by Patrick O'Hely, the Bishop of Mayo, who sailed with him. He had hoped, said the bishop, to make a speedy passage to Ireland, and thence to send intelligence of some glorious victory over the enemies of the Church, 'but the course of events has been quite otherwise'. The wind was against them when they left Lisbon. Falling in with an English ship, they attacked and took her, but, at the bishop's request, James 're-frained from massacring the prisoners', sending them ashore under escort to be dealt with by the Inquisition instead. Then, after battling for over a month with adverse winds, they were compelled to put in to Bayona in Galicia. Here they were robbed of their ship one feast day while they were at mass, by its Breton master and mariners, who sailed away with it across the bay to Brittany. So it was necessary to pursue it there, and Fitzmaurice remained at St. Malo, where his wife also was, while Bishop O'Hely went to Paris to get a warrant for the ship's restitution. The robbers, said the bishop, had, as well as stealing the ship, warned the Queen of England to be on her guard against the forthcoming attack on Ireland. The bishop is petulant about the whole affair; had his advice been followed, he complains, his Holiness would never have made a vain show by displaying the standard of the Church unsupported by military force, to be derided by their enemies; nor would James ever have left the Roman court had he not expected to be provided with forces by the Collector Apostolic in Portugal. However, he adds resignedly, such an enterprise once begun cannot be abandoned without disgrace and disaster; it must now be prosecuted, and James should be helped to Ireland by his Holiness, for no one else will do so.

Apparently no one did, for in St. Malo and other Breton ports James spent the spring and early summer, presumably with his wife. News of him, his piracies and his misfortunes, trickled through to Lisbon, Spain and Rome. He has captured an English ship, chased another which escaped, has arrived at Vannes. In Lisbon his career was followed with interest by the Bishop of Killaloe (who had got out of sailing with him by having his bulls stolen by pirates). 'We have waited for exact tidings of the most illustrious James. We learn he is at St. Malo, with two English ships he captured at sea, and has got from a Breton nobleman, M. de la Roche, four ships with soldiers. He had them nearly a month and a half ago, so that with the first wind he might sail to Ireland.'

But the wind, it seemed, blew continuously from the wrong quarter; in May the illustrious James was still at St. Malo.

Cardinal Galli, a not very patient cleric, who thought his Holiness had helped James just about enough, began to write sharply about the delay. 'The affairs of Geraldine and Stukely begin to occasion the Pope some annoyance.' He has, he says, been told by the Bishop of Mayo that Geraldine is staying at St. Malo with his wife until the bishop brings an order from Paris to certain sailors to restore his goods. He is demanding more money from the Pope, saying he will still go to Ireland, though he does hear that close watch is being kept on the Irish coasts. The Pope, writes the cardinal, is getting tired of it, having had enough and to spare of this kind of thing, to say nothing (which means, as it usually does, that he says a great deal) of the Pope's disgust at the expense. The cardinal, a suspicious man, would like to know the true version of the Breton robbery: 'Geraldine may have magnified every slight excuse for not going upon this troublesome business of Ireland, but taking his rest with his wife at St. Malo.'

There followed a period when everyone but Geraldine thought

that Geraldine should come to Lisbon to join forces with Sir Thomas Stukely for a joint invasion. It was no good: the minority of one was in a strong position, and prevailed. 'The said James is in good quarters at Nantes, in the house of a nobleman.' 'Geraldine is still at Nantes. From Lisbon they write that they are trying to cause him to return there, to confer with Stukely.' In June he was in Paris, a little further from Lisbon. From there he wrote to Galli explaining his delay and difficulties; and added that he would like it if two or three learned Jesuits were sent to Scotland and Ireland to arouse the Catholics from their torpor. The Pope, still hopeful and enthusiastic for the enterprise, sent him more money, sympathizing with his calamities and hoping he will resume his plans. He went again to Brittany, to wait opportunity for crossing to Ireland: he had become to Fontana 'that gentleman who tarried in Brittany'. Sir Amyas Paulet, English ambassador in Paris, wrote that he and his wife lived lavishly at Dinan, with a household of eighteen persons, 'which argues that he finds liberal friendship in this country, and there is no appearance that he is preparing for any new voyage'. He raised a loan of a hundred crowns in Dinan on seven silver cups that he pledged; it was not enough; he moved himself and his family to Spain and settled in a villa a league and a half from Madrid, living at great expense; he already, writes the irritated Nuncio, begins to importune me for aid.

It is obvious that much continental opinion must have been mobilized one way and another in favour of James leaving the Continent for Ireland. But he managed to resist it throughout that year. Galli, writing in October one of his acid letters to Madrid, said 'This clumsy dance of Geraldine and Stukely has by this time cost the Pope more than 50,000 crowns'. He urged that Geraldine, with two ships and a thousand soldiers 'picked up wherever he can find them', be dispatched forthwith on the expedition.

At the end of the year, the determined and capable Dr. Nicholas Sanders took a hand. A man of the most inflexible driving-power, the hope of the Spanish Party among the English Catholics, an extremist who never ceased to wage his bitter war of propaganda against the Elizabethan government, and believed that his country would never be saved from ruin until it was taken over by his Most Catholic Majesty, Dr. Sanders knew none of the human shrinkings and shiftings of his colleagues in the great enterprise. Yet even he, though his sojourn at Lisbon in the winter of 1578-9 could not soften his purpose or disintegrate his intention, was defeated by it. With his customary able efficiency, and backed by Madrid (the Nuncio wrote of him 'I trust more in the prudence, foresight and religious convictions of that man than I should in a whole army') he bought a ship secretly in Lisbon (in so far as anything done in Lisbon is ever secret), equipped it with troops and arms, and was preparing to depart with it to join Fitzgerald in Galicia, when, owing to the indiscretion of one of his men in claiming to be a papal soldier and exempt from local jurisdiction, the secret broke, to the alarm and displeasure of the new king, who was particularly anxious, in view of the growing menace from Spain, to remain on terms with England. The belligerent Dr. Sanders was turned out of Portugal, his ship confiscated and his troops disbanded. According to the testimony of an Irish friar, Sanders went to Fitzgerald at Bayona with the news that after all he had come with neither ships nor men. James, with his usual grandeur, returned, 'I care for no soldiers at all; you and I are enough; therefore let us go'. And, after some further months spent in getting hold of two more not very large ships, go at last they did, in June 1579. James had with him his wife ('me good bedfellow', as he calls her, in writing to his Desmond cousins), the indispensable Dr. Sanders, who was to be legate, two bishops (including Patrick O'Hely of Mayo), a few friars, a few English laymen, some Spanish and Italian soldiers, a general who was to lead the Irish army when they raised one, and a fine papal banner.

'James Fitzmaurice, the Irishman,' wrote the Spanish ambassador in London, on June 20th, 'is now said to be on the coast of Cornwall with a ship of 800 tons and two small ones, with which he has captured a Bristol vessel, throwing all the crew into the sea. In consequence of this, Humphrey Gilbert, who was robbing on the coast, has been ordered to go in pursuit of the Irishman, who, although he has so few ships, is causing them some anxiety.'

They landed in Dingle Bay; the enterprise of Ireland had begun. It was brief. Rebellion blazed up and was stamped out; everyone knows the story. In Brittany, the faithful M. de la Roche was making ready ships to send after the expedition; he was Fitzmaurice's close friend; they had arranged that their children would marry each other. But the Brittany ships never got to

Ireland; there was not time. James Fitzmaurice Fitzgerald was killed two months after landing, in a skirmish, by one of those hostile relatives in whom Irishmen abound. In spite of the scepticism of his supporters and his own reluctance, he had, anyhow, got to Ireland in the end.

BIBLIOGRAPHY

Cal S.P. Rome (1577, 1578, 1579).
Cal. S.P. Spain (1571, 1577, 1578, 1579).
Cal. S.P. Foreign (1577, 1578).
Cal. Carew MSS. (1576, 1580).
Historiae Catholicae Iberiae Compendium, PHILIP O'SULLIVAN BEARE (1621).
Dictionary of National Biography.

2. DON STUCLEY

Sir Thomas Stukely

[1578]

IF the Lisbon atmosphere had cooled the ardour, sharpened the worldly wisdom, heightened the love of life, and slowed down the spirit which had flamed so hotly in Rome, of the bold and ardent James Fitzgerald and of so many religious and patriotic bishops and priests his countrymen, it more easily and sensationally changed and deflected the aims of their English rival and colleague in the invasion dream, Sir Thomas Stukely from Devonshire. The crafty, buccaneering opportunism of Stukely sounds a different note, more complex, less heated, than theirs. This enterprising and versatile pirate (for such had been for a time his profession), who claimed Henry VIII for his father, 'this bubble of emptiness and meteor of ostentation', as Fuller called him, this restless soldier of fortune, offering his services to foreign courts, full of grandiose projects for colonizing Florida, conquering Ireland, burning the English navy in the Thames and conquering England, finally for conquering the Moors in Africa, won a strange hold on the imagination of his contemporaries. There must have been about him a magnificence; he did things on the grand scale; he was a 'glorioso'. He was, says Fuller, 'valued the less by others because over-prized by himself' — but this does not greatly appear; in fact, though it was apt to wear thin after a time, he seems to have had a remarkable knack of putting his own valuation of himself across, particularly abroad. Queen Elizabeth wrote, as early as 1560, that she found it strange, the credit he seemed to be in, 'considering the general discredit wherein he remaineth'. For he had, on his own half-authorized piracies, spent the queen's money and ships without return — the unforgivable sin. As to Burghley, he detested the rakehell fellow. 'Out of Ireland', he wrote, 'ran away Thomas Stukley, a defamed person almost through all Christendom, and a faithless beast rather than a man, fleeing first out of England for notable piracies and out of Ireland for treacheries not pardonable.' They were not, indeed, of the kind that rulers pardon; in 1569 the Spanish ambassador in London was writing to his king that 'Thomas Stukely claims to be in favour of handing over the country to your Majesty ... He and some of the barons intend to send to Spain to ask your Majesty to approve of this design'. Yet Sir Henry Sidney could write of him as 'discreet, faithful to the queen'. Discreet is a two-faced word; faithful he never was, to man or cause. A Catholic conspirator, he yet took the oath of allegiance, then, in June 1570, was off to the Continent (the best Tom Tiddler's ground he could think of, now that Florida had failed him, and Ireland and the Barbary seas), to embrace the career of continental salesman of the British Isles to the highest bidder: he wrote to the queen that he desired to live abroad for conscience' sake. The queen and council, wrote King Philip's Spanish correspondent in London, were thrown by this gentleman's intention into the utmost alarm; 'I know him', the writer explained, 'for an excellent Christian.'

So for the next eight years disconcerting rumours of the fitting out of expeditions to be led by Stukely into Ireland kept the queen's government on the *qui vive*; they were chequered, dizzy, up-and-down years for Stukely, but they led him at last, after much patient effort, from Rome to the mouth of the Tagus, in a ship furnished by the Pope for the invasion of Ireland, on a fine April morning of 1578. In Lisbon his name had for years been a recurrent rumour, his Irish expedition a legend; in 1574 a Lisbon correspondent had reported 'nine great ships prepared here for Stuckly to pass into Ireland'; and in the October of 1577 he was believed to be secretly in Lisbon; 'it is reported as true', someone wrote from thence, 'that Stewkly is here. He is kept close in the Spanish ambassador's house'. But we have no evidence that he visited Lisbon until this April morning of 1578, when he lay outside Belem and sent in a message to Roberto Fontana, the Apostolic Collector in Lisbon, that he was about to enter the port. Fontana was perturbed; he had just received orders from Rome that he must by all means prevent this from occurring; the Vatican had its reasons. The Collector sent back a message to the seas beyond Belem that his Most Illustrious Lordship was to remain where he was; next morning he sailed out himself to urge him to do so.

For the process known as being seen through, which had gradually flawed Sir Thomas's relations, once so satisfactory, with the court of Madrid, had set in now with the Vatican; it was an inevitable development in his relationships with those to whom he offered the Stukely service. Good at impressing and imposing for a time, he had magnificently imposed on King Philip, coming over with Ireland in one hand, for His Majesty's first course, England in the other, for his second, both so easy to take if he would let Mr. Stukely manage it. 'In June, Mr. Stukely came with a great ship and many gentlemen, and made an offer to the king about the conquest of Ireland', Mr. Robert Huggins reported from Madrid to Sir Henry Norris. 'It is marvellous matter to hear what shameful and dishonest brags they make. If great words may win such a realm as England, it is won every day. All their foundation is to take some port and fortify themselves. . . .'

Philip, a cautious though a dreaming man, had not believed it would be as easy as that. But he had welcomed the enterprising salesman, giving him a handsome establishment in Madrid and a lavish pension, making him general of the great expedition that was to sail. 'He is called Duke of Ireland', Huggins wrote, 'and keeps a greater port than any two dukes in the court; for his table only the king gives him 500 reals a day . . . It will be March or April before they can get ready.'

Those first months in Spain had been the grandest phase in Stukely's grandiose life.

> Then did Tom Stucley glitter all in gold,
> Mounted upon his gennett white as snow.
> Shining as Phoebus in King Philip's court;
> There like a lord famous Don Stucley lived,
> For so they called me in the court of Spain. . . .

Such was the legend dramatized by Peele; and it is apparent that for a time Stukely had been a brilliant and a happy figure in Madrid, kept by the king, befriended by that good patron of English Catholic émigrés, the English Duchess of Feria, hated and envied by the Archbishop of Cashel, who had long since appointed himself leader of the Irish enterprise, and now saw himself pushed into the shade by this plausible braggart Devonian, who despised the Irish nation, in his heart agreeing with the Spanish courtiers and rulers who spoke of them as 'the savages', as if they had been South Sea Islanders. The archbishop set himself to show up Stukely as a person of trifling consequence and disreputable past; Stukely reciprocated, and got the best of it; he was the more resourceful and intelligent. The archbishop had only one merit, said Walsingham: he 'mislikes that Stukely should have the glory of the enterprise to which they both pretend, and he would be glad to do anything to impeach the same'. He had done what he could. But Stukely was capable of arranging for his own decline from favour without help. Within a year his enemies had begun to report that his prodigality had somewhat lessened his credit; he had 'expended great sums of the king's money upon his vain pomps'; 'his accustomed manners have decayed his credit'. Honours had been heaped on him; he had been made a knight of the Order of Calatrava, and called Duke of Ireland, Marquis of Leinster, and other noble names; he had moved in an atmosphere of piety, he had got his absolution from heresy from Rome. Still, he had gone down; he had come back from a trip to find his allowance and Madrid lodging stopped; he went to live in a village outside, and talked of going to Rome.

And to Rome he had presently gone, to intrigue and quarrel with rival conspirators, and to dazzle the old Pope with his imposing airs and by the offer of the crown of Ireland to his Holiness's son. He had sustained his reputation for piety by pilgrimages and devout conversation; he had asked the Pope for the realm of Ireland to hold in fee of the See of Rome, with the title of Archduke; 'he makes great vaunts in Rome, but he begins to be as well known there as he was in Spain'. But not so well known in either as he came later to be. His expeditionary plans were still papally approved and furthered; finally the day had arrived when, together with James Fitzgerald, he had been furnished with money, a ship, a troop of Italian soldiers and a gang of bandits,

and been seen off with the papal blessing to Lisbon. Father
Parsons had written to Campion that he 'took away with him at
midnight out of their beds all the Irishmen in Rome'. This would
have over-weighted the already leaky ship; but he had taken
(against their wills, for they did not trust the Marquis of Ireland
a stone's throw from Rome, nor were their hearts set on invading
their native land) the Bishop of Killaloe and eight Irish priests
and students.

So the enterprising Marquis of Ireland, Knight of Calatrava,
Baron of Ross and Idron, Viscount of the Morough and Kensh-
lagh, Earl of Wexford and Catherlough, General of the most Holy
Father Pope Gregory XIII, had sailed off from Civita Vecchia in
the *St. John of Genoa* in February 1578. Rumours of his voyage
had flown like alarm signals about land and sea. The Queen of
England had been much concerned. Impossible to know which
powers were involved in the adventure; even Portugal might be
dragged in. 'It appears', the Master of the Merchant Adventurers
at Hamburg had written to Secretary Walsingham, 'that the
counterfeit English duke who has lately been at Rome is now
going with soldiers to Portugal, whence some suspicion might be
gathered that the preparation for Africa is meant some other
way . . . It is told me by an archpapist that the great army of ships
prepared in Spain and Portugal will divide, one half for Ireland,
the other for Friesland'.

But the great army of ships preparing in Portugal had had
another effect on the dreams of the counterfeit English duke, as
he had sailed down the Spanish coast, putting in at ports by the
way. King Sebastian's African adventure dazzled and seduced
him from his and the Pope's purpose before ever he sailed into the
Portuguese seas. At some point in his leisurely voyage, Vatican
suspicions must have uneasily stirred concerning his developing
intentions; hence that urgent order to the Collector in Lisbon,
couched in quite different terms from the previous message from
Rome, in which Cardinal Galli had commended the marquis and
his expedition 'for the defence of the poor Catholics of that island
against the heretics' to the Collector's care and aid if the ship
should call at Lisbon. Rumours had reached Rome which made
it seem inadvisable that the Ireland-bound marquis should encounter that waiting fleet in the Lisbon river and its Africa-
dreaming king.

Fontana did his best. 'I made all possible effort', he wrote to Galli, 'to stop Stukely's ship entering Lisbon.' Sailing out to meet the ship in the seas beyond Belem, 'in his cabin I told him why he should not have entered this port, whereat he seemed to marvel'. The marquis explained that so small and poor a ship would be quite unsafe for the Irish adventure, and that therefore he thought it well to postpone this for two or three months, which would allow him to join first in the African expedition, which was also an enterprise for the holy faith, after which he might proceed with the Irish invasion under better conditions. The cards were now on the table; it was obvious that the marquis intended Africa. Fontana reminded him of his mission and his oath to his Holiness; he answered by blaming those in Rome who had provided him with so poor a ship, and by begging the collector to get him an audience with the king.

Fontana sailed back to Belem, where, at the monastery His Majesty was attending the funeral of his grandmother; he was interested in the marquis's arrival; he ordered him to be brought to the monastery by night. This was done. Before the audience, Fontana walked in the cloister with the marquis and warned him of what the king might suggest to him regarding the African expedition; the marquis must insist, instead, on help with ships for Ireland. Stukely said little to the Collector about the Irish project, only remarking that James Fitzmaurice was merely a private gentleman who had a feud with an earl, and would be of little or no use in Ireland. Then he was admitted to the king; the interview lasted about an hour; His Majesty, Stukely told Fontana afterwards, had been most insistent on his going to Africa with him; in vain, Stukely explained, he had tried to persuade His Majesty to help him against Ireland instead; it was quite useless. He had obtained leave to disembark his troops at Cascais.

Fontana, conferring next day with the king's minister of finance, found this confirmed. The king would do nothing against England, with whom he was in peace and friendship; he said that the only defensible pretext for the tarrying of Stukely's ship in Lisbon was that she was bound for Africa. Respect for England's queen preponderated in him over everything else. In vain Fontana represented the Pope's indignation and disgust at this hitch in the holy enterprise he had backed and financed; in vain he pleaded for the loan or hire of one or two ships. In vain he told

Stukely what was his duty to the Pope; the marquis replied that, should the King of Portugal constrain him, he had no power to resist. Fontana suggested he might take his ship away to a Spanish port; he explained that it wasn't navigable, and that the soldiers would mutiny, disembarkation here having been promised them. The king's proposal was, said he, a piece of luck, since the ship was in such a sorry plight, and munitions so lacking, that it was impossible to go forward to Ireland.

Fontana told the king that he must at least send a courier to Rome for leave thus to divert his Holiness's expedition, and do nothing till he got it. To which Sebastian returned that he would do so, but might have to start for Africa before the answer came. The Collector perceived that he was up against the closed mind of obstinate royalty. All he could do was to try to secure some of the money advanced by the Vatican, and to note with grim satisfaction how little love and understanding prevailed between the marquis and any of his companions, whether Irish bishops or other. He 'is not in the good graces of any Irishman of conse-quence, nor yet of the other Englishman, Baron Dacres, who was loath to go on the ship with him and is minded to part company with him. If you permit me to say so, the little accord and less love that is between them, and the little stability and prudence that they evince, make me very mistrustful of them ... The five or six priests that were brought in custody have been complaining that Stukely has ill-treated them, and protesting that, hated as he is in Ireland, he will lead them all to death'. It was obvious that few Irishmen abroad had any more notion than the English marquis of visiting their native land. Even the homing intention of James Fitzmaurice, now in Brittany with his wife, seemed to be cooling considerably.

As to Stukely, behind the façade of bland and accommodating willingness reluctantly coerced by royal bullying, that he pre-sented to the papal representatives in Lisbon, he concealed, or did not conceal, a quite unalterable intention. He had, Cardinal Galli believed, made up his mind to switch his expedition before ever he came into Lisbon, and had indeed entered Lisbon with no other design: 'he had no other occasion to add more than a hundred miles to his voyage by touching at Lisbon'; he could have got his ship repaired at Cadiz, if that was, as he maintained, his aim. 'I am sure Stukely readily agreed to go to Africa; he was forewarned by the Collector that the king was resolved to detain him, but he went out of his way to put it there. This is God's affair', the cardinal added, a little crossly, renouncing responsibility.

No doubt Stukely thought so too. Africa had been to him a land of promise, since his old associate Hawkins had plundered the Barbary seas for slaves and gold. Other, more flattering, reasons for his preference have been suggested. 'Some thought', said Fuller, 'he quitted the Irish design partly because loath to be pent up in an island (the Continent of Africa affording more elbow-room for his achievements), partly because, so mutable a mind, he ever loved his last project (as mothers do the youngest child), best. Others conceive he took this African in order to his Irish design; such his confidence of conquest, that his breakfast on the Turks would the better enable him to dine on the English in Ireland.' So mutable a mind must remain in some obscurity to us, as it did to his contemporaries. The Nuncio in Madrid notes, writing to Galli in Rome, that this man 'is one that would have his feet in many shores at one and the same time, and neglects his duty to give his whole attention to what he thinks may turn out most to his advantage', and this analysis seems fairly obvious.

The figure Lisbon saw was that of a man delighted to be where he was. There is an account of him by an English merchant, William Pillen, who had his bark in Lisbon at the time and watched the renowned marquis arrive. The Lisbon merchants had got it firmly in their rather thick heads for some months that Stukely was already in Lisbon, even before the coming of Fitzmaurice, but kept close in the Spanish ambassador's house so that no one saw him. Lisbon gossip held obstinately to this interesting rumour, which was only dispelled by the marquis's actual arrival in April. Mr. Pillen saw the 'great ship of 700 tons' and about 700 soldiers, and reported them mustered before the king and well liked by him. Stukely, said he, was called by no other name than marquis, and had an Irish bishop and three or four priests. For a fortnight he kept on board, and entertained resorters, but afterwards a residence was prepared for him in Lisbon, where he kept house. Pillen and other merchants went aboard his ship, and asked him if he knew a brother of Pillen's in Rome. Afterwards Pillen supped with the marquis and a knight of Spain, and with one Cleyborne, the ship's master, a Lancashire man, who got six ducats a month. Stukely used to ride about Lisbon with a page before and behind him, in the degree of a marquis. He told Pillen that the King of Spain had proffered him great titles of honour and he had refused them, but the Pope's title of Marquis of Leinster and Baron or Earl of Washford he could not refuse; that, though they said in England he was going to Ireland, he was not appointed for it; that he knew Ireland as well as the best, and that there was nothing to be got there but hunger and lice. 'They say', said he, 'that I am a traitor to Her Majesty; 'tis they are traitors that say so. I will ever accept her as my queen. It is true that there is in England my cruel enemy Cecil the Treasurer, whom I care not for. I have had 1000 ducats of the Pope, and I have 1000 ducats a month, and I am to serve the King of Portugal in Africa against the Moors.' There was no likelihood, thought Pillen of Stukely's invading Ireland, except the king prepared the whole navy for him.

While thus posing before the merchants, Stukely was writing his excuses and explanations to Rome and to the Nuncio in Spain. He thanked God he had reached this port in safety; it seemed to him almost a miracle, as the ship was practically falling to pieces. It was a nuisance about the king, who was almost compelling him to go and serve him 'in the enterprise of Barbary. I refused, but am powerless . . . I would rather die a thousand deaths, were that possible, than give up the voyage to Ireland'. Meanwhile, he had received and embraced various of the Nuncio's friends.

The tension grew, as the situation defined itself. Sharp letters came from Rome; the unfortunate Collector, Fontana, was pressed by Galli to persuade the king to let Stukely go, and to impress on Stukely the disgust of his Holiness at his wavering. 'You are to let the marquis know that he must continue his voyage, and persuade the king, in the Pope's name, to provide for his needs.' Fontana did his best with both instructions, but in vain. The Spanish Nuncio sent his chamberlain to Lisbon to report on the situation. Fontana was delighted to see him, so that he could share the responsibilities for the difficult business, and 'the many various and intricate complications to which, hydra-like, it daily gives birth'. The Nuncio's chamberlain, interviewing the king at Cintra, got the same answer that Fontana had. He reported to Madrid that he found in Stukely such instability, between him and his soldiers such distrust, among the soldiers themselves such dissension, as could not be exceeded. Stukely, he said, was abandoned by all the Irish who had come on his ship; they said the Pope could not constrain them to go to Ireland against their will. 'In a word, the business is a sea of confusion.'

It was indeed. The one thing that emerged was that the Pope could not constrain anyone to go to Ireland, neither Stukely, nor the Irish on his ship, nor Fitzmaurice in Brittany, who declined to come to Lisbon to confer with Stukely, though Stukely had sent a man post-haste to St. Malo to summon him. Stukely, mentioning this to Galli, added cheerfully that when he did go to Ireland he made sure of conquering it speedily, 'in which case the said James is to be left there as governor, with some worthy prelate', pending Stukely's 'rapid reduction of England'. Meanwhile the Irish bishop and priests were behaving insufferably, and so were the Italian troops, among whom feuds raged, the Corsican gentlemen endeavouring to kill the Sienese gentlemen, and even exhorting the Lisbonians to 'join with them in killing these Sienese'. All were unjustly treated by Stukely, and all hated him. 'The marquis is hated by the Irish; the Englishmen are not on good terms with him; and he is hated by the Italian soldiers.' Lisbon, in short, was a storm-centre; probably the only tranquil person concerned in these doings was the young king, steadily, fanatically, exaltedly proceeding with his preparations for conquering the infidels of Africa.

On June 5th the Madrid Nuncio wrote to Rome that it was now evident how past hoping for was the Irish expedition. He hoped in God, however, that his Holiness would not lack other means of chastising 'that accursed woman'. It was now, alas, obvious that her chastisement was not going to come at present through her loyal subject the Marquis of Leinster. Even Galli had pretty well given up his hope of 'harassing that lady' with this weapon. He wrote grimly that Stukely might, provided James Fitzmaurice was not yet in Ireland, serve the king in Africa for a time, and go to Ireland on his return, if he first paid back his Holiness the expenses of transporting the army to Lisbon, and if the papal munitions and arms were kept in safe custody by Fontana. Fontana must see to this; and attempting to do so became one of the major problems in the Collector's harassed life. The king was vague and uninterested, his minister of finance thrifty, Sir Thomas crafty. Fontana wrote on June 16th that Stukely had been offering the Pope's arms to the king for Africa 'as if they were his own'. 'I complained', the Collector added.

Poor Fontana seems to have been assigned all the ungrateful tasks. The astute, businesslike, and by now very angry Cardinal Galli, lashing Stukely with his scorn and disgust and that of the Pope, in letters to everyone concerned, wrote his last word to Stukely himself on June 20th. 'His Holiness remains fully satisfied of your integrity of purpose, and makes no doubt that your behaviour will afford clear evidence of it, for the Pope deems you valiant, sincere and honourable.' Fontana at the same time was told to 'bid the marquis not to harass the captain and soldiers of his Holiness, as we understand he does'.

But it was too late for any admonitions to be of much use in Lisbon, for on June 27th Stukely sent Galli a note from Lagos, as he passed it *en route* for Africa. He has embarked, he says, with the papal troops under his command, to serve the King of Portugal in Africa. He has left the papal munitions and arms at Lisbon. Galli is to believe no reports and slanders circulated by heretics. He is sending Captain Cleyborne and his Italian secretary to counteract these. Alas, in this endeavour Captain Cleyborne proved singularly unhelpful; he did not care about the marquis, and thought him 'quite unfit to be entrusted with the conduct of this or any other business'; what reports and slanders he circulated we hardly like to guess.

But the marquis was well away on his chosen adventure; and, as it turned out, never had to face the awkward problem of Ireland, or any other, for he was killed at the battle of Alcacer with King Sebastian, a year before James Fitzmaurice Fitzgerald conducted his invading fleet into Dingle Bay.

In the anonymous contemporary play, Stukely is killed in Africa by his own Italian soldiers, who remark in doing so, 'If he had kept his oath he swore unto the Pope, we had been safe in Ireland, where now we perish here in Afric'. But, except Afric, nothing could have been less safe than Ireland; the Marquis of Leinster had known that too well, as had all his followers and companions; when Africa took him, he had at least made himself safe for ever from the menace of that island, for whose conquest he had charmed so much money, so much honour, favour and rich living, so many remarkable titles, even a ship, out of the various potentates whom he had temporarily persuaded of his fitness for the great task of delivering Ireland from England, England from heresy, schism, and the governance of 'that wicked lady' her queen.

It was remarkable how these expeditionary plans would wilt in the charming port of Lisbon, among our amiable and not too uncomfortably enterprising oldest allies. Regarded from the Lisbon quays, England and Ireland, whence merchants daily arrived with their cargocs of cloth, whither they daily embarked laden with tuns of wine, kegs of olives, oranges, almonds and salt, seemed distressingly near; among the great traffic of shipping coming and going in the Tagus between Belem and the Cais do Trigueiro, one vessel with a few foreign troops, a little hardly gained ammunition, a handful of English and Irish émigrés, and a papal banner, seemed distressingly small and solitary, not to say silly, for the subjugation of the British Isles. It was a mistake, as Cardinal Galli, that shrewd business man, had known, to put into Lisbon. Better, if fervour for the Enterprise of England were to be maintained, to remain among the homesick, *têtes-montés* pensioned exiles at the court of Madrid, among the quarrelling, intriguing refugees, with their wishful delusions and hopes, in the city of Rome, blowing grandiose bubbles which gleamed so rosily in that improbable exotic light, bubbles which, when blown to Portugal, drifted like spindrift and vanished in the Atlantic mists off Belem.

So, one may assume, thought the Irish priests whom Stukely had brought by compulsion from Rome and left stranded in Lisbon. 'The Irish priests', Fontana wrote to Galli after the fleet had sailed for Africa, 'now say they desire to go to Madrid, not Ireland. . . .'

But in October they were still in Lisbon, for Madrid had provided neither invitation nor transport money, and neither had Rome. 'Here is the bishop who was sent from Rome with all those other Irish priests and clerks, who incessantly pester me, now for money to go to Rome, and now for succour to enable them to live, saying they are here on the Pope's service.' To do them justice, they had never wanted to come to Lisbon.

Besides these unhappy stranded men, there remained, to remind Lisbon of the Marquis of Leinster, a mass of unpaid debts owed by 'that fraudulent and deceitful man', some costly jewels of his which would pay some of them, the memory of an imposing figure riding the steep streets of the city in the degree of a marquis, with a page in front and another behind, lavishly entertaining all who came, and a small, ornate crucifix, placed on the altar of St. Vincent's church by the Augustinian canons: it had been blessed for indulgences by his Holiness at the instance of the devout Thomas Stukely.

BIBLIOGRAPHY

Cal. S.P. Rome (1578).
Cal. S.P. Spain (1569, 1570, 1571, 1578).
Cal. S.P. Foreign (1570, 1571, 1572, 1574, 1575, 1577, 1578).
Cal. S.P. Dom. Add. (1574, 1578).
Historiae Catholicae Iberiae Compendium, PHILIP O'SULLIVAN BEARE (1621).
Worthies of England, THOMAS FULLER (1661).
The Battle of Alcazar, GEORGE PEELE (1594).
The Play of Stucley.
Biography of Sir Thomas Stucley, RICHARD SIMPSON (The School of Shakespeare, 1872).
The Celtic Peoples and Renaissance Europe, DAVID MATHEW (1933).

AMBASSADORS

I. HIBERNIAN STRANGFORD

Lord Strangford

[1803-1807]

IN the year 1801, young Lord Strangford, an Irish peer of just
twenty-one, fresh from Trinity College, Dublin, and a Foreign
Office clerk, was living in rooms in Bury Street, St. James's, just
below his friend Tom Moore, translating some of the minor
poems of Camoens into bright, sentimental and piping English
verse, rather in the style, and occasionally in the cantering,
extremely un-Portuguese metres, of the already celebrated Moore.
Moore thought them, naturally, very good, and advised publication. In 1803, after two years' industry, a slim little volume
emerged from the publishing house of James Carpenter of Old
Bond Street, entitled *Poems from the Portuguese of Luis de Camoens*.
The translator declared in his introductory foreword that he
wished to introduce his countrymen to another side of the great
Portuguese epic poet that was to be found in the Lusiads, translated some years before by Mr. Mickle; a side no less real, no less
the true Camoens. He offered his effort to the world with diffidence, as 'the private amusement of a young mind, which, when
obliged to relax from severer studies, preferred literary trifling
to total inactivity'. As translations, they are loose and do not
reflect Camoens: as poetry, they are sometimes pretty, always
trivial, and often foolish. As,

> When the girl of my heart is on perjury bent
> The sweetest of oaths hides the falsest intent,
> And suspicion abash'd from her company flies,
> When she smiles like an angel and swears by her eyes.

And so on. Camoens says this, but says it in a better metre and
with a less artificial sprightliness. Strangford is better when less
obviously *à la* Moore, as in

Prythee, Cupid, hence, — desist;
Why should I increase the list
Of boys whose sole delights consist
In kissing, and in being kiss'd?

But there was nothing important either about the translations or, to say the truth, about the originals. The poems have a commentary of notes, in one of which the moral youth remarks that 'The chaste discretion of delicate love is admirably portrayed in this little Poem. Happy for our Author had he always obeyed its dictates!' In another note he praises auburn locks and blue eyes in a woman above all other conceptions of beauty (it seems odd how many of Camoens's Portuguese lady-loves were blondes), archly adding that this is delicate ground for him to tread on. As he was blue-eyed and auburn himself, as well as being a rival aristocrat, this naturally annoyed Byron, who alluded to his vanity in *English Bards*.

But that was six years later. At first the effort of the young peer was received with general acclaim. It suited the fashion of the moment; its author was young, titled, personable, well-connected; and apparently knew Portuguese, a language seldom known, though it was all the fashion to visit the land where it was spoken. Not too often did peers write works of intelligence, and, as Dr. Johnson had observed, when a man of high birth turns author, he deserves to be treated with benevolence. Viscount Strangford's Camoens became the rage, and not only among young ladies. Even Byron, then at Cambridge, admired it at first, before it had become too popular for him to stomach. Only Southey dissented, in the *Annual Review* for 1803; he called it a literary fraud. He was followed by a few carpers and critics, who attacked the freedom of the translations, the influence of Moore on the verse, and the amorous themes, for which, unfairly comparing them with the Lusiads, they blamed the translator. Byron even decided that they were somewhat immoral. In a spasm of denigrating spite, he wrote the passage in *English Bards* —

Hibernian Strangford! with thine eyes of blue,
And boasted locks of red or auburn hue,
Whose plaintive strain each love-sick miss admires,
And o'er harmonious fustian half expires,

> Learn, if thou canst, to yield thine author's sense,
> Nor vend thy sonnets on a false pretence.
> Thinks't thou to gain thy verse a higher place
> By dressing Camoens in a suit of lace?
> Mend, Strangford! mend thy morals and thy taste;
> Be warm, be pure, be amorous, but be chaste:
> Cease to deceive; thy pilfered harp restore,
> Nor teach the Lusian bard to copy Moore.

But the enthusiasm of society never waned, and the lyrics ran through many editions; they were exactly what elegant readers liked.

Strangford won a reward more substantial than literary success. He was read at court, and royalty decided (greatly to its credit, said *Blackwood*) that he was obviously just the man they wanted at the Lisbon legation. They offered him the post of Secretary of Legation; and at the age of twenty-two he arrived in Lisbon, where Lord Robert Fitzgerald had succeeded John Hookham Frere as ambassador the year before.

Thus began the diplomatic career of Percy Clinton Sydney Smythe, sixth Viscount Strangford. One looks at his portrait, painted a few years later, after his Lisbon exploits: there are the celebrated blue eyes, large, set too near together, the curly red hair, aquiline nose, firm, thin-lipped mouth, cleft chin, long cravatted neck, the stylish bottle shoulders of his epoch (wonderful how people got them, how they get everything necessary to be in the mode), uniform and decorations. A Spanish commentator says the portrait reveals noble race, *mucho de gran señor*, and shows him *un apuesto dandy*. If he was this, his first years at the Lisbon legation probably suited him well enough. They also left him time for his literary occupations, which consisted mainly in preparing new and amended editions of his celebrated poems.

For the rest, there were his chancellery duties, and the social life of Lisbon, of the diplomatic circle, and of a second-rate and unintelligent court reigned over by a crazy old queen and her son, the Prince Regent, a weak, obstinate, vacillating man, pulled this way and that by everyone in turn. The young British diplomat was popular in this society, which just suited him; he made friends with Portuguese *literati*, who admired his cult of their national poet, with foreigners of distinction, with (it was said of him) lower and looser company than these, and with the British fashionable set, which came to Portugal for the winter and spring, either for health or entertainment, or to enjoy the amenities of the little court of the Duke of Sussex, who was there for his asthma and was firmly directing the growth at court of the *partido ingles*, with the assistance of his brother of Kent and of Admiral Campbell. The English party was locked in a swaying struggle of influence with the French party: it was vital that it should win; the fortunes of Portugal, of Great Britain and of Europe might depend on it. All the efforts of British diplomacy were employed to this end. The Duke of Sussex might be in Lisbon for his asthma; he might even be there, as clericalists have always insisted, in order to propagate Freemasonry in Portugal; but his presence was an ace in the British pack. Everyone liked him; he was even friendly with the French embassy. Madame Junot, the French ambassadress, arriving in 1805 soon after he hàd left, wrote, 'When I arrived at Lisbon, a very agreeable man had just left it — Prince Augustus, Duke of Sussex. He used to come often to the French embassy. I have regretted him.' She even paid him the compliment of getting his name and title right, in the most un-French manner. As to the British ambassador, she found 'Sir Robert Fitzgerald' charming; quiet and reserved, he had the manners *du grand monde*, and sustained the violent hostility of General Lannes, who preceded General Junot as French ambassador. Lord Robert took precedence of Lannes at audiences; 'with all the disdain of a peer of England and all the ease of a courtier, he passed before the general of the French Republic . . . the general became insane with rage. I shall get the better of him, he cried.' So one day, as both ministers were driving to court at Queluz, Lannes' coach knocked Lord Robert's into a ditch and left the ambassador there while he drove triumphantly on to the royal audience. Lannes, a violent and patriotic man, hated the whole British embassy staff, including the young Secretary of Legation, who at that time seemed to spend his time harmlessly enough, dividing it, says Mme Junot, between sleeping and translating Camoens. Junot in Paris, when the emperor offered him the Lisbon embassy, did not at all care for the idea of it; Lannes had told him that England was all-powerful there, that there was no society but that which was under English influence, that the French royalist émigrés were a nuisance, and the court a perfect bear-garden; the Lannes had not liked it at all. However, it was the emperor's wish; Portugal was the key to Europe, the bone for which the two mighty age-old enemies contended, and might well become the base for vital operations, with its front door on to the Atlantic, its back door into Europe; the good-will of the Portuguese court if possible, its domination by fear if not, might tip the scales of empire. Junot agreed to go to Lisbon, to practise there the uncongenial wiles of diplomacy.

So to Lisbon he went, with his sharp-eyed and sharp-tongued young wife, whom the emperor warned against gossip, against quarrelling, against any indiscretion in talk which might lessen the reputation of the new French court in hostile or inquisitive eyes. To this lively and inaccurate female pen we owe an account of social and diplomatic life in Lisbon before 1805, before the departure of Lord Robert Fitzgerald left his First Secretary as chargé d'affaires (he was made Minister Plenipotentiary in November, 1806) through two fateful years of crisis. Mme Junot admired Lord Robert, who had good manners and was a handsome man, though reserved; Lady Robert, on the contrary, was 'quite a virago', with large legs, large arms, flaming eyes, and large teeth which made one afraid she might bite if one went too near, so extreme was her hatred of everything French. As to 'milord Strankford', that sleepy and dandified young nobleman, he had translated Camoens — 'non que je pense que cela serve beaucoup enpolitique', but it showed, thought Mme Junot, with her customary inexactitude, that he knew Portugal perfectly and had resided there many years. And he was an agreeable and well-bred man, though somewhat near-sighted. All the same, the English domination over the Portuguese court at this time was detestable, and the chief cause of the malady that preyed on Portugal all these years, when the Prince Regent was England's slave and half the nobility aped English ways. France complained of this partiality, of Cochrane's squadron lying in the mouth of the Tagus, of the English pirates who seemed to have taken the Portuguese ports for their bases, of the entry into Lisbon of a convoy of British troops. 'If they have no concerted plan with Portugal', protested Junot, 'why do they enter this port? If they are come to occupy it, my mission as ambassador is over'. He complained too of the fleet of Portuguese cruisers lying off Gibraltar being under the command of Admiral Campbell, which he held to be a violation of neutrality. The prince, always anxious to be conciliatory, revoked this command, but British violations of neutrality and French protests still continued. When the news of Trafalgar reached Lisbon, the British ships in the Tagus celebrated it by firing their guns all night, just as if, complained Mme Junot, they had been at home in Portsmouth harbour.

Rocked to and fro by these two mighty forces, the imperial menace and the ancient ally, the wavering and alarmed regent and his advisers did their best to keep a nervous foot in both camps and to incur no one's displeasure. In 1806 Junot was recalled to Paris and Lord Robert Fitzgerald to London, leaving the First Secretary in charge. Now came the chance of the elegant young peer, who had passed his time, apart from his unexacting chancellery duties, in social intercourse, Camoens, dissipation and the doze. He found himself in charge of the trickiest of situations; Napoleon was bound to pounce on Portugal within a year or so; Portugal must somehow be saved for Britain; the French party must be routed at court, the government persuaded that Britain was the only healthy ally; Portugal must consent to defend herself and be defended (in moderation) by her protector.

Efforts to save Portugal redoubled; Lord Rosslyn came out with a mission of generals and admirals to consider the situation. Lisbon was full of British agents, who subsidized and tried to hearten the down-at-heels French royalist émigrés, working on their hate of Bonaparte and their natural craving for subsistence. British squadrons kept coming in and out of the Tagus, a demonstration of menacing force to the French, of reliable assistance (if only they would use it) to the Portuguese. Lord Strangford in his dispatches informed Canning constantly of the temperature of the patient, on whose health he diligently and (he believed) skilfully worked. Quite early the plan was decided on (by the British) that if Portugal should be invaded and occupied by the French, the royal family and ministers should be transported to Brazil, to carry on the Portuguese government from overseas until their country should be liberated. The only difficulty was, and this was Strangford's task, to make this favourite and ancient British plan acceptable to the home-loving and not very enterprising Prince Regent, who had far too many moods of not seeing why he could not really be quite happy at his dear Queluz even under French occupation. He was probably entirely right: he was of the stuff of which contented quislings rather than émigré governments are made.

In August 1806 there arrived in Lisbon a formidable British mission of investigation, under the leadership of Lord Rosslyn. With him were the redoubtable Admiral Lord St. Vincent and General Simcoe, with the young lawyer Henry Brougham as secretary. They were in Portugal to find out and report on the Portuguese situation: would Portugal put up a defence against the French when they came? was she in a state, military and naval, to do so? was it of any use to offer British help? They were charged to discover all this, and, further, to warn and convince the government that the French really did intend invasion. If defence seemed out of the question, they were to persuade or coerce the court to emigrate. Setting about their task, they came up against, first, an unconvincible incredulity about the French menace; the Prince Regent was sure he could appease the French and keep them off by the use of tact and a little obligingness; secondly, a profound reluctance to emigrate. Lord St. Vincent thought it a hopeless case. 'The reluctance to remove was universal and deep-rooted; nor could any arrangement the expected invader might offer prove less palatable than expatriation and banishment for life across the Atlantic to pampered voluptuaries the extent of whose excursions had hitherto been the distance between the town and the country palace.'

But the admiral, who had no notion of having a perfectly good British project defeated by pampered Portuguese obstinacy, went ahead with preparations for the Atlantic trip, enjoining the strictest secrecy on all concerned. His scheme had a fine and breath-taking naval simplicity. The Prince Regent had to go to Brazil; Britain had said so. Well then, go to Brazil he should, and if he wouldn't go for himself he must be taken forcibly by the navy. His scheme, as he outlined it to the rather startled Brougham, who had the caution of the lawyer rather than the dash of the navy, was to persuade the prince to pay a visit to the flagship *Hibernia*, then to sail off to Rio with him that same night, after he had been induced to issue a proclamation transferring the seat of government. The admiral felt no doubt that, great as the royal ill-humour and even indignation might be at first, yet a few hours' conversation would obtain this proclamation. His favourites would be sent for, including d'Aranjo if he cared to come, which he probably would not; as to the queen, her unfortunate mental condition would necessitate her being conveyed on board by night. Should the prince for any reason decline to enter the boat which should take him to the *Hibernia*, he would be forced; the admiral would take him by one arm, Sir Pultney Malcolm by the other, 'the men' would help, and the prince and his attendants would be on the boat in no time. Brougham asked if the prince should be invited to a collation on the *Hibernia*, as had occurred before. The admiral, who had his own ideas as to what was right, replied, 'Certainly not; for, considering what was intended, it might be thought contrary to good taste'. Brougham said that he conceived the plan to be so little grounded on good faith as to make this distinction something of a refinement. But the admiral said, that was as one happened to feel it.

Brougham says 'There could be little doubt that Lord St. Vincent had borrowed this plan from Cortes's seizure of the Emperor Montezuma'. When he put this to the admiral, he did not deny it, but said there were material differences, as there was in his project no treachery and no cruelty.

What would have been the effect on the international situation had this admirable kidnapping scheme been carried out we shall never know, since, for some reason not quite clear, it faded out; possibly on orders from London, or perhaps it failed to commend itself to Lord Rosslyn. Rosslyn reported to the Foreign Office in September that there were no grounds for expecting from the Portuguese any vigorous efforts in their own defence, that no British force it would be practicable to send out would stop a French invasion, and that any such force which arrived would excite terror and despair in government and populace. The British mission resolved itself into an intelligence inquiry into the state of Spain, whither it sent a number of spies, and into the imminence of the French attack. The squadron became a centre for a friendly and flourishing Anglo-Portuguese social life. 'We were in perpetual masquerade', St. Vincent wrote later to his brother, 'the whole time of our stay in the Tagus, not less than a thousand Portuguese on board the *Hibernia* every day; some days three or four thousand, nobles, priests, merchants, shopkeepers, farmers with their wives and families, piscadors, etc. etc.;

and what is more extraordinary, many of the clergy and some people of high rank came to our worship, and were struck with the solemnity of it, for the Prebend of York is dignified, expressive, and solemn in his manner, with a fine voice and excellent articulation. With these advantages, no wonder that he stole away the congregation from our ambassador's chapel, for Mr. Hill is a bad stick in the desk and pulpit . . . When this was reported to the old Patriarch (who is a great friend of mine, as is the Pope's Nuncio) he laughed, and said he must prohibit the ecclesiastics from our worship, as we should convert them to heresy. All the Ministers, both domestic and foreign, dined on board, except the Spanish and French . . . The nuns of several convents admitted me to conversations, one of them without the grille, and very beautiful two or three of them were: they sent me cakes, sweetmeats and toys, and seemed as if they wished to be amongst us. We certainly had their prayers, and I believe by the direction of the Patriarch, who considers me as the preserver of Portugal from French and Spanish bondage . . . I also engaged a box at the Opera, which franked the Captains and other principal officers . . . But these were necessary, though expensive appendages to an embassy extraordinary. I have every reason to believe that we had the blessings of the whole country, from the Prince Regent to the meanest peasant, on our leaving the Tagus.' There is indeed little doubt that the Prince Regent blessed the departure of these cordial, imposing and nagging visitors who so menaced his ease.

The squadron left the Tagus in October. Brougham remained. After visiting the north and starting an intelligence service from Oporto, he stayed for a time in Lisbon, waiting to be sent to Madrid. He was lonely and bored. 'To me who know nobody here' (and Strangford failed to introduce him) 'I assure you it is a *triste séjour*', he wrote to Lord Rosslyn. He did not take to Strangford, and demurred to Rosslyn's suggestion that he should put him *au fait* with their sources of intelligence. 'I would rather divulge it to another than Lord Strangford, who is somewhat too flighty and uncertain in his movements to gain my confidence.' He thought him very extravagant, too, in his payment of spies. He did his best (though Brougham's best was not likely to be particularly good) to maintain cordial relations; but by November 8th relations must have been something less than cordial.

'In conformity with your desire,' Brougham wrote to Rosslyn, 'I have very carefully and with no small labour and exertion of patience kept perfectly well with Strangford. This was necessary for public business; but I appeal to you, who know him, how difficult a thing it was. My temper has been tried perpetually by his infinite childishness in doing business, and indeed in doing everything else; and really, however unpleasant to say so, there is a defect about him which I can still less pardon than his want of common sense. I mean his *total want* of that first-rate quality which gives a man's words the right to be believed. I can scarcely express this more *delicately*. He has *on all subjects* the above disease, to a degree quite unexampled.

'However, let that pass. I have done my part of the business, and I am sure have humoured him in everything, to his merest caprices, and to his very heart's content. I only lament that the consequences of his character here are a total want of respect either from common society or from those he has to do business with. I don't wish to judge him harshly, but I can scarcely wonder at this, from what I know and see of him. Certainly he is not the man to change a ministry here. Pray discourage him from writing *loose* letters to you, for his silliness makes him brag of it everywhere, and so, I suppose, do his blackguard companions, to the great annoyance of one who has so real a respect and friendship for you as I have.'

The situation hinted at in the last sentence is cryptic; that is, it is not clear just what Strangford wrote loose letters to Lord Rosslyn about, what he and his blackguard companions bragged of, or how Rosslyn was involved: all that emerges is that Brougham disliked Strangford, and believed him to be a liar and to be generally despised in Lisbon. Knowing Brougham's temper, one would be rash to take this too literally; but, when weighing Strangford's later statements about his diplomatic exploits as against Napier's accusations, it may be borne in mind.

It does more credit to Brougham's self-control than to Strangford's perceptions that, five and twenty years later, Strangford alluded to the time when he and Brougham 'were brother secretaries together at the court of Lisbon, and lived together like Helen and Hermione'. He was a young man who believed himself liked.

1807 wore on, and so did the international war of nerves. The anti-British party among Portuguese courtiers and ministers too often gained the ascendant; Strangford had to use all his influence to make the poor prince see the light again. (His mother the queen, being mad, could see no light but that of the infernal fires which she knew from her confessor were awaiting her just round the corner. In a crisis, she was less than no good.) The French were for ever demanding the expulsion and expropriation of the British in Portugal. That was the last thing the prince had a mind to do; but sometimes, to appease the potential enemy, he came near promising it. He was induced at last to promise his royal brother of Great Britain that he would do no such thing, and also to declare that, should the French actually invade, he really would go with the court and government to Brazil. But when the news arrived on September 2nd that the invasion force had started on its way, still the prince would not agree to departure. 'During an interview of nearly an hour and a half', wrote Strangford, 'I employed every argument in my power to induce His Royal Highness to accept the only solution that can enable him to exist as an independent sovereign, and although I have not succeeded in persuading him to immediate adoption of it, still I trust that I have weakened his reluctance.' 'His Majesty's Government', he wrote a little later, 'need not be under any doubt respecting the intention of the Prince Regent. I am fully convinced that he has made up his mind as to the eventual necessity of retiring to South America.'

When a firm ultimatum arrived from Talleyrand that the British were to be expelled and their goods sequestered, the ports closed against their ships, and the British minister and consul given their passports, the Regent, terribly put about, characteristically saw nothing for it but to agree, and at the same time to make a secret convention with Britain transferring the royal seat to Brazil. Both his mentors thus, as he hoped, appeased, he began the dilatory equipment of a fleet, still greatly hoping not to have to go in it, and gave the English time to depart with their property if they wished before issuing the decree against them. He finally signed it with agonies of remorse, casting his pen from him five times before he could bring himself to use it. He then buried himself in the convent at Mafra, a prey to apprehension and regret, while his government seized British property and detained British persons. 'Il chassa les Anglais', recorded Mme Junot, with some glee. 'He ordered confiscations, he had the chief members of the English Factory arrested. All Buenos Ayres, the quarter of Lisbon where the English live, was a place of trouble and terror. The English fled. Lisbon seemed about to become a prey to horrible anarchy.'

The British minister, his king and country thus affronted, had the British arms removed from his residence, demanded his passports, and retired on to the flagship of the British squadron which had just arrived in the Tagus under Sir Sidney Smith. 'The conduct of this court', he observed, 'is marked by the strongest infatuation.' The government had been for some time desperately urging him to depart; d'Aranjo, the foreign minister, now wrote that His Royal Highness, to whom he had greatly endeared himself, lamented his absence and hoped it might be short. Strangford reached the *Hibernia* on November 18th, and suggested to Sir Sidney Smith that he should blockade the Tagus. A few days later, he determined on another visit to the palace, 'to represent to a misguided and unfortunate sovereign the peril of his present situation, and to point out to him in the plain and simple language of truth the only means of safety'. He wrote to request an audience under a flag of truce.

From this point in the drama, and indeed before this, there are four different versions of what happened, and of Lord Strangford's part in it. There is General Sir William Napier's version of it, as set out in his *History of the Peninsular War*, and in the bombardment of notes and counter-notes which he subsequently exchanged with Strangford about it; there is Strangford's version as given in his dispatches to the Foreign Office; there is his slightly modified and deflated version as given in his replies to Napier; and there is the lively and palpably largely imaginary version of Mme Junot, who, not being in Lisbon herself at the time, had it on hearsay. The Regent, according to her, became sunk in gloom and fear of assassination; he gave up hunting; he stayed at home. 'But he received visits to distract him. And whom do you suppose he received? The ambassador of England: yes, the ambassador of England, who had left Lisbon, but only for form's sake, and had been aboard an English fleet outside the bar beyond Belem. Every evening the ambassador landed and came to pay his court to the Prince of Brazil. One cannot imagine that he found it a great pleasure, but it was necessary to remove this family of Bragança to where Napoleon could not strike it except with anathemas. The conduct of the British ambassador was logical, if that of the prince was absurd ... One day the ambassador brought him the *Moniteur*; the unhappy prince read, "The house of Bragança has ceased to reign in Europe". "You see, sir", said the Englishman, "the usurper himself indicates to you the only means of safety which remains. Come to America!" The prince began to cry like a child. He ran to and fro like a poor madman in this palace which they told him to abandon and which he had never so much loved. Sometimes he went to the apartment of his mother, fell on his knees and asked for her blessing. But she repulsed him with fury, and cried in a bitter and sinister voice, "Al fuego! al fuego d'infierno! Todos a l'infierno!" And her frightened son fled from this septuagenarian mother who could only curse and blaspheme. He ran to his wife. There he found a new storm. "Behind me", she cried, tearing her dress with her hands. "Behind me! You are only a miserable coward!" And the unfortunate, thus rebuffed, was on the point of becoming as mad as his mother. At last he learnt that the advance guard of the French army had slept at Abrantes on the 22nd; he decided to depart, and on November 27th, 1807, all the Bragança family embarked on different ships ...' No one was ready. The Prince of Brazil arrived at Belem in a closed carriage, with his nephew, Don Pedro of Spain. He had received alarming reports from the police, and was afraid the people would oppose his departure. They took with them all the money of Portugal, most of the jewels. They took everything. And what did they leave? War (if anyone wished to make it), misery and shame. The prince had desired to wish his people good-bye, but he had been warned that they were in an ill humour and would make a bad response. So the poor fugitive determined to go alone to the port. Suddenly his remarkable head was recognized by people on the quays; his name ran from mouth to mouth, with curses. Police officers supported the trembling prince into the boat. Ancient respect prevented the people from showing their feelings, but these were evident. Then the queen and princesses and all the royal family arrived, each separately, and embarked in silence, except the queen, who, on descending from her carriage, had such a violent attack that she seemed about to expire. She refused obstinately to embark; they had to embark her by force. There followed the

Council of State and the ministers, and the chief noble families; about 13,800 people went. The disorder which always faithfully accompanies everything done in Portugal reached such a point that it became a burlesque.

Thus Mme Junot, who says she had it from her husband, who marched in at the head of the French invaders next day but one, in time to see the ships with the House of Bragança on board disappearing beyond the bar. Junot, who is represented by British historians as furious at the escape, is said by his wife to have been greatly relieved. 'Et qu'en aurais-je fait?' he said to her. 'We had enough of Ferdinand VII at Valencia. The emperor's will was to get rid of the Braganças.'

Lord Strangford's account of the events which led up to the royal embarkation, as he gave it in his dispatches at the time, is no doubt more (more, but not wholly) reliable. His dispatch dated from the flagship *Hibernia* on November 29th (but according to his enemies actually written later from London) relates the sequence of events as he wished them to appear. After a few days on the *Hibernia*, he resolved to go into Lisbon and propose to the government that they should either surrender their fleet to Britain or use it to sail for Brazil at once. 'I accordingly requested an audience of the Prince Regent . . . and proceeded to Lisbon on the 27th in H.M. ship *Confiance*, bearing a flag of truce. I had immediately most interesting communications with the court of Lisbon, the particulars of which shall be fully detailed in a future dispatch. It suffices to mention in this place that the Prince Regent wisely directed all his apprehensions to a French army, and all his hopes to an English fleet.' Strangford promised him the protection of a British squadron on his retreat from Lisbon and his voyage to Brazil. On November 29th, after the issue of a decree announcing the royal plans and appointing a regency to govern in Lisbon, the fleet left the Tagus, Strangford accompanying the prince over the bar, 'having resolved', as he wrote in a fuller dispatch on the 30th, 'not to lose sight of His Royal Highness until the Measure of Departure should be fully accomplished. And I have had much reason to be satisfied with this determination . . . everything depended on the degree of encouragement and consolation afforded to His Royal Highness, to whose mind it was continually necessary to present the Measure under the most agreeable and captivating forms'. The ambassador made it his object tactfully to 'destroy all hopes of accommodation with the invaders, terrify him with dark and gloomy descriptions of the capital which I had just left, and then dazzle him suddenly with the brilliant prospects before him . . .' 'I am convinced', he added, 'that I have entitled England to establish with the Brazils the relation of Sovereign and Subject, and to require obedience to be paid as the price of protection.'

It will be seen that Lord Strangford agreed with Mme Junot that the House of Bragança was emigrated mainly through his own assiduous diplomatic efforts. The British government was also convinced of this; a warm letter of thanks was sent to Strangford conveying his king's approbation of his valuable achievement, and he was honoured with the red ribbon. Next year he was sent, at the request of the Prince of Brazil, to be ambassador to the Portuguese court at Rio. After Napoleon's fall, his task was to persuade the prince that he had better now return to Lisbon; but John, whose line was always 'J'y suis, j'y reste', and who, now that he had got to Brazil, rather liked it, had had enough of crossing the Atlantic, and would not this time be persuaded to do so. Later, he fell out with Strangford over the slave trade, and asked for his recall. Strangford, a Foreign Office pet, was sent, with undiminished reputation, to Stockholm, to negotiate between Sweden and Denmark; for doing this so well he was much thanked by Castlereagh and sent to Constantinople. He wrote to his mother in elation of his 'late services in restoring tranquillity to the north of Europe . . . Blessed are the peacemakers! Diamond snuff-boxes and letters of thanks from the different sovereigns have poured in from all quarters, and certainly if I were a vain man the events of the last three months would have turned my head'.

All had gone well with him (except that he had married a woman who nagged the servants) from the days of his brilliant Lisbon début. He was known everywhere as the man who had saved the house of Bragança from French clutches. In 1808 someone wrote a tragedy in five acts on the subject of the emigration; it was called *The Fall of Portugal, or the Royal Exiles*. The British ambassador, Lord Montford, is the hero of this piece, Bellegarde, the French ambassador, plays the part of devil's advocate to the prince, who is transformed into a fine and resolute character —

> His soul on fire, and resolutely bent
> On emigration. Little did I think
> His placid, lamb-like spirit could assume
> The lion's port, and be at once the king.

Thus the disappointed Bellegarde. Then,

> Lord Montford comes,
> Ambassador from England; round him throng
> The raptured populace, whose voice proclaims him
> The true, th' unshaken friend of Portugal.

Lord Montford says,

> And lo! the naval power of Britain waits
> To bear ye to her bosom, from oppression
> The fair asylum of th'unfortunate,
> Or yield safe conduct to your Indian realms.

The Prince replies, very properly,

> The generous zeal of England warms our hearts.

Bellegarde, arriving on this scene, breaks out in rage,

> Your bias, Sir, towards your British friends,
> As you have deign'd to call them, is well known,
> And too well known your rancour to Napoleon,
> Whose deeds of greatness and propitious star
> Create him Europe's master, Europe's Lord.

Montford retorts,

> Bellegarde, thou wilt except one little Isle,
> That to the power of France disdains to yield,

and has the last word. The embarkation scene is not at all as Mme Junot has it, for the prince departs amid the loving plaudits of his people.

From a different angle, the *Gospel Magazine* (December 1807) approved Lord Strangford's feat, for

'The religious and discerning reader of the Bible will not lament the exportation of a family wedded to all the worst errors of popery, and whose subjects were on that account the most ignorant, the most crude and besotted in Christendom. He, setting political and momentary advantages aside, will rather rejoice that a more liberal system than the former will soon be introduced into Portugal. It is undeniable that, wherever the new French influence has prevailed, religious liberty has followed of course.'

Such were the agreeable plaudits among which Lord Strangford basked; had he been (as he remarked) a vain man, he would doubtless have enjoyed it. There were only a few captious dissentients who raised unimportant voices in periodicals, and whom Strangford ignored.

Then, in 1828, came a disconcerting broadside from General Sir William Napier, who published his *History of the War in the Peninsula*. Napier put the events of 1807 quite differently. The Prince Regent, he said, having, to please the French, made his attack on the British merchants, shut his ports against British ships, and dismissed the British minister from his court, was reluctant to leave, until the reception of a *Moniteur* dated November 13th announced in startling terms that 'the House of Bragança had ceased to reign'. Lord Strangford, whose previous efforts to make the royal family emigrate had entirely failed, had been then on board the British squadron, with the intention of returning to England. Admiral Sir Sidney Smith, however, had stepped in and threatened to attack Lisbon if the prince hesitated longer, and, thus menaced from the ocean by the admiral and from the land by the French, he embarked with his court and sailed for Brazil. Lord Strangford's dispatch, dated November 29th from the *Hibernia*, but actually written on December 19th in London, was so worded as to create a notion that it had been his exertions during November 27th and 28th that had precipitated the emigration, whereas actually the Prince Regent, yielding to the combined pressure of the admiral's threats and of the *Moniteur*, had embarked on the 27th, *before Lord Strangford reached Lisbon*, and sailed without having had an interview with that nobleman, who consequently had no opportunity either to advance or retard the event. The result, however, was that Lord Strangford had received the red ribbon and Sir Sidney Smith no honour at all, though it was owing to his vigorous negotiations that the emigration took place.

There ensued a fusillade of pamphlets. Strangford published *Observations on some passages in Colonel Napier's 'History of the War in the Peninsula'*. He disposed of Sir Sidney Smith's successful negotiations by commenting that the admiral's only communication with the Portuguese government had been one letter, written under Strangford's authority, proclaiming measures of hostility should the prince not depart. And the emigration had been decided on November 24th, before this letter was received. It was not the result of sudden alarm, but of many months of pressure on Strangford's part. The blockade of the Tagus had been his idea, not Sir Sidney's. When he had written from the *Hibernia* to ask for an audience, he had not known that the Prince had already embarked, though the reply to his letter told him this, and naturally he knew it when he left the *Hibernia*. He went to Lisbon to make sure that the voyage was really to take place, and to reassure the Prince Regent as to his relations with England. He arrived in Lisbon on the night of the 28th (having, as he had said truly in his dispatch, left the *Hibernia* on the 27th, for the winds were adverse), and almost immediately saw the Portuguese prime minister, who was already on board ship. He then proceeded to the Prince Regent's ship, and, notwithstanding Colonel Napier's assertion to the contrary, had a long and most confidential interview with him. 'His resolution to depart was irrevocably taken. It required no confirmation from me. I had then, as Colonel Napier states, no power either to advance or to retard the emigration. But when did I ever assume that I *had*? or take credit to myself for anything which passed at that last interview with His Royal Highness? . . . I have now sufficiently shown (1) that the emigration was *not* owing to the negotiations of Sir Sidney Smith, (2) that it *was* owing to a series of transactions and engagements between August 13th and November 17th. That I had some little share in these transactions was not only the belief of His Majesty's government, formed at the time from my dispatches and other contemporaneous information', but continued to be so when all the evidence had been considered. That his services might have been over-rated and over-paid, Lord Strangford was ready to admit. But he did not think it proper to claim, like Colonel Napier, the right of deciding whom his sovereign ought and ought not to honour.

To these observations Colonel Napier made a reply. His opinions, he said, were unchanged, as Lord Strangford had admitted most of his points and skilfully evaded others. He repeated his charges, supporting them by evidence from someone who had been informed by some Portuguese gentlemen who went with the court to Brazil how disgusted they had been at Rio when Strangford's account of the affair had appeared, and how exceedingly false they (the Portuguese gentlemen) had found it. The colonel compared the dispatch of November 29th with Strangford's account of the same events in his *Observations*, and found them noticeably different. 'I assert it again. A dispatch stating that Lord Strangford proceeded to Lisbon on the 27th and immediately had most interesting communications with the court of Lisbon, does not convey the idea that Lord Strangford arrived in the night of the 28th and saw the Prince Regent on board ship. This goes to the pith of the question.' 'It is clear as a Lisbon sun', said Napier, disagreeably, 'that this weak prince would have vacillated until Junot reached his palace, had not the *Moniteur* put an end to his hopes of mollifying the French, and Sir Sidney's vigorous negotiations put an end to his indolence. If therefore the red riband was a reward for inducing the splendid and magnanimous running away of the Prince Regent, it should be cut into three parts, one for Lord Strangford, one for Sir Sidney, one for the writer of the *Moniteur*.'

Strangford, grieved by this obdurate incredulity, issued *Further Observations*, repeating his denials and assertions. The Prince Regent, now said by Napier to have cast doubt in Rio on his account, had never done so while he had been in Brazil with him.

There the dispute had to be left. Strangford sought to bring a criminal libel suit against the editor of the *Sun* for saying, while commenting on the controversy, that his lordship 'would hardly be believed upon his oath, certainly not upon his honour at the Old Bailey'. It is interesting to note that the counsel for the defence was Lord Brougham, who justified the offensive passage by Lord Strangford's own admissions in the controversy. Possibly he remembered those months in Lisbon two and twenty years ago, and how the chargé d'affaires had seemed to him to have, on all subjects, to a degree quite unexampled, the total want of that first-rate quality which gives a man's words the right to be believed. The suit was dismissed.

Nevertheless, historians have sided with Strangford and against Napier, whose bias was apparent and whose charges were many of them unfair. Lockhart stated that Napier's accusations had been inaccurate and repelled. The British government upheld Strangford, and heaped on him continued honours. Club gossip took sides for and against him, according to their taste, judgment, and politics. He figures in later accounts — Fonblanque (whose narrative is wildly inaccurate) and Ruiz-Guiñazù — as the man who saved the Lisbon situation practically single-handed by his ceaseless persuasions. And indeed he deserves much credit for his diplomacy; it obviously cannot be dismissed as Napier dismisses it. All the same, and whatever the truth or the falsehood of the other assertions and counter-assertions may be, Napier was right on one essential point: Strangford's dispatch of November 29th did give a carefully false impression of the situation and of the part played in it at the last by its writer; 'and really', as Brougham had put it long before, 'however unpleasant to say so, there is a defect about him. . . .'

Strangford, after representing his country in successive important capitals, ended his days, as he had begun them, in literature.

BIBLIOGRAPHY

F.O. Portugal 63/ 47, 50, 51, 52, 55, 56 (Record Office).
Lord Strangford y la Revolucion de Mayo, ENRIQUE RUIZ-GUIÑAZU (1937).
Lives of the Lords Strangford, E.B. DE FONBLANQUE (1877).
Memoires, LAURE JUNOT, DUCHESSE D'ABRANTÉS (1831-4).
Souvenirs d'une ambassade et d'un séjour en Espagne et Portugal, LAURE JUNOT, DUCHESSE D'ABRANTÉS (1837).
Life and Times, LORD BROUGHAM (1871).
Memoirs of the Earl of St. Vincent, JEREDIAH TUCKER (1844).
History of the war in the Peninsula, SIR W. F. P. NAPIER (1828).
Observations on some passages in Colonel Napier's War in the Peninsula, VISCOUNT STRANGFORD (1828).
Further Observations, VISCOUNT STRANGFORD (1828).
A Reply to Lord Strangford's Observations, SIR W. F. P. NAPIER (1828).
Poems from the Portuguese of Luis de Camoens, VISCOUNT STRANGFORD (1803).
English Bards and Scotch Reviewers, LORD BYRON (1809).
La Litterature Portugaise en Angleterre à l'Époque Romantique, FÈLIX WALTER (1927).
The Fall of Portugal, or the Royal Exiles, J. WOOLCOT (1808).
The Gospel Magazine, December (1807).

2. THE WORRIED WHIG

Lord and Lady William Russell

[1832-1834]

ON May 23rd, 1832, when Dom Pedro's expeditionary fleet, laden with British and other volunteers, was within a week of sailing from the Azores to Portugal to depose the usurping

Miguel after his four years' escapade, the British Foreign Office issued to Lord William Russell instructions for the special mission on which he was being sent to Lisbon. With him were going two colonels, Badcock and Hare; these were to be observation officers, sent by Lord William about the country and into Spain to find out what the Spanish were up to and report if the troops they had massed near the frontier crossed it to assist Miguel against his brother. Palmerston's instructions were, watch the movements of Spanish troops; should they cross the frontier, immediately tell Admiral Parker, commanding His Majesty's squadron off the Tagus, and 'the Admiral will pass at once from a state of passive and impartial neutrality to active military co-operation with one of the contending parties'. Should this occur, Lord William and his staff were to embark on H.M. squadron and land at the nearest point to Dom Pedro's headquarters, where they should remain, offering him every assistance and advice. In the meantime, 'Your Lordship's known discretion renders it unnecessary for me to caution you against anything that might appear like partiality or interference in the political differences which divide the Portuguese nation', and he was to instruct the colonels also to this effect. As there was no accredited minister to Dom Miguel's government, any representations to it should be made through Mr. Hoppner the consul.

A delicate and tricky situation, and one calling for all his Lordship's known discretion. Lord William really had discretion, as well as a natural moderation and fairness, and great dislike of violence; in fact, Portugal during the war of the two brothers was scarcely the place for him. He was a sensitive man: he hated cruelty, he was shocked by injustice; he had a quality of gentleness rare in his profession, which was soldiering. The second son of the Duke of Bedford, he had fought through the Peninsular War, distinguished himself after it by his efficient command of a difficult Irish regiment, been Wellington's aide-de-camp in Paris and Cambrai from 1816 to 1818, married the brilliant, beautiful and dominating Elizabeth Rawdon, retired on half pay in 1828, and commenced diplomat in 1830, at the age of forty; it was possibly too late; the shocking conduct of foreign governments vexed and hurt him more deeply than if it had been from youth his task to deal with it. He was a true Russell Whig; 'at least as strong a Whig as Lord John' (his younger brother) 'and more nearly

Radical', it was said of him. He also, like Lord John, had the hampering Russell shyness; 'the predominant feature and organic deficiency of the Russell family is shyness', said Disraeli, much later; and one of Lord William's Berlin Legation remembered in his own old age that his chief had been 'so shy that when he came into a room he made every one else there shy too and conversation dried up. But all the same, he was a great man for making love to the ladies'. They made love to him too, it seems; the enthusiastic young daughter of the King of Wurtemburg (to which court he was sent after leaving Lisbon) used to push love letters to the attractive though middle-aged British envoy under his door. 'Lord William, with his demure look, is a gay deceiver', Lady Granville said of him in Paris in 1817. He was, apparently, a man whom every one liked, including Harriette Wilson, whom he met at the opera in his youth, and began to stammer humbly that he could not hope to deserve her, 'a poor little wretch without fortune or wit'. Harriette told him he was well-looking, well-bred, and high-born. 'I felt really desirous to encourage the most humble little gentlemanlike being I had ever met with.'

That was many years back; since then, Lord William had developed in confidence and firmness; he showed no diffidence in his brief Portuguese mission.

Embarking in the *Britannia*, Lord William and his two colonels arrived in the Tagus on June 9th. Dom Miguel, said Badcock, was all about the place, cruising up and down the Tagus in his yacht. Lord William, and his staff were officially quartered in a hotel; for himself and his wife and children, who were soon to follow him from England, the Quinta d'Amara in Junqueira was assigned as residence. The colonels put up at Reeves's. Lord William immediately waited, with Mr. Hoppner the consul, on Viscount Santarem, the 'shabby and miserable little new-made nobleman' who had succeeded the constitutionally minded Villa Real at the Foreign Office four years ago after Miguel had dissolved the Cortes, and of whom the *Times* correspondent in Lisbon had optimistically prophesied that he could not long 'withstand the contempt of Sir Frederick Lamb and all the foreign ministers'; however, here he still was. Lord William informed him of the views and instructions of the British government, and requested a passport for Colonel Badcock to go to the Spanish frontier. The arrival of Dom Pedro's expedition, he wrote to London, was expected daily; meanwhile, Lisbon was in a miserable state; the most respectable persons, including ladies, were hourly arrested and crammed into prisons already far too full. 'Were I to give your Lordship a description of the misery of this country, you would believe I was writing a romance . . . The whole system is compound of stupidity, imbecility and injustice . . . carried on with a degree of cruelty and contempt of the laws surpassing anything I ever heard of. The nights are employed in arresting the most respectable inhabitants, among them ladies of the greatest worth, and for no other reason than that of being respectable.' The arrests were made by the 'Royalist Volunteers', a gang of the dregs and scum of the populace, who beat their victims with large sticks; 'in short, this is the most odious of all tyrannies, a mob government'. 'Amidst the terror and abject mental slavery to which these people are reduced', it was difficult to get information as to the chances of Pedro's success; no one could be sure whether the army, for instance, would receive its lawful sovereign with shouts of joy or with bullets. The officers were mostly Miguelists; the soldiers had been accustomed always when constitutions were mooted to go about singing 'Give us five vintems a day and viva the Constitution; give us a vintem more and death to the Constitution'. Colonel Badcock, who spent a nervous few days on the Spanish frontier, suspected everywhere as a Pedro agent and greeted with anglophobe rage and shouts for Miguel, returned to Lisbon reporting that Spain seemed at present unlikely to invade.

Dom Pedro's expeditionary force, full of British volunteers, landed near Oporto in June; Lord William thought it should have been in Cascais Bay instead, but was optimistic about its quick victory — 'my belief is that very few shots will be fired'. His own position in Lisbon grew no easier; he fell out with the Portuguese government for allowing Admiral Parker's ships to be fired on from the tower of Belem as they entered the port; he showed that Britain's representative could get tough when affronted, and began to move from neutrality to something a good deal more like non-belligerency. He wanted His Majesty's government to interfere and shorten the war; he had now ceased to be optimistic about this; he foresaw that, unless Britain would take Portugal under her protection, as she had formerly been used to do, the country would become a desert, and English influence be completely destroyed. His Majesty should at once recognize Queen Maria. The state of the country was appalling, with mobs bursting open the prisons and massacring the political prisoners, monks doing violent religious propaganda among the army, the constitutional party cowed with fear. The ambassador's own house was daily filled with men beseeching him to save their lives. One word from England, and these victims would be delivered. The mass of the people, cowed by four years of cruelty, were 'more like sheep driven into a fold by a ferocious dog than human beings who can feel and reason, and it is painful to see mankind so degraded'.

It may have been the constant presence in her house of these unfortunate refugees that produced a cooling effect on the constitutionalist sympathies, perhaps never very ardent, of Lady William Russell. That intellectual, beautiful and strong-minded woman, bred and brought up in a brilliant circle of gay and intelligent people, used in girlhood to distinguished French émigrés, from whom she cannot have imbibed principles precisely democratic, for two years after her marriage living at Cambrai and Paris with Wellington and his mission, the centre of the newly restored French aristocratic society, in which the émigrés had come again to their own, had not even by the Russells or by Holland House been turned into a good Whig. Discounting Creevey's comment, 'she is a bitter Tory' (for Creevey disliked her), one must accept the implication of her eldest son's adjuration in her later life, 'My dear mother, when will you understand that the Russells are Whigs?' She was accused while at Lisbon of Miguelism; there was, it seems, a newspaper campaign against her both in London and, after the constitutionalists came to power, in Lisbon. Her friends acquitted her of this; but she had, if rumour is to be believed, her Miguelist moments; or rather, for she had too cultivated a mind to be Corcunda, apostolical or anti-liberal (though she became in later life a Roman Catholic) moments when she was definitely tired of frightened constitutionalists fleeing to William for refuge, moments when, possibly, she compared these cowed people with the courageous, cultured, witty émigrés she had known, and exclaimed impatiently, 'a plague on both your houses'. That she was kind to those in danger and trouble, independently of their politics, there is testimony from many witnesses; she urgently and repeatedly appealed to Miguel for the release of the mother of three young persons whose parents were imprisoned as constitutionalists, and so effectively that other such prison orphans thronged about her with similar petitions, and she established a reputation as mother-releaser that she was to sustain after Miguel was driven out and the imprisoned parents were of the other colour; according to a *Times* correspondent she interceded with Pedro for Lord Beresford's Viscountess Juramenha, at the request of that lady's children, gave her asylum, and sheltered her until she was shipped off to France. 'She has rescued others', wrote this correspondent, 'indifferent to their political sentiments, but beyond this has in no way meddled in the unhappy differences of Portugal. The discharge of her domestic duties and her literary pursuits have too great a hold upon her time to allow her to meddle with politics.'

This is as may be. It was not Lady William's reputation, this retired life of quiet domesticity, unheedful of politics. She had temptations; her beauty, her intellect, her lively intelligence, drew to her people of high position. Her husband had written of her three years before to his favourite brother, Lord John, 'In England you all treat Bessy as if she was an ordinary person. But on the continent she is treated like the most distinguished person in Europe, and, in fact, she is. Sovereigns, potentates, princes, ministers, men of letters, and simple individuals seek her acquaintance, and vie with each other to show her attention. Talents and virtue are more respected on the continent than in England'.

Lisbon under Miguel was a dull and cowed society; it gave Lady William's gifts little scope; there were few social gatherings; she, the Aurora of Byron's *Beppo*, 'whose bloom could after dancing dare the dawn', had been courted as a girl by everyone, commended always as the handsomest young woman present; 'the sweetest, to my fancy', said Monk Lewis, 'is Miss Rawdon, and she has wit, too, and sprightly humour. I wonder what coronet she will get to put upon her pretty head'. This, from Monk Lewis, who hated a blue and inveighed against learned woman, is high praise. There are hints that she was a trifle overwhelming: 'like the Tower of Babel', said Harriet Granville, who much liked and admired the beautiful young woman; 'tall, unbending, and gifted with tongues'. Lady Granville describes Lord William, looking 'quiet and pleased, but a little small between his accomplished bride and exigeante mother-in-law, who talks all the time as if Lady William was dead — "from the time I lost my poor Bessy",' etc. And now, grown into an ambassadress, 'really beautiful, grown into a very large woman, brighter and clearer than anything I ever saw', Lady William, hitherto surrounded with intellect, fashion and wit, found her lot cast among narrow-minded clericalist and absolutist fidalgos, a ridiculous and illiterate court, and nerve-ridden constitutionalists in terror of their lives. It was discouraging. She sought, no doubt, in her intellectual and digni- fied way, such consolations as offered themselves. Foremost, rumour said, among these was Señor Cordova, the handsome Spanish minister at Miguel's court; much trouble and scandal was to assault the Russells on account of this friendship later, after the expulsion of the Miguelites.

But at present their troubles were of other kinds. Lord William grew increasingly shocked at the goings-on in Lisbon. Papers by priests threatened a Sicilian Vespers in which no Pedroist, male or female, should be spared; in October Lord William's porter, a gentle and harmless Englishman, was murdered by police guards while on duty outside his master's house; there was no apology or punishment of the murderers, an inquest was refused, and the soldiers said it would not be the last English life taken. 'A pre- meditated insult to me', said Lord William, and called on Captain Hillyer to enter the Tagus with two ships of the squadron to pro- tect English lives. It was the sort of brutal outrage that made him furious; it was one of those bursts of anglophobia that caused Miguelists to see red, and rush murderously at any Englishman, however harmless, that they saw, as the Evora mobs had rushed at the young Tory Lord Porchester in 1828, and a fierce major at the mild Sir Augustus West to break his ribs, though, had the major known, Sir Augustus was court physician to Miguel and his mother and agent to Lord Beresford. It was enough that these gentlemen, and Lord William's poor porter, were Englishmen.

Impelled by compassion and rage, Lord William spent much time and ingenuity in rescuing hunted liberals and putting them on British ships. Here he was apt to fall foul of Admiral Parker, who was a bluff naval Tory. Lord William wrote to his brother John that he had had 'another violent breeze with the Admiral, for having put five poor devils on board Edward's ship. He is a great fool, and very injurious to English interests here. However, we are now the best friends in the world again. If I had such a man as Codrington here, I could knock this horrible Government on the head. Pray lend a favourable ear to Palmella and do all he wants, do a little wrong to do a great good; really your policy towards this country is not right'.

From the beginning of 1833 to the end of his mission, Russell's dispatches were a constant plea for British mediation; like Lord Falkland in another civil war, he ingeminated peace, peace, and desired to throw himself between the embattled sides. He wrote that there was a great desire in Lisbon for British intervention to place Maria on the throne. Many of the aristocracy supporting Miguel were now convinced that he would ruin Portugal: but against a tyranny with powers of life and death, the scaffold always at the ready, and police patrolling the city night and day, few expressions hostile to the government would be heard.

Probably Russell, with Whiggish hopefulness, under-estimated the fanatical fidelity to their cause of Miguel's supporters. The apparent popular desire for absolutism he put down to self-interest and fear. 'There is no doubt that the Constitution is ardently desired by the enlightened, though the mass of the people, guided by the clergy, is strongly opposed to it; but it is difficult while a state of terror exists to ascertain the real wishes of the people.' He surmised that three-quarters of the Lisbon citizens, mostly the wealthier and more industrious, were for the queen, but they remained trembling in their houses. Nor did Dom Pedro and his advisers inspire much confidence; the moderate party 'remain patient spectators of the contest, convinced that whichever faction wins, they will be the sufferers'. Indeed, Russell increasingly felt, as all Pedro's British supporters felt, and as all interveners in Iberian politics have felt, that the liberal side ran the risk of being sacrificed to jealous and petty intrigues.

Then, in July 1833, Charles Napier won his spectacular victory over the Miguelist fleet off Cape St. Vincent, the Duke of Terceira marched up through the Algarve and took over Lisbon from Miguel, ran up the blue and white flag on the fortress of St. George, and proclaimed Queen Maria da Gloria. His salute to the constitutional flag was returned by His Majesty's squadron in the Tagus: Great Britain had acknowledged the queen. The populace, said Russell, behaved with moderation, only killing a few of the more obnoxious royalists; at night there were illuminations and joy and bonfires of Miguelist furniture. But Bourmont's army was waiting outside the capital to attack. Russell wrote home suggesting that a British force be put on shore and Bourmont be warned that an attempt on the city would be taken as an act of aggression against Great Britain. To let Lisbon be re-taken with a passive British fleet looking on from the Tagus 'appears to me to be an act to which we could not submit without dishonour. I am most anxious to have further instructions from your Lordship on this subject'.

But Lisbon was not re-taken. On July 28th Dom Pedro of Bragança arrived in the Tagus with his government; he was received with immense joy.

Thus opened the constitutionalist regime that was so to discourage the good Whig after the detested years of tyranny. The administration became at once of a feverish activity 'neither directed by wisdom nor discretion'. The moderate Palmella was displaced; crude and sweeping reforms were made by peremptory decree; the Church was threatened with confiscations greater than it could bear; the clergy were given a handle for anti-government propaganda; national prejudices were flouted at a moment when every means should have been taken to unite people behind the constitution; Dom Pedro's advisers were hopelessly unfitted for their task.

Such as the new government was, the British ambassador was to be now accredited to it, after the interregnum of four years since Sir Frederick Lamb had handed his irate resignation to the usurping Miguel. On August 7th the Foreign Secretary wrote to Lord William Russell charging him with the special mission of re-opening diplomatic relations with Portugal, and 'treating of such other matters as may arise until the arrival of the Minister whom His Majesty may appoint as his permanent representative at the Court of Lisbon'. Russell wrote his thanks for being charged with this mission 'until a more efficient person shall replace me'. His dispatch and Palmerston's both leave it uncertain whether the decision to replace him was already taken, had been taken from the first, or whether it was not yet made. There may have been an exchange of letters off the official record. The suspension was generally considered to have been caused by indiscretion, the indiscretion of Lady William, against whose alleged Miguelist leanings a newspaper campaign was waged busily both in London and in Lisbon after the liberal occupation. The spiteful Princess Lieven put it maliciously in a letter to Lady Cowper that autumn: 'Lady William Russell took it into her head that Don Pedro's cause was not the right one, and, imagining perhaps that her husband's instructions gave her special privileges at the expense of your Government's proclaimed neutrality, she took the Miguelites under her protection in order to re-establish the balance, showing special favour to Mr. Cordova, the Spanish minister at the Court of Miguel. This Cordova is very handsome and intelligent. Her papers fell into the hands of the Pedroites at the taking of Lisbon, and among them were discovered little green and pink billets-doux which contained a mixture of politics, literature and other matters, addressed by Lady William to the Spanish Minister. She subsequently demanded leave to go into M. Bourmont's camp at Cintra, but the permission was refused, and she never went to pay her respects to Dona Maria. That is the whole story. It is the Hollands who are most excited about the affair, and since Lady Holland is the only one who has talked about the matter, omitting the amorous side of it which she condones, no harm has come of it, apart from her saying of Lady William that she thinks her imperious nature and love of domination very difficult to forgive. She finds these qualities unbecoming in a woman. Dearest, now we have settled Lady William's affair. You know, of course, that as a result of all this they are being sent to Stuttgart. . . .'

Some months earlier than this, apparently in August or September, Lord Brougham, that champion of interference, wrote privately to Lord Holland, 'I never saw anything so disgraceful as William Russell letting that cursed *woman* (I might give her another name) lead him by the nose in this way. Recalling him would be very painful; but at any rate Lord Anglesey should go, as you suggest, and then if he likes to stay William Russell should come home. I certainly should prefer his being recalled; but if he is virtually superseded it comes to the same thing and lets him down more gently. I have written to Lord Grey fully my mind on this; and except that his nature is always to have a prepossession against whatever anybody suggests, merely because they suggest it, I should hope he will do it'.

Whatever the facts about the recall, it is certain that there was high indignation among Lisbon liberals at the kindness shown by the Russells (and Admiral Parker) to the Miguelist refugees who now haunted their house and were entertained on British ships. Lord William, wrote Charles Napier (now a Portuguese admiral and in command of the Lisbon Arsenal) was known as a friend of liberty; 'his name alone was a guarantee for his principles'. But he was known also for his humanity; he would turn away no persecuted political refugee seeking asylum, and this impartial kindness made him enemies among the victim-hunting extremists. 'Lady William', said Napier, 'was supposed to lean the other way, and for no better reason than because she afforded occasional protection to a Miguelist who fancied himself in danger; but be it remembered that when Miguel's party ruled in Lisbon with an iron sceptre, and that red-hot, her house was always open for the protection of the unfortunate constitutionalists.' Napier's view of the ambassadress was endorsed both by Colonel Badcock and the *Times* correspondent who described her rescue of mothers, including the Viscountess Juramenha. He also cleared her of the imputation of not having waited on the young queen, which was current gossip against her. She was ill, said her defender, when the queen arrived in Lisbon, but the moment she could get about she waited on Her Majesty, as was the duty of the wife of a British minister. 'Though neither a Miguelite nor a constitutionalist, democrat nor fanatic, she hates tyranny and injustice, because she can feel for those who suffer oppression; it is hateful to her to see mothers torn from their children, and she, it is hoped, never will be deterred by any slander from interfering to prevent such cruelty. Women had better never meddle with politics, for they are generally mischievous when they do so; but they may be permitted to indulge in the performance of humane and generous acts. Are those brave and manly who attack an admirable lady? And, however valuable the freedom of the press truly is, it never can be permitted to malign the character of a distinguished female.'

So wrote 'A Lover of Truth and a Constitutional Liberal' from Lisbon. But there was no doubt that Lord William came under a cloud of suspicion in constitutionalist circles, partly through the embassy rescues, partly through the friendship of himself and his wife with the persecuted nobility in Lisbon, partly through his constant urging of moderation on Pedro's immoderate advisers and administrators. Here he was obeying the instructions of his government. His Majesty's government, Palmerston wrote to him, were sure that Queen Maria's government would never think of resorting when in power to the oppression and persecution of which they themselves had so loudly and so justly complained. There must, he urged, be a general amnesty, there must be moderate men in power, and nothing must be done to incite Spain to aggression; on this His Majesty's government had a right to insist, since if Spain did invade they were bound by treaty to send a protecting force. 'I will press on the government', Russell replied, 'the necessity of moderation.' And from that moment until his departure nine months later, he did not cease to do so; it naturally gave him, with the immoderate men who ruled in Lisbon, a reputation for lukewarmness in their cause. The foreign minister, in reply to his good advice, said quite so, but Portugal was full of abuses which must be cut away at once; after the first operations, things would proceed more quietly. Russell told him he regretted that not more of the aristocracy were in the government, as a guarantee that this important part of the community were not going to be oppressed.

While he thus pressed moderation on Dom Pedro, the envoy pressed on his own government, still more urgently, mediation or intervention to end the war. Neither pressure was effective. Dom Pedro's government would not be moderate, King William's clung to strict non-intervention unless Spain should invade.

Meanwhile, Bourmont's army lay at Santarem; the ravages of his troops were shocking; Lisbon was threatened again. Admiral Parker had arranged to embark British merchants if it should be taken; the inhabitants of the country round were fleeing into the city with their goods; everywhere the priests and monks were rousing the populace for Miguel. British merchants so far forgot themselves as to take sides in demonstrations for the queen; the ambassador sent the consul a letter to read to them, 'to recall them to a proper sense of the conduct that became them, and from which they had widely departed'. He told them that, under the protection of neutrality, they must not publicly take sides and embarrass their ambassador and endanger British property. The merchants replied that they were surprised at such a charge, having always been congratulated by Mr. Hoppner the consul on their remarkable neutrality. But then Mr. Hoppner was, Lord William wrote to Lord John, something of a *sanguinaire sans-culotte*, who had been rather mistakenly placed in Lisbon at this crisis. With his own campaign for moderation, conciliation and toleration as the only road to unity and peace, the only way to secure the allegiance of the wavering and uneasy Lisbon nobility to the unrelenting Pedro, Mr. Hoppner, though he loyally co-operated, had no great sympathy, nor had the British merchants. Many noblemen, rebuffed and confiscated, left Lisbon and joined Miguel; the British consul thought them a good riddance.

It was a tense time. 'Bourmont', wrote Charles Greville in London, 'is marching on Lisbon with 18,000 men; *regna il terror nella città*. William Russell, in a fit of enthusiasm, says the capital must be saved even at the cost of a war. Admiral Parker says he shall land 1200 marines and make them occupy the forts. Our government are in great confusion and alarm, and have dispatched a swift steamer to Parker to desire him to do no such thing; but the steamer will probably arrive too late, and if Bourmont is really there we shall cut a pretty figure with our non-intervention, for Parker will probably have to surrender the forts to Miguel ... Pedro has committed since he was in Lisbon every folly and atrocity he could squeeze into so small a space of time; imprisoning, confiscating, granting monopolies, attacking the Church, putting forth the Constitution in its most offensive shape. I suspect we shall have made a sad mess of this business.'

So Lord William was thinking. Bourmont was driven back from Lisbon in September, and the situation in the capital became easier. But the war did not grow less savage. It worked on Russell's humane and sensitive mind with cruel insistence; he could think of little but how to stop it. He sent Colonel Hare to Bourmont's headquarters with a letter proposing its end. 'J'ose espérer que le moment de terminer cette affreuse guerre soit arrivé.' General Bourmont replied that it had not arrived, since the majority of Portugal was for Miguel. In his camp, any officer who suggested negotiation was punished.

In September the *Lord of the Isles*, a large steamer from Britain, entered S. Martinho and disembarked a horde of foreign officers talking Spanish, French and English and inquiring for Miguel; among them was the redoubtable British Miguelist naval officer, Captain Elliot. The Foreign Minister in Lisbon called it, as well he might, a foreign invasion, and told the British ambassador that it gave the queen a right to claim help from Great Britain; 'he asks me', wrote Russell, 'to tell you of the Regent's hope for it'.

Russell hoped for it too. 'The war is now carried on by foreigners for general principles, or for non-Portuguese interests, consequently I think the government should receive His Majesty's support.' But His Majesty's government was firm; the war must not be spread by any British action.

On September 23rd the young Queen Maria arrived in Lisbon 'amidst the shouts of her delighted subjects', who dressed up in their blue and white favours and hurried to the court to congratulate her. The British envoy had an early audience; he liked the plump little queen, and saw in her the one hope for a united Portugal.

Meanwhile his Miguelist countrymen were behaving vexatiously and giving him trouble. One of the passengers who had arrived on the *Lord of the Isles*, suspected of being an agent of Captain Elliot's and spying for the enemy, was arrested by order of Sir Charles Napier, now commanding the Arsenal as a Portuguese admiral, and sent to prison. Russell, learning of the outrage, 'took fire', as Napier put it, and when this humane Whig took fire, he blazed. In his view the very roots of British privilege were struck at; he wrote to the Foreign Minister asserting that Admiral Cape St. Vincent had no right of arrest over British subjects; the Foreign Minister did not concede this point, but released the prisoner and sent him out of Portugal. Napier thought the ambassador quite wrong; Russell thought the admiral dangerously irresponsible, as indeed he always was. He himself was nothing if not constitutional.

But he did not see his way to interfering on behalf of Sir John Campbell, a British Miguelist officer who had been captured at sea in a British merchant schooner carrying on him enemy dispatches, and imprisoned in St. George's castle, from whence he wrote long and eloquent letters of appeal to his country's representative, complaining that he had been kidnapped from a British ship on the high seas. 'I cannot submit to injustice . . . I trust to the high feeling of a British nobleman and a British officer.'

Russell answered his passionate appeals with judicial care and not without kindness. The legal case was being decided (ultimately against the prisoner) by crown lawyers in England; meanwhile he advised the Portuguese government to set Sir John free on bail. They refused. 'Sir John Campbell is known as one of our most active enemies; he fell into our hands leaving a blockaded port, charged with dispatches from Viscount Santarem.' 'You may', Russell mildly suggested to Sir John, 'find this argument not unreasonable.'

Himself he found it reasonable enough. Possibly too he found it inadvisable to insist on the liberation of yet another British Miguelist; constitutionalists were suspicious people, and the Russells were suspect. They suffered, said Colonel Badcock, from being impartially kind to all sides. A rumour had started, said he, that Lord William was to be recalled and Lord Howard de Walden sent out in his place. 'The truth was', added the colonel, who admired the ambassador and his lady greatly, 'that Lord William Russell, one of the most humble and kind-hearted of men, could not, in his neutral position, please everybody: and if anyone went nineteen steps with a party and did not take the twentieth, he was considered an enemy to the cause. It was impossible for an individual to be placed in a more awkward situation than he was continually; and I know no one that would get so well through the innumerable difficulties with which he had to contend. The Legation was kept up in the best style possible, and persons of all rank of all parties were invited. Lady William Russell had also her share of enemies. This highly talented and accomplished lady, who did the honours of her station with great *éclat*, and in the most charming manner, was disliked by some people because the goodness of her heart made her feel for the misfortunes of all, and do acts of kindness to those who differed from her politically.'

It was true that Lady William had her share of enemies; but it does not seem invariably to have been on account of the goodness of her heart. Creevey, for instance, meeting her at dinner soon after the Russells' return from Portugal, wrote crossly, 'I have never seen a woman that I hate so much as Lady William Russell, without knowing her or ever having exchanged a word with her. There is a pretension, presumption, and a laying down the law about her that are quite insufferable. Then her base ingratitude to those who formerly fed and clothed her — Fanny Brandling, the Fawkses and others — sinks her still lower in my hatred of her'.

It looks as if Creevey had been snubbed. Possibly Lady William, with whom he had not 'exchanged a word', had neglected him for Rogers, who was also present; perhaps she had been too highbrow for female propriety, for her conversation, wrote an admiring friend after her death, revealed a familiarity with classic thought and 'to Cicero, Thucydides, Euripides, and other masters of thought and style, she ever turned with unfailing pleasure'. This friend however added that 'with all these rare attainments, no kind of pedantry or superiority was ever present'.

However this may have been, and it is obvious that Lovell Badcock, a gay colonel of Hussars with an eye for handsome ladies but no particular partiality for bluestockings, admired and liked her very much, Lady William, as well as her husband, whom no one ever disliked personally, came in for a good deal of criticism in Lisbon. They did shelter and befriend suspicious characters, and try to protect the constitutional aristocracy from the persecutions of the democratic party, receiving them on British ships. There was, wrote Russell, a long-festering wound in the constitutionalist ranks; it broke out in collisions between the aristocratic and democratic principles. Russell, a constitutionalist aristocrat, saw that such collisions must end in disaster. So indeed, in his view, must most of the measures of the present government. Everything they did was foolish: they abolished tithes without making any provision for the parish priests, already ill enough disposed towards them, and now thrown on the charity of their parishioners and stirring them up still more assiduously and successfully for Miguel; they dissolved convents, alienated moderates who might, given a chance, have come round to their cause, managed finance with the usual idiocy; they could scarcely, in so brief a time, have done worse. This, thought Russell, was no way to end the war. He himself carried on a constant and vain campaign for an armistice.

He sent to the Foreign Office on December 20th a pessimistic summary of the prospects and situation. 'A retrospective view of the state of Portugal shows us seventeen months of barbarous and vindictive civil war destroying the resources of a country previously impoverished by bad government. The prospective view shows us the Belligerents in a formidable attitude without apparent means of putting an end to the war by force of arms: and even the complete triumph of either party presents nothing but the prospect of Confiscation, Persecution and Bloodshed, leading rapidly to another Revolution. The Rival Brothers have placed themselves at the head of the extreme factions of the nation: both parties so intent on revenging themselves for the evils they have suffered, that the real interests of Portugal are lost sight of in the deadly hatred that animates the combatants. One Party proclaims Religion as its device, and outrages all its precepts' (Lord William himself was a truly religious man) 'the other invokes Liberty, and all its acts are despotic. It is evident that neither of these parties will ever yield to the other; or if forced to yield for the moment, it will only be to again collect its strength and renew the struggle; therefore the state and prospects of Portugal give no hope of permanent tranquillity, or of establishing the throne of the Queen on a solid foundation.' What with the Carlists too, the whole peninsula might be involved in anarchy and a struggle of Principle that would endanger the peace of Europe.

This dispatch was taken to England by a Portuguese messenger who was charged by the Regent to ask England's aid.

Meanwhile, Russell devoted himself to his two improbable aims — the fusion of the aristocratic and democratic parties in one ministry, and the mediation of England and Spain. On this he wrote a personal letter to Palmerston. 'If you object to sending troops (to which there are grave objections), why not an *armed mediation*? Assemble a force in Ireland, and let the Spanish assemble a force on the frontier, and then dictate peace to both parties. I see no other way of getting out of this mess. Really I am ashamed of my own cause, for we have got rid of one despotism to set up another, which I bore patiently as long as I saw a prospect of having the Constitution, but now it is very distant. Miguel will wear these people out, and their own follies and vices will be their ruin. I am still at work to make a fusion of parties, but the difficulties are immense . . . I hope Lord Howard will be able to manage better than I have done. I have worked incessantly to obtain Peace, and shall leave War. I found a despotism, and I shall leave a despotism, and little prospect of peace or good government unless you take things into your own hands.'

On December 28th he wrote that he expected Lord Howard any day, and that this might be his last dispatch, so he described again at some length the dismal state of Portugal and the provenance and arrangement of its parties. The two parties, he said, were nearly equal, 'one drawing its strength from fanaticism, the other from an ardent desire to reform abuse and improve the country by free institutions'. But while extraordinary unity held the absolutists, the friends of freedom were weakened by dissension; the party in power wanted to cut out abuses by the roots at once, while those not in the ministry thought reform should be gradual; one was the aristocratic, the other the democratic party, and they had already sown the seeds of deadly feud; there would be another revolution before any government could have permanent security. England should interfere, and at once.

There was a touching faith and optimism in Lord William's endeavours. His letters, and the Portuguese struggle as observed by liberalism in England, so worked on Lord Grey that in January 1834 he resigned the premiership because he could not persuade the Cabinet to send an expedition to Portugal to give Miguel the *coup de grâce*. He was persuaded by king and cabinet to resume power, and the incident passed without public knowledge.

Neither an armed expedition nor a mediating body was sent to Portugal. 1834 began; Russell's mission was nearing its end. He began the year by attempting mediation between the turbulent English chaplain Mr. Seeley and his quarrelsome flock; Russell proposed that the clergyman should be sent to England and ex-.changed for another. 'I see no hope of reconciling the clergyman and the merchants.' It was a business as hopeless as, but more easily settled than, the larger quarrels that he tried to reconcile. These grew no milder. Russell was still writing home about armed mediation when, on February 14th, Lord Howard de Walden arrived, bringing Russell's letter of recall, which expressed His Majesty's approbation of his conduct in Portugal and appointed him to Wurtemburg. Having paid his farewells, been entertained at a good-bye dinner, refused a box of gold bars from the government, and had a rest at Cintra, Lord William sailed from Lisbon at the beginning of April 1834, stopping at Vigo to visit Napier, who was enjoyably riding a vicious pony about the north and capturing towns as it were by telephone.

Russell may have been glad to leave his thankless post to someone else. His successor found it as depressing as he had. 'Howard', wrote Greville, on April 3rd, 'writes from Lisbon, disgusted with the men he has to deal with. . . .' On June 5th, 'Lord William Russell told me he did not think Pedro would be able to keep possession of the country, and that another revolution would probably take place whenever the Foreign Troops in his pay were disbanded; the party against him is too strong . . . The country is in a dreadfully ruined state'.

The Russells were well out of Portugal, even though Lisbon is a more attractive city than Stuttgart. The acrimonious disputes which Peninsular civil wars seem to engender, even in onlookers, continued to rage in London round the late ambassador, his wife, and Admiral Parker, who had, it was said, received on his ship refugees from Pedro, having refused refugees from Miguel, and had taken Count Taipa to a ball. The ambassador had been too neutral. His defenders maintained that he had been scrupulously obedient to his instructions, and that whatever he had done he would have been abused; while, as to the interference of Lady William, 'who has so often been accused by a part of the public press, I do not believe that it ever existed but in the heated imaginations of those who propagated the report'. The imagination of Lady Holland having, it seems, been somewhat heated on the subject, a quarrel and coldness ensued between her and Lady William.

However, the Russells departed presently for Wurtemburg. Meeting them at Baden-Baden next year, the irritable Princess Lieven, herself in a state of egotistical fury with the universe, made the inept comment, 'Oh! if only I had something to distract my mind! The William Russells are here, but they are no use to me. They are as kind as possible, but that is not enough — they have no ideas or intelligence'. It is fair to add that this was a passing mood; later the Russells were 'friends of the right sort', though she was, naturally, pleased to hear that 'dear William Russell' had temporarily eloped with a Jewess. For her part she preferred men to women; she admitted Lady William to be 'fairly clever', but added 'I will tell you who has ten times more esprit, and that is Lord William'.

From Stuttgart Lord William went to Berlin. 'I have no doubt', wrote Lord Grey, 'he will do very well there.' Better, possibly, than coping with the impossible brothers in Portugal, though in Berlin this good Whig would find other worries — no constitution, an autocratic, though well-meaning monarch, and a discouraging *Demagogenhetzerei*.

It is perhaps worth quoting a few more contemporary judgments on these two. There is no doubt that some people liked Lady William and some did not; opinions ranged from Creevey's 'never saw a woman that I hate so much' and Lady Holland's accusations of selfishness and coldness, to the paean of enthusiasm uttered by a friend after her death in 1874 — 'the attraction of a lively fancy, varied literary knowledge, a tone of conversation which revealed a familiarity with classic thought, together with a charm of manner peculiar to herself. Although *grande dame* if ever there was one, she put her visitors at their ease, and did the honours of the salon with grace and cordiality. The company of learned men was always agreeable to her'. She held her salon in Audley Square, and knew, says Locker-Lampson, 'every one whom other people would have liked to know'. Queen Victoria used to visit her, though she herself would never go to court after the insulting treatment of her cousin, Lady Flora Hastings. The young Prince of Wales too used to come in after dinner; very creditable to him, thought Lady William's French daughter-in-law, for the company he met there was sufficiently *sérieux*. It has been surmised that the young man was sent to Audley Square by his parents to improve his mind.

On Lord William few adverse comments have survived. As Creevey once observed, he was 'quite what a Russell ought to be'. Charles Greville, who thought rather less well of Russells, for they were too radical for him, criticized William for not resigning from the Berlin embassy in 1841, when the Tories came in, for 'with his violent politics and his bitterness against, and abuse of, the present Government, he ought not to have thought of staying there'. But 'the place suited his finances, and was convenient for his amour with Mme de Heber'.

Nearly twenty years before this, young Henry Fox had written of Lord William and his wife, when they were guests at Holland House, 'She is totally unlike anyone else I know. Her expressions are very peculiar and well chosen; she is accused by many' (the accusers included his mother) 'of coldness and want of heart, I believe unjustly. She is certainly fond of William and of her delightful child. William is in my opinion by far the most amiable of the Russells; there is a warmth of heart and tenderness of manner that is delightful, nor is he at all deficient in understanding. His admiration and love for her is just and great as it ought to be'.

This civilized, sensitive, humane and just man, set to deal with *les frères ennemis* and the savage business of civil war in the Peninsula, a situation that he was convinced it was a country's duty to end, if need be by force, became perhaps more eager for strong action than was convenient or discreet. Through his dispatches runs a heightening note of tension; possibly his government agreed with Lord Brougham's comment, that it was in his family to do rash things.

BIBLIOGRAPHY

F.O. Portugal 63/ 384, 398, 399, 400, 401, 402, 416 (Record Office).
Rough Leaves from a Journal kept in Spain and Portugal, LT.-COL. LOVELL BADCOCK (1835).
The Times (April and September 1828, December 1833, January and February, 1834).
Life and Letters of Admiral Sir Charles Napier, H. N. WILLIAMS (1917).
Account of the War of Succession in Portugal, SIR CHARLES NAPIER (1836).
Memoirs, CHARLES GREVILLE (August 24th, 1833, April 3rd, June 5th, 1834, December 15th, 1841).
The Lieven-Palmerston Correspondence, edited LORD SUDLEY (1943).
Creevey Papers, edited SIR HERBERT MAXWELL (1903).
Chronicles of Holland House, EARL OF ILCHESTER (1937).
Correspondence of Princess Lieven and Earl Grey, G. LE STRANGE (1890).
Journal of the Hon. Henry Edward Fox, EARL OF ILCHESTER (1923).
Life and Times, LORD BROUGHAM (1871).
Memoir of Lady William Russell, MRS. HARVEY (1874).
Memoirs, HARRIETTE WILSON (1825).
Life of Lord John Russell, SPENCER WALPOLE (1889).
Early correspondence of Lord John Russell, ROLLO RUSSELL (1913).
Diary of a Lady in Waiting, LADY CHARLOTTE BURY (1920).
Letters of Harriet Countess Granville 1810-45, F. LEVESON GOWER (1894).
Lord Grey of the Reform Bill, G. M. TREVELYAN (1920).
My Confidences, F. J. LOCKER-LAMPSON (1891).
Elizabeth Lady Holland to her son, EARL OF ILCHESTER (1946).

LEARNED CONSUL

John Whitehead
[1756-1805]

JOHN WHITEHEAD was British consul in Oporto for close on fifty years. His consular career began in the stormy days of the formation of the Altô Douro Wine Company, when the Oporto taverners and the British wine shippers alike rose in rebellion against this intolerable grievance. The shippers sent impassioned memorials to the Portuguese government, to the British envoy in Lisbon, to Mr. Pitt in London, to everyone, declaring themselves outraged and ruined, their treaties set at naught, by this upstart company which had been set up by a malicious anti-British minister to destroy their trade. In all their protests and memorials, the shippers and merchants were valiantly led by their consul, a philosophical, eccentric and absent-minded scholar, who remained personally calm while presenting these fiery memorials for his countrymen.

Mr. Whitehead was not a man of heat. The chief distinction of his consular career was that he designed the magnificent British Factory House and superintended its building; it was opened in 1790; Mr. Whitehead's portrait, wearing a brown wig, hangs in the noble dining-room. He piloted his indomitable and vociferous Factory through an eventful half century, and died in his job two years before the French occupation.

All this we know of him in his consular capacity. But an unusually vivid and lifelike portrait of him as a man was given by Captain Arthur Costigan who, with his companion Lord Freeman, stayed with him when he visited Oporto in 1778. Costigan greatly enjoyed the jolly Oporto company and good Christmas fare, after the hardships of travelling up from Algarve and stopping at wretched Portuguese hostels. Lord Freeman's French valet in particular had been lavish in his curses on the country and its fare. But once in Oporto, the Christmas pies, fat turkeys, fine sirloins, jellies and creams, cheered them all up. They admired the affluent style in which the foreign merchants, and especially the British, who were by far the most numerous, lived, and the natives followed their good example.

The visitors were asked out to dinners and assemblies all the time, but, said Captain Costigan, they would scarcely have missed if they had not been so invited, for 'we possess so extraordinary and valuable a landlord as the Gentleman who insisted on our taking up our residence in his house, who is no other than the British Consul here, and the most entertaining companion I have met with anywhere'. Unlike the consul at Faro, who had been dumb, morose and pensive, Mr. Whitehead was 'versatile, sprightly and communicative in the highest degree, and has a wonderful skill in adapting himself to all companies and languages he happens to meet with'. Whereas the Faro consul had passed his time in the counting-house among his clerks, and in attending to a large family of children, 'his colleague of Porto, living in a very large house, has no Counting-House nor family to mind, and though far enough from being a young man, is still a bachelor'. He owned a fine library, of which he gave his guests the freedom; John Carlos, the young Portuguese ordinand who was Costigan's guide and interpreter, could scarcely be torn from it.

Young Lord Freeman asked the consul if he might borrow a Bible. 'The Consul stared, and told him it was really one of the last requests he expected to be made him by an English officer. However, he carried us to a long shelf, where we found copies of almost all the editions which have been printed, from Cardinal Ximenes's Complutensian Polyglot down to Dean Ryder's Family Bible. Lord Freeman said he was already pretty well acquainted with that invaluable book, but as his young companion John Carlos had never seen one, he was willing to introduce it to his acquaintance. There was something humorous and sarcastic in the very arrangement of the consul's books. On the same shelf with the Bibles were to be found translations of the Koran, and *Le Système de la Nature*, with Bryant's *Antient Mythology* and Gebelin's *Monde Primitif*. On another shelf was *Don Quixote*, neighboured by *Saint Ignatius of Loyola* and Bunyan's *Holy War*, and a voluminous *Life of Saint Iago of Spain*; 'among several volumes of the absurd and unintelligible jargon of the Thomists and Scotists and other schoolmen' (the Captain was, it seems, no Thomist, whatever the consul may have been) there were mixed Dr. Beattie's *Essay on Truth* and Locke's *Essay on the Human understanding*; Spanish and Portuguese Lenten and missionary sermons were contrasted with the works of Bishop Tillotson and other protestants; Hume's essays stood next to St. Austin, and 'the fiery and impatient Martin Luther' to the 'zealous and declaiming Cardinal Baronius'. In fact, the consul had an excellent theological library, which no doubt was of assistance to the chaplain, the Reverend Herbert Hill, also a great reader.

Besides these, the consul had an admirable collection of books on the arts and sciences, particularly mathematics, in which he was an ingenious theorist and dabbler; he had a manuscript collection of his own problems and theorems, and two huge terrestrial and celestial globes, on which he was constantly at work making alterations in the light of modern science and discoveries, marking in the currents, Pacific islands, and heavenly bodies. He had an observatory platform (from which he had seen Venus in the morning above the sun, with one side illuminated like a beautiful ivory ball); he had microscopes, a camera obscura, and an apparatus for electrical experiments which had convinced the neighbouring priests and people that he was a magician who, with the Devil's help, drew the thunderbolts down into his garden, and brought on him two visits from the Commissaries of the Coimbra Inquisition; but these gentlemen, 'comparing the Consul's established virtuous character with such a black accusation, could not help thinking it absurd; and, what was perhaps no less fortunate for the Consul, their visits happened at a time when the Inquisition, being entirely under the control of the Marquis of Pombal, durst not take any step without his express permission; the Consul received their visits respectfully, entertained them very politely, and, explaining to them the whole process of his experiments, the nature and qualities of fire, in a philosophical manner, but in terms they readily comprehended, he sent them away perfectly well satisfied, and enraged at the ridiculous accusations of their ignorant countrymen'.

The consul, wrote Costigan, was a most uncommon character. When young he had been in business in London, but the attractions of a life of dissipation in the metropolis had more charms for his youth; he decided that 'the universality of his genius was not to be limited by the trammels of commerce, of which he retained only what is necessary for executing the office of Consul, and at the same time that he discharged it with all the punctuality and care of a man of honour, it leaves him sufficient time to follow the bent of his own natural genius and inclination'. He was certainly an excellent host, and devoted himself to improving the education of John Carlos in the higher mathematics, for which the young man showed astonishing aptitude. Leaving his zealous pupil in the library, the consul spent his days showing the sights of the city and country to his other guests. He took them walking about the steep streets, showed them the grand new convents and churches, where he was on the most cordial terms with the friars, and explained to the inquiring Lord Freeman as they walked the history of the doctrine of the Immaculate Conception. 'To walk much about this city', says Costigan, 'is, I assure you, rather a violent exercise, not one street in it being upon a level excepting that where the most part of the English inhabit.' The consul, undaunted by this physical exertion, accompanied it by theological and historical discourses and stories of Portuguese life that enthralled his audience and kept young Lord Freeman from brooding over the absence of a letter from his mistress. Indeed, their host was a mine of entertaining stories, as they rode about the country together, visiting Braga, Guimaraens, and an old friend of the consul's, a jovial canon, who had picked up from the English the conviviality of the bottle, and proudly introduced them to his daughter, with 'She is of my own making, Gentlemen, what do you think of her? It is true I was never married' (said the good old fellow, laughing) '*sed homo sum, et nihil humani a me alienum puto*; I am obliged to call her my niece here, among these hypocritical people, and she has four brothers, all stout young fellows, three of them are now abroad serving their King and Country, and I intend renouncing my stall in favour of the fourth'. Here the consul observed to the canon that he was persuaded he had no occasion to apologize to the company present for producing creditable and useful subjects to the state, which was, he thought, 'the duty of every good citizen'. The good canon proceeded to lament the mad and most unfortunate celibacy decrees, and to inform his sympathetic audience how much the interests and cares of paternity had improved his character.

Lord Freeman said he had never heard a churchman in the country utter so much sterling good sense before, and the canon's daughter wept, overcome with filial affection and gratitude. 'It was a scene truly affecting; I loved it, and at the same time wished to get out of it. The Consul made a motion to go to rest, and we all supported him.' After they had left this touching scene of family life, the consul told his friends that he had educated the

canon's daughter in English, and that she had read many English
books which her father would have forbidden her had he known
of it, for, though otherwise a man of sense, his mind was so be-
wildered and stuffed with saints, miracles and hocus-pocuses
that there was no talking with him on it.

As they rode from Braga to Guimaraens, the consul was lost in
dreams of a proposition that he had propounded, concerning an
ellipse and a spherical triangle, which neither he nor his friend
and fellow mathematician the Scotch physician in Porto had been
able yet to solve. He rode with his reins dropped on his mule's
neck, pencil and paper in hand, wrapped in a profound reverie,
till the mule stumbled and came down, throwing its rider over its
head into the mud, where he lay still lost in thought while his
mule quietly reposed. 'Damn it all,' remarked the consul presently, realizing the situation, 'I believe my villainous Rozinante
has thrown me.'

Getting back to Porto, the consul sent out notes to some friends
to come to supper, since it was the last night before his visitors set
out for Lisbon. After dinner, they all retired for a siesta, weary
after their long ride. But the consul happened to catch sight of the
paper with his design of the ellipse and triangle, and immediately
again became absorbed; instead of going to his siesta, he went out
to see his friend the Scotch physician, with whom he was wont to
have prolonged sessions and hot altercations on such topics. The
two gentlemen discussed the matter until nine of the evening,
when the doctor's lady summoned him to the tea-table and the
consul went home, his head full of calculations, to find a company
assembled for supper whom he had not the smallest recollection of
inviting. Indeed, there would have been no supper for them to
eat, for the consul had given no orders to his housekeeper, but that
his sister, a married lady living in the city, had got wind of
the situation in time and sent in food and servants from her own
house.

Next day Costigan and Lord Freeman set off for Lisbon, the
consul seeing them on their way as far as the house of a fidalgo,
where he, the consul, had asked the party to dinner. The fidalgo's
family and household were undressed, unshaved and shabby; the
conversation at dinner was of horses, bull-feasts, and the Chapters
of the different Orders of Religious. Costigan, who had military
notions of smartness, was displeased with these slovenly fidalgos;

but the tolerant consul told him 'it was not the style here for people of fashion to dress till after they had slept their sesta'.

With much regret and hearty embraces the travellers took leave of their host, whom they sadly missed as they rode on to Coimbra and Lisbon to pursue the highly complicated love affairs of Lord Freeman and his acquaintances.

They left behind them at Consul Whitehead's the young theological student John Carlos, who was anxious to continue the improvement of his mind by the perusal of the consul's books and the advantage of his conversation and instruction. He continued it to such purpose that in a few weeks Captain Costigan had a long letter from him explaining that he had now seen the light of reason and good sense, and found it impossible to proceed in his plan of taking priest's orders. His constant employment, he wrote, had been in the worthy consul's library, 'where I spend every moment I can curtail from the dinners and suppers we are asked to; for though they are excellent, and vouch most favourably for the hospitality of the Portonians, yet, as I am now becoming daily more sensible of the bad quality and insufficiency of the mental sustenance with which I have been hitherto supplied, I am resolved to improve by the present favourable opportunity of remedying so great a defect'.

Such a young man was bound to get on. But he was embarrassingly situated, for he was engaged by the last will and testament of his benefactor to take the university courses at Coimbra and become a priest. Unfortunately Euclid had enlightened him, ushering him into the higher walks of that elegant science; astronomy and experimental philosophy had opened to him the enchanting secrets of Nature, and perusal of the Bible, which showed him a Christian religion quite different from, and generally opposite to, the tenets in which he had been educated, completed his undoing. 'The result of all my inquiries to this present moment has been, that if the New Testament contains the pure elements of the Christian doctrine, how different, opposite and corrupted are the established religions of this, as well as of most other countries of Europe.' It was indeed, as many before and since this poor youth have found, a grave dilemma. 'Am I to renounce the faith in which I have been brought up, to embrace another of the many opinions I see before me, and the most of them perhaps equally erroneous?' — and, in doing so, to sacrifice his career? He missed

Lord Freeman and the captain, as they had been always willing, and almost always able, to give him satisfactory solutions to his problems. The consul he found less forthcoming on religious topics; perhaps theological questions bored him, his mind being wrapped in calculations, triangles and oblate spheroids. He would answer inquiries on any other subject, 'yet, as often as I have attempted to bring the discourse upon the topic of Theology, I find he always fights off, and cannot be brought to deliver any opinion'. At last the distracted young man told his host about the will on which his subsistence depended, and how he would soon be obliged to take Holy Orders, and was therefore anxious to know as much as possible about the past and present state of the religion he was to profess. 'The Consul, seeing me thus in earnest, and that he was under a sort of necessity of explaining himself on the subject, desired me to sit down last night, after we had done drinking tea, and spoke to me as follows.' The consul's discourse was long and eloquent, and John Carlos was able, apparently, to quote it verbatim in his letter. He began by insisting that all he said must be taken as his private opinion only, and that he had no more wish to obtrude it on any one else than he would desire that a man six feet high should reduce himself to five foot seven, which was his own height, or that another man should wear a wig and a brown coat as he did, instead of his own hair and a scarlet one if he preferred that (which, besides the Factory portrait, provides us with the only picture of Mr. Whitehead that we have). He went on to maintain that all constraint put on men's minds was abominable; anyone who would shackle people's understanding, direct their sentiments, and make them think as he chooses, especially in matters of mere speculation, as all established worships are, must descend from the devil. Christianity, that pure and noble system, had been immediately contaminated wherever it had been established, ever since the times of the bloody Constantine, who set it upon the imperial throne. 'As to that particular Sect of the Christian religion in which you have been educated, now going fast out of date wherever Reason and Good Sense have re-affirmed their due influence ... I should be extremely vexed to see so fine a young man as yourself engage precipitately in it before you are thoroughly acquainted with the ground you tread on!' He advised him therefore to spend a year in studying both sides of the question, reading church history, conversing with persons of all persuasions 'and if, after only a twelvemonth's application in the manner I have prescribed, you do not renounce every idea of becoming a Priest, then I will voluntarily disclaim every pretension to the use of Reason and Common Sense'.

'Here', the young man concludes his letter, 'the Consul ended his surprising discourse'. And we have, unfortunately, no more of this engaging and eccentric mathematician, who continued for nearly thirty years to preside over his countrymen's welfare at Oporto, for the affairs of Captain Costigan, Lord Freeman, and John Carlos now shift to Lisbon.

BIBLIOGRAPHY

Sketches of Society and Manners in Portugal, CAPTAIN ARTHUR COSTIGAN (1787).
Oporto Old and New: A Historical Record of the Port Wine Trade, CHARLES SELLERS (1899).
State Papers, Portugal, 89/50 (Record Office).

PRISONERS OF DOM MIGUEL

I. TORY NOBLEMAN
Lord Porchester
[1827-1828]

VISCOUNT PORCHESTER (he was to become the Earl of Carnarvon) had every right to feel aggrieved when he was dragged off to gaol in Evora with a furious Miguelista mob yelling round him, 'Death to the Freemason! Cut off his ears!' For, though these were entirely normal Miguelist cries, as natural to the Apostolical party as barking to a dog, he had really done nothing at all to deserve them, beyond being an Englishman. He was not a Freemason; he would never have dreamed of being a Freemason; he was not a radical, not a democrat, not a reformer (he detested the Reform Bill when it came), not even a Whig. He was, in fact, a Tory through and through; had it not been that many of his Portuguese friends were eminent constitutionalists he would probably have supported Dom Miguel as zealously as did most of his party in England. Yet the undiscriminating Miguelists would have lynched him with the fury with which they flung themselves upon those who approved Dom Pedro and his infernal Charter. It was excessively unfair.

Further, Lord Porchester was an admirer of the Portuguese, and more particularly of that aristocratic Portuguese society which mainly supported Dom Miguel. He was a civilized traveller, without those insular prejudices which obscured the view of so many British tourists and residents in Portugal. He did not go about complaining of bigotry, superstition and processions; he scarcely even complained of dirt. He appreciated, admired and described, and got on well with everyone, except the Miguelist mob. A traveller for pleasure, rich, cultivated, well-informed and civil, with a passion for sight-seeing and a stately flow of words about all he saw and heard, the young gentleman (he was twenty-seven) arrived in Lisbon on the steam packet *Duke of York* on August 3rd, 1827, put up at Reeves's, and spent ten days seeing the sights and meeting the best people, under the ciceronage of his friend Sir Arthur de Capel Brooke and of Mr. Forbes, the chargé d'affaires. He met, among others, some eminent constitutionalists, the Count da Puente and Count Villa Flor, who had at the beginning of the year commanded the government troops against the Miguelists. He celebrated King George IV's birthday at a party at General Sir William Clinton's, where the band pleased the distinguished Portuguese guests by playing Portuguese airs during dinner. After ten pleasant days, Lord Porchester, accompanied by his friend Colonel Lambert of the Guards, visited Cintra, passing on the way Queluz, where the queen mother resided in sullen state, holding no communication with her daughter the Regent 'and offering up ceaseless prayers for the return of her banished son and for the restoration of the ancient rule'.

Having stayed at and admired Cintra, Lord Porchester returned to Lisbon, and a few days later left it to ride to Oporto. The several weeks' journey was agreeable; he saw the sights of interest *en route*, Mafra, Torres Vedras, Alcobaça, Coimbra; everywhere he had introductions or old friends; he found Sir Edward Blakeney in Mafra palace, in charge of the British expeditionary force which was quartered in barracks next the convent and which by its excellent behaviour had won the approval even of the monks; he found also three old Etonian friends among the officers; one of these, Lord William Paulet, gave him letters of introduction to Coimbra. He got on well with the monks of Alcobaça, who were very gentlemanly, possessing those manners which only birth or long acquaintance with good society can confer. He learned afterwards that they were Bernadines, who restrict themselves to persons of condition, 'a limitation which has kept up the respectability of their order, amid the comparative degradation of part of the profession'. So unlike the Franciscans, who, from poverty and other causes, 'have fallen into the hands of persons selected from the lower classes, who, as might be naturally expected, sometimes disgrace the brotherhood by their excesses. The monks of the higher orders are generally restrained by considerations of policy and self-respect, are often swayed by higher motives, and almost always throw a decent veil over any violations of the convent rules'. Here Lord Porchester protests against general and unfair denunciations of the monastic orders. Writing after the suppression of the convents, he deplores it as a disaster to agriculture and the lives of the poor; they should have been preserved, reformed, and improved, so as to resemble in some degree 'our college institutions'.

He retired to rest in the cell placed at his disposal for the night by his kind hosts, musing over the doom that awfully awaited their proud establishment; unless he only thought of this later, after the event. And so on to Coimbra, where he bathed in the Mondego, saw the university, and was greeted by a labourer with the only cry of 'Vivan los Ingleses' which he heard in Portugal; he attributed it to the popularity of the British troops stationed in the neighbourhood.

Once in Oporto, the known character and rank, said W. H. G. Kingston, of this highly-talented and amiable nobleman 'at once gave him the entrée into the best society, and he therefore has described the nobility of Portugal in true and very pleasing colours'. His Lisbon acquaintance, Count Villa Flor, was now governor of the city, and showed him every hospitality. He met the most intelligent and cultivated Portuguese, admired their courtesy and amiable manners, their kindness, the lively gaiety of the females, though he admitted that these, not being highly educated, had little conversation on general subjects. The best English society he held to have more intellectual culture, but less exquisite politeness. He was very hospitably treated by everyone, including the British consul and chaplain and the gentlemen of the Factory; he was present at the enthusiastic celebration of Dom Pedro's birthday, when Villa Flor gave a grand dinner and proposed the health of his sovereign and of Great Britain's. He made a tour into the wine district and Tras-os-Montes, where he met with universal kindness from everyone, both officials and private individuals, for this was before the great revulsion of feeling against the English that accompanied the Miguel revolution and that was later to endanger his life in the Alemtejo.

After several months in north Portugal, he was in Lisbon again by the end of the year, and in February, after his four years of exile, there arrived, on a ship from England (where they had been coaching him in the Charter) the ominous Infante Dom Miguel, to take over the Regency from his sister. He was received with the thunder of guns and shouts of 'Viva el rey absoluto!' He took the oath to the constitution; but it was rumoured that he had avoided kissing the sacred book, and those constitutionalists who observed his sullen, embarrassed and furtive manner feared the worst. With the swiftness of a mountain storm, popular feeling swelled into hysteria; mobs rioted about, shouting against the constitution and

'Down with the Charter' and expressing noisily their preference for an absolute monarchy. Constitutionalists were attacked in the streets; Miguel looked on with sinister complacency. On March 10th Lord Porchester dined with the Marquis of Fronteira at Bemfica; he met the Villa Flors, and other eminent constitutionalists; it was the last time, for in three days they were exiles at sea. Doom was at hand; the revolution was proceeding at a dizzy pace; ministers and officials were sacked, and Miguelists put in their places. The queen mother, the day she had waited and prayed for at last arrived, rode the whirlwind and directed the storm, organizing risings and conspiracies everywhere, driving violently ahead, while her son, frightened of what might come to him, shut himself up in his palace and would eat no food not prepared by his faithful nurse. Lord Porchester, no devotee of constitutions himself, felt that the young Regent was muffing his chances, he should have accepted the Charter, which 'could not, I think, have been detrimental to the established interests of the country, at a time when an immense majority of the nation were attached to his person'; indeed, 'among the Portuguese, with whom the love of liberty is of recent date, and altogether subservient to their hereditary sense of loyalty, the constitution was not sufficiently rooted in the hearts of the people to have interfered with the attachment which would soon have grown up for a young and popular prince'.

Thus the Tory viscount, with a rather wistful hankering, muses. Had he been Miguel's counsellor, he would have urged compromise, moderation, a seeming acceptance of the Charter, as the way to real power . . . Then the conflict would have been avoided, and the excesses both of Miguel now and of Pedro six years later averted. Lord Porchester disliked excesses; he was for a tranquil and moderate, but firm-handed and undemocratic rule, that preserved the ancient forms of State, Church, and Property, but tried to balance the budget. The constitutional party of 1828 he thought moderate and conservative; that of 1834 revolutionary and disastrous. Analysing the reasons for the conservatism of his liberal friends of 1828, he decided that it was because they were the leaders of society, men of rank and stake in the country, swayed by many of the prejudices of the old regime, and friendly to representative government rather from the force of circumstances than from any natural bias towards constitutional doctrines. They were, in brief, good Tories; the class which must, Lord Porchester was sure, in the end steer the ship of any state into haven, the class without which any ship will drive on to the rocks.

But there was no room in Portugal now for the good Tory or the good Whig; passions were ablaze and ruthless ruin gathered impetus. Sir William Clinton was kicked violently by a mule; the queen mother bought the mule. While she petted and praised it, she and her confessor prepared lists of constitutionalists for arrests; these hid in the city and escaped in the night on to neutral ships in the Tagus. Lord Porchester rowed out to the frigate of the British admiral to say good-bye to the Villa Flors and the Fronteiras, who had sought refuge there. They were depressed; their eyes filled with tears as they looked on Lisbon that they were leaving. Villa Flor said, 'However, I have not abandoned the cause; honour is preserved'.

There followed days and nights of fear and tension in the city; British ships overflowed with fugitives. Anti-British feeling rose; British troops were still occupying the forts, which annoyed the court. General Saldanha arrived in the Tagus; finding revolution afoot, he dared not land, but hid on a neutral vessel till he could escape. On April 3rd Clinton's troops left Portugal. Clinton, says Porchester, had won everyone's regard; the departure of the troops left Lisbon apprehensive, and Porchester socially dull, for now nearly all his friends, English and Portuguese, were gone. He decided to leave Lisbon and explore the south of Portugal. Before he left, Sir Frederick Lamb took him to the Ajuda palace and presented him to Dom Miguel, who said little, but looked placid.

Against informed advice, Lord Porchester then set out across the Tagus for the wild south, where Miguelist feeling ran high, and the word 'constitution' had the snarl of an oath, and priests fanned up religious and patriotic hate in the peasantry, and the life of a known constitutionalist would have been uninsurable for twenty-four hours by any intelligent firm; indeed, it was becoming a little like this even with known Englishmen, who were all (except a few Roman Catholics) tarred with the capacious brushes of heresy, liberalism, constitutionalism and Freemasonry. Even a Tory viscount who was as dark as a Spaniard (Lord Porchester's fortunate case) was in grave peril, as he was to find.

After a beautiful ride (he describes country well) he reached Setubal, which he has the grace not to call St. Ubes, and put up at an inn kept by an English Catholic, an enlightened young man, who conducted him in the evening to the scene of a Miguelist meeting, where wild-looking people, largely fishermen, shouted round a band which played the ultra-royalist hymn; cries of 'Miguel the absolute king! Death to the Malhados! Death to the infamous Constitutionalists!' filled Lord Porchester with the sense that an awful hour of vengeance was at hand. Never had he seen the human face distorted by such a variety of horrible passions, 'passions cradled in fanaticism, nursed in silence and in gloom, but now roused to madness and ready to break down every barrier opposed to their gratification'. All seemed transported by love of the Infante, hatred of his opponents, and almost frenzied devotion to the Church. No English spectator, used to the more tepid attitude of churchmen in his native land, but must have felt that a little of this spirit imported into parochial church councils would rejoice the heart of any vicar. Such thoughts may or may not have occurred to Lord Porchester as, definitely alarmed, he watched the inhabitants of Setubal, inflamed as they were by music, hymns, wine, and egged on by religious zealots; there were also fireworks to excite further.

At length began the discouraging cry of 'Death to the English!' Lord Porchester, thankful for his dark complexion, felt that the time to retire had arrived. The crowd, ripe for attack and vengeance, now began to surge into Setubal, urged on by their leaders and by drums. Lord Porchester was borne along with it; many fierce inquiring glances were cast upon him; one savage-looking fellow seized him by the coat, and called him a Freemason, and told him to shout for the absolute king; an awkward moment, for his accent would have given him away. But his assailant lost his hold and was swept on with the crowd; taking what cover he could, he made his way back to the inn, among groups of demoniacs who resembled wild beasts. All night the houses of constitutionalists were attacked and sacked; most of them had taken warning and fled. Dom Miguel was, by universal acclamation, proclaimed King of Setubal.

Next morning all seemed tranquil in the town. After a few days Lord Porchester pushed on further on his journey, which was a mixed quest after fine scenery and political excitement; the former he approached with sensitive and romantic appreciation, the latter with mingled interest and trepidation. It must have made his later experiences as Tory M.P. for Wootton Bassett during the Reform Bill seem comparatively safe and dull. Though he had a servant with him, intercourse with the natives was difficult, since he appears to have known no Portuguese. In the wilder districts people fled in terror at the approach of strangers, so that it was not easy to ask the way. If the fleeing peasantry were pursued, they vanished into cistus-bushes, establishing alibis as complete and unbreakable as Daphne's.

Lord Porchester rode across the Monchique range into Algarve, where he met with kind hospitality from local gentry and officials and learned that many of the ladies wore portraits of Dom Miguel next their hearts. He found the Alemtejo in a still more advanced state of Miguelist hysteria; the towns he arrived in were, as likely as not, in the throes of revolution, holding meetings, drawing up petitions to the Infante to abolish all democratic institution, proclaiming him as absolute king. At Beja he was startled by a shrill, prolonged screaming as of pigs being killed or women undergoing massacre; it turned out to be nuns crying 'Dom Miguel, absolute king of Portugal'. In the same town he went to church in the evening, and heard a sermon about the princely saint, his glorious return from exile, the wickedness of those who opposed his claims, and the necessity of a crusade against God's enemies. General excitement animated the congregation.

Riding out of Beja towards Evora next day, Lord Porchester met men hurrying fiercely about, and heard that the long-expected revolt in the provinces had broken out, and that the people were rising *en masse* against the constitutionalists. The young Englishmen felt the position precarious; revolution had drawn round him a fiery circle, and there seemed no way out of it. Evora was already in commotion. Entering its gate, he was first received by the guard politely, as a Spaniard; inspection of his passport revealed the truth, and the guard's manner changed. Crowds flocked round, asking the visitor the reason of his journey; he had no reason to allege beyond English tourism and curiosity; it was not satisfactory; they began crying out that he was English, that his nation was planning a war against the Faith and against their King Miguel. The sentinel arrested him for investigation; he was conducted to the mayor, then to the Corregidor, accompanied by swelling crowds; neither official dared release him, in the face of mob tumult and rage; at last the Secretary of Police ordered him to be removed to prison. He broke into vehement protests (either in Portuguese, Spanish or English, or possibly French). He appealed to class feeling, reminding them that by Portuguese law fidalgos cannot be put in common gaols; he appealed to caution, mentioning the privileges of an Englishman and the British ambassador; whether he was understood or not, his feeling was, and a militia man suggested that he should be confined in the guard room instead of the gaol. Here, accompanied by his servant, whom he with difficulty protected from being dragged away to prison, he spent the night and day, with hostile crowds shouting at him through the window; as evening came on, and an attack on the guard room was obviously intended after dark, the Governor, who knew too well the violence of his fellow townsmen, had him transferred to the prison, which he entered with relief.

He remained there for several days; the Corregidor dared not release him, with the citizens of Evora clamouring for his blood; his own might well have been shed instead had he done so. So his victim languished in gaol, with Evora shouting every evening outside his window (fortunately strongly barred) 'Death to the prisoners! Death to the English! Death to all Freemasons'! in the most disgusting voices. He passed the nights in nightmare misgivings as to the outcome of it all; the Minister of Police in Lisbon had been sent a statement of his case, and he had himself written to the British ambassador, Sir Frederick Lamb; but he knew that Miguel's strange behaviour must have caused a rift between Portugal and Great Britain, and it was rumoured in Evora that Lamb had actually departed. Even if he had not, would the Evora authorities dare to enforce an order from Lisbon against the feeling of the mob? Worse, were the walls thick enough, the bars strong enough? Would they hold against an attack?

In the face of the risk of all this, and of a frightful and inglorious death, Lord Porchester's spirits became extremely depressed. He was woken one morning by horrifying yells; drums beat to arms, and infuriated crowds rushed along the streets *en pleine revolution*, looking and sounding dreadful, all aflame for blood and murder, armed with clubs, knives, muskets and pikes. The gaoler, very nervous and trying to fortify the prison doors with iron bars, told the prisoners that the Imperial troops had re-entered the city, and it was against them that the citizens were agitating themselves so formidably. Apprehensively Lord Porchester listened, as all day long the noise of battle swayed in the city; at last the gaoler came in and announced the total defeat of the regular troops and their expulsion from the town; the Arsenal had been seized; the Corregidor had been attacked and dragged to prison for attempting to restrain the mob. Lord Porchester awaited the attack on the prisons and made up his mind for death; but it seemed that the rioters were exhausted, or glutted with prey, for they passed the prison by. The worst was over; next day there was more calm and order; the insurrectionists took possession of the city and had no more need of revolt. Hope revived in Lord Porchester's breast; one evening as he sat listening to the perpetual chant for Miguel, letters were brought him informing him of the interference of the British embassy, and an order of release from the mayor. He at once went to the Town Hall and requested the release of his servant Juan, a ruffian from the Spanish border; but this was not granted; no British ambassador had interfered for Juan, and it was very certain that no Spanish ambassador would do so; Lord Porchester had to leave him in prison for the present.

He had himself some delay in leaving Evora, as he could not get his baggage mules out of the inn-keeper who was keeping them; a tourist of great spirit and curiosity, and by no means to be cowed by danger, he walked about Evora and inspected the cathedral and the temple of Diana, then went to the inn and argued about his mules; a hostile crowd took the inn-keeper's part, and he was strongly advised to seek refuge again in the prison, where he passed a day and night while negotiating with the mayor to order the release of his animals. He did not get off till dusk next day; he was armed with a passport for Lisbon, made out in the name of King Miguel the First — the first passport made out in that style for an Englishman.

So he and his muleteer took the perilous road back through the wild Alemtejo, and at last reached Aldea Gallega safely, and crossed the Tagus to Black Horse Square. Here his friend Mr. Forbes met him, and told him that the Corps Diplomatique had suspended functions, owing to their respective governments' disapproval of Miguel. Sir Frederick Lamb was still in Lisbon, and helped to persuade the police to order the release of Juan from Evora gaol. This done, Lord Porchester sailed for England. Gazing on beautiful Portugal with regret, he sighed for the sad days on which she had fallen, and perhaps for the immoderation with which Dom Miguel was ruining his chances of giving his country a beneficent oligarchic and monastic rule.

With relief Lord Porchester landed in his own country, and 'trod once more upon the soil of native, peaceful, and then unreformed England' — a land still fit for Tories to live in.

Two years later, in February 1830, there was a debate on Portugal in the House of Lords. In its course, Lord Carnarvon made what was, for a Tory peer, an unusual speech—a speech, he said, that he would never have made but for his own experiences. He referred to 'the brave and unfortunate victims of Dom Miguel's tyranny, the extent of whose sufferings, he begged leave to say, were but little known in this country'. Had the British government, he maintained, supported Donna Maria, the lawful sovereign, Miguel would not have succeeded in his perfidious usurpation, for he had no money, and no party but the priests, and his expulsion would have been bloodless. Strange words, and heard with disapprobation by Lord Aberdeen, who had just been declaring that Miguel, though he may have been a rascal, had a right to the throne.

But Lord Carnarvon knew about Miguel, and that goings on such as his and those of his party disqualified him from any rights to any throne.

BIBLIOGRAPHY

Portugal and Galicia, THE EARL OF CARNARVON (1836).
The Times (February, 1830).
Lusitanian Sketches, W. H. G. KINGSTON (1845).

2. ROWDY RADICAL

William Young

[1814-1828]

MR. WILLIAM YOUNG'S style and type were quite different from Lord Porchester's. Mr. Young was rather a cheerful, rowdy, vulgar man; a Londoner by extraction, a half-pay British officer, who had lived at Leiria since the end of the war in 1814; he was doing business for Lloyds underwriters; he had married a Portuguese. He was one of those unusual Englishmen accused by the Portuguese of Freemasonry who actually was a Freemason. He spent his time quarrelling with the clergy, whom he did not like, nor they him. 'More than three-quarters of the regular and irregular clergy of Portugal are men capable of conniving at or practising every vice that disgraces human nature'; that was his tone. He resented their influence over 'the female mind'; he may have been thinking of Mrs. Young. As to Freemasonry, 'they invariably stigmatize with the name of *Freemason* every man who attempts to use any arguments in favour of religious or political freedom ... although, in three cases out of four, they are entirely ignorant of the nature and objects of masonic institutions. Indeed the great majority consider the English constitution and Freemasonry are one and the same'.

When first Mr. Young went to live at Leiria he found the place rather dull; 'I always tried to promote any kind of amusement, and, being rather of a lively disposition, I was mostly at the head of anything of that kind'. So, in 1817, he helped to build a theatre, and got up plays in it. Some of the clergy disapproved of this; a bishop, when complained to about it, told Mr. Young he must be cautious in the selection of plays and farces, for many were unfit to be performed in Leiria. The inhabitants of the town were happy and friendly, even though in ignorance and subjection. And so they would be still, said Mr. Young, embarking with animus on one of his favourite topics, but for the interference in Portuguese affairs of a most objectionable Englishman (Marshal Lord Beresford, whom he abuses anonymously throughout his book) who had ruined the country.

Mr. Young's own account of the doings that led to his arrest in 1828 is not very detailed or coherent (he was no practised author) but the charges against him were set forth at his trial. His was a long and black record of pro-constitutionalism. It would appear that he celebrated the Oporto revolt of 1820 against the Regency, and the proclamation of the constitution, by riding in a triumphal car through Leiria playing a violin. Then he gave a dinner party, at which all the wrong toasts were given, and rockets let off for the constitution. He replied to this accusation, 'I have often given dinners to my friends, and I have often let off rockets'; and no doubt he had; he was an exuberant, rocketty man. But there is no doubt that he was particularly exuberant at the proclamation of the constitution, the annoyance of the clergy, and the expulsion of

Lord Beresford and his officers. His accusers said that he seemed on this occasion to experience the greatest pleasure, making festivals, dancing, and performing plays, and inducing others to do the same. Obviously Leiria made merry, while the clergy looked on in disgust. These, however, had their day again, after the counter-revolution of 1823, and, still better (though more briefly), during the *abrilada*, Miguel's attempted coup of April and May 1824, when he issued his proclamation threatening death to all Freemasons and exhorting loyal Portuguese to make an end of that infernal race, who had conspired to murder their king. The Leiria clergy had the pleasure of reading this aloud in church, to the consternation of many of the citizens, and of assisting in the compilation of a list of local suspects alleged to be Freemasons; a list which no doubt featured prominently Mr. William Young.

But Mr. Young had his revenge, for he was (it was one of the crimes with which he was charged) the first to spread in Leiria a few days later the glad tidings of the collapse of the coup, the king's safe flight to a British warship, and the exile of his impetuous son. The list of Freemasons was kept safely, against more favourable times. Before these arrived, there came the definitely unfavourable time of the constitutional Charter brought by Sir Charles Stuart from Dom Pedro in Brazil on his accession. Mr. Young, on this auspicious occasion for liberals, was said to have behaved in just the same way as he had in 1820—violin, dinner party, rockets, theatricals, dancing and all. It was apparent that constitutions went to his head.

The Leiria clergy bided their time, and, sure enough, it came, for in the Iberian peninsula one has only to wait. *Rei Chegou*; early in 1828 Miguel arrived back from abroad, his principles unweakened, indeed reinforced, by his residence at Vienna under the astute tutelage of Metternich; promptly usurping the throne, he issued fresh proclamations against 'the infernal clubs of Freemasons and lovers of freedom'. Mr. Young was in Lisbon at the time of the usurpation; the scenes, he reported, were dreadful — arrests, imprisonments, flights, riotings, tumultuous Miguelist mobs terrorizing liberals, all the frantic expressions of a Portuguese change of government. But soon came the stirring news from Oporto; the army there had revolted against Miguel, proclaimed Pedro as their king; the students of Coimbra marched out to join them. Here was some good news for Mr. Young to spread; he rode up from Lisbon on a mule, ringing a bell, and proclaiming the glad tidings about the countryside; he was again in his triumphant constitutional British mood, the same mood in which the Lisbon correspondent of the *Times* wrote on May 22nd, 'The city of Oporto has become once more the cradle of Portuguese liberty'. But, if Mr. Young was in this mood when he reached his home in Leiria, it did not last. That evening his house was surrounded by militia and the inevitable mob that collects when constitutionalists are in trouble; the militia, commanded by a major, entered, and seized him as he was drinking tea with Mrs. Young, to the accompaniment of cries from the mob of 'Bring him out! Cut off his ears! He is a Freemason!' He was dragged from the room with blows, stoned by the mob in the streets, and taken to gaol, where he was confined in the privy. All night and next day the mob rioted outside, shouting about cutting off the ears of Freemasons — 'Bring him out and cut off his ears! Die, you spotted English devil!' and so forth. Mr. Young, very sick from the smell, could not eat. He thought Portuguese mobs peculiarly dreadful, because egged on by priests and monks. He was prepared to die; but if they tried torture or mutilation, he decided that he would not stand it tamely. For several days the clamouring went on. Other prisoners visited the privy; both he and they were embarrassed; 'in this painful situation I met Sir John Milley Doyle', also a prisoner of Miguel. The only bright spot was that his wife sent him in food, with paper and pencil concealed in it; he sent back a note telling her to write to his friends in Lisbon.

Later, he was transferred to a room occupied by Sir John Milley Doyle; the mob threw missiles at the window, and continued to shout. On the eighteenth day of his imprisonment he was taken to the senate house for examination; he was accused of being an Englishman, a republican, a Freemason, a hater of King Miguel I, and of having committed the offences already described. He was then sent to Lisbon, to be imprisoned in Castle St. George till tried. It was a detestable prison, full of vermin (which he had the British middle class habit of alluding to as 'these gentry'). As an Englishman, he felt ashamed and embarrassed among the Portuguese political prisoners, who reproached Great Britain for being about, as they inaccurately gathered from the *Lisbon Gazette*, to recognize Miguel. 'Look what your country is doing to ruin us', they would say. 'They brought us a constitution, sent us troops to support it, then sent them away, and will ultimately recognize the usurper. Had Mr. Canning lived, this would not have been the case. Miguel would never have done this without feeling certain of the support of the British government; someone in England sends him instructions, and tells him the sentiments of the government. We know the *great man* [Beresford] sends letters by the packets, and we know who delivers them to the old queen.'

In such melancholy conversation, the prisoners wiled away their days. They discussed the situation, the departure of the British squadron, the departure of the foreign ambassadors, which however desirable as a gesture, left their nationals unprotected; the probable attitude of the Countess of Juramanha, now just widowed, towards her late protector Lord Beresford (the affairs of this detested marshal were an obsession with Mr. Young) and their chances of deliverance. These, for the Portuguese constitutionalists, were slight indeed; the British had better fortune, for, though their ambassador had been recalled their consul remained to look after their interests, and, in the case of Mr. Young, Lloyds in London interceded with the British government, so successfully that Lord Aberdeen, the Foreign Secretary, was persuaded to send a note through the consul to Miguel's government about this troublesome and apparently obnoxious fellow who had got himself into gaol in Lisbon, no doubt through his own fault, for the fellow appeared to be a noisy radical, of the kind that gives us a bad name with foreigners.

Anyhow, when Mr. Young was brought up for trial in August, and charged with his tale of crimes (which now included having seduced the troops in Oporto during the rising of last May), though the trial took a long time and involved many witnesses, nothing was proved against him which seemed to make wise the further detention of an Englishman in prison; he was sentenced to be deported, signing an agreement never to return to Portugal. This was also the fate of Sir John Milley Doyle; and on September 7th both were put on board the *Magnet* for England. Before he left, Mr. Young drew up an eloquent remonstrance against his treatment and sent it to Mr. Matthews the consul.

On arriving in England he wrote his book about it. It is not a very good book; he laboured, when he wrote it, under considerable annoyance; and his two detested bugbears, Marshal Beresford and the Portuguese clergy, make too frequent and too unbalanced appearances. He begins, 'As all the injuries and persecutions I have sustained in Portugal have arisen solely on account of my being a British subject, and as such suspected of being inimical to the detestable mental and political slavery which it is the constant object of the Catholic clergy to perpetuate . . .' He ends with a warning that there will assuredly be a revolution against the present atrocious rule, and 'unless a desperate effort be made to rescue Portugal from the fangs of this second Nero, we may expect, ere many months elapse, to hear of the streets of Lisbon being deluged with blood'.

Meanwhile, he left behind him in Portugal, he said, over ten thousand politicals in prison, over five thousand in hiding, and there were about five thousand emigrants. About twenty-three thousand persons were ruined; including many British merchants; the streets of Lisbon were full of the shut and boarded shops of those whose property had been confiscated, their persons seized or chased from the country.

Lord Carnarvon would not have cared for Mr. Young; but, had they met, they would have had one topic in common.

An odd postscript to Mr. Young's case is the comment of Colonel Hodges that, in the autumn of 1831, when recruiting for Dom Pedro was going on in England, and the rallying-point of intrigues against it was the Portuguese consul-general, this gentleman was surrounded by 'humble admirers of the modern Nero', among whom was Mr. William Young, who had been so cruelly treated in 1828. It seems probable that Colonel Hodges misunderstood Mr. Young's attitude: if he was right, Mr. Young had performed an odd somersault indeed.

BIBLIOGRAPHY

Portugal in 1828: *Sketches of the state of private society and of religion under Don Miguel, with a narrative of the Author's residence there and of his persecution and confinement as a state prisoner,* WILLIAM YOUNG, H. P. British service (1828).

The Times (April, May, 1828).

Narrative of an Expedition to Portugal under His Imperial Majesty Don Pedro, G. LLOYD HODGES (late Colonel in the service of the Queen of Portugal (1833).

F.O. 63/333, 334, 331

THE EARL OF ESSEX AND THE
BISHOP'S BOOKS

[1596]

'THE reader in Duke Humphrey's library' (in the Bodleian)
'may perhaps have noticed, scattered up and down upon
the shelves, a number of volumes bound in black leather, tooled
in gilt, and stamped with a coat of arms; and if he is a student of
heraldry he will have been able to identify the arms as those of
Ferdinand Martins Mascarenhas, Bishop of Faro from 1594 to
1618, and later Grand Inquisitor of Portugal.' Thus, some years
ago, the *Bodleian Quarterly Record*, which appends a list of the books
in question, and rather unappetizing they on the whole are; just
such books of theology, scholastic philosophy, biblical commentary, homilies and canon law, as one might expect from a bishop of
the period.

They were presented to the newly founded Bodleian in 1598
by the Earl of Essex, who may have welcomed the chance to be
creditably rid of them. Possibly, when he stole them from the
unfortunate bishop's palace two years before, he had not time to
look into them much, but only perceived that they looked very
well on the shelves. Anyhow, it was a characteristic Renaissance
gesture, to sack and burn the city and palace, but to save fine
books from the flames.

The English fleet, under Essex and Lord Howard of Effingham,
had just been sacking and burning Cadiz; Raleigh, Lord Thomas
Howard, Sir William Monson and Sir Francis Vere were among
those present. Essex's design of permanently occupying Cadiz had
been vetoed; the city was fired and left, after having been plundered
of everything worth carrying off, except the fine mules and jennets,
which were knocked on the head before the fire, and the fine
Andalusian women, who were not molested. 'Not a woman has
been attacked or carried off to England', wrote a canon of Cadiz,
in some surprise at such moderation. And no one, he added, had
been tortured to get hold of his money. Apparently English
manners on the Continent had improved since the Reformation.
Still, the troops had done pretty well. 'We had enjoyed the town

of Cadiz a fortnight, and our men were grown rich by the spoil of it', wrote Sir William Monson, who had been Essex's flag-captain. 'What the Generals have gotten, I know least; they protest it is little', was Raleigh's comment; the soldiers and sailors were satiated with booty; they would have been happy to abandon further enterprises and sail for home. But their leaders, the young and ardent Essex, the elderly and fatigued but still undaunted Howard, had other unformulated plans. They sailed uncertainly in the sweltering and almost windless heat along the Algarve coast, keeping a wary but optimistic eye on the Portugal seaboard, seeking some unguarded beach where they might land, get water and victuals, and destroy something. Coming to the creek that runs up to Faro, capital of Algarve and a bishop's seat, they anchored, and three officers went ashore to see the lie of the land. They returned with a discouraging report: no water, and Faro evacuated of inhabitants and valuables. However, the army was landed; having destroyed, as usual, the tunny fisheries, it encamped for the night. Next morning it marched on Faro, Essex walking on foot at the head of his men, leading his horse by the bridle; an exhausting and uncomfortable march through deep hot sand beneath a burning tropical sun. Faro they found a deserted city. They took possession; Essex 'quarted himself' in the bishop's palace for two days, while a force pushed on to Loulé (also wisely abandoned by the Portuguese), burned it, rounded up a hundred cows and oxen and some pigs, were guided 'by an old Portugal to a well of good fresh water', and so returned to Faro, finding those unfortunate soldiers who had from sickness dropped out by the way 'pitifully mangled, some with their hands chopped off'. Essex meanwhile had, presumably, been having a look at the library of Bishop Mascarenhas. They were handsomely bound volumes, and it was something of a triumph to return to England with a Portuguese bishop's library; besides, it would seem a shame to let them burn. To be sure they did not seem very exciting; but Essex, a militant puritan, could put up with a good deal of theo-logy. The bishop's books bore such names as *Comm. in 3ᵃᵐ partem Thomae*, 1590-95, *Questionarum conciliationis sacrae Scripturae*, 1587, *Exegemata in Habacuc.*, 1595, *Breviloquium scholasticae theologiae.*, 1584, *Compendium moralium conceptum*, 1588, *Controversiae theologicae* 1586. They were, in short, a good, up to date, finely printed and bound clerical library, and Essex thought they would adorn his shelves and edify his visitors and perhaps be a useful training in the theological controversy which was part of an Elizabethan gentleman's equipment. He had, it is supposed, also collected some books from Cadiz.

Besides this library, there was little of value to take in Faro: but such as it was the army took it, not wishing to go away empty-handed. Having done this, they set Faro on fire, and marched to the coast where their boats waited for them. But they reached it too late; the boats had to return for them next day. To the disgust of their crews, and of Admiral Howard awaiting them on his flag-ship, the boats were sent back laden not with the army but with the army's plunder, including the weighty load of the bishop's books. The admiral protested. The men, said he, were tired with continual rowing; 'there hath been great abuses; for when the boats have been sent up for the ordnance, or to bring weak men, they have been sent back with luggage, every man seeking for his own profit. I have not had the leisure with any of my boats to water'.

By evening the force was re-embarked. No one but Essex wanted to stay and attack Lagos; the men complained that the food and water would run out, which was considered at least by Monson to be a ruse for getting home; 'the riches of Cadiz kept them that had got much from attempting more'. Raleigh as usual was cautious; a favourable wind got up, and the fleet rounded Cape St. Vincent, to rendezvous off Lisbon for the discussion of further plans. And here they vanish from our story and from the Portugal coast, straggling home each to tell his story of the expedition in the way most creditable to himself and to his friends. ('I', wrote Raleigh to Cecil, 'was not second to any in the fight against the galleons and gallies.' And so on.)

Essex had, to console him for the cutting short of his adventure, his handsome new library of about two hundred books. But possibly theology and commentaries soon palled; anyhow two years later he presented the two hundred to Sir Thomas Bodley for his new library at Oxford — a generous gesture from a Cambridge man, who possibly reflected (forestalling the comment on the presentation to Cambridge of the library of another bishop over a century later) how much that loyal body wanted learning. Anyhow, the Bodleian got the books. Many of them had, it seems, been censored and mutilated by the Inquisition; Dr. James, the first Bodleian librarian, referred in 1611 to books 'brought from

Cales, wherein diverse sentences were put forth by the Inquisitors'. This was a subject on which he felt strongly. He inveighed against the inquisitorial habit of mutilation in a treatise fourteen years later. 'They fail not with the pen to blot out all the places that are to be expunged ... This is plainly manifested ... out of the books themselves that come unto us by divine providence' (an admirable name for piracy) 'especially from the College of Cadiz ... some whole leaves pasted together, the sentences blotted, and the books tormented in a pitiful manner, that it would grieve any man's heart to see them ... It is no marvel then if Massarena the Bishop or any other offered such large sums for to have had the books again; they feared belike that their knavery would come forth, and the mystery be unfolded of this work of darkness, which since that time hath layen no more secret in corners, but is now known to the body of all Christendom'. This was to put Essex's theft on the highest plane of public interest.

As to the poor bishop, he had lost his beloved library, and the fact that he and his fellow townsmen had all fled to safety before the English pirates without striking a blow for their city and its treasures did not detract from his anger and grief. He writes an account of the raid in his preface to a tract, *De auxiliis divinae gratiae*, published in Lisbon in 1604. Essex and his troops were 'hostes impii, insolentes, iracundi, piratea non minus ab humanitate quam a religione abhorrentes'. By ill fortune they had taken, among other things, a library 'non vulgaris, quae mihi in pretio et deliciis'; for a long time he had sought it, offered to buy it back, but nowhere found the robbers; it may have been burnt, or perished somehow and somewhere; 'mihi non dubium periisse'.

A lament which must wring the hearts of all who have lost their libraries. The bishop could not guess that the savage heretic pirates might have installed his beloved books with care on the shelves of learned libraries of their own.

BIBLIOGRAPHY

The Bodleian Quarterly Record, K. M. POGSON (1922).
The Successors of Drake, JULIAN S. CORBETT (1900).
Naval Tracts, SIR WILLIAM MONSON (pub. 1732).
Commentaries, SIR FRANCIS VERE (pub. 1657).
Life and Letters of Sir Walter Raleigh, E. EDWARDS (1868).
Cal. S.P. Spain (1596).

TWO CAPTAINS AND A MAJOR

I. THE MAJOR ABROAD
Major William Dalrymple
[1774]

MAJOR DALRYMPLE is chiefly known to-day because Beckford took a copy of his *Travels* with him to Portugal and Spain, in 1787, and found it 'dry, tiresome and splenetic'. 'Methinks', he says on one occasion, after mentioning a carpet manufactory at Arroyolas which employed about three hundred persons, 'I begin to write as dully as Major W. Dalrymple, whose dry journal of travels through a part of Spain I had the misfortune of reading in the coach this morning, as we jogged and jolted along the dreary road between Arroyolas and Venta do Duque'. Beckford was right; Major W. Dalrymple was dull. One wonders what made Beckford select his book for his travels; there were many more interesting and amusing works lately published about Portugal; he might have travelled with Baretti, or Richard Twiss, or even Udal ap Rhys, with less ennui. One would not, I think, greatly like the major if one met him; his style is ponderous, and disjointed, many of his facts and descriptions extremely dull, and he sounds like a bully. He breaks out from time to time into a kind of heavily frisking bawdiness, at other times into contemptuous abuse. The book is, he says, composed from his journal and from letters. Garrisoned at Gibraltar, he set out to visit Madrid, then went on for a five months' tour. He was afraid his narrative might prove as dry and tedious as the road was dull and dreary; 'but it will serve to show how very far behind the rest of Europe is this nation in improvements and conveniences for travelling'.

With this commendable object, he produced his book. He got a certain amount of interest out of his travels; he noted churches, monasteries, buildings, manufactures, quintas, modes of agriculture, the state of the army, food and drink, and 'the sex'. He shows nice feelings sometimes; as when in Oporto he 'feasted most voluptuously with the consul and Factory, who were remarkably civil and attentive; the only thing that I disliked amongst them was their supercilious treatment of the Portuguese, from whom they derive their wealth and opulence'. They complained much of the Portuguese Wine Company, but the major thought it not a bad thing, and that it improved the wine sent to England, which was often shockingly adulterated and bad. From Oporto he travelled to Lisbon, seeing all the proper things on the way; he noted at Coimbra the university (where learning was neglected), the monasteries (expensively endowed), the observatory (under an English colonel), and the little wooden toothpicks. Travelling on, he observed a French hat manufacture at Pombal, an English glass factory at Marinha, a handsome Gothic church at Batalha, a convent at Alcobaça, 'a most extensive and large pile of building in the Gothic taste, with some modern additions that disfigure it exceedingly . . . I dined with the prior, who entertained me with great civility. What a shame it is that those celestial pastors should possess so much worldly wealth, thereby wallowing in sloth and idleness, a nuisance to society! There is a cambric manufacture established at this place under the guidance of some Scotch and Irish manufacturers. There is an old Moorish tower here, but of no great import'. And so on to Caldas, Obidos, and Mafra, a stupendous work, 'a stately palace with bare walls, a sumptuous convent for supercilious priests'. Then Cintra, with its umbrageous quintas, romantic and agreeable and cool, but not all it was cracked up to be. Finally Lisbon; and 'I am now to give you the best account I could obtain of this unfortunate metropolis'. He does so, and contrives to make it pretty dull. But he cheers up a little when he describes a skit on Brazilians he had seen at the theatre (which included the most indecent dance he had ever beheld), the cellar of the Marquis of Pombal, and the sparkling black eyes and white teeth of the sex. 'Love', says he, 'is the darling passion of both sexes, and it is wonderful their perseverance to obtain their object. Jealousy prevails, yet the eyes of Argus do not prevent intrigue, which, when discovered, is often severely avenged.' He continues his commentary on love with a rather surprising statement, which shows the kind of thing people liked to tell him and that he liked to hear and repeat — 'Sapphic love rises predominant here; the stories I have heard of the females, who indulge themselves in this passion, are almost incredible'. The people, he goes on, are in general temperate eaters and drinkers; but in the large towns 'from their intercourse with my countrymen, we find some drunkards: beef and boiled rice is their favourite food. I had an opportunity of dining twice with some people of rank, but elegance did not prevail at their tables: they are as familiar with their servants as if their equals, nay, they even go so far as to take a principal servant into their party at cards, if one be wanting to make up the set; yet the people of family pique themselves much on their birth, and would not keep company with a bourgeois.

'Adieu, my dear friend', he ends this letter, 'live happily in that country where the hard hand of tyranny cannot exert its iron rule.'

So saying, off went the major to Spain, to observe the iron rule of tyranny there also.

No, Beckford would not have got on with the major, and nor, probably, should we.

BIBLIOGRAPHY

Travels through Spain and Portugal in 1774, MAJOR WILLIAM DALRYMPLE (1777). *Italy; with Sketches of Spain and Portugal*, WILLIAM BECKFORD (1834).

2. TRIP OF A CAPTAIN OF FOOT

Captain Richard Croker

[1780-1781]

'IN the course of a varied life, now advanced', wrote Captain Richard Croker from the custom house where, in 1789, he was employed, 'no circumstance has happened to the writer of these sheets more extraordinary than that he should have become the author of a book. The incitements to this undertaking were forcible and urgent, and the Author has considered this publication in some respects a duty'.

So Captain Croker, late of the 99th Regiment of Foot, thus incited, put together the letters he had written (to some unnamed correspondent who had expressed a desire that he should write them) between July 1780 and his return to England the next year. It seems that the captain had been ordered with his regiment to Jamaica; his first letter is dated from Hilsea Barracks, which he was delighted to leave, as they were unhealthy and inconvenient. The regiment embarked from Portsmouth on July 7th in high spirits, on the ship *Morant*. But the *Morant* did not get to Jamaica, nor did the 99th Foot, for a month later they were captured by the *Burgogne*, a French man-of-war, and landed presently in Spain. The French officers, Captain Croker noticed, were very economical on shore; he comments shrewdly that 'the levity of a Frenchman is seldom discovered where his purse is concerned: of an Englishman, more frequently in that respect than any other'. The officers of the 99th stayed at Arcos, but were sent into Portugal in December, and arrived in Lisbon (or anyhow, Captain Croker and some others did) on the 21st. Croker, like so many who know some Spanish, was annoyed by the Portuguese language; he had apparently hoped it would be much the same, and put the blame that it wasn't on its speakers; 'from the pert and quick manner in which the Portuguese speak', he 'could not understand a word'. To make up for this, he found the Portuguese women handsomer than the Spanish.

He, and presumably the officers with him, of whom he mentions only one Captain M., were landed in Lisbon's outskirts (presumably Belem), and after a long and dirty walk came to Williams's hotel in Buenos Ayres, an ordinary frequented by strangers of the best rank; at dinner that day there was a large party, chiefly English and French. The hotel's management and cooking were English, 'which might induce a person to forget he is in Portugal and believe himself in a much better country'. The captain proposed to spend ten days or a fortnight there, to recruit after the journey. He employed the time in observing and commenting on Lisbon, and his comments are those of a cheerful English captain finding himself abroad in a rather odd country, where he manages to put in a pretty good time, though in the main rather bored. First he observed that Lisbon had a number of good inns and lodging-houses, and that consumptives were sent there by their doctors from every part of Europe; whether he shared William Hickey's depressing estimate of their prospects of recovery, he does not mention. He perhaps thought their prospects lessened by the lack of amusement in Lisbon; the rigid piety of the queen, he observes, has shut up all places of amusement, and neither opera nor plays are permitted. Unless Lisbon was just then doing vicarious penance for some act of sacrilege, which was sometimes the case under Queen Maria, the captain was mistaken about this; he cannot have looked hard enough. Lisbon was not gay, but it did have religious drama and Italian opera; possibly the latter was suspended during advent. Anyhow, all that Captain Croker found to entertain' him was the hospitality provided by his own countrymen. The balls given by the British Factory occurred once a fortnight; there was one the evening the officers arrived; one hopes that they got there, but they probably had scarcely time. However, 'the Gentlemen of the Factory live in a very sociable and pleasant manner, and are particularly civil and hospitable to all strangers that visit this city'. (So much for the spiteful Frenchman Carrère, who tried to make out that all the gaiety and hospitality in Lisbon was French and that English parties were no good. English visitors knew better.) The tolerant captain, whose motto was *chacun à son gôut*, added that the churches were always open, 'and to connoisseurs in music and pictures, religious ceremonies and parade, will doubtless afford great satisfaction'. He himself, not being a connoisseur in any of these arts, preferred the exhibition of the Portuguese ladies at their lattices. They were often very handsome, he thought, with very fine hair, elegantly mixed with flowers and feathers; they were apparently (as he knew no Portuguese, he could not go further than this) sprightly and gay, and dressed for show. It was a little dull to find that no woman above the meanest condition ever walked in the streets.

Captain Croker shared with Captain M. a calash, in which they drove about the city. They paid their respects to Mr. Walpole, who received them politely and did them the honour to return their visit in two days; they also waited on Sir John Hort, the consul, and were treated by him with great amiability and kindness. What must have been still more gratifying and useful, Mr. Maine, a banker, and brother to Lord Newhaven, to whom the Lisbon English had the highest obligations, behaved in the most friendly manner and supplied the officers with money.

It does not seem that Croker went outside Lisbon; probably there was not time. He knew that the gentlemen of the Factory had country houses amidst the orange-gardens of Cintra, but believed this to be 'a pleasant village on the opposite side of the Tagus'. Wherever it was, 'here they retire from the fatigues of business and enjoy in honourable leisure the comforts of this enchanted spot, where even at this season the vivid green and golden fruit of orange-trees everywhere abound'. So Croker was informed; but he admits that they had not time to visit it, as they were anxious to go to England by the next packet, there being 'nothing in Lisbon to induce a wish to continue in it an hour, the good fare and excellent wine of the English hotel only excepted'. They did not, in fact, continue in Lisbon long, but went off to Oporto to sail from there. Croker approved of Oporto, where 'the example and encouragement of the British Factory have been attended with singularly good effects; the appearance of the country and the manners of the inhabitants in the vicinity of that city improve daily', and an activity and spirit of industry prevailed, unknown in any other province of Portugal. No doubt, like Captain Costigan and Lord Freeman two years before, the officers enjoyed the hospitable tables of the estimable British merchants, and no doubt Croker's view of the excellent effects of their example on the surrounding Portuguese was all the rosier for it.

He concludes his study of the country with a comment on the religious excesses of the royal family. 'Their present Majesties are so much given to piety, that there is no road to preferment but by the influence of the Church; their whole confidence', he remarks with some natural surprise, 'is placed in things above; they and their ministers are continually employed in attendance on masses and religious processions; all other objects are over-looked or forgotten'. Of this the captain could not approve, par-ticularly since among the objects overlooked or forgotten were the navy and army, which were in a hopeless state. Nothing, he thought, could preserve the independence of Portugal for a month but the torpid state of the Spanish government; the Spaniards had the advantage in numbers; in military spirit and activity, the two were on a level.

As to the Portuguese people, he thought the men, being of mixed blood, combined the less good qualities of all races; the women (less mixed, it seems) were, on the other hand, handsome, lively and gay. In spite of this, 'you will not be surprised that we have resolved to visit England by the first opportunity'.

So they (presumably Croker and Captain M.) embarked on some date in January on the *Hampden* packet. This ship kept two good tables, but unfortunately leaked. On the way home it was chased, but not caught, by a French frigate.

So ended Captain Croker's adventure in Spain and Portugal,

which resulted eighteen years later in the extraordinary circumstance of his becoming the author of a book. Whether he ever looked back, either from barracks with the 99th Regiment of Foot, or, later in life, from the custom house, and wished, a little wistfully, that he had stayed longer in Portugal, seen a little more of it, gone to Cintra across the Tagus (had he studied a map since then?) and seen those golden oranges on their green trees, gone to Setubal, which he would have called St. Ubes, even explored the Algarve, or pushed north from Porto to the mountain country and the lovely port of Vianna — whether, arranging those old letters for his book that so surprised him, he found in them anything wanting, any lack of understanding of the foreign land in which for him and Captain M. the only good things had been the cooking and fare at Williams's hotel, the hospitality of their countrymen, and perhaps the faces of some of the women at their lattices — whether he ever desired to see again the view from the hotel windows of the Tagus and its ships, there is no indication in his book. Memory may have fed the vein of romance in the soul of a British captain of foot; he may have wished he had written fuller or different letters; on the other hand, it is very probable that he did not.

BIBLIOGRAPHY

Travels through several provinces of Spain and Portugal, etc., RICHARD CROKER, ESQ., Captain in the late 99th Regiment of Foot (1799).

3. UNDECEIVING THE DISTRESSED NATIVES

Captain Walter Bromley

[1810-1812]

WALTER BROMLEY, an officer of the Welch Fusiliers (holding, at the time of which he writes, the rank of captain) was one of those amiable characters, to be met with from time to time in British history of all periods, who are filled with compassion for the miseries around them, or (even more) far from them, and spend their time, money and energies in pleas and endeavours for this or that 'unhappy state of affairs'. Bromley turned his eyes on 'the deplorable state of the Indians' in North America, on the miseries 'in some of the inland counties', on the wretched, poverty-stricken and unconverted condition of the inhabitants of the Iberian Peninsula. He printed appeals for all these poor creatures, often at his own expense; and for the enlightenment of the Iberians he laboured faithfully throughout his service during the Peninsular Wars.

He had not always been thus. Though born of religious parents in a country village, and imbibing in his youth principles of religion of the purest kind, he unfortunately 'indulged a violent passion for a military life' and commenced his career in that profession at the age of fifteen: he does not say in what capacity, but presumably in the ranks. The Welch Fusiliers were apparently an abandoned set, for 'from this moment, all outward appearance of religion vanished', and Walter 'mixed in a crowd of dissipated youth'. With the usual lack of precision so regrettable among converts, he passed over the details of his exploits, 'Suffice it to say, without entering into the details of the various species of vice which I readily embarked in, that I was considered a pleasant jovial companion'. He remained in this course of sin and folly for twenty-one years. Then, in November 1810, his regiment (the 23rd), arrived in Lisbon from Nova Scotia. He had with him his son, aged twelve; he does not refer to his wife. He got a billet in Lisbon with a respectable family who supported a priest, and there he learnt Portuguese. With the priest, a kindly and amiable man, he made friends, and found him 'much concerned that I was not a Catholic, without which I could not be saved'. Walter did not at this time care about religion, though he had become rather a moral character, having apparently turned over a new leaf after his dissipated youth. In March 1811, he left Lisbon to pursue Massena; having successfully done so, he returned in June, to send his son home. The boy had not wasted his time; he had explained the Church of England Prayer Book to the priest, who had changed his mind and now, polite and open-minded clergyman, thought there was little difference between Roman Catholicism and Protestantism, and that there were mistakes in both. Seeing how elegantly Master Bromley's prayer book was bound in red morocco, he concluded that the English must pay some attention to religion. Captain Bromley perceived that this was the moment to strike. He had himself lately become religious; he

433

had with some difficulty borrowed a Bible from a brother officer, and 'commenced perusal of it with uncommon eagerness and attention; and from this period I formed the design, assisted by Divine Providence, of endeavouring to redeem the lost time by first ascertaining the state of religion among the inhabitants of the Peninsula', and then to improve it. So, finding his friend the priest in this promising mood, he presented him with some tracts, which he got from a Lieutenant Hacket, whose mother, a pious lady in Dublin, had sent them for distribution among the Roman Catholic soldiers in the regiment. Hacket, who took after his mother, declared himself willing to act as agent for the distribution of Portuguese Bibles if they were sent out to him. All the Portuguese when asked said they would gladly receive the Bible or any other good books; they had not read it yet, but, from the glowing descriptions of it given them by the British captain and lieutenant, they felt sure they would enjoy it. 'I am certain', said Bromley, 'the generality of the people are disgusted by the fanaticism of their priests, for whenever I described the blessings the English enjoyed by the unrestrained perusal of the Bible, some of them declared they would spare no expense or trouble in endeavouring to obtain it. I made it a rule, the moment I entered a house, to commence the topic, which never gave offence.'

Indeed, Portuguese parents felt this book of the British officers might be just the thing for their sons and daughters, in whom respect for priests and morality had been much upset by the influence of the French occupation; there had been an alarming weakening of morals, particularly among females, owing to intercourse with foreign troops. Meanwhile, pending the arrival of Bibles, Lieutenant Hacket's tracts proved to be extremely useful. Their effect was often remarkable, particularly on priests. One of these, whom Bromley met on the Spanish frontier, was converted forthwith, and began to travel in tracts. He was particularly impressed by a questionnaire which asked how a rational man in the nineteenth century could submit to be forbidden to read what he chose, and other sensible questions. Bromley had put this tract and others in a place where the priest could find them as if by chance; having done so and perused them, the grateful priest exclaimed 'Oh God bless you, my dear captain', and embraced him with tears of joy, observing that he had always had a presentiment that the English would be the first to open the eyes of his ignorant countrymen. He immediately began the translation of the above tract into his own language, with remarkable results; he would collect the parishioners of a neighbouring church, whose curate was 'a base illiterate fellow', in a field, and admonish them in the most affectionate manner to be no longer deceived by the false doctrines of their minister. A few years ago, and a few years later, such conduct could not have been indulged in with impunity, either in Portugal or Spain; but Jacobinism had left its taint, and the mighty Inquisition had fallen low indeed.

It was a golden opportunity for the distribution of Bibles. Bromley suggested the army as distributors. Though indeed 'it is a melancholy fact that in the 23rd regiment it would be difficult at times to procure even one English Bible, and this scarcity I believe exists throughout the whole army in the Peninsula'. Had they only some Bibles, the army would be able to undeceive very many of the inhabitants, and the most beneficial result might be produced. But Bibles in Portuguese did not arrive: one does not know what the British and Foreign Bible Society were thinking of. 'Would to God', said Bromley, 'that some of my pious countrymen could be induced by this statement to visit the seat of war, and lend an ear to the supplications of the distressed inhabitants on the frontier of Portugal!'

The character of these distressed inhabitants was, Bromley found, most estimable. He had travelled about alone, with much property, and never met with insult or attack — so different from Great Britain. Drunkenness too was unknown; so little did the Portuguese soldiers value wine that they sold their ration to the British. Of the British character, Bromley did not think very much; in particular, British women and girls, whom he found frailer than their brothers. In London, or any large English town, it was impossible to walk the streets 'without shedding a tear of sorrow at the deplorable state of society, when innumerable females, scarcely arrived at the age of puberty, often staggering with intemperance, are become so hardened in iniquity as to outdo, in oaths and imprecations, the oldest practitioners of this frail sex'. Often, Captain Bromley mused, this iniquity on the part of young British females was the fault of their parents, who, when 'the object of their care has been enticed from the happy circle of the family fireside by some refined intriguer in high life, to remain from home past the usual hour of retirement, shut her out', so that in a few weeks she becomes a wretched example of disease and human depravity.

Yet these young women, these parents, had enjoyed the inestimable benefits of the Bible. If Captain Bromley ever paused to ask himself whether it was indeed wise to introduce this book among Portuguese young women, Portuguese parents, who behaved, it seemed, so well without it, he does not tell us. He pursued his beneficent way, laying tracts about where the inhabitants could pick them up, sending to Mrs. Hacket of Dublin for more, amiably leading all conversations round to the Bible, affectionately undeceiving priests and people, being courteously treated by all, until the 23rd regiment left the Peninsula. Then, solicited by many religious friends and ministers of the Gospel, and before his interest shifted to the deplorable state of North American Indians, he published *The Distressed and Destitute State of the Inhabitants of Spain and Portugal respecting Moral and Religious Instruction, from the most recent Investigation*, by an Old Officer returned from the Army in Spain.

Twenty years later, his projects were achieved through the agency of a less amiable and honest, a more arrogant and violent man, who probably distributed Bibles less effectively than Captain Bromley would have, but wrote about it a better book.

BIBLIOGRAPHY

The Distressed and Destitute State of the Inhabitants of Spain and Portugal respecting Moral and Religious Instructions, from the most recent Investigation, WALTER BROMLEY (1813).

INDEX

MORE ABOUT PENGUINS, PELICANS
AND PUFFINS

For further information about books available from Penguins please write to Dept EP, Penguin Books Ltd, Harmondsworth, Middlesex UB7 0DA.

In the U.S.A.: For a complete list of books available from Penguins in the United States write to Dept DG, Penguin Books, 299 Murray Hill Parkway, East Rutherford, New Jersey 07073.

In Canada: For a complete list of books available from Penguins in Canada write to Penguin Books Canada Ltd, 2801 John Street, Markham, Ontario L3R 1B4.

In Australia: For a complete list of books available from Penguins in Australia write to the Marketing Department, Penguin Books Australia Ltd, P.O. Box 257, Ringwood, Victoria 3134.

In New Zealand: For a complete list of books available from Penguins in New Zealand write to the Marketing Department, Penguin Books (N.Z.) Ltd, P.O. Box 4019, Auckland 10.

In India: For a complete list of books available from Penguins in India write to Penguin Overseas Ltd, 706 Eros Apartments, 56 Nehru Place, New Delhi 110019.

PENGUIN TRAVEL BOOKS

☐ *A Time of Gifts* **Patrick Leigh Fermor**   £3.50

In 1933 the author set out to walk to Constantinople. This award-winning book carries him as far as Hungary and is, to Philip Toynbee, 'more than just a Super-travel-book' and, according to Jan Morris, 'a masterpiece'.

☐ *A Reed Shaken by the Wind* **Gavin Maxwell**   £2.95

Staying in reed houses on tiny man-made islands, Maxwell journeyed through the strange, unexplored marshlands of Iraq. His unusual book is 'a delight' – *Observer*

☐ *Third-Class Ticket* **Heather Wood**   £3.95

A rich landowner left enough money for forty Bengali villagers to set off, third-class, and 'see all of India'. This wonderful account is 'wholly original, fantastic, but true' – *Daily Telegraph*

☐ *Slow Boats to China* **Gavin Young**   £3.95

On an ancient steamer, a cargo dhow, a Filipino kumpit and twenty more agreeably cranky boats, Young sailed from Piraeus to Canton in seven crowded and colourful months. 'A pleasure to read' – Paul Theroux

☐ *Granite Island* **Dorothy Carrington**   £3.95

The award-winning portrait of Corsica that magnificently evokes the granite villages, the beautiful mountains and olive trees as well as the history, beliefs, culture and personality of its highly individualistic island people.

☐ *Venture to the Interior* **Laurens van der Post**   £3.50

A trek on foot through the breathtaking scenery and secret places of Central Africa, described by one of the great explorers and travellers of our time.

PENGUIN TRAVEL BOOKS

☐ *Brazilian Adventure* **Peter Fleming** £2.95

'. . . To explore rivers Central Brazil, if possible ascertain fate Colonel Fawcett . . .' – this is the exciting account of what happened when Fleming answered this advertisement in *The Times*.

☐ *Mani* **Patrick Leigh Fermor** £3.95

Part travelogue, part inspired evocation of the people and culture of the Greek Peloponnese, this is 'the masterpiece of a traveller and scholar' – *Illustrated London News*

☐ *As I Walked Out One Midsummer Morning*
Laurie Lee £1.95

How he tramped from the Cotswolds to London, and on to Spain just before the Civil War, recalled with a young man's vision and exuberance. 'A beautiful piece of writing' – *Observer*

☐ *The Light Garden of the Angel King* **Peter Levi** £3.50

Afghanistan has been a wild rocky highway for nomads and merchants, Alexander the Great, Buddhist monks, great Moghul conquerors and the armies of the Raj. Here, brilliantly, Levi discusses their journeys and his own.

☐ *The Worst Journey in the World*
Apsley Cherry-Garrard £5.95

An account of Scott's last Antarctic Expedition, 1910–13. 'It is – what few travellers' tales are – absolutely and convincingly credible' – George Bernard Shaw

☐ *The Old Patagonian Express* **Paul Theroux** £2.50

From blizzard-stricken Boston down through South America, railroading by luxury express and squalid local trains, to Argentina – a journey of vivid contrasts described in 'one of the most entrancing travel books' – C. P. Snow

PENGUIN TRAVEL BOOKS

☐ *Hindoo Holiday* **J. R. Ackerley**   £3.50

Ackerley's journal of his career as companion to the Maharajah of Chhokrapur in the twenties. 'Radiantly delightful . . . A book difficult to praise . . . temperately' – Evelyn Waugh

☐ *The Marsh Arabs* **Wilfred Thesiger**   £4.95

'This voyage through desert waters will remain, like his *Arabian Sands*, a classic of travel writing' – *The Times*

☐ *A Pattern of Islands* **Arthur Grimble**   £2.95

Full of gleaming humour and anecdotes, this is the true story (and a popular classic) of an Englishman living among the fishermen, sorcerers, fighters and poets of the Pacific islands.

These books should be available at all good bookshops or news-agents, but if you live in the UK or the Republic of Ireland and have difficulty in getting to a bookshop, they can be ordered by post. Please indicate the titles required and fill in the form below.

NAME _____ BLOCK CAPITALS

ADDRESS _____

_____

_____

Enclose a cheque or postal order payable to The Penguin Bookshop to cover the total price of books ordered, plus 50p for postage. Readers in the Republic of Ireland should send £IR equivalent to the sterling prices, plus 67p for postage. Send to: The Penguin Bookshop, 54/56 Bridlesmith Gate, Nottingham, NG1 2GP.

You can also order by phoning (0602) 599295, and quoting your Barclaycard or Access number.

Every effort is made to ensure the accuracy of the price and availability of books at the time of going to press, but it is sometimes necessary to increase prices and in these circumstances retail prices may be shown on the covers of books which may differ from the prices shown in this list or elsewhere. This list is not an offer to supply any book.

This order service is only available to residents in the UK and the Republic of Ireland.